Keto Air Fryer Cookbook For Beginners

by Robin Clayton

Contents

INTRODUCTION

Have you ever wondered what is the secret behind the perfect restaurant-style foods? And how can you cook fast foods as good as the professionals? Well, I am about to reveal the mystery. But, before I do that, I would like to share with you more about my Air Fryer experience.

A few years ago, my husband and I originally saw an Air Fryer on a food website and it seemed like a good idea. We found out that the Air Fryer uses rapid air technology to cook fried food to perfections with a drizzle of healthy oil. We were leading a healthy lifestyle, but I must admit, we used to eat junk food occasionally and rarely. We didn't own a deep fryer but we loved indulging in some junk food cravings from time to time. After all, nothing says the Saturday night better than a good movie with pizza and a large bowl of chips! An Air Fryer seemed like the perfect alternative to expensive restaurant meals and unhealthy take-outs. Above all, a deep-fried food with a massive amount of fat is something to be avoided at all costs. I didn't know that the Air Fryer was going to change the way we cooked and ate forever and ever. My family had fallen in love with it. From this point of view, I can say that it was one of the best things to ever enter my kitchen!

I started by making fried veggies, French fries, fish and pork chops in it. Then I ventured into more complicated meals, and shortly thereafter, I started the keto diet. Due to a combination of circumstances, I was at my highest weight so I needed to change something in my current diet. Actually, I've never been on a diet in the past. I did my research and decided to try a low carb dietary regimen. In addition, I decided to give my Air Fryer a try during this diet. To my surprise, I have enjoyed keto foods in my Air Fryer and started losing weight quickly. My family is much healthier now, and we still eat fried foods. However, we make our own fried foods in our Air Fryer and it is much healthier than typical fast food that is loaded with calories, unhealthy fats, and sodium. Plus, the Air Fryer always helps me to avoid that awkward "there's-nothing-to-eat" situation, especially on the weeknights. When I use my Air Fryer as a regular oven, a family dinner can be a reality any night of the week. In my extensive testing, I found that the Air Fryer can cook much faster than conventional cooking methods. I have literally taken the art of baking and frying to the next level. That's how this book was created.

Are you searching for Air Fryer recipes that are adjusted for the ketogenic diet? Are you looking for the best "make-it-again" Air Fryer dishes? Well, you are in the right place. The Air Fryer can deliver amazing results with minimal effort and take your cooking routine up a notch! In other words, if you like home-cooked meals but you don't want to give up eating fried foods, the Air Fryer is your number one choice! If you are thinking of cutting down on fat consumption, the Air Fryer can provide amazing results. If you're lucky enough to own an Air Fryer, then you're probably aware of how much this kitchen gadget can do for you. In this collection, we'll explore an extensive range of dishes, from breakfast and meat dishes to snacks, desserts and vegetarian dishes. A considerable majority of these recipes can be prepared in less than 30 minutes, making meal planning a breeze. Believe me, many other food aficionados have known this secret for years. Your food cooks faster and retains more valuable nutrition than those prepared using conventional cooking methods. Ultimately, everyone likes the taste of fried foods such as chicken nuggets, fish sticks, or chicken wings. It is too tempting to ignore, right?

What Can You Do with Your Air Fryer?

If you're reading this cookbook, you probably already know what an Air Fryer is, but in case you don't, let me introduce you to the wonders of my favorite kitchen gadget. The Air Fryer is an "all-in-one" kitchen appliance that promises to replace a deep fryer, convection oven, and microwave; it also lets you sauté your foods. The Air Fryer is a unique kitchen gadget designed to fry food in a special chamber using super-heated air. In fact, the hot air circulates inside the cooking chamber using the convection mechanism, cooking your food evenly from all sides. It uses so-called Maillard effect – a chemical reaction that gives fried food that distinctive flavor. Simply put, thanks to the hot air, your foods get that crispy exterior and a moist interior and does not taste like the fat.

Why use an Air Fryer? I'm asked this question time and time again so my answer is always the same: It all boils down to versatility, health, and speed. It means that I can "set it and forget it" until it is done. Unlike most cooking methods, there's no need to keep an eye on it. I can pick the ingredients, turn the machine on and walk away – no worries about overcooked or burned food. Another great benefit of using an Air Fryer is that unlike the heat in your oven or on a stove top, the heat in the cooking chamber is constant and it allows your food to cook evenly. Plus, it is energy-efficient and space-saving solution.

Is an Air Fryer worth buying? It is a personal matter. You should keep in mind personal factors such as your kitchen equipment, counter space, budget, cooking preferences, and the size of your family. However, there are numerous benefits you'll get from using an Air Fryer. Here are the top three benefits of using an Air Fryer.

Fast cooking and convenience. The Air Fryer is an electric device so you just need to press the right buttons and go about your business. It heats up in a few minutes so it can cut down cooking time; further, hot air circulates around your food, cooking it quickly and evenly. Roast chicken is perfectly cooked in 30 minutes, baby back ribs in less than 25 minutes and beef chuck or steak in about 15 minutes. You can use dividers and cook different foods at the same time. The Air Fryer is a real game changer, it is a cost-saving solution in many different ways. I also use my Air Fryer to keep my food warm. Air Fryer features an automatic temperature control, eliminating the need to slave over a hot stove. A digital screen and touch panel allow you to set the cooking time and the temperature according to your recipe and personal preferences.

Healthy eating. Yes, there is such a thing as healthy fried food and the Air Fryer proves that! The Air Fryer inspires me every day so that I enjoy cooking healthy and well-balanced meals for my family. Recent studies have shown that air-fried foods contain up to 80% less fat in comparison to foods that are deep-fried. Deep-fried food contributes to obesity, type 2 diabetes, high cholesterol, increased risk of heart disease, and so on. Plus, fats and oils become harmful under the high heat, which leads to increased inflammation in your body and speeds up aging. Further, these oils release cancer-causing toxic chemicals. Moreover, the spills of fats and oils injure wildlife and produce other undesirable effects on the planet Earth.

According to the leading experts, you should not be afraid of healthy fats and oils, especially if you follow the ketogenic diet. Avoid partially hydrogenated and genetically modified oils such as cottonseed oil, soybean oil, corn oil, and rice bran oil. You should also avoid margarine since it is loaded with trans-fats. Good fats and oils include olive oil, coconut oil, avocado oil, sesame oil, nuts and seeds. Air-fried foods are really delicious and have the texture of regular fried food but they do not taste like fat. French fries are only the beginning. Perfect ribs, hearty casseroles, fast snacks, and delectable desserts turn out great in this revolutionary kitchen gadget. When it comes to healthy dieting that does not compromise flavor, the Air Fryer is a real winner.

The ultimate solution to losing pounds and maintain a healthy weight. One of the greatest benefits of owning an Air Fryer is the possibility to maintain an ideal weight in an easy and healthy way. The best part is – it doesn't mean that you have to give up fried fish fillets, saucy steaks, and scrumptious desserts. Choosing a healthy-cooking technique is the key to success. Air frying actually requires less fat compared to many other cooking methods, making your weight loss diet more achievable.

Basic Keto Diet Rules

What separates a fit person from the couch potato is action. Doing the work! So, I decided to change my diet and find an adequate nutrition plan. I knew – I should find a meal plan that I will actually follow! Then, I discovered the ketogenic diet and I thought it could be worth considering. Fortunately, I was right! The ketogenic diet is a low-carb, adequate-protein, and high-fat and diet plan. This eating plan involves a significant reduction in carbohydrate intake and replacing it with lean protein and good fats. It means no more junk food, sugar, cereals, and grains. How does it work? On the ketogenic diet, your body produces less glucose and more ketones. Cutting out carbs can lower insulin levels in the blood. Then, your body and your brain accordingly use ketones as energy after you have been on the ketogenic diet for 7 to 8 days. Consequently, you can lose body fat and improve your physical health, cognitive function, and mental performance.

Basically, you should eat protein-rich foods such as fish, seafood, poultry, full-fat dairy products, eggs, and vegetarian keto foods (e.g. nutritional yeast, tofu, tempeh, Shirataki noodles, and seaweed). You should also consume whole foods such as nuts, seeds, and low-carb vegetables. When it comes to the keto beverages, you can consume coffee, tea, sparkling water, and zero carb energy drinks. Foods to avoid on the ketogenic diet include grains, rice, common types of flour, legumes, starchy vegetables, fruits, and sugars. Finally, I can lose pounds and reduce appetite by eating big portions of fatty and high-protein foods. Plus, I am finally free of counting calories and I couldn't be happier than this! When it comes to the keto diet macros, keto requires getting 5% carbs, 20% protein, and 75% fats of total daily calories. Most ketoers stick to this formula as well.

Why I Choose the Keto Diet?

There are numerous science-based benefits of the keto diet. They range from significant weight loss and improved cognitive functions to therapeutic applications.
The ketogenic diet has been shown to reduce bad cholesterol and improve heart health. It can boost brain function and prevent Alzheimer's disease, dementia and other brain malfunctions. The ketogenic diet may help treat metabolic syndrome and hypertension. Further, this dietary regimen, with lower insulin levels, may help treat diabetes too. Moreover, studies found that it may slow down the growth of cancer cells. Some clinical trials have proven that you can experience increased memory and mental clarity on the ketogenic diet. In addition to improved mental performance, the stabilization of insulin levels can lead to increased energy levels, too.

How to Lose Weight on the Ketogenic Diet?

Calorie counting. Many nutritionists claim that you do not have to count calories on the ketogenic diet. I think it is good advice when it comes to healthy weight maintenance. Otherwise, if you tend to lose weight, you should track your calorie intake. It sounds daunting but, trust me, counting calories and macros is easier than you think. Still, do not go too low and do not consume fewer than 1000 calories per day because it could be counterproductive!

Ketosis can help you reduce hunger. The appetite suppression is one of the greatest advantages of the keto diet. According to experts, ketosis may significantly boost your metabolism. You can practice intermittent fasting to get the most out of keto. Recent studies have shown that a combination of intermittent fasting and keto-friendly foods can help you maintain ketosis and achieve better results.

Healthy fats. A related point to consider is a type of fat you should consume on a healthy diet. The whole story about fat is confusing, but I think it would be enough to stay away from margarine, processed vegetable oils, and store-bought spreads. I think that many ketoers eat more fat than they need to satisfy their caloric requirements. Keep in mind that high-fat foods can slow down or stop your efforts, even if you only eat healthy fats and very few carbs. It is obvious that you should eat high-quality fat to burn fat but you should be careful and eat smart. If you eat high-quality fats such as olive oil, coconut oil, avocado and nuts in small amount, your body won't need too many calories; your body needs a small amount of fat to feel full and satisfied. Do not be obsessed with calories and fatty foods. Once you get used to it, you can add a bit more fat while continuing to eat fewer carbs; this strategy helps me maintain my weight long term. Plus, I can use my Air Fryer to prepare fried foods without too much oil. Win-win!

Stay hydrated. Drink enough water to get the most out of the ketogenic diet. On a low-carb diet, we are skipping various salty carbohydrates, so it's crucial that you increase your intake of essential electrolytes such as potassium, magnesium, sodium, and calcium.

Physical activity. And last but not least, doing a regular physical activity can help you lose weight faster and make you feel good about yourself. On the ketogenic diet, you can practice low-intensity cardio workouts such as jogging as well as interval training. Doubtlessly, weight lifting is one of the best workouts for people on a low-carb diet. Protein-rich foods are building blocks that can help prevent injuries and muscle loss as well as reduce appetite. Plus, keto-friendly foods can help you gain muscle and improve endurance.

A Few Words about This Recipe Collection

This recipe collection features keto foods such as poultry, fish, meat, vegetables, healthy fats, nuts, seeds, eggs, and dairy products! Every recipe includes the suggested serving size, approximate cook time, the ingredient list, and step-by-step instructions. Each recipe is accompanied by nutritional analysis, so you can easily create your meal plan. You can also use my sample menu for three weeks on a ketogenic diet. My recipes are designed to help you create tasty, restaurant-quality meals, from old-fashioned grandma's recipes to ethnic-inspired dishes and the hottest culinary trends. These recipes are pretty simple to prepare in the Air Fryer, it's all just going to take practice. I hope you won't run out of inspiration with these 550 recipes! Bon Appétit!

3-Week Meal Plan

This is a sample menu for three weeks on a ketogenic diet plan.

DAY 1

Breakfast – Omelet with Mushrooms and Peppers

Snack – Must-Serve Thai Prawns

Lunch – Smoked Beef Burgers; 1 handful of iceberg lettuce

Dinner – Spicy Braised Vegetables

DAY 2

Breakfast – 1 hard-boiled egg; 1 slice of bacon; 1 shake with 1/2 cup of coconut milk and protein powder

Lunch – Spicy Holiday Roast Beef; 1 serving of cauliflower rice

Dinner – Decadent Frittata with Roasted Garlic and Sausage; 1 medium tomato

Dessert – Chocolate Rum Lava Cake

DAY 3

Breakfast – Double Cheese Crêpes

Lunch – Mexican Stuffed Peppers with Pork and Cheese

Snack – Bacon Wrapped Onion Rings

Dinner – Favorite Broccoli with Garlic Sauce; Italian Shrimp Scampi

DAY 4

Breakfast – Omelet with veggies; 1 slice of bacon

Lunch – Pork Chops Romano; 1 serving of coleslaw

Dinner – Zingy Dilled Salmon

Dessert – Blackberry and Cocoa Butter Cake

DAY 5

Breakfast – Italian Creamy Frittata with Kale

Snack – Brussels Sprout Crisps

Lunch – Spicy Pork Curry; 1 serving of cauliflower rice

Dinner – Grandma's Spicy Wings; Thai Zucchini Balls

DAY 6

Breakfast – Eggs Florentine with Spinach

Lunch – Peppery Pork Roast with Herbs; 1 serving of cabbage salad

Dinner – Green Beans with Cheese

Dessert – Vanilla Orange Custard

DAY 7

Breakfast – Muffins with Brown Mushrooms

Lunch – Marinated Chicken Drumettes with Asparagus; 1 large tomato

Dinner – Filipino Fried Bangus

DAY 8

Breakfast – Scrambled eggs; 1 tomato; 1/2 cup of Greek-style yogurt

Lunch – Pork Kebabs with Serrano Pepper; 1 serving of cauliflower rice

Dinner – Paprika Crab Burgers

Dessert – Ultimate Lemon Coconut Tart

DAY 9

Breakfast – Spicy Eggs with Sausage and Swiss Cheese; 1/2 cup of unsweetened almond milk

Lunch – Chicken with Bacon and Herbs de Provence; 1 serving of cabbage salad

Snack – Cheesy Eggplant Crisps

Dinner – Thai Zingy Turkey Bites; Restaurant-Style Roasted Vegetables

DAY 10

Breakfast – Western Eggs with Ham and Cheese

Snack – Chicken Wings in Barbecue Sauce

Lunch – Top Chuck with Mustard and Herbs; 1/2 tomato

Dinner – Cottage Cheese Stuffed Chicken Rolls; a dollop of sour cream; 2 tablespoons tomato paste

DAY 11

Breakfast – 1 tablespoon of peanut butter; 1 slice of keto bread

Lunch – Curried Halibut Fillets; 1 serving of cabbage salad

Snack – Broccoli and Pecorino Toscano Fat Bombs

Dinner – Pollock with Kalamata Olives and Capers

DAY 12

Breakfast – Scrambled Egg Muffins with Cheese

Snack – Paprika Bacon Shrimp

Lunch – Christmas Filet Mignon Steak; 1 serving of low-carb grilled vegetables

Dinner – Parmesan Broccoli Fritters; 1/2 cup of full-fat Greek yogurt

DAY 13

Breakfast – Frittata with Porcini Mushrooms

Lunch – Irish Whisky Steak

Dinner – Orange Swiss Roll

DAY 14

Breakfast – Vegetarian Tofu Scramble

Lunch – Spicy Tuna Casserole; 1 handful of baby spinach with 1 teaspoon of mustard and 1 teaspoon of olive oil

Dinner – Bacon-Wrapped Hot Dogs; Famous Fried Pickles

Dessert – Perfectly Puffy Coconut Cookies

DAY 15

Breakfast – Scrambled eggs; 1 tomato; 1/2 cup of Greek-style yogurt

Lunch – Farmhouse Pork with Vegetables

Snack – Sage Roasted Zucchini Cubes

Dinner – Pecan Crusted Tilapia; Bell Peppers with Spicy Mayo

DAY 16

Breakfast – 2 hard-boiled eggs; 1/2 cup of Greek-style yogurt

Lunch – Chicken Tenders with Parmesan and Lime

Dinner – Cod Fillets with Lemon and Mustard

Dessert – Snickerdoodle Cinnamon Cookies

DAY 17

Breakfast – Baked Eggs with Linguica Sausage; 2 slices of Cheddar cheese

Lunch – 30-Minute Hoisin Pork Loin Steak; 1 fresh bell pepper

Dinner – Curried Fish Patties with Green Beans; 1 cucumber

DAY 18

Breakfast – Cheesy Cauliflower Balls; 2-3 olives
Lunch – Turkey Meatballs with Manchego Cheese
Snack – Brussels Sprouts with Feta Cheese
Dinner – Fish Fingers with Dijon Mayo Sauce

DAY 19

Breakfast – Baked Denver Omelet with Sausage
Lunch – Piri Piri Chicken; 1 serving of steamed broccoli; 1 cucumber
Dinner – Cajun Fish Fritters; Easy Sesame Broccoli
Dessert – French Blueberry Flan

DAY 20

Breakfast – Baked Eggs with Beef and Tomato; 1 medium tomato with 2-3 Kalamata olives
Lunch – Cheesy Ground Pork Casserole
Snack – Saucy Chicken Wings with Sage
Dinner – Easy Turkey Breasts with Basil

DAY 21

Breakfast – Greek Omelet with Halloumi Cheese
Lunch – Balsamic London Broil with Garlic; 1 serving of cabbage salad
Snack – Crispy Crackling Bites
Dinner – Fish and Cauliflower Cakes; Easy Vegetable Kabobs

ULTIMATE KETO FOOD LIST

Fish & Seafood
Anchovy
Bass
Carp
Flounder
Haddock
Halibut
Mackerel
Salmon
Sardines
Sole
Tilapia
Trout
Tuna
Clams
Crab Meat
Lobster
Mussels
Oysters
Shrimp
Squid

Cheese
American
Blue Cheese
Cheddar
Cottage Cheese
Cream Cheese
Feta
Gouda
Mozzarella
Parmesan
Provolone
Ricotta
Swiss

Dairy & Dairy Substitutes & Eggs
Almond Milk (unsweetened)
Coconut Cream
Coconut Milk (unsweetened)
Greek Yogurt
Sour Cream ((full-fat)
Soy Milk (unsweetened)
Whipped Cream (unsweetened)
Eggs

Flours, Meals & Powders
Acorn Flour
Almond Flour
Almond Meal
Cocoa Powder
Coconut Flour
Flax Seed Meal
Protein Powder
Psyllium Husk
Sesame Seed Flour
Splenda

Poultry
Chicken: Breast, Legs, Wings
Duck
Goose
Quail
Turkey: Breast, Ground, Bacon

Fats & Oils
Almond Butter, Oil
Avocado Oil
Butter
Cocoa Butter, Oil
Coconut Oil
Fish Oil
Flax Seed Oil
Grape Seed Oil
Hemp Seed Oil
Macadamia Oil
Full Fat Mayonnaise
Olive Oil
Walnut Oil

Seeds
Chia
Flax
Hemp
Pumpkin
Safflower
Sesame
Sunflower

Nuts
Almonds
Brazil Nuts
Coconut
Hazelnuts
Macadamias
Pecans
Pistachios
Walnuts

Vegetables	Fruits	Meat
Arugula	Avocado	Corned beef
Asparagus	Blackberry	Ground beef, 70-90% lean
Bok Choy	Blueberry	Beef, Hot Dog/Frankfurter
Broccoli, Broccoli Rabe	Cranberry	Beef Tongue
Cabbage	Lemon	Beef Ribs
Cauliflower	Lime	Beef Roast
Celery	Green Olive	Beef Sausage
Chard	Raspberry	Beef Steak
Chicory Greens	Strawberry	Filet Mignon
Cucumber	Rhubarb	Beef Rib Eye
Eggplant	Tomato	Beef Round
Endive		Beef Sirloin
Fennel		Beef Strip Loin
Garlic		Bologna (pork, beef, chicken)
Green Bean		Lamb, Chops
Jalapeno		Pepperoni (pork, beef)
Lettuce: Green Leaf, Romaine		Pork Bacon
Parsley		Pork Chops
Radish		Ham
Spinach		Liverwurst
Soy Bean		Pork Loin
Zucchini		Prosciutto
Artichoke		Sausage
Brussels Sprouts		Veal
Carrots		Venison
Celery		
Kale		
Kohlrabi		
Mushrooms		
Okra		
Onion		
Peppers: Sweet or Hot Red, Sweet Yellow		
Pumpkin		
Snow Pea		
Spaghetti Squash		
Turnips		

VEGETABLES & SIDE DISHES

1. Tomato Bites with Creamy Parmesan Sauce

(Ready in about 20 minutes | Servings 4)

Per serving: 428 Calories; 38.4g Fat; 4.5g Carbs; 18.8g Protein; 2.3g Sugars; 1.3g Fiber

INGREDIENTS

For the Sauce:
1/2 cup Parmigiano-Reggiano cheese, grated
4 tablespoons pecans, chopped
1 teaspoon garlic puree
1/2 teaspoon fine sea salt
1/3 cup extra-virgin olive oil

For the Tomato Bites:
2 large-sized Roma tomatoes, cut into thin slices and pat them dry
8 ounces Halloumi cheese, cut into thin slices
1/3 cup onions, sliced
1 teaspoon dried basil
1/4 teaspoon red pepper flakes, crushed
1/8 teaspoon sea salt

DIRECTIONS

Start by preheating your Air Fryer to 385 degrees F.

Make the sauce by mixing all ingredients, except the extra-virgin olive oil, in your food processor.

While the machine is running, slowly and gradually pour in the olive oil; puree until everything is well - blended.

Now, spread 1 teaspoon of the sauce over the top of each tomato slice. Place a slice of Halloumi cheese on each tomato slice. Top with onion slices. Sprinkle with basil, red pepper, and sea salt.

Transfer the assembled bites to the Air Fryer cooking basket. Drizzle with a nonstick cooking spray and cook for approximately 13 minutes. Arrange these bites on a nice serving platter, garnish with the remaining sauce and serve at room temperature. Bon appétit!

2. Simple Green Beans with Butter

(Ready in about 12 minutes | Servings 4)

Per serving: 73 Calories; 3.0g Fat; 6.1g Carbs; 1.6g Protein; 1.2g Sugars; 2.1g Fiber

INGREDIENTS

3/4 pound green beans, cleaned
1 tablespoon balsamic vinegar
1/4 teaspoon kosher salt

1/2 teaspoon mixed peppercorns, freshly cracked
1 tablespoon butter
2 tablespoons toasted sesame seeds, to serve

DIRECTIONS

Set your Air Fryer to cook at 390 degrees F.

Mix the green beans with all of the above ingredients, apart from the sesame seeds. Set the timer for 10 minutes.

Meanwhile, toast the sesame seeds in a small-sized nonstick skillet; make sure to stir continuously.

Serve sautéed green beans on a nice serving platter sprinkled with toasted sesame seeds. Bon appétit!

3. Creamy Cauliflower and Broccoli

(Ready in about 20 minutes | Servings 6)

Per serving: 133 Calories; 9.0g Fat; 9.5g Carbs; 5.9g Protein; 3.2g Sugars; 3.6g Fiber

INGREDIENTS

1 pound cauliflower florets
1 pound broccoli florets
2 ½ tablespoons sesame oil
1/2 teaspoon smoked cayenne pepper

3/4 teaspoon sea salt flakes
1 tablespoon lemon zest, grated
1/2 cup Colby cheese, shredded

DIRECTIONS

Prepare the cauliflower and broccoli using your favorite steaming method. Then, drain them well; add the sesame oil, cayenne pepper, and salt flakes.

Air-fry at 390 degrees F for approximately 16 minutes; make sure to check the vegetables halfway through the cooking time.

Afterwards, stir in the lemon zest and Colby cheese; toss to coat well and serve immediately!

4. Mediterranean-Style Eggs with Spinach

(Ready in about 15 minutes | Servings 2)

Per serving: 274 Calories; 23.2g Fat; 5.7g Carbs; 13.7g Protein; 2.6g Sugars; 2.6g Fiber

INGREDIENTS

2 tablespoons olive oil, melted
4 eggs, whisked
5 ounces fresh spinach, chopped
1 medium-sized tomato, chopped

1 teaspoon fresh lemon juice
1/2 teaspoon coarse salt
1/2 teaspoon ground black pepper
1/2 cup of fresh basil, roughly chopped

DIRECTIONS

Add the olive oil to an Air Fryer baking pan. Make sure to tilt the pan to spread the oil evenly.
Simply combine the remaining ingredients, except for the basil leaves; whisk well until everything is well incorporated.
Cook in the preheated Air Fryer for 8 to 12 minutes at 280 degrees F. Garnish with fresh basil leaves. Serve warm with a dollop of sour cream if desired.

5. Spicy Zesty Broccoli with Tomato Sauce

(Ready in about 20 minutes | Servings 6)

Per serving: 70 Calories; 3.8g Fat; 5.8g Carbs; 2g Protein; 6.6g Sugars; 1.5g Fiber

INGREDIENTS

For the Broccoli Bites:
1 medium-sized head broccoli, broken into florets
1/2 teaspoon lemon zest, freshly grated
1/3 teaspoon fine sea salt
1/2 teaspoon hot paprika
1 teaspoon shallot powder
1 teaspoon porcini powder

1/2 teaspoon granulated garlic
1/3 teaspoon celery seeds
1 ½ tablespoons olive oil
For the Hot Sauce:
1/2 cup tomato sauce
1 tablespoon balsamic vinegar
1/2 teaspoon ground allspice

DIRECTIONS

Toss all the ingredients for the broccoli bites in a mixing bowl, covering the broccoli florets on all sides.
Cook them in the preheated Air Fryer at 360 degrees for 13 to 15 minutes. In the meantime, mix all ingredients for the hot sauce.
Pause your Air Fryer, mix the broccoli with the prepared sauce and cook for a further 3 minutes. Bon appétit!

6. Cheese Stuffed Mushrooms with Horseradish Sauce

(Ready in about 15 minutes | Servings 5)

Per serving: 180 Calories; 13.2g Fat; 6.2g Carbs; 8.6g Protein; 2.1g Sugars; 1g Fiber

INGREDIENTS

1/2 cup parmesan cheese, grated
2 cloves garlic, pressed
2 tablespoons fresh coriander, chopped
1/3 teaspoon kosher salt
1/2 teaspoon crushed red pepper flakes
1 ½ tablespoons olive oil

20 medium-sized mushrooms, cut off the stems
1/2 cup Gorgonzola cheese, grated
1/4 cup low-fat mayonnaise
1 teaspoon prepared horseradish, well-drained
1 tablespoon fresh parsley, finely chopped

DIRECTIONS

Mix the parmesan cheese together with the garlic, coriander, salt, red pepper, and the olive oil; mix to combine well.
Stuff the mushroom caps with the cheese filling. Top with grated Gorgonzola.
Place the mushrooms in the Air Fryer grill pan and slide them into the machine. Grill them at 380 degrees F for 8 to 12 minutes or until the stuffing is warmed through.
Meanwhile, prepare the horseradish sauce by mixing the mayonnaise, horseradish and parsley. Serve the horseradish sauce with the warm fried mushrooms. Enjoy!

7. Broccoli with Herbs and Cheese

(Ready in about 25 minutes | Servings 4)

Per serving: 103 Calories; 9.1g Fat; 4.9g Carbs; 1.9g Protein; 1.2g Sugars; 0.4g Fiber

INGREDIENTS

1/3 cup grated yellow cheese
1 large-sized head broccoli, stemmed and cut small florets
2 1/2 tablespoons canola oil

2 teaspoons dried rosemary
2 teaspoons dried basil
Salt and ground black pepper, to taste

DIRECTIONS

Bring a medium pan filled with a lightly salted water to a boil. Then, boil the broccoli florets for about 3 minutes.
Then, drain the broccoli florets well; toss them with the canola oil, rosemary, basil, salt and black pepper.
Set your Air Fryer to 390 degrees F; arrange the seasoned broccoli in the cooking basket; set the timer for 17 minutes. Toss the broccoli halfway through the cooking process.
Serve warm topped with grated cheese and enjoy!

8. Family Favorite Stuffed Mushrooms

(Ready in about 16 minutes | Servings 2)

Per serving: 179 Calories; 14.7g Fat; 8.5g Carbs; 5.5g Protein; 4.6g Sugars; 2.6g Fiber

INGREDIENTS

2 teaspoons cumin powder
4 garlic cloves, peeled and minced
1 small onion, peeled and chopped
18 medium-sized white mushrooms

Fine sea salt and freshly ground black pepper, to your liking
A pinch ground allspice
2 tablespoons olive oil

DIRECTIONS

First, clean the mushrooms; remove the middle stalks from the mushrooms to prepare the "shells".
Grab a mixing dish and thoroughly combine the remaining items. Fill the mushrooms with the prepared mixture.
Cook the mushrooms at 345 degrees F heat for 12 minutes. Enjoy!

9. Spanish-Style Eggs with Manchego Cheese

(Ready in about 40 minutes | Servings 4)

Per serving: 153 Calories; 11.9g Fat; 3.2g Carbs; 9.3g Protein; 1.7g Sugars; 0.9g Fiber

INGREDIENTS

1/3 cup grated Manchego, cheese
5 eggs
1 small onion, finely chopped
2 green garlic stalks, peeled and finely minced
1 ½ cups white mushrooms, chopped
1 teaspoon dried basil

1 ½ tablespoons olive oil
3/4 teaspoon dried oregano
1/2 teaspoon dried parsley flakes or 1 tablespoon fresh flat-leaf Italian parsley
1 teaspoon porcini powder
Table salt and freshly ground black pepper, to savor

DIRECTIONS

Start by preheating your Air Fryer to 350 degrees F. Add the oil, mushrooms, onion, and green garlic to the Air Fryer baking dish. Bake this mixture for 6 minutes or until it is tender.
Meanwhile, crack the eggs into a mixing bowl; beat the eggs until they're well whisked. Next, add the seasonings and mix again. Pause your Air Fryer and take the baking dish out of the bakset.
Pour the whisked egg mixture into the baking dish with sautéed mixture. Top with the grated Manchego cheese.
Bake for about 32 minutes at 320 degrees F or until your frittata is set. Serve warm. Bon appétit!

10. Famous Fried Pickles

(Ready in about 20 minutes | Servings 6)

Per serving: 58 Calories; 2g Fat; 6.8g Carbs; 3.2g Protein; 0.9g Sugars; 0.4g Fiber

INGREDIENTS

1/3 cup milk

1 teaspoon garlic powder

2 medium-sized eggs

1 teaspoon fine sea salt

1/3 teaspoon chili powder

1/3 cup all-purpose flour

1/2 teaspoon shallot powder

2 jars sweet and sour pickle spears

DIRECTIONS

Pat the pickle spears dry with a kitchen towel. Then, take two mixing bowls.

Whisk the egg and milk in a bowl. In another bowl, combine all dry ingredients.

Firstly, dip the pickle spears into the dry mix; then coat each pickle with the egg/milk mixture; dredge them in the flour mixture again for additional coating.

Air fry battered pickles for 15 minutes at 385 degrees. Enjoy!

11. Fried Squash Croquettes

(Ready in about 22 minutes | Servings 4)

Per serving: 152 Calories; 10.02g Fat; 9.4g Carbs; 5.8g Protein; 0.3g Sugars; 0.4g Fiber

INGREDIENTS

1/3 cup all-purpose flour

1/3 teaspoon freshly ground black pepper, or more to taste

1/3 teaspoon dried sage

4 cloves garlic, minced

1 ½ tablespoons olive oil

1/3 butternut squash, peeled and grated

2 eggs, well whisked

1 teaspoon fine sea salt

A pinch of ground allspice

DIRECTIONS

Thoroughly combine all ingredients in a mixing bowl.

Preheat your Air Fryer to 345 degrees and set the timer for 17 minutes; cook until your fritters are browned; serve right away.

12. Tamarind Glazed Sweet Potatoes

(Ready in about 24 minutes | Servings 4)

Per serving: 103 Calories; 9.1g Fat; 4.9g Carbs; 1.9g Protein; 1.2g Sugars; 0.3g Fiber

INGREDIENTS

1/3 teaspoon white pepper

1 tablespoon butter, melted

1/2 teaspoon turmeric powder

5 garnet sweet potatoes, peeled and diced

A few drops liquid Stevia

2 teaspoons tamarind paste

1 1/2 tablespoons fresh lime juice

1 1/2 teaspoon ground allspice

DIRECTIONS

In a mixing bowl, toss all ingredients until sweet potatoes are well coated.

Air-fry them at 335 degrees F for 12 minutes.

Pause the Air Fryer and toss again. Increase the temperature to 390 degrees F and cook for an additional 10 minutes. Eat warm.

13. Roasted Cauliflower with Pepper Jack Cheese

(Ready in about 25 minutes | Servings 2)

Per serving: 271 Calories; 23g Fat; 8.9g Carbs; 9.8g Protein; 2.8g Sugars; 4.5g Fiber

INGREDIENTS

1/3 teaspoon shallot powder

1 teaspoon ground black pepper

1 ½ large-sized heads of cauliflower, broken into florets

1/4 teaspoon cumin powder

½ teaspoon garlic salt

1/4 cup Pepper Jack cheese, grated

1 ½ tablespoons vegetable oil

1/3 teaspoon paprika

DIRECTIONS

Boil cauliflower in a large pan of salted water approximately 5 minutes. After that, drain the cauliflower florets; now, transfer them to a baking dish.

Toss the cauliflower florets with the rest of the above ingredients.

Roast at 395 degrees F for 16 minutes, turn them halfway through the process. Enjoy!

14. Mexican-Style Cauliflower Fritters

(Ready in about 48 minutes | Servings 6)

Per serving: 190 Calories; 14.1g Fat; 4.7g Carbs; 11.5g Protein; 1.3g Sugars; 1.3g Fiber

INGREDIENTS

2 teaspoons chili powder

1 1/2 teaspoon kosher salt

1 teaspoon dried marjoram, crushed

2 1/2 cups cauliflower, broken into florets

1 1/3 cups tortilla chip crumbs

1/2 teaspoon crushed red pepper flakes

3 eggs, whisked

1 ½ cups Queso cotija cheese, crumbled

DIRECTIONS

Blitz the cauliflower florets in your food processor until they're crumbled (it is the size of rice). Then, combine the cauliflower "rice" with the other items.

Now, roll the cauliflower mixture into small balls; refrigerate for 30 minutes.

Preheat your Air Fryer to 345 degrees and set the timer for 14 minutes; cook until the balls are browned and serve right away.

15. Cheesy Omelet with Mixed Greens

(Ready in about 17 minutes | Servings 2)

Per serving: 409 Calories; 29.5g Fat; 6.9g Carbs; 27.9g Protein; 3g Sugars; 1.4g Fiber

INGREDIENTS

1/3 cup Ricotta cheese

5 eggs, beaten

1/2 red bell pepper, seeded and sliced

1 cup mixed greens, roughly chopped

1/2 green bell pepper, seeded and sliced

1/2 teaspoon dried basil

1/2 chipotle pepper, finely minced

1/2 teaspoon dried oregano

DIRECTIONS

Lightly coat the inside of a baking dish with a pan spray.

Then, throw all ingredients into the baking dish; give it a good stir.

Bake at 325 degrees F for 15 minutes.

16. Decadent Omelet with Oyster Mushrooms

(Ready in about 42 minutes | Servings 2)

Per serving: 362 Calories; 29g Fat; 7.2g Carbs; 19g Protein; 2.8g Sugars; 1.4g Fiber

INGREDIENTS

3 king oyster mushrooms, thinly sliced
1 lemongrass, chopped
1/2 teaspoon dried marjoram
5 eggs
1/3 cup Swiss cheese, grated
2 tablespoons sour cream
1 1/2 teaspoon dried rosemary

2 teaspoons red pepper flakes, crushed
2 tablespoons butter, melted
1/2 red onion, peeled and sliced into thin rounds
½ teaspoon garlic powder
1 teaspoon dried dill weed
Fine sea salt and ground black pepper, to your liking

DIRECTIONS

Melt the margarine in a skillet that is placed over a medium flame. Then, sweat the onion, mushrooms, and lemongrass until they have softened; reserve.

Then, preheat the Air Fryer to 325 degrees F. Then, crack the eggs into a mixing bowl and whisk them well. Then, fold in the sour cream and give it a good stir.

Now, stir in the salt, black pepper, red pepper, rosemary, garlic powder, marjoram, and dill.

Next step, grease the inside of an Air Fryer baking dish with a thin layer of a cooking spray. Pour the egg/seasoning mixture into the baking dish; throw in the reserved mixture. Top with the Swiss cheese.

Set the timer for 35 minutes; cook until a knife inserted in the center comes out clean and dry.

17. Italian Tomatoes with Goat Cheese

(Ready in about 20 minutes | Servings 4)

Per serving: 237 Calories; 20.4g Fat; 0.9g Carbs; 13g Protein; 0.9g Sugars; 0.5g Fiber

INGREDIENTS

6 ounces goat cheese, sliced
2 shallots, thinly sliced
2 Pantano Romanesco tomatoes, cut into 1/2-inch slices
1 ½ tablespoons extra-virgin olive oil

3/4 teaspoon sea salt
Fresh parsley, for garnish
Fresh basil, chopped

DIRECTIONS

Preheat your Air Fryer to 380 degrees F.

Now, pat each tomato slice dry using a paper towel. Sprinkle each slice with salt and chopped basil. Top with a slice of goat cheese.

Top with the shallot slices; drizzle with olive oil. Add the prepared tomato and feta "bites" to the air fryer food basket.

Cook in the Air Fryer for about 14 minutes. Lastly, adjust seasonings to taste and serve garnished with fresh parsley leaves. Enjoy!

18. Swiss Creamed Eggs

(Ready in about 25 minutes | Servings 2)

Per serving: 388 Calories; 27g Fat; 6g Carbs; 29g Protein; 2.6g Sugars; 0.7g Fiber

INGREDIENTS

1 teaspoon garlic paste
1 ½ tablespoons olive oil
1/2 cup crème fraîche
1/3 teaspoon ground black pepper, to your liking
1/3 cup Swiss cheese, crumbled

1 teaspoon cayenne pepper
1/3 cup Swiss chard, torn into pieces
5 eggs
1/4 cup yellow onions, chopped
1 teaspoon fine sea salt

DIRECTIONS

Crack your eggs into a mixing dish; then, add the crème fraîche, salt, ground black pepper, and cayenne pepper.

Next, coat the inside of a baking dish with olive oil and tilt it to spread evenly. Scrape the egg/cream mixture into the baking dish. Add the other ingredients; mix to combine well.

Bake for 18 minutes at 292 degrees F. Serve immediately.

19. Italian-Style Broccoli

(Ready in about 25 minutes | Servings 4)

Per serving: 110 Calories; 10g Fat; 4.9g Carbs; 1.9g Protein; 1.2g Sugars; 3.1g Fiber

INGREDIENTS

1/3 cup Asiago cheese
1 large-sized head broccoli, stemmed and cut small florets
2 1/2 tablespoons canola oil

1 tablespoon Italian seasoning blend
Salt and ground black pepper, to taste

DIRECTIONS

Bring a medium pan filled with a lightly salted water to a boil. Then, boil the broccoli florets for about 3 minutes.
Then, drain the broccoli florets well; toss them with the canola oil, rosemary, basil, salt and black pepper.
Set your Air Fryer to 390 degrees F; arrange the seasoned broccoli in the cooking basket; set the timer for 17 minutes. Toss the broccoli halfway through the cooking process.
Serve warm topped with grated cheese and enjoy!

20. Bell Peppers with Spicy Mayo

(Ready in about 20 minutes | Servings 2)

Per serving: 346 Calories; 34.1g Fat; 9.5g Carbs; 2.3g Protein; 4.9g Sugars; 2.1g Fiber

INGREDIENTS

4 bell peppers, seeded and sliced (1-inch pieces)
1 onion, sliced (1-inch pieces)
1 tablespoon olive oil
1/2 teaspoon dried rosemary
1/2 teaspoon dried basil

Kosher salt, to taste
1/4 teaspoon ground black pepper
1/3 cup mayonnaise
1/3 teaspoon Sriracha

DIRECTIONS

Toss the bell peppers and onions with the olive oil, rosemary, basil, salt, and black pepper.
Place the peppers and onions on an even layer in the cooking basket. Cook at 400 degrees F for 12 to 14 minutes.
Meanwhile, make the sauce by whisking the mayonnaise and Sriracha. Serve immediately.

21. Easy Sesame Broccoli

(Ready in about 15 minutes | Servings 3)

Per serving: 160 Calories; 13.2g Fat; 7.7g Carbs; 6.5g Protein; 1.4g Sugars; 5g Fiber

INGREDIENTS

1 pound broccoli florets
2 tablespoons sesame oil
1/2 teaspoon shallot powder
1/2 teaspoon porcini powder
1 teaspoon garlic powder

Sea salt and ground black pepper, to taste
1/2 teaspoon cumin powder
1/4 teaspoon paprika
2 tablespoons sesame seeds

DIRECTIONS

Start by preheating the Air Fryer to 400 degrees F.
Blanch the broccoli in salted boiling water until al dente, about 3 to 4 minutes. Drain well and transfer to the lightly greased Air Fryer basket.
Add the sesame oil, shallot powder, porcini powder, garlic powder, salt, black pepper, cumin powder, paprika, and sesame seeds.
Cook for 6 minutes, tossing halfway through the cooking time. Bon appétit!

22. Easy Vegetable Kabobs

(Ready in about 30 minutes | Servings 4)

Per serving: 86 Calories; 6.9g Fat; 5.9g Carbs; 1.1g Protein; 2.9g Sugars; 1.1g Fiber

INGREDIENTS

1 medium-sized zucchini, cut into 1-inch pieces
2 red bell peppers, cut into 1-inch pieces
1 green bell pepper, cut into 1-inch pieces
1 red onion, cut into 1-inch pieces

2 tablespoons olive oil
Sea salt, to taste
1/2 teaspoon black pepper, preferably freshly cracked
1/2 teaspoon red pepper flakes

DIRECTIONS

Soak the wooden skewers in water for 15 minutes.
Thread the vegetables on skewers; drizzle olive oil all over the vegetable skewers; sprinkle with spices.
Cook in the preheated Air Fryer at 400 degrees F for 13 minutes. Serve warm and enjoy!

23. Cauliflower Croquettes with Colby Cheese

(Ready in about 25 minutes | Servings 4)

Per serving: 274 Calories; 19g Fat; 8.8g Carbs; 16.4g Protein; 2.5g Sugars; 2.7g Fiber

INGREDIENTS

1 pound cauliflower florets
2 eggs
1 tablespoon olive oil
2 tablespoons scallions, chopped
1 garlic clove, minced

1 cup Colby cheese, shredded
1/2 cup parmesan cheese, grated
Sea salt and ground black pepper, to taste
1/4 teaspoon dried dill weed
1 teaspoon paprika

DIRECTIONS

Blanch the cauliflower in salted boiling water about 3 to 4 minutes until al dente. Drain well and pulse in a food processor.
Add the remaining ingredients; mix to combine well. Shape the cauliflower mixture into bite-sized tots.
Spritz the Air Fryer basket with cooking spray.
Cook in the preheated Air Fryer at 375 degrees F for 16 minutes, shaking halfway through the cooking time. Serve with your favorite sauce for dipping. Bon appétit!

24. Mediterranean Tomatoes with Feta Cheese

(Ready in about 20 minutes | Servings 2)

Per serving: 148 Calories; 9.4g Fat; 9.4g Carbs; 7.8g Protein; 6.6g Sugars; 0.6g Fiber

INGREDIENTS

3 medium-sized tomatoes, cut into four slices, pat dry
1 teaspoon dried basil
1 teaspoon dried oregano

1/4 teaspoon red pepper flakes, crushed
1/2 teaspoon sea salt
3 slices Feta cheese

DIRECTIONS

Spritz the tomatoes with cooking oil and transfer them to the Air Fryer basket. Sprinkle with seasonings.
Cook at 350 degrees F approximately 8 minutes turning them over halfway through the cooking time.
Top with the cheese and cook an additional 4 minutes. Bon appétit!

25. Cauliflower Fritters with Mustard and Cheese

(Ready in about 30 minutes | Servings 2)

Per serving: 331 Calories; 31g Fat; 8.7g Carbs; 6.3g Protein; 2.8g Fiber

INGREDIENTS

1/2 pound cauliflower florets
2 garlic cloves, minced
1/2 cup goat cheese, shredded
Sea salt and ground black pepper, to taste

1/2 teaspoon shallot powder
1/4 teaspoon cumin powder
1/2 cup sour cream
1 teaspoon Dijon mustard

DIRECTIONS

Place the cauliflower florets in a saucepan of water; bring to the boil; reduce the heat and cook for 10 minutes or until tender.
Mash the cauliflower using your blender; add the garlic, cheese, and spices; mix to combine well.
Form the cauliflower mixture into croquettes shapes.
Cook in the preheated Air Fryer at 375 degrees F for 16 minutes, shaking halfway through the cooking time. Serve with the sour cream and mustard. Bon appétit!

26. Fried Yellow Beans with Blue Cheese and Pecans

(Ready in about 15 minutes | Servings 3)

Per serving: 236 Calories; 21g Fat; 7.9g Carbs; 6.5g Protein; 0.5g Sugars; 2.1g Fiber

INGREDIENTS

3/4 pound wax yellow beans, cleaned
2 tablespoons peanut oil
4 tablespoons Romano cheese, grated
Sea salt and ground black pepper, to taste

1/2 teaspoon red pepper flakes, crushed
2 tablespoons pecans, sliced
1/3 cup blue cheese, crumbled

DIRECTIONS

Toss the wax beans with the peanut oil, Romano cheese, salt, black pepper, and red pepper.
Place the wax beans in the lightly greased cooking basket.
Cook in the preheated Air Fryer at 400 degrees F for 5 minutes. Shake the basket once or twice.
Add the pecans and cook for 3 minutes more or until lightly toasted. Serve topped with blue cheese and enjoy!

27. Dilled Asparagus with Cheese

(Ready in about 15 minutes | Servings 3)

Per serving: 132 Calories; 11.2g Fat; 2.2g Carbs; 6.5g Protein; 1g Sugars; 3.3g Fiber

INGREDIENTS

1 bunch of asparagus, trimmed
1 tablespoon olive oil
1/2 teaspoon kosher salt

1/4 teaspoon cracked black pepper, to taste
1/2 teaspoon dried dill weed
1/2 cup goat cheese, crumbled

DIRECTIONS

Place the asparagus spears in the lightly greased cooking basket. Toss the asparagus with the olive oil, salt, black pepper, and dill.
Cook in the preheated Air Fryer at 400 degrees F for 9 minutes.
Serve garnished with goat cheese. Bon appétit!

28. Zucchini Parmesan Crisps

(Ready in about 20 minutes | Servings 4)

Per serving: 157 Calories; 9.5g Fat; 7.4g Carbs; 12g Protein; 0.4g Sugars; 1.2g Fiber

INGREDIENTS

1 pound zucchini, peeled and sliced
1 egg, lightly beaten

1 cup parmesan cheese, preferably freshly grated

DIRECTIONS

Pat the zucchini dry with a kitchen towel.
In a mixing dish, thoroughly combine the egg and cheese. Then, coat the zucchini slices with the breadcrumb mixture.
Cook in the preheated Air Fryer at 400 degrees F for 9 minutes, shaking the basket halfway through the cooking time.
Work in batches until the chips is golden brown. Bon appétit!

29. Italian-Style Sausage Casserole

(Ready in about 20 minutes | Servings 4)

Per serving: 508 Calories; 40g Fat; 5.3g Carbs; 30.2g Protein; 1.3g Sugars; 4.2g Fiber

INGREDIENTS

1 pound Italian sausage
2 Italian peppers, seeded and sliced
1 cup mushrooms, sliced
1 shallot, sliced
4 cloves garlic
1 teaspoon dried basil

1 teaspoon dried oregano
1/4 teaspoon black pepper
1/4 teaspoon cayenne pepper
Sea salt, to taste
2 tablespoons Dijon mustard
1 cup chicken broth

DIRECTIONS

Toss all ingredients in a lightly greased baking pan. Make sure the sausages and vegetables are coated with the oil and seasonings.
Bake in the preheated Air Fryer at 380 degrees F for 15 minutes.
Divide between individual bowls and serve warm. Bon appétit!

30. Rustic Roasted Green Beans

(Ready in about 10 minutes + chilling time | Servings 4)

Per serving: 280 Calories; 23.3g Fat; 8.8g Carbs; 9.3g Protein; 4.2g Sugars; 2.4g Fiber

INGREDIENTS

3/4 pound trimmed green beans, cut into bite-sized pieces
Salt and freshly cracked mixed pepper, to taste
1 shallot, thinly sliced
1 tablespoon lime juice
1 tablespoon champagne vinegar
1/4 cup extra-virgin olive oil

1/2 teaspoon mustard seeds
1/2 teaspoon celery seeds
1 tablespoon fresh basil leaves, chopped
1 tablespoon fresh parsley leaves
1 cup goat cheese, crumbled

DIRECTIONS

Toss the green beans with salt and pepper in a lightly greased Air Fryer basket.
Cook in the preheated Air Fryer at 400 degrees F for 5 minutes or until tender.
Add the shallots and gently stir to combine.
In a mixing bowl, whisk the lime juice, vinegar, olive oil, and spices. Dress the salad and top with the goat cheese. Serve at room temperature or chilled. Enjoy!

31. Garlic Fried Mushrooms

(Ready in about 15 minutes | Servings 4)

Per serving: 338 Calories; 22.3g Fat; 8g Carbs; 26.1g Protein; 2.3g Sugars; 1.2g Fiber

INGREDIENTS

1 pound button mushrooms

1 ½ cups pork rinds

1 cup parmesan cheese, grated

2 eggs, whisked

1/2 teaspoon salt

2 tablespoons fresh parsley leaves, roughly chopped

DIRECTIONS

Pat the mushrooms dry with a paper towel.

To begin, set up your "breading" station. Mix the pork rinds and parmesan cheese in a shallow dish. In a separate dish, whisk the eggs. Start by dipping the mushrooms into the eggs. Press your mushrooms into the parm/pork rind mixture, coating evenly.

Spritz the Air Fryer basket with cooking oil. Add the mushrooms and cook at 400 degrees F for 6 minutes, flipping them halfway through the cooking time.

Sprinkle with the salt. Serve garnished with fresh parsley leaves. Bon appétit!

32. Greek-Style Roasted Vegetable Salad

(Ready in about 20 minutes | Servings 4)

Per serving: 183 Calories; 15.8g Fat; 9.7g Carbs; 3.1g Protein; 4.8g Sugars; 3.7g Fiber

INGREDIENTS

1 red onion, sliced

1 pound cherry tomatoes

1/2 pound asparagus

1 cucumber, sliced

2 cups baby spinach

2 tablespoons white vinegar

1/4 cup extra-virgin olive oil

2 tablespoons fresh parsley

Sea salt and pepper to taste

1/2 cup Kalamata olives, pitted and sliced

DIRECTIONS

Begin by preheating your Air Fryer to 400 degrees F.

Place the onion, cherry tomatoes, and asparagus in the lightly greased Air Fryer basket. Bake for 5 to 6 minutes, tossing the basket occasionally.

Transfer to a salad bowl. Add the cucumber and baby spinach.

Then, whisk the vinegar, olive oil, parsley, salt, and black pepper in a small mixing bowl. Dress your salad; add Kalamata olives.

Toss to combine well and serve.

33. Summer Vegetable Fritters

(Ready in about 20 minutes | Servings 2)

Per serving: 172 Calories; 13.4g Fat; 7.6g Carbs; 6.5g Protein; 4g Sugars; 1.5g Fiber

INGREDIENTS

1 zucchini, grated and squeezed

1 cup cauliflower florets, boiled

4 tablespoons Romano cheese, grated

2 tablespoons fresh shallots, minced

1 teaspoon fresh garlic, minced

1 tablespoon peanut oil

Sea salt and ground black pepper, to taste

1 teaspoon cayenne pepper

DIRECTIONS

In a mixing bowl, thoroughly combine all ingredients until everything is well incorporated.

Shape the mixture into patties. Spritz the Air Fryer basket with cooking spray.

Cook in the preheated Air Fryer at 365 degrees F for 6 minutes. Turn them over and cook for a further 6 minutes

Serve immediately and enjoy!

34. Veggies with Middle-Eastern Tahini Sauce

(Ready in about 20 minutes | Servings 4)

Per serving: 185 Calories; 14.8g Fat; 9.2g Carbs; 6.9g Protein; 3.8g Sugars; 3.1g Fiber

INGREDIENTS

1 pound cauliflower florets
1 pound button mushrooms
2 tablespoons olive oil
1/2 teaspoon white pepper
1/2 teaspoon dried dill weed
1/2 teaspoon cayenne pepper
1/2 teaspoon celery seeds
1/2 teaspoon mustard seeds

Salt, to taste
Yogurt Tahini Sauce:
1 cup plain yogurt
2 heaping tablespoons tahini paste
1 tablespoon lemon juice
1 tablespoon extra-virgin olive oil
1/2 teaspoon Aleppo pepper, minced

DIRECTIONS

Toss the cauliflower and mushrooms with olive oil and spices. Preheat your Air Fryer to 380 degrees F.
Add the cauliflower to the cooking basket and cook for 10 minutes.
Add the mushrooms, turn the temperature to 390 degrees and cook for 6 minutes more.
While the vegetables are cooking, make the sauce by whisking all ingredients. Serve the warm vegetables with the sauce on the side. Bon appétit!

35. Rainbow Cheese and Vegetable Bake

(Ready in about 50 minutes | Servings 4)

Per serving: 233 Calories; 17.2g Fat; 9.7g Carbs; 11.1g Protein; 4.6g Sugars; 3.2g Fiber

INGREDIENTS

1 pound cauliflower, chopped into small florets
2 tablespoons olive oil
1/2 teaspoon red pepper flakes, crushed
1/2 teaspoon freshly ground black pepper
Salt, to taste
3 bell peppers, thinly sliced

1 serrano pepper, thinly sliced
2 medium-sized tomatoes, sliced
1 leek, thinly sliced
2 garlic cloves, minced
1 cup Monterey cheese, shredded

DIRECTIONS

Start by preheating your Air Fryer to 350 degrees F. Spritz a casserole dish with cooking oil.
Place the cauliflower in the casserole dish in an even layer; drizzle 1 tablespoon of olive oil over the top. Then, add the red pepper, black pepper, and salt.
Add 2 bell peppers and 1/2 of the leeks. Add the tomatoes and the remaining 1 tablespoon of olive oil.
Add the remaining peppers, leeks, and minced garlic. Top with the cheese.
Cover the casserole with foil and bake for 32 minutes. Remove the foil and increase the temperature to 400 degrees F; bake an additional 16 minutes. Bon appétit!

36. Classic Cauliflower Hash Browns

(Ready in about 30 minutes | Servings 2)

Per serving: 157 Calories; 11.2g Fat; 7.3g Carbs; 8g Protein; 2.6g Sugars; 2.6g Fiber

INGREDIENTS

2/3 pound cauliflower, peeled and grated
2 eggs, whisked
1/4 cup scallions, chopped
1 teaspoon fresh garlic, minced

Sea salt and ground black pepper, to taste
1/4 teaspoon ground allspice
1/2 teaspoon cinnamon
1 tablespoon peanut oil

DIRECTIONS

Boil cauliflower over medium-low heat until fork-tender, 5 to 7 minutes Drain the water; pat cauliflower dry with a kitchen towel.
Now, add the remaining ingredients; stir to combine well.
Cook in the preheated Air Fryer at 395 degrees F for 20 minutes. Shake the basket once or twice. Serve with low-carb tomato sauce.

37. Vegetable and Egg Salad

(Ready in about 35 minutes | Servings 4)

Per serving: 298 Calories; 23.3g Fat; 7.5g Carbs; 15g Protein; 2.6g Sugars; 2.6g Fiber

INGREDIENTS

1/3 pound Brussels sprouts
1/2 cup radishes, sliced
1/2 cup mozzarella cheese, crumbled
1 red onion, chopped
4 eggs, hardboiled and sliced

Dressing:
1/4 cup olive oil
2 tablespoons champagne vinegar
1 teaspoon Dijon mustard
Sea salt and ground black pepper, to taste

DIRECTIONS

Start by preheating your Air Fryer to 380 degrees F.

Add the Brussels sprouts and radishes to the cooking basket. Spritz with cooking spray and cook for 15 minutes. Let it cool to room temperature about 15 minutes.

Toss the vegetables with cheese and red onion.

Mix all ingredients for the dressing and toss to combine well. Serve topped with the hard-boiled eggs. Bon appétit!

38. Simple Stuffed Bell Peppers

(Ready in about 20 minutes | Servings 2)

Per serving: 378 Calories; 38g Fat; 7.6g Carbs; 5.5g Protein; 4.1g Sugars; 2.6g Fiber

INGREDIENTS

2 bell peppers, tops and seeds removed
Salt and pepper, to taste
2/3 cup cream cheese

2 tablespoons mayonnaise
1 tablespoon fresh celery stalks, chopped

DIRECTIONS

Arrange the peppers in the lightly greased cooking basket. Cook in the preheated Air Fryer at 400 degrees F for 15 minutes, turning them over halfway through the cooking time.

Season with salt and pepper.

Then, in a mixing bowl, combine the cream cheese with the mayonnaise and chopped celery. Stuff the pepper with the cream cheese mixture and serve.

39. Japanese Tempura Bowl

(Ready in about 20 minutes | Servings 3)

Per serving: 324 Calories; 19.2g Fat; 9.5g Carbs; 21.6g Protein; 1.9g Sugars; 2g Fiber

INGREDIENTS

7 tablespoons whey protein isolate
1 teaspoon baking powder
Kosher salt and ground black pepper, to taste
1/2 teaspoon paprika
1 teaspoon dashi granules
2 eggs
1 tablespoon mirin

3 tablespoons soda water
1 cup parmesan cheese, grated
1 onion, cut into rings
1 bell pepper
1 zucchini, cut into slices
3 asparagus spears
2 tablespoons olive oil

DIRECTIONS

In a shallow bowl, mix the whey protein isolate, baking powder, salt, black pepper, paprika, dashi granules, eggs, mirin, and soda water. In another shallow bowl, place grated parmesan cheese.

Dip the vegetables in tempura batter; lastly, roll over parmesan cheese to coat evenly. Drizzle each piece with olive oil.

Cook in the preheated Air Fryer at 400 degrees F for 10 minutes, shaking the basket halfway through the cooking time. Work in batches until the vegetables are crispy and golden brown. Bon appétit!

40. Balsamic Keto Vegetables

(Ready in about 15 minutes | Servings 3)

Per serving: 170 Calories; 14g Fat; 9.7g Carbs; 4.2g Protein; 4.5g Sugars; 2.9g Fiber

INGREDIENTS

1/2 pound cauliflower florets
1/2 pound button mushrooms, whole
1 cup pearl onions, whole
Pink Himalayan salt and ground black pepper, to taste
1/4 teaspoon smoked paprika

1 teaspoon garlic powder
1/2 teaspoon dried thyme
1/2 teaspoon dried marjoram
3 tablespoons olive oil
2 tablespoons balsamic vinegar

DIRECTIONS

Toss all ingredients in a large mixing dish.
Roast in the preheated Air Fryer at 400 degrees F for 5 minutes. Shake the basket and cook for 7 minutes more.
Serve with some extra fresh herbs if desired. Bon appétit!

41. Winter Vegetables with Herbs

(Ready in about 25 minutes | Servings 2)

Per serving: 141 Calories; 11.3g Fat; 8.1g Carbs; 2.5g Protein; 2.9g Sugars; 2.6g Fiber

INGREDIENTS

1/2 pound broccoli florets
1 celery root, peeled and cut into 1-inch pieces
1 onion, cut into wedges
2 tablespoons unsalted butter, melted
1/2 cup chicken broth

1/4 cup tomato sauce
1 teaspoon parsley
1 teaspoon rosemary
1 teaspoon thyme

DIRECTIONS

Start by preheating your Air Fryer to 380 degrees F. Place all ingredients in a lightly greased casserole dish. Stir to combine well.
Bake in the preheated Air Fryer for 10 minutes. Gently stir the vegetables with a large spoon and cook for 5 minutes more.
Serve in individual bowls with a few drizzles of lemon juice. Bon appétit!

42. Traditional Indian Kofta

(Ready in about 35 minutes | Servings 4)

Per serving: 259 Calories; 19.1g Fat; 9.1g Carbs; 12.9g Protein; 3.3g Sugars; 3.4g Fiber

INGREDIENTS

Veggie Balls:
3/4 pound zucchini, grated and well drained
1/4 pound kohlrabi, grated and well drained
2 cloves garlic, minced
1 tablespoon Garam masala
1 cup paneer, crumbled
1/4 cup coconut flour

1/2 teaspoon chili powder
Himalayan pink salt and ground black pepper, to taste
Sauce:
1 tablespoon sesame oil
1/2 teaspoon cumin seeds
2 cloves garlic, roughly chopped
1 onion, chopped

1 Kashmiri chili pepper, seeded and minced
1 (1-inch) piece ginger, chopped
1 teaspoon paprika
1 teaspoon turmeric powder
2 ripe tomatoes, pureed
1/2 cup vegetable broth
1/4 full fat coconut milk

DIRECTIONS

Start by preheating your Air Fryer to 360 degrees F. Thoroughly combine the zucchini, kohlrabi, garlic, Garam masala, paneer, coconut flour, chili powder, salt and ground black pepper.
Shape the vegetable mixture into small balls and arrange them in the lightly greased cooking basket.
Cook in the preheated Air Fryer at 360 degrees F for 15 minutes or until thoroughly cooked and crispy. Repeat the process until you run out of ingredients.
Heat the sesame oil in a saucepan over medium heat and add the cumin seeds. Once the cumin seeds turn brown, add the garlic, onions, chili pepper, and ginger. Sauté for 2 to 3 minutes.
Add the paprika, turmeric powder, tomatoes, and broth; let it simmer, covered, for 4 to 5 minutes, stirring occasionally.
Add the coconut milk. Heat off; add the veggie balls and gently stir to combine. Bon appétit!

43. Shrimp and Cauliflower Casserole

(Ready in about 25 minutes | Servings 4)

Per serving: 209 Calories; 8.6g Fat; 6.2g Carbs; 24.6g Protein; 3.1g Sugars; 1.9g Fiber

INGREDIENTS

1 pound shrimp cleaned and deveined
2 cups cauliflower, cut into florets
2 bell pepper, sliced

1 shallot, sliced
2 tablespoons sesame oil
1 cup tomato paste

DIRECTIONS

Start by preheating your Air Fryer to 360 degrees F. Spritz the baking pan with cooking spray.
Now, arrange the shrimp and vegetables in the baking pan. Then, drizzle the sesame oil over the vegetables. Pour the tomato paste over the vegetables.
Cook for 10 minutes in the preheated Air Fryer. Stir with a large spoon and cook for a further 12 minutes. Serve warm.

44. Brussels Sprout Salad with Pancetta

(Ready in about 35 minutes + chilling time | Servings 4)

Per serving: 157 Calories; 9.9g Fat; 8.5g Carbs; 10.4g Protein; 2.3g Sugars; 3.3g Fiber

INGREDIENTS

2/3 pound Brussels sprouts
1 tablespoon olive oil
Coarse sea salt and ground black pepper, to taste
2 ounces baby arugula
1 shallot, thinly sliced
4 ounces pancetta, chopped

Lemon Vinaigrette:
2 tablespoons extra virgin olive oil
2 tablespoons fresh lemon juice
1 tablespoon honey
1 teaspoon Dijon mustard

DIRECTIONS

Start by preheating your Air Fryer to 380 degrees F.
Add the Brussels sprouts to the cooking basket. Brush with olive oil and cook for 15 minutes. Let it cool to room temperature about 15 minutes.
Toss the Brussels sprouts with the salt, black pepper, baby arugula, and shallot.
Mix all ingredients for the dressing. Then, dress your salad, garnish with pancetta, and serve well chilled. Bon appétit!

45. Keto Buddha Bowl

(Ready in about 20 minutes | Servings 3)

Per serving: 329 Calories; 32.3g Fat; 8.6g Carbs; 3.4g Protein; 3.5g Sugars; 3g Fiber

INGREDIENTS

1 (1-pound) head cauliflower, food-processed into rice-like particles
2 bell pepper, spiralized
Coarse sea salt and ground black pepper, to taste
3 cups baby spinach
2 tablespoons champagne vinegar

4 tablespoons mayonnaise
1 teaspoon yellow mustard
4 tablespoons olive oil, divided
2 tablespoons cilantro leaves, chopped
2 tablespoons pine nuts

DIRECTIONS

Start by preheating the Air Fryer to 400 degrees F.
Place the cauliflower florets and bell peppers in the lightly greased Air Fryer basket. Season with salt and black pepper; cook for 12 minutes, tossing halfway through the cooking time.
Toss with the baby spinach. Add the champagne vinegar, mayonnaise, mustard, and olive oil. Garnish with fresh cilantro and pine nuts. Bon appétit!

46. Italian-Style Eggplant with Mozzarella Cheese

(Ready in about 45 minutes | Servings 4)

Per serving: 402 Calories; 36g Fat; 8.7g Carbs; 12.1g Protein; 5g Sugars; 3.9g Fiber

INGREDIENTS

1 pound eggplant, sliced
1 tablespoon sea salt
1/2 cup Romano cheese, preferably freshly grated
Sea salt and cracked black pepper, to taste

1 egg, whisked
4 ounces pork rinds
1/2 cup mozzarella cheese, grated
2 tablespoons fresh Italian parsley, roughly chopped

DIRECTIONS

Toss the eggplant with 1 tablespoon of salt and let it stand for 30 minutes. Drain and rinse.

Mix the cheese, salt, and black pepper in a bowl. Then, add the whisked egg.

Dip the eggplant slices in the batter and press to coat on all sides. Roll them over pork rinds. Transfer to the lightly greased Air Fryer basket.

Cook at 370 degrees F for 7 to 9 minutes. Turn each slice over and top with the mozzarella. Cook an additional 2 minutes or until the cheese melts.

Serve garnished with fresh Italian parsley. Bon appétit!

47. Fennel with Shirataki Noodles

(Ready in about 20 minutes + chilling time | Servings 3)

Per serving: 208 Calories; 10.2g Fat; 9.7g Carbs; 1.7g Protein; 4.7g Sugars; 3.9g Fiber

INGREDIENTS

1 fennel bulb, quartered
Salt and white pepper, to taste
1 clove garlic, finely chopped
1 green onion, thinly sliced
1 cup Chinese cabbage, shredded

2 tablespoons rice wine vinegar
2 tablespoons sesame oil
1 teaspoon ginger, freshly grated
1 tablespoon soy sauce
1 1/3 cups Shirataki noodles, boiled

DIRECTIONS

Start by preheating your Air Fryer to 370 degrees F.

Now, cook the fennel bulb in the lightly greased cooking basket for 15 minutes, shaking the basket once or twice.

Let it cool completely and toss with the remaining ingredients. Serve well chilled.

48. Authentic Peperonata Siciliana

(Ready in about 25 minutes | Servings 4)

Per serving: 165 Calories; 14.4g Fat; 8.8g Carbs; 1.7g Protein; 4.3g Sugars; 1.8g Fiber

INGREDIENTS

4 tablespoons olive oil
4 bell peppers, seeded and sliced
1 serrano pepper, seeded and sliced
1/2 cup onion, peeled and sliced
2 garlic cloves, crushed

1 large tomato, pureed
Sea salt and black pepper
1 teaspoon cayenne pepper
4 fresh basil leaves
8 Sicilian olives green, pitted and sliced

DIRECTIONS

Brush the sides and bottom of the cooking basket with 1 tablespoon of olive oil. Add the peppers, onions, and garlic to the cooking basket. Cook for 5 minutes or until tender.

Add the tomatoes, salt, black pepper, and cayenne pepper; add the remaining tablespoon of olive oil and cook in the preheated Air Fryer at 380 degrees F for 15 minutes, stirring occasionally.

Divide between individual bowls and garnish with basil leaves and olives. Bon appétit!

49. Asparagus Salad with Boiled Eggs

(Ready in about 10 minutes + chilling time | Servings 4)

Per serving: 239 Calories; 18.4g Fat; 9.3g Carbs; 8.3g Protein; 5.3g Sugars; 2.8g Fiber

INGREDIENTS

1/4 cup olive oil
1 pound asparagus, trimmed
1 cup cherry tomatoes, halved
1/4 cup balsamic vinegar
2 garlic cloves, minced

2 scallion stalks, chopped
1/2 teaspoon oregano
Coarse sea salt and ground black pepper, to your liking
2 hard-boiled eggs, sliced

DIRECTIONS

Start by preheating your Air Fryer to 400 degrees F. Brush the cooking basket with 1 tablespoon of olive oil.
Add the asparagus and cherry tomatoes to the cooking basket. Drizzle 1 tablespoon of olive oil all over your veggies.
Cook for 5 minutes, shaking the basket halfway through the cooking time. Let it cool slightly.
Toss with the remaining olive oil, balsamic vinegar, garlic, scallions, oregano, salt, and black pepper.
Afterwards, add the hard-boiled eggs on the top of your salad and serve.

50. Super-Crispy Asparagus Fries

(Ready in about 20 minutes | Servings 4)

Per serving: 217 Calories; 14.4g Fat; 7.7g Carbs; 13.2g Protein; 1.2g Sugars; 0.5g Fiber

INGREDIENTS

2 eggs
1 teaspoon Dijon mustard
1 cup Parmesan cheese, grated

Sea salt and ground black pepper, to taste
18 asparagus spears, trimmed
1/2 cup sour cream

DIRECTIONS

Start by preheating your Air Fryer to 400 degrees F.
In a shallow bowl, whisk the eggs and mustard. In another shallow bowl, combine the Parmesan cheese, salt, and black pepper.
Dip the asparagus spears in the egg mixture, then in the parmesan mixture; press to adhere.
Cook for 5 minutes; work in three batches. Serve with sour cream on the side. Enjoy!

51. Asian Cauliflower Rice with Eggs

(Ready in about 20 minutes | Servings 4)

Per serving: 149 Calories; 11g Fat; 6.1g Carbs; 7.4g Protein; 2.6g Sugars; 1.7g Fiber

INGREDIENTS

2 cups cauliflower, food-processed into rice-like particles
2 tablespoons peanut oil
1/2 cup scallions, chopped
2 bell pepper, chopped

4 eggs, beaten
Sea salt and ground black pepper, to taste
1/2 teaspoon granulated garlic

DIRECTIONS

Grease a baking pan with nonstick cooking spray.
Add the cauliflower rice and the other ingredients to the baking pan.
Cook at 400 degrees F for 12 minutes, checking occasionally to ensure even cooking. Enjoy!

52. Easy Shepherd's Pie

(Ready in about 30 minutes | Servings 5)

Per serving: 214 Calories; 18.5g Fat; 8.5g Carbs; 4.4g Protein; 3.9g Sugars; 2.2g Fiber

INGREDIENTS

2 tablespoons olive oil
2 bell peppers, seeded and sliced
1 celery, chopped
1 onion, chopped
2 garlic cloves, minced
1 cup cooked bacon, diced
1 ½ cups beef bone broth

5 ounces green beans, drained
Sea salt and freshly ground black pepper, to taste
8 ounces cauliflower pulsed in a food processor to a fine-crumb like consistency
1/2 cup milk
2 tablespoons butter, melted

DIRECTIONS

Heat the olive oil in a saucepan over medium-high heat. Now, cook the peppers, celery, onion, and garlic until they have softened, about 7 minutes

Add the bacon and broth. Bring to a boil and cook for 2 minutes more. Stir in green beans, salt and black pepper; continue to cook until everything is heated through.

Transfer the mixture to the lightly greased baking pan.

Microwave cauliflower rice for 5 minutes.

In a small bowl, combine the cauliflower, milk, and melted butter. Stir until well mixed and spoon evenly over the vegetable mixture. Smooth it with a spatula and transfer to the Air Fryer cooking basket.

Bake in the preheated Air Fryer at 400 degrees F for 12 minutes. Place on a wire rack to cool slightly before slicing and serving. Bon appétit!

53. Zucchini Casserole with Cooked Ham

(Ready in about 30 minutes | Servings 4)

Per serving: 325 Calories; 20.9g Fat; 7.9g Carbs; 26.6g Protein; 2.8g Sugars; 2.1g Fiber

INGREDIENTS

2 tablespoons butter, melted
1 zucchini, diced
1 bell pepper, seeded and sliced
1 red chili pepper, seeded and minced
1 medium-sized leek, sliced
3/4 pound ham, cooked and diced

5 eggs
1 teaspoon cayenne pepper
Sea salt, to taste
1/2 teaspoon ground black pepper
1 tablespoon fresh cilantro, chopped

DIRECTIONS

Start by preheating the Air Fryer to 380 degrees F. Grease the sides and bottom of a baking pan with the melted butter.

Place the zucchini, peppers, leeks and ham in the baking pan. Bake in the preheated Air Fryer for 6 minutes.

Crack the eggs on top of ham and vegetables; season with the cayenne pepper, salt, and black pepper. Bake for a further 20 minutes or until the whites are completely set.

Garnish with fresh cilantro and serve. Bon appétit!

POULTRY

54. Asian Spicy Turkey

(Ready in about 35 minutes | Servings 6)

Per serving: 279 Calories; 16.2g Fat; 2.4g Carbs; 29g Protein; 1.4g Sugars; 2.2g Fib

INGREDIENTS

1 tablespoon sesame oil
2 pounds turkey thighs
1 teaspoon Chinese Five-spice powder
1 teaspoon pink Himalayan salt
1/4 teaspoon Sichuan pepper

1 tablespoon Chinese rice vinegar
2 tablespoons soy sauce
1 tablespoon chili sauce
1 tablespoon mustard

DIRECTIONS

Preheat your Air Fryer to 360 degrees F.
Brush the sesame oil all over the turkey thighs. Season them with spices.
Cook for 23 minutes, turning over once or twice. Make sure to work in batches to ensure even cooking
In the meantime, combine the remaining ingredients in a wok (or similar type pan) that is preheated over medium-high heat. Cook and stir until the sauce reduces by about a third.
Add the fried turkey thighs to the wok; gently stir to coat with the sauce.
Let the turkey rest for 10 minutes before slicing and serving. Enjoy!

55. Spicy Chicken Drumsticks with Herbs

(Ready in about 40 minutes | Servings 6)

Per serving: 280 Calories; 18.7g Fat; 2.6g Carbs; 24.1g Protein; 1.4g Sugars; 0.5g Fiber

INGREDIENTS

6 chicken drumsticks
Sauce:
6 ounces hot sauce
3 tablespoons olive oil

3 tablespoons tamari sauce
1 teaspoon dried thyme
1/2 teaspoon dried oregano

DIRECTIONS

Spritz the sides and bottom of the cooking basket with a nonstick cooking spray.
Cook the chicken drumsticks at 380 degrees F for 35 minutes, flipping them over halfway through.
Meanwhile, heat the hot sauce, olive oil, tamari sauce, thyme, and oregano in a pan over medium-low heat; reserve.
Drizzle the sauce over the prepared chicken drumsticks; toss to coat well and serve. Bon appétit!

56. Classic Chicken with Peanuts

(Ready in about 25 minutes | Servings 4)

Per serving: 354 Calories; 17.4g Fat; 6.3g Carbs; 40g Protein; 1.4g Sugars; 0.7g Fiber

INGREDIENTS

1 ½ pounds chicken tenderloins
2 tablespoons peanut oil
1/2 cup parmesan cheese, grated
Sea salt and ground black pepper, to taste

1/2 teaspoon garlic powder
1 teaspoon red pepper flakes
2 tablespoons peanuts, roasted and roughly chopped

DIRECTIONS

Start by preheating your Air Fryer to 360 degrees F.
Brush the chicken tenderloins with peanut oil on all sides.
In a mixing bowl, thoroughly combine grated parmesan cheese, salt, black pepper, garlic powder, and red pepper flakes. Dredge the chicken in the breading, shaking off any residual coating.
Lay the chicken tenderloins into the cooking basket. Cook for 12 to 13 minutes or until it is no longer pink in the center. Work in batches; an instant-read thermometer should read at least 165 degrees F.
Serve garnished with roasted peanuts. Bon appétit!

57. Turkey with Paprika and Tarragon

(Ready in about 40 minutes | Servings 6)

Per serving: 217 Calories; 7.5g Fat; 1.2g Carbs; 34.7g Protein; 0.5g Sugars; 0.3g Fiber

INGREDIENTS

2 pounds turkey tenderloins
2 tablespoons olive oil
Salt and ground black pepper, to taste

1 teaspoon smoked paprika
2 tablespoons dry white wine
1 tablespoon fresh tarragon leaves, chopped

DIRECTIONS

Brush the turkey tenderloins with olive oil. Season with salt, black pepper, and paprika.
Afterwards, add the white wine and tarragon.

Cook the turkey tenderloins at 350 degrees F for 30 minutes, flipping them over halfway through. Let them rest for 5 to 9 minutes before slicing and serving. Enjoy!

58. Italian-Style Chicken with Roma Tomatoes

(Ready in about 45 minutes | Servings 8)

Per serving: 315 Calories; 17.1g Fat; 2.7g Carbs; 36g Protein; 1.7g Sugars; 0.9g Fiber

INGREDIENTS

2 teaspoons olive oil, melted
3 pounds chicken breasts, bone-in
1/2 teaspoon black pepper, freshly ground
1/2 teaspoon salt
1 teaspoon cayenne pepper

2 tablespoons fresh parsley, minced
1 teaspoon fresh basil, minced
1 teaspoon fresh rosemary, minced
4 medium-sized Roma tomatoes, halved

DIRECTIONS

Start by preheating your Air Fryer to 370 degrees F. Brush the cooking basket with 1 teaspoon of olive oil.
Sprinkle the chicken breasts with all seasonings listed above.
Cook for 25 minutes or until chicken breasts are slightly browned. Work in batches.
Arrange the tomatoes in the cooking basket and brush them with the remaining teaspoon of olive oil. Season with sea salt.
Cook the tomatoes at 350 degrees F for 10 minutes, shaking halfway through the cooking time. Serve with chicken breasts. Bon appétit!

59. Duck Breasts with Candy Onion and Coriander

(Ready in about 25 minutes | Servings 4)

Per serving: 362 Calories; 18.7g Fat; 4g Carbs; 42.3g Protein; 1.3g Sugars; 2.5g Fiber

INGREDIENTS

1 ½ pounds duck breasts, skin removed
1 teaspoon kosher salt
1/2 teaspoon cayenne pepper
1/3 teaspoon black pepper

1/2 teaspoon smoked paprika
1 tablespoon Thai red curry paste
1 cup candy onions, halved
1/4 small pack coriander, chopped

DIRECTIONS

Place the duck breasts between 2 sheets of foil; then, use a rolling pin to bash the duck until they are 1-inch thick.
Preheat your Air Fryer to 395 degrees F.
Rub the duck breasts with salt, cayenne pepper, black pepper, paprika, and red curry paste. Place the duck breast in the cooking basket.
Cook for 11 to 12 minutes. Top with candy onions and cook for another 10 to 11 minutes.
Serve garnished with coriander and enjoy!

60. Paprika Chicken Legs with Turnip

(Ready in about 30 minutes | Servings 3)

Per serving: 207 Calories; 7.8g Fat; 3.4g Carbs; 29.5g Protein; 1.6g Sugars; 0.5g Fiber

INGREDIENTS

1 pound chicken legs
1 teaspoon Himalayan salt
1 teaspoon paprika

1/2 teaspoon ground black pepper
1 teaspoon butter, melted
1 turnip, trimmed and sliced

DIRECTIONS

Spritz the sides and bottom of the cooking basket with a nonstick cooking spray.
Season the chicken legs with salt, paprika, and ground black pepper.
Cook at 370 degrees F for 10 minutes. Increase the temperature to 380 degrees F.
Drizzle turnip slices with melted butter and transfer them to the cooking basket with the chicken. Cook the turnips and chicken for 15 minutes more, flipping them halfway through the cooking time.
As for the chicken, an instant-read thermometer should read at least 165 degrees F.
Serve and enjoy!

61. Turkey Burgers with Crispy Bacon

(Ready in about 30 minutes | Servings 4)

Per serving: 308 Calories; 16.4g Fat; 7.4g Carbs; 30.9g Protein; 4.4g Sugars; 0.6g Fiber

INGREDIENTS

2 tablespoons vermouth
2 strips Canadian bacon, sliced
1 pound ground turkey
1/2 shallot, minced
2 garlic cloves, minced

2 tablespoons fish sauce
Sea salt and ground black pepper, to taste
1 teaspoon red pepper flakes
4 tablespoons tomato ketchup

4 tablespoons mayonnaise
4 (1-ounce) slices Cheddar cheese
4 lettuce leaves

DIRECTIONS

Start by preheating your Air Fryer to 400 degrees F. Brush the Canadian bacon with the vermouth.
Cook for 3 minutes. Flip the bacon over and cook an additional 3 minutes.
Then, thoroughly combine the ground turkey, shallots, garlic, fish sauce, salt, black pepper, and red pepper. Form the meat mixture into 4 burger patties.
Bake in the preheated Air Fryer at 370 degrees F for 10 minutes. Flip them over and cook another 10 minutes.
Serve turkey burgers with the ketchup, mayonnaise, bacon, cheese and lettuce; serve immediately.

62. Chicken Sausage Casserole

(Ready in about 50 minutes | Servings 4)

Per serving: 300 Calories; 17.8g Fat; 9.7g Carbs; 25.3g Protein; 4.7g Sugars; 2.3g Fiber

INGREDIENTS

8 ounces zucchini, spiralized
1 pound smoked chicken sausage, sliced
1 tomato, pureed
1/2 cup Asiago cheese, shredded

1 tablespoon Italian seasoning mix
3 tablespoons Romano cheese, grated
1 tablespoon fresh basil leaves, chiffonade

DIRECTIONS

Salt the zucchini and let it stand for 30 minutes; pat it dry with kitchen towels.
Then, spritz a baking pan with cooking spray; add the zucchini to the pan. Stir in the chicken sausage, tomato puree, Asiago cheese, and Italian seasoning mix.
Bake in the preheated Air Fryer at 325 degrees F for 11 minutes.
Top with the grated Romano cheese. Turn the temperature to 390 degrees F and cook an additional 5 minutes or until everything is thoroughly heated and the cheese is melted.
Garnish with fresh basil leaves. Bon appétit!

63. Turkey Tenderloins with Gravy

(Ready in about 50 minutes | Servings 4)

Per serving: 276 Calories; 16,4g Fat; 5.2g Carbs; 26.9g Protein; 2.3g Sugars; 1.9g Fiber

INGREDIENTS

1 pound turkey tenderloins
1 tablespoon Dijon-style mustard
1 tablespoon olive oil
Sea salt and ground black pepper, to taste
1 teaspoon Italian seasoning mix

1 cup turkey stock
1/2 teaspoon xanthan gum
4 tablespoons tomato ketchup
4 tablespoons mayonnaise
4 pickles, sliced

DIRECTIONS

Rub the turkey tenderloins with the mustard and olive oil. Season with salt, black pepper, and Italian seasoning mix.
Cook the turkey tenderloins at 350 degrees F for 30 minutes, flipping them over halfway through. Let them rest for 5 to 7 minutes before slicing.
For the gravy, in a saucepan, place the drippings from the roasted turkey. Add in turkey stock and bring to a boil.
Stir in xanthan gum and whisk to combine. Let simmer another 5 to 10 minutes until starting to thicken. Gravy will thicken more as it cools.
Serve turkey tenderloins with gravy, tomato ketchup, mayonnaise, and pickles. Serve and enjoy!

64. Old-Fashioned Turkey Chili

(Ready in about 40 minutes | Servings 4)

Per serving: 271 Calories; 15.7g Fat; 7.6g Carbs; 25.7g Protein; 3.6g Sugars; 1.4g Fiber

INGREDIENTS

1/2 medium-sized leek, chopped
1/2 red onion, chopped
2 garlic cloves, minced
1 jalapeno pepper, seeded and minced
1 bell pepper, seeded and chopped
2 tablespoons olive oil
1 pound ground turkey, 85% lean 15% fat

2 cups tomato puree
2 cups chicken stock
1/2 teaspoon black peppercorns
Salt, to taste
1 teaspoon chili powder
1 teaspoon mustard seeds
1 teaspoon ground cumin

DIRECTIONS

Start by preheating your Air Fryer to 365 degrees F.
Place the leeks, onion, garlic and peppers in a baking pan; drizzle olive oil evenly over the top. Cook for 4 to 6 minutes.
Add the ground turkey. Cook for 6 minutes more or until the meat is no longer pink.
Now, add the tomato puree, 1 cup of chicken stock, black peppercorns, salt, chili powder, mustard seeds, and cumin to the baking pan.
Cook for 24 minutes, stirring every 7 to 10 minutes.
Bon appétit!

65. Rustic Chicken Drumettes with Chives

(Ready in about 30 minutes | Servings 3)

Per serving: 319 Calories; 11.3g Fat; 2.4g Carbs; 49.5g Protein; 0.5g Sugars; 1.4g Fiber

INGREDIENTS

1/3 cup almond meal
1/2 teaspoon ground white pepper
1 teaspoon seasoning salt
1 teaspoon garlic paste

1 teaspoon rosemary
1 whole egg + 1 egg white
6 chicken drumettes
1 heaping tablespoon fresh chives, chopped

DIRECTIONS

Start by preheating your Air Fryer to 390 degrees.
Mix the almond meal with white pepper, salt, garlic paste, and rosemary in a small-sized bowl.
In another bowl, beat the eggs until frothy.
Dip the chicken into the flour mixture, then into the beaten eggs; coat with the flour mixture one more time.
Cook the chicken drumettes for 22 minutes. Serve warm, garnished with chives.

66. Piri Piri Chicken

(Ready in about 1 hour 30 minutes | Servings 6)

Per serving: 517 Calories; 21g Fat; 1.9g Carbs; 47g Protein; 0.6g Sugars; 0.4g Fiber

INGREDIENTS

12 chicken wings
1 ½ ounces butter, melted
1 teaspoon onion powder
1/2 teaspoon cumin powder
1 teaspoon garlic paste
For the Sauce:

2 ounces piri piri peppers, stemmed and chopped
1 tablespoon pimiento, deveined and minced
1 garlic clove, chopped
2 tablespoons fresh lemon juice
1/3 teaspoon sea salt
1/2 teaspoon tarragon

DIRECTIONS

Steam the chicken wings using a steamer basket that is placed over a saucepan with boiling water; reduce the heat.

Now, steam the wings for 10 minutes over a moderate heat. Toss the wings with butter, onion powder, cumin powder, and garlic paste.

Let the chicken wings cool to room temperature. Then, refrigerate them for 45 to 50 minutes.

Roast in the preheated Air Fryer at 330 degrees F for 25 to 30 minutes; make sure to flip them halfway through.

While the chicken wings are cooking, prepare the sauce by mixing all of the sauce ingredients in a food processor. Toss the wings with prepared Piri Piri Sauce and serve.

67. Chicken Sausage in Dijon Sauce

(Ready in about 20 minutes | Servings 4)

Per serving: 575 Calories; 52g Fat; 2.5g Carbs; 22.4g Protein; 0.8g Sugars; 0.5g Fiber

INGREDIENTS

4 chicken sausages
1/4 cup mayonnaise
2 tablespoons Dijon mustard

1 tablespoon balsamic vinegar
1/2 teaspoon dried rosemary

DIRECTIONS

Arrange the sausages on the grill pan and transfer it to the preheated Air Fryer.

Grill the sausages at 350 degrees F for approximately 13 minutes. Turn them halfway through cooking.

Meanwhile, prepare the sauce by mixing the remaining ingredients with a wire whisk. Serve the warm sausages with chilled Dijon sauce. Enjoy!

68. Ethiopian-Style Chicken with Cauliflower

(Ready in about 30 minutes | Servings 6)

Per serving: 234 Calories; 12.3g Fat; 4.7g Carbs; 25.4g Protein; 1.4g Sugars; 2.1g Fiber

INGREDIENTS

2 handful fresh Italian parsleys, roughly chopped
½ cup fresh chopped chives
2 sprigs thyme
6 chicken drumsticks
1 ½ small-sized head cauliflower, broken into large-sized florets

For the Berbere Spice Rub Mix:
2 teaspoons mustard powder
1/3 teaspoon porcini powder
1 ½ teaspoons berbere spice
1/3teaspoon sweet paprika
1/2 teaspoon shallot powder
1teaspoon granulated garlic
1 teaspoon freshly cracked pink peppercorns
1/2 teaspoon sea salt

DIRECTIONS

Simply combine all items for the berbere spice rub mix. After that, coat the chicken drumsticks with this rub mix on all sides. Transfer them to the baking dish.

Now, lower the cauliflower onto the chicken drumsticks. Add thyme, chives and Italian parsley and spritz everything with a pan spray. Transfer the baking dish to the preheated Air Fryer.

Next step, set the timer for 28 minutes; roast at 355 degrees F, turning occasionally. Bon appétit!

69. Herbed Parmesan Chicken Breasts

(Ready in about 35 minutes | Servings 6)

Per serving: 231 Calories; 9.6g Fat; 1.9g Carbs; 32.3g Protein; 0.1g Sugars; 0.2g Fiber

INGREDIENTS

3 boneless and skinless chicken breasts, cut into small pieces
1/3 cup cooking wine (such as Sauvignon Blanc)
1teaspoon fresh sage leaves, minced
1 teaspoon freshly cracked black pepper
1/3 cup Parmigiano-Reggiano cheese, freshly grated

3 cloves garlic, minced
2 tablespoons olive oil
1 teaspoon seasoned salt
1 teaspoon fresh rosemary leaves, minced

DIRECTIONS

Warm the oil in a sauté pan over a moderate flame. Then, sauté the garlic until just fragrant.
Next, remove the pan from the heat; pour in the cooking wine. Add the seasonings and toss until everything is well combined. Pour this mixture into a lightly-oiled baking dish.
Toss in the pieces of chicken breasts; roast in the preheated Air Fryer at 325 degrees F for 32 minutes. Scatter grated cheese over the chicken and serve on individual plates.

70. Chicken Breasts with Peppers and Tarragon

(Ready in about 40 minutes | Servings 4)

Per serving: 221 Calories; 6.0g Fat; 4.0g Carbs; 35.9g Protein; 2.2g Sugars; 0.7g Fiber

INGREDIENTS

2 cups of roasted vegetable broth
2 chicken breasts, cut into halves
3/4 teaspoon fine sea salt
1/4 teaspoon mixed peppercorns, freshly cracked
1 teaspoon cumin powder
1 ½ teaspoons sesame oil

1 ½ tablespoons Worcester sauce
1/2 cup of spring onions, chopped
1 Serrano pepper, deveined and chopped
1 bell pepper, deveined and chopped
1 tablespoon tamari sauce
1/2 chopped fresh tarragon

DIRECTIONS

Place the vegetable broth and chicken breasts in a deep saucepan; cook for 10 minutes; reduce the temperature and let it simmer for additional 10 minutes.
After that, allow the chicken to cool slightly; shred the chicken using a stand mixer or two forks.
Toss the shredded chicken with the salt, cracked peppercorns, cumin, sesame oil and the Worcester sauce; air-fry them at 380 degrees F for 18 minutes; check for doneness.
Meanwhile, in a non-stick skillet, cook the remaining ingredients over a moderate flame. Cook until the onions and peppers are tender and fragrant.
Remove the skillet from the heat, add the shredded chicken and toss to combine. Serve right away!

71. The Best Pizza Chicken Ever

(Ready in about 20 minutes | Servings 4)

Per serving: 561 Calories; 38.3g Fat; 2.1g Carbs; 49.3g Protein; 0.6g Sugars; 0.5g Fiber

INGREDIENTS

4 small-sized chicken breasts, boneless and skinless
1/4 cup pizza sauce
1/2 cup Colby cheese, shredded
16 slices pepperoni

Salt and pepper, to savor
1 ½ tablespoons olive oil
1 ½ tablespoons dried oregano

DIRECTIONS

Carefully flatten out the chicken breast using a rolling pin.
Divide the ingredients among four chicken fillets. Roll the chicken fillets with the stuffing and seal them using a small skewer or two toothpicks.
Roast in the preheated Air Fryer grill pan for 13 to 15 minutes at 370 degrees F. Bon appétit!

72. Chicken with Creamy Rosemary Sauce

(Ready in about 20 minutes + marinating time | Servings 4)

Per serving: 362 Calories; 27.9g Fat; 6.9g Carbs; 20.1g Protein; 0.5g Sugars; 0.7g Fiber

INGREDIENTS

1/2 cup full-fat sour cream
1 teaspoon ground cinnamon
½ teaspoon whole grain mustard
1 ½ tablespoons mayonnaise
1 pound chicken thighs, boneless, skinless, and cut into pieces
1 ½ tablespoons olive oil

2 heaping tablespoons fresh rosemary, minced
1/2 cup white wine
3 cloves garlic, minced
1/2 teaspoon smoked paprika
Salt and freshly cracked black pepper, to taste

DIRECTIONS

Firstly, in a mixing dish, combine chicken thighs with olive oil and white wine; stir to coat.
After that, throw in the garlic, smoked paprika, ground cinnamon, salt, and black pepper; cover and refrigerate for 1 to 3 hours.
Set the Air Fryer to cook at 375 degrees F. Roast the chicken thighs for 18 minutes, turning halfway through and working in batches.
To make the sauce, combine the sour cream, whole grain mustard, mayonnaise and rosemary. Serve the turkey with the mustard/rosemary sauce and enjoy!

73. Nacho-Fried Chicken Burgers

(Ready in about 25 minutes | Servings 4)

Per serving: 234 Calories; 12.3g Fat; 2.4g Carbs; 26.1g Protein; 0g Sugars; 0.3g Fiber

INGREDIENTS

1 palmful dried basil
1/3 cup parmesan cheese, grated
2 teaspoons dried marjoram
1/3 teaspoon ancho chili powder
2 teaspoons dried parsley flakes
1/2 teaspoon onion powder
Toppings, to serve

1/3 teaspoon porcini powder
1 teaspoon sea salt flakes
1 pound chicken meat, ground
2 teaspoons cumin powder
1/3 teaspoon red pepper flakes, crushed
1 teaspoon freshly cracked black pepper

DIRECTIONS

Generously grease an Air Fryer cooking basket with a thin layer of vegetable oil.
In a mixing dish, combine chicken meat with all seasonings. Shape into 4 patties and coat them with grated parmesan cheese.
Cook chicken burgers in the preheated Air Fryer for 15 minutes at 345 degrees F, working in batches, flipping them once.
Serve with toppings of choice. Bon appétit!

74. Exotic Chicken Breasts

(Ready in about 30 minutes | Servings 4)

Per serving: 471 Calories; 28.6g Fat; 1.2g Carbs; 48g Protein; 1.1g Sugars; 0g Fiber

INGREDIENTS

1/2 teaspoon grated fresh ginger
1/3 cup coconut milk
1/2 teaspoon sea salt flakes
3 medium-sized boneless chicken breasts, cut into small pieces
1 ½ tablespoons sesame oil

3 green garlic stalks, finely chopped
1/2 cup dry white wine
1/2 teaspoon fresh thyme leaves, minced
1/3 teaspoon freshly cracked black pepper

DIRECTIONS

Warm the sesame oil in a deep sauté pan over a moderate heat. Then, sauté the green garlic until just fragrant.
Remove the pan from the heat and pour in the coconut milk and the white wine. After that, add the thyme, sea salt, fresh ginger, and freshly cracked black pepper. Scrape this mixture into a baking dish.
Stir in the chicken chunks.
Cook in the preheated Air Fryer for 28 minutes at 335 degrees F. Serve on individual plates and eat warm.

75. Chicken Vegetable Medley with Fontina Cheese

(Ready in about 25 minutes | Servings 4)

Per serving: 361 Calories; 29.4g Fat; 3.9g Carbs; 19.3g Protein; 1.3g Sugars; 1.1g Fiber

INGREDIENTS

3 eggs, whisked

1/2 teaspoon dried marjoram

1/3 cup Fontina cheese, grated

1 teaspoon sea salt

1/3 teaspoon red pepper flakes, crushed

2 cups leftover keto vegetables

1/2 red onion, thinly sliced

2 cups cooked chicken, shredded or chopped

3 cloves garlic, finely minced

DIRECTIONS

Simply mix all of the above ingredients, except for cheese, with a wide spatula.

Scrape the mixture into a previously greased baking dish.

Set your Air Fryer to cook at 365 degrees F for 22 minutes. Air-fry until everything is bubbling. Serve warm topped with grated Fontina cheese. Bon appétit!

76. Turkey Meatballs Pecorino Romano and Mint

(Ready in about 15 minutes | Servings 6)

Per serving: 241 Calories; 17.5g Fat; 1.1g Carbs; 23.0g Protein; 0g Sugars; 0.1g Fiber

INGREDIENTS

1 pound ground turkey

1 tablespoon fresh mint leaves, finely chopped

1 teaspoon onion powder

1 ½ teaspoons garlic paste

1 teaspoon crushed red pepper flakes

1/4 cup melted butter

3/4 teaspoon fine sea salt

1/4 cup grated Pecorino Romano

DIRECTIONS

Simply place all of the above ingredients into the mixing dish; mix until everything is well incorporated.

Use an ice cream scoop to shape the meat into golf ball sized meatballs.

Air fry the meatballs at 380 degrees F for approximately 7 minutes; work in batches, shaking them to ensure evenness of cooking.

Serve with a simple tomato sauce garnished with fresh basil leaves. Bon appétit!

77. Spicy Turkey Patties with Chive Mayonnaise

(Ready in about 20 minutes | Servings 6)

Per serving: 252 Calories; 15.9g Fat; 10.0g Carbs; 17.1g Protein; 2.7g Sugars; 0.8g Fiber

INGREDIENTS

For the Turkey Sliders:

3/4 pound turkey mince

1/4 cup pickled jalapeno, chopped

1 tablespoon oyster sauce

1-2 cloves garlic, minced

1 tablespoon chopped fresh cilantro

2 tablespoons chopped scallions

Sea salt and ground black pepper, to savor

For the Chive Mayo:

1 cup mayonnaise

1 tablespoon chives

1 teaspoon salt

Zest of 1 lime

DIRECTIONS

In a mixing bowl, thoroughly combine all ingredients for the turkey patties.

Mold the mixture into 6 even-sized slider patties. Then, air-fry them at 365 degrees F for 15 minutes.

Meanwhile, make the Chive Mayonnaise by mixing the rest of the above ingredients. Serve warm.

78. Red Thai Turkey Drumsticks in Coconut Milk

(Ready in about 25 minutes | Servings 2)

Per serving: 298 Calories; 16.3g Fat; 5.3g Carbs; 32.3g Protein; 1.5g Sugars; 2.6g Fiber

INGREDIENTS

1 tablespoon red curry paste
1/2 teaspoon cayenne pepper
1 ½ tablespoons minced ginger
2 turkey drumsticks

1/4 cup coconut milk
1 teaspoon kosher salt, or more to taste
1/3 teaspoon ground pepper, to more to taste

DIRECTIONS

First of all, place turkey drumsticks with all ingredients in your refrigerator; let it marinate overnight.
Cook turkey drumsticks at 380 degrees F for 23 minutes; make sure to flip them over at half-time. Serve with the salad on the side.

79. Fried Turkey with Lemon and Herbs

(Ready in about 45 minutes | Servings 6)

Per serving: 244 Calories; 16g Fat; 8g Carbs; 11g Protein; 3.9g Sugars; 0.7g Fiber

INGREDIENTS

1 ½ tablespoons yellow mustard
1 ½ tablespoons herb seasoning blend
1/3 cup tamari sauce
1 ½ tablespoons olive oil

1/2 lemon, juiced
3 turkey drumsticks
1/3 cup pear or apple cider vinegar
2 sprigs rosemary, chopped

DIRECTIONS

Dump all ingredients into a mixing dish. Let it marinate overnight.
Set your air fryer to cook at 355 degrees F.
Season turkey drumsticks with salt and black pepper and roast them at 355 degrees F for 28 minutes. Cook one drumstick at a time.
Pause the machine after 14 minutes and flip turkey drumstick. Bon appétit!

80. Chicken Sausage with Nestled Eggs

(Ready in about 20 minutes | Servings 6)

Per serving: 211 Calories; 14.6g Fat; 5.9g Carbs; 14.7g Protein; 1.4g Sugars; 0.7g Fiber

INGREDIENTS

6 eggs
2 bell peppers, seeded and sliced
1 teaspoon dried oregano
1 teaspoon hot paprika
1 teaspoon freshly cracked black pepper

6 chicken sausages
1 teaspoon sea salt
1 1/2 shallots, cut into wedges
1 teaspoon dried basil

DIRECTIONS

Take four ramekins and divide chicken sausages, shallot, and bell pepper among those ramekins. Cook at 315 degrees F for about 12 minutes.
Now, crack an egg into each ramekin. Sprinkle the eggs with hot paprika, basil, oregano, salt, and cracked black pepper. Cook for 5 more minutes at 405 degrees F.
Bon appétit!

81. Parmesan Chicken Nuggets

(Ready in about 10 minutes | Servings 4)

Per serving: 347 Calories; 23.6g Fat; 1.5g Carbs; 30.5g Protein; 0.5g Sugars; 0g Fiber

INGREDIENTS

1 pound chicken breast, ground

1 teaspoon hot paprika

2 teaspoon sage, ground

1/3 teaspoon powdered ginger

1/2 teaspoon dried thyme

1/3 teaspoon ground black pepper, to taste

1 teaspoon kosher salt

2 tablespoons melted butter

3 eggs, beaten

1/2 cup parmesan cheese, grated

DIRECTIONS

In a mixing bowl, thoroughly combine ground chicken together with spices and an egg. After that, stir in the melted butter; mix to combine well.

Whisk the remaining eggs in a shallow bowl.

Form the mixture into chicken nugget shapes; now, coat them with the beaten eggs; then, dredge them in the grated parmesan cheese.

Cook in the preheated Air Fryer at 405 degrees F for 8 minutes. Bon appétit!

82. Tangy and Buttery Chicken

(Ready in about 20 minutes | Servings 4)

Per serving: 264 Calories; 18.6g Fat; 0.9g Carbs; 23.6g Protein; 0.4g Sugars; 0.1g Fiber

INGREDIENTS

½ tablespoon Worcestershire sauce

1 teaspoon finely grated orange zest

2 tablespoons melted butter

½ teaspoon smoked paprika

4 chicken drumsticks, rinsed and halved

1 teaspoon sea salt flakes

1 tablespoon cider vinegar

1/2 teaspoon mixed peppercorns, freshly cracked

DIRECTIONS

Firstly, pat the chicken drumsticks dry. Coat them with the melted butter on all sides. Toss the chicken drumsticks with the other ingredients.

Transfer them to the Air Fryer cooking basket and roast for about 13 minutes at 345 degrees F. Bon appétit!

83. Easy Turkey Kabobs

(Ready in about 15 minutes | Servings 8)

Per serving: 360 Calories; 31g Fat; 3.9g Carbs; 14.2g Protein; 0.2g Sugars; 0.6g Fiber

INGREDIENTS

1 cup parmesan cheese, grated

1 ½ cups of water

14 ounces ground turkey

2 small eggs, beaten

1 teaspoon ground ginger

2 ½ tablespoons vegetable oil

1 cup chopped fresh parsley

2 tablespoons almond meal

3/4 teaspoon salt

1 heaping teaspoon fresh rosemary, finely chopped

1/2 teaspoon ground allspice

DIRECTIONS

Mix all of the above ingredients in a bowl. Knead the mixture with your hands.

Then, take small portions and gently roll them into balls.

Now, preheat your Air Fryer to 380 degrees F. Air fry for 8 to 10 minutes in the Air Fryer basket. Serve on a serving platter with skewers and eat with your favorite dipping sauce.

84. Turkey Breasts with Greek Mustard Sauce

(Ready in about 1 hour 13 minutes | Servings 4)

Per serving: 471 Calories; 23.6g Fat; 4.1g Carbs; 56g Protein; 2.4g Sugars; 0.3g Fiber

INGREDIENTS

1/2 teaspoon cumin powder

2 pounds turkey breasts, quartered

2 cloves garlic, smashed

½ teaspoon hot paprika

2 tablespoons melted butter

1 teaspoon fine sea salt

Freshly cracked mixed peppercorns, to savor

Fresh juice of 1 lemon

For the Mustard Sauce:

1 ½ tablespoons mayonnaise

1 ½ cups Greek yogurt

1/2 tablespoon yellow mustard

DIRECTIONS

Grab a medium-sized mixing dish and combine together the garlic and melted butter; rub this mixture evenly over the surface of the turkey.

Add the cumin powder, followed by paprika, salt, peppercorns, and lemon juice. Place in your refrigerator at least 55 minutes.

Set your Air Fryer to cook at 375 degrees F. Roast the turkey for 18 minutes, turning halfway through; roast in batches.

In the meantime, make the mustard sauce by mixing all ingredients for the sauce. Serve warm roasted turkey with the mustard sauce. Bon appétit!

85. Country-Style Nutty Turkey Breast

(Ready in about 30 minutes | Servings 2)

Per serving: 395 Calories; 19.5g Fat; 1.1g Carbs; 51.5g Protein; 0.4g Sugars; 0.5g Fiber

INGREDIENTS

1 ½ tablespoons coconut aminos

1/2 tablespoon xanthan gum

2 bay leaves

1/3 cup dry sherry

1 ½ tablespoons chopped walnuts

1 teaspoon shallot powder

1 pound turkey breasts, sliced

1 teaspoon garlic powder

2 teaspoons olive oil

1/2 teaspoon onion salt

1/2 teaspoon red pepper flakes, crushed

1 teaspoon ground black pepper

DIRECTIONS

Begin by preheating your Air Fryer to 395 degrees F. Place all ingredients, minus chopped walnuts, in a mixing bowl and let them marinate at least 1 hour.

After that, cook the marinated turkey breast approximately 23 minutes or until heated through.

Pause the machine, scatter chopped walnuts over the top and air-fry an additional 5 minutes. Bon appétit!

86. Eggs and Sausage with Keto Rolls

(Ready in about 40 minutes | Servings 6)

Per serving: 494 Calories; 30.1g Fat; 9.2g Carbs; 45.1g Protein; 2.3g Sugars; 2.1g Fiber

INGREDIENTS

1 teaspoon dried dill weed

1 teaspoon mustard seeds

6 turkey sausages

3 bell peppers, seeded and thinly sliced

6 medium-sized eggs

1/2 teaspoon fennel seeds

1 teaspoon sea salt

1/3 teaspoon freshly cracked pink peppercorns

Keto Rolls:

1/2 cup ricotta cheese, crumbled

1 cup part skim mozzarella cheese, shredded

1 egg

1/2 cup coconut flour

1/2 cup almond flour

1 teaspoon baking soda

2 tablespoons plain whey protein isolate

DIRECTIONS

Set your Air Fryer to cook at 325 degrees F. Cook the sausages and bell peppers in the Air Fryer cooking basket for 8 minutes.

Crack the eggs into the ramekins; sprinkle them with salt, dill weed, mustard seeds, fennel seeds, and cracked peppercorns. Cook an additional 12 minutes at 395 degrees F.

To make the keto rolls, microwave the cheese for 1 minute 30 seconds, stirring twice. Add the cheese to the bowl of a food processor and blend well. Fold in the egg and mix again.

Add in the flour, baking soda, and plain whey protein isolate; blend again. Scrape the batter onto the center of a lightly greased cling film.

Form the dough into a disk and transfer to your freezer to cool; cut into 6 pieces and transfer to a parchment-lined baking pan (make sure to grease your hands).

Bake in the preheated oven at 400 degrees F for about 14 minutes.

Serve eggs and sausages on keto rolls and enjoy!

87. Bacon-Wrapped Turkey with Cheese

(Ready in about 20 minutes | Servings 12)

Per serving: 568 Calories; 34.6g Fat; 0.7g Carbs; 59g Protein; 0.6g Sugars; 0.1g Fiber

INGREDIENTS

1 ½ small-sized turkey breast, chop into 12 pieces
12 thin slices Asiago cheese
Paprika, to taste

Fine sea salt and ground black pepper, to savor
12 rashers bacon

DIRECTIONS

Lay out the bacon rashers; place 1 slice of Asiago cheese on each bacon piece.
Top with turkey, season with paprika, salt, and pepper, and roll them up; secure with a cocktail stick.
Air-fry at 365 degrees F for 13 minutes. Bon appétit!

88. Italian-Style Spicy Chicken Breasts

(Ready in about 20 minutes | Servings 4)

Per serving: 390 Calories; 12.6g Fat; 7.5g Carbs; 54g Protein; 4.5g Sugars; 1.7g Fiber

INGREDIENTS

2 ounces Asiago cheese, cut into sticks
1/3 cup tomato paste
1/2 teaspoon garlic paste
2 chicken breasts, cut in half lengthwise
1/2 cup green onions, chopped
1 tablespoon chili sauce

1/2 cup roasted vegetable stock
1 tablespoon sesame oil
1 teaspoon salt
2 teaspoons unsweetened cocoa
1/2 teaspoon sweet paprika, or more to taste

DIRECTIONS

Sprinkle chicken breasts with the salt and sweet paprika; drizzle with chili sauce. Now, place a stick of Asiago cheese in the middle of each chicken breast.
Then, tie the whole thing using a kitchen string; give a drizzle of sesame oil.
Transfer the stuffed chicken to the cooking basket. Add the other ingredients and toss to coat the chicken.
Afterward, cook for about 11 minutes at 395 degrees F. Serve the chicken on two serving plates, garnish with fresh or pickled salad and serve immediately. Bon appétit!

89. Classic Chicken Nuggets

(Ready in about 20 minutes | Servings 4)

Per serving: 327 Calories; 17g Fat; 1.3g Carbs; 40g Protein; 0.2g Sugars; 1g Fiber

INGREDIENTS

1 ½ pounds chicken tenderloins, cut into small pieces
1/2 teaspoon garlic salt
1/2 teaspoon cayenne pepper
1/4 teaspoon black pepper, freshly cracked

4 tablespoons olive oil
2 scoops low-carb unflavored protein powder
4 tablespoons Parmesan cheese, freshly grated

DIRECTIONS

Start by preheating your Air Fryer to 390 degrees F.
Season each piece of the chicken with garlic salt, cayenne pepper, and black pepper.
In a mixing bowl, thoroughly combine the olive oil with protein powder and parmesan cheese. Dip each piece of chicken in the parmesan mixture.
Cook for 8 minutes, working in batches.
Later, if you want to warm the chicken nuggets, add them to the basket and cook for 1 minute more. Enjoy!

90. Thai Chicken with Bacon

(Ready in about 50 minutes | Servings 2)

Per serving: 612 Calories; 44.1g Fat; 8.6g Carbs; 52g Protein; 2.5g Sugars; 2.1g Fiber

INGREDIENTS

4 rashers smoked bacon
2 chicken filets
1/2 teaspoon coarse sea salt
1/4 teaspoon black pepper, preferably freshly ground
1 teaspoon garlic, minced

1 (2-inch) piece ginger, peeled and minced
1 teaspoon black mustard seeds
1 teaspoon mild curry powder
1/2 cup coconut milk
1/2 cup parmesan cheese, grated

DIRECTIONS

Start by preheating your Air Fryer to 400 degrees F. Add the smoked bacon and cook in the preheated Air Fryer for 5 to 7 minutes. Reserve.

In a mixing bowl, place the chicken fillets, salt, black pepper, garlic, ginger, mustard seeds, curry powder, and milk. Let it marinate in your refrigerator about 30 minutes.

In another bowl, place the grated parmesan cheese.

Dredge the chicken fillets through the parmesan mixture and transfer them to the cooking basket. Reduce the temperature to 380 degrees F and cook the chicken for 6 minutes.

Turn them over and cook for a further 6 minutes. Repeat the process until you have run out of ingredients.

Serve with reserved bacon. Enjoy!

91. Thanksgiving Turkey with Mustard Gravy

(Ready in about 50 minutes | Servings 6)

Per serving: 384 Calories; 8.2g Fat; 2.5g Carbs; 51.5g Protein; 0.2g Sugars; 0.2g Fiber

INGREDIENTS

2 teaspoons butter, softened
1 teaspoon dried sage
2 sprigs rosemary, chopped
1 teaspoon salt
1/4 teaspoon freshly ground black pepper, or more to taste

1 whole turkey breast
2 tablespoons turkey broth
2 tablespoons whole-grain mustard
1 tablespoon butter

DIRECTIONS

Start by preheating your Air Fryer to 360 degrees F.

To make the rub, combine 2 tablespoons of butter, sage, rosemary, salt, and pepper; mix well to combine and spread it evenly over the surface of the turkey breast.

Roast for 20 minutes in an Air Fryer cooking basket. Flip the turkey breast over and cook for a further 15 to 16 minutes. Now, flip it back over and roast for 12 minutes more.

While the turkey is roasting, whisk the other ingredients in a saucepan. After that, spread the gravy all over the turkey breast.

Let the turkey rest for a few minutes before carving. Bon appétit!

92. Loaded Turkey Meatloaf with Cheese

(Ready in about 50 minutes | Servings 6)

Per serving: 324 Calories; 19.3g Fat; 2.7g Carbs; 35.5g Protein; 1.1g Sugars; 0.6g Fiber

INGREDIENTS

2 pounds turkey mince
1/2 cup scallions, finely chopped
2 garlic cloves, finely minced
1 teaspoon dried thyme

1/2 teaspoon dried basil
3/4 cup Colby cheese, shredded
1 tablespoon tamari sauce
Salt and black pepper, to your liking

1/4 cup roasted red pepper tomato sauce
3/4 tablespoons olive oil
1 medium-sized egg, well beaten

DIRECTIONS

In a nonstick skillet, that is preheated over a moderate heat, sauté the turkey mince, scallions, garlic, thyme, and basil until just tender and fragrant. Then set your Air Fryer to cook at 360 degrees. Combine sautéed mixture with the cheese and tamari sauce; then form the mixture into a loaf shape.

Mix the remaining items and pour them over the meatloaf. Cook in the Air Fryer baking pan for 45 to 47 minutes. Eat warm.

93. Country-Style Turkey Thighs with Vegetables

(Ready in about 1 hour 15 minutes | Servings 4)

Per serving: 393 Calories; 20.6g Fat; 6.2g Carbs; 46.1g Protein; 2.1g Sugars; 1.7g Fiber

INGREDIENTS

1 red onion, cut into wedges
1 carrot, trimmed and sliced
1 celery stalk, trimmed and sliced
1 cup Brussel sprouts, trimmed and halved
1 cup roasted vegetable broth
1 tablespoon apple cider vinegar
4 turkey thighs

1/2 teaspoon mixed peppercorns, freshly cracked
1 teaspoon fine sea salt
1 teaspoon cayenne pepper
1 teaspoon onion powder
1/2 teaspoon garlic powder
1/3 teaspoon mustard seeds

DIRECTIONS

Take a baking dish that easily fits into your device; place the vegetables on the bottom of the baking dish and pour in roasted vegetable broth.

In a large-sized mixing dish, place the remaining ingredients; let them marinate for about 30 minutes. Lay them on the top of the vegetables.

Roast at 330 degrees F for 40 to 45 minutes. Bon appétit!

94. Aromatic Turkey Breast with Mustard

(Ready in about 1 hour | Servings 4)

Per serving: 321 Calories; 17.4g Fat; 1.2g Carbs; 37.6g Protein; 0.1g Sugars; 0.5g Fiber

INGREDIENTS

1/2 teaspoon dried thyme
1 ½ pounds turkey breasts
1/2 teaspoon dried sage
3 whole star anise

1 ½ tablespoons olive oil
1 ½ tablespoons hot mustard
1 teaspoon smoked cayenne pepper
1 teaspoon fine sea salt

DIRECTIONS

Set your Air Fryer to cook at 365 degrees F.

Brush the turkey breast with olive oil and sprinkle with seasonings.

Cook at 365 degrees F for 45 minutes, turning twice. Now, pause the machine and spread the cooked breast with the hot mustard.

Air-fry for 6 to 8 more minutes. Let it rest before slicing and serving. Bon appétit!

95. Rustic Turkey Breasts

(Ready in about 50 minutes + marinating time | Servings 4)

Per serving: 385 Calories; 20.6g Fat; 7.6g Carbs; 40.1g Protein; 1.9g Sugars; 0.9g Fiber

INGREDIENTS

1 ½ pounds turkey breasts, boneless and skinless
1/2 palmful chopped fresh sage leaves
1 ½ tablespoons freshly squeezed lemon juice
1/3 teaspoon dry mustard
1/3 cup dry white wine

3 cloves garlic, minced
2 leeks, cut into thick slices
1/2 teaspoon smoked paprika
2 tablespoons olive oil

DIRECTIONS

Combine sage leaves, lemon juice, mustard, garlic, and paprika in a small-sized mixing bowl; mix thoroughly until everything is well combined.

Then, smear this mixture on the turkey breast. Add white wine and let it marinate about 2 hours.

Transfer to the Air Fryer cooking basket along with the leeks. Drizzle olive oil over everything.

Bake at 375 degrees F for 48 minutes, turning once or twice. Bon appétit!

96. Spicy Egg and Ground Turkey Bake

(Ready in about 30 minutes | Servings 6)

Per serving: 298 Calories; 15.6g Fat; 5.4g Carbs; 16g Protein; 1.9g Sugars; 0.7g Fiber

INGREDIENTS

1 ½ pounds ground turkey
6 whole eggs, well beaten
1/3 teaspoon smoked paprika
2 egg whites, beaten
Tabasco sauce, for drizzling

2 tablespoons sesame oil
2 leeks, chopped
3 cloves garlic, finely minced
1 teaspoon ground black pepper
1/2 teaspoon sea salt

DIRECTIONS

Warm the oil in a pan over moderate heat; then, sweat the leeks and garlic until tender; stir periodically.
Next, grease 6 oven safe ramekins with pan spray. Divide the sautéed mixture among six ramekins.
In a bowl, beat the eggs and egg whites using a wire whisk. Stir in the smoked paprika, salt and black pepper; whisk until everything is thoroughly combined. Divide the egg mixture among the ramekins.
Air-fry approximately 22 minutes at 345 degrees F. Drizzle Tabasco sauce over each portion and serve.

97. Saucy Chicken with Leeks

(Ready in about 20 minutes + marinating time | Servings 6)

Per serving: 390 Calories; 15.6g Fat; 7.2g Carbs; 51.9g Protein; 2.8g Sugars; 1.4g Fiber

INGREDIENTS

2 leeks, sliced
2 large-sized tomatoes, chopped
3 cloves garlic, minced
½ teaspoon dried oregano

6 chicken legs, boneless and skinless
½ teaspoon smoked cayenne pepper
2 tablespoons olive oil
A freshly ground nutmeg

DIRECTIONS

In a mixing dish, thoroughly combine all ingredients, minus the leeks. Place in the refrigerator and let it marinate overnight.
Lay the leeks onto the bottom of an Air Fryer cooking basket. Top with the chicken legs.
Roast chicken legs at 375 degrees F for 18 minutes, turning halfway through. Serve with hoisin sauce.

98. Tangy Chicken with Parsley and Lime

(Ready in about 30 minutes + marinating time | Servings 2)

Per serving: 390 Calories; 20.6g Fat; 4.7g Carbs; 46.9g Protein; 0.6g Sugars; 1.9g Fiber

INGREDIENTS

1 1/2 handful fresh parsley, roughly chopped
Fresh juice of 1/2 lime
1 teaspoon ground black pepper

1 1/2 large-sized chicken breasts, cut into halves
1 teaspoon kosher salt
Zest of 1/2 lime

DIRECTIONS

Preheat your Air Fryer to 335 degrees F.
Toss the chicken breasts with the other ingredients and let it marinate a couple of hours.
Roast for 26 minutes and serve warm. Bon appétit!

99. Chili Chicken Sliders

(Ready in about 20 minutes | Servings 4)

Per serving: 366 Calories; 9.6g Fat; 4.4g Carbs; 61.6g Protein; 2.3g Sugars; 0.9g Fiber

INGREDIENTS

1/3 teaspoon paprika

1/3 cup scallions, peeled and chopped

3 cloves garlic, peeled and minced

1 teaspoon ground black pepper, or to taste

1/2 teaspoon fresh basil, minced

1 ½ cups chicken, minced

1 ½ tablespoons coconut aminos

1/2 teaspoon grated fresh ginger

1/2 tablespoon chili sauce

1 teaspoon salt

DIRECTIONS

Thoroughly combine all ingredients in a mixing dish. Then, form into 4 patties.

Cook in the preheated Air Fryer for 18 minutes at 355 degrees F.

Garnish with toppings of choice. Bon appétit!

100. Lime and Mustard Marinated Chicken

(Ready in about 30 minutes + marinating time | Servings 4)

Per serving: 255 Calories; 13.5g Fat; 1.7g Carbs; 30.3g Protein; 0.8g Sugars; 0.3g Fiber

INGREDIENTS

1/2 teaspoon stone-ground mustard

1/2 teaspoon minced fresh oregano

1/3 cup freshly squeezed lime juice

2 small-sized chicken breasts, skin-on

1 teaspoon kosher salt

1teaspoon freshly cracked mixed peppercorns

DIRECTIONS

Preheat your Air Fryer to 345 degrees F.

Toss all of the above ingredients in a medium-sized mixing dish; allow it to marinate overnight.

Cook in the preheated Air Fryer for 26 minutes. Bon appétit!

101. Chicken Legs with Dilled Brussels Sprouts

(Ready in about 30 minutes | Servings 2)

Per serving: 365 Calories; 20.1g Fat; 5.3g Carbs; 36.6g Protein; 0.2g Sugars; 4.3g Fiber

INGREDIENTS

2 chicken legs

1/2 teaspoon paprika

1/2 teaspoon kosher salt

1/2 teaspoon black pepper

1/2 pound Brussels sprouts

1 teaspoon dill, fresh or dried

DIRECTIONS

Start by preheating your Air Fryer to 370 degrees F.

Now, season your chicken with paprika, salt, and pepper. Transfer the chicken legs to the cooking basket. Cook for 10 minutes.

Flip the chicken legs and cook an additional 10 minutes. Reserve.

Add the Brussels sprouts to the cooking basket; sprinkle with dill. Cook at 380 degrees F for 15 minutes, shaking the basket halfway through.

Serve with the reserved chicken legs. Bon appétit!

102. Turkey Meatballs with Manchego Cheese

(Ready in about 15 minutes | Servings 4)

Per serving: 386 Calories; 24g Fat; 0.9g Carbs; 40.1g Protein; 0.3g Sugars; 0.2g Fiber

INGREDIENTS

1 pound ground turkey
1/2 pound ground pork
1 egg, well beaten
1 teaspoon dried basil
1 teaspoon dried rosemary

1/4 cup Manchego cheese, grated
2 tablespoons yellow onions, finely chopped
1 teaspoon fresh garlic, finely chopped
Sea salt and ground black pepper, to taste

DIRECTIONS

In a mixing bowl, combine all the ingredients until everything is well incorporated.
Shape the mixture into 1-inch balls.
Cook the meatballs in the preheated Air Fryer at 380 degrees for 7 minutes. Shake halfway through the cooking time. Work in batches.
Serve with your favorite pasta. Bon appétit!

103. Ranch Chicken Wings

(Ready in about 25 minutes | Servings 3)

Per serving: 285 Calories; 20.2g Fat; 7.3g Carbs; 19.2g Protein; 0.5g Sugars; 3.6g Fiber

INGREDIENTS

1/4 cup almond meal
1/4 cup flaxseed meal
2 tablespoons butter, melted
6 tablespoons parmesan cheese, preferably freshly grated

1 tablespoon Ranch seasoning mix
2 tablespoons oyster sauce
6 chicken wings, bone-in

DIRECTIONS

Start by preheating your Air Fryer to 370 degrees F.
In a resealable bag, place the almond meal, flaxseed meal, butter, parmesan, Ranch seasoning mix, and oyster sauce. Add the chicken wings and shake to coat on all sides.
Arrange the chicken wings in the Air Fryer basket. Spritz the chicken wings with a nonstick cooking spray.
Cook for 11 minutes. Turn them over and cook an additional 11 minutes. Serve warm with your favorite dipping sauce, if desired. Enjoy!

104. Easy Turkey Breasts with Basil

(Ready in about 1 hour | Servings 4)

Per serving: 416 Calories; 22.6g Fat; 0g Carbs; 49g Protein; 0g Sugars; 0.2g Fiber

INGREDIENTS

2 tablespoons olive oil
2 pounds turkey breasts, bone-in skin-on
Coarse sea salt and ground black pepper, to taste

1 teaspoon fresh basil leaves, chopped
2 tablespoons lemon zest, grated

DIRECTIONS

Rub olive oil on all sides of the turkey breasts; sprinkle with salt, pepper, basil, and lemon zest.
Place the turkey breasts skin side up on a parchment-lined cooking basket.
Cook in the preheated Air Fryer at 330 degrees F for 30 minutes. Now, turn them over and cook an additional 28 minutes.
Serve with lemon wedges, if desired. Bon appétit!

105. Wine Marinated Turkey Wings

(Ready in about 30 minutes + marinating time | Servings 4)

Per serving: 346 Calories; 20.1g Fat; 2g Carbs; 35g Protein; 0.2g Sugars; 0.3g Fiber

INGREDIENTS

1 teaspoon freshly cracked pink peppercorns
1 ½ pound turkey wings, cut into smaller pieces
2 teaspoon garlic powder

1/3 cup white wine
1/2 teaspoon garlic salt
1/2 tablespoon coriander, ground

DIRECTIONS

Toss all of the above ingredients in a mixing dish. Let it marinate at least 3 hours.
Air-fry turkey wings for 28 minutes at 355 degrees F. Bon appétit!

106. Chinese Turkey with Hoisin Sauce

(Ready in about 45 minutes + marinating time | Servings 4)

Per serving: 469 Calories; 26.3g Fat; 9.6g Carbs; 45.2g Protein; 3.4g Sugars; 0.5g Fiber

INGREDIENTS

2 pounds turkey drumsticks
2 tablespoons balsamic vinegar
2 tablespoons dry white wine
1 tablespoon sesame oil
1 sprig rosemary, chopped

Salt and ground black pepper, to your liking
2 ½ tablespoons butter, melted
For the Hoisin Sauce:
2 tablespoons hoisin sauce
1 tablespoon mustard

DIRECTIONS

Add the turkey drumsticks to a mixing dish; add the vinegar, wine, sesame oil, and rosemary. Let them marinate for 3 hours.
Then, preheat the Air Fryer to 350 degrees F.
Season the turkey drumsticks with salt and black pepper; spread the melted butter over the surface of drumsticks.
Cook turkey drumsticks at 350 degrees F for 30 to 35 minutes, working in batches. Turn the drumsticks over a few times during the cooking.
While the turkey drumsticks are roasting, prepare the Hoisin sauce by mixing the ingredients. After that, drizzle the turkey with the sauce mixture; roast for a further 5 minutes.
Let it rest about 10 minutes before carving and serving. Bon appétit!

107. Melt-in-Your-Mouth Chicken Breasts

(Ready in about 30 minutes | Servings 4)

Per serving: 299 Calories; 7.g Fat; 4.5g Carbs; 51g Protein; 1.4g Sugars; 2.1g Fiber

INGREDIENTS

2 chicken breasts, cut into bite-sized chunks
1/3 cup almond flour
1 cup scallions, chopped
1 celery, chopped

For the Sauce:
1/4 cup dry white wine
2 tablespoons coconut aminos
1/2 cup of chicken broth

DIRECTIONS

Start by preheating your Air Fryer to 365 degrees F. Toss the chicken chunks with the almond flour, covering well.
Air-fry the chicken for 20 minutes in the preheated cooker. Pause the Air Fryer and add the vegetables into the cooking basket cook for a further 5 to 7 minutes.
Meanwhile, in a sauté pan, whisk the remaining ingredients over a moderate flame; then, turn the heat to medium-low and simmer for 2 to 3 minutes.
Serve the chicken with the warm sauce and enjoy!

108. Tender Buttermilk Chicken

(Ready in about 1 hour 20 minutes | Servings 4)

Per serving: 297 Calories; 13.7g Fat; 5.5g Carbs; 37.2g Protein; 2.9g Sugars; 2.1g Fiber

INGREDIENTS

3/4 cup of buttermilk
1 ½ pounds chicken tenders
1/2 cup coconut flour
2 tablespoons flaxseed meal
Salt, to your liking

1/2 teaspoon pink peppercorns, freshly cracked
1 teaspoon shallot powder
1/2 teaspoon cumin powder
1 ½ teaspoon smoked cayenne pepper
1 tablespoon sesame oil

DIRECTIONS

Place the buttermilk and chicken tenders in the mixing dish; gently stir to coat and let it soak for 1 hour.
Then, mix the coconut flour with flaxseed meal and all seasonings. Coat the soaked chicken tenders with the coconut flour mixture; now, dip them into the buttermilk.
Finally, dredge them in the coconut flour mixture.
Brush the prepared chicken tenders with sesame oil and lower them onto the bottom of a cooking basket.
Air-fry for 15 minutes at 365 degrees F; make sure to shake them once or twice. Bon appétit!

109. Chicken with Bacon and Herbs de Provence

(Ready in about 25 minutes | Servings 4)

Per serving: 296 Calories; 13.7g Fat; 6.9g Carbs; 34.7g Protein; 2.9g Sugars; 2.3g Fiber

INGREDIENTS

4 medium-sized skin-on chicken drumsticks
1 ½ teaspoons herbs de Provence
Salt and pepper, to your liking
1 tablespoon rice vinegar
2 tablespoons olive oil

2 garlic cloves, crushed
12 ounces crushed canned tomatoes
1 small-size leek, thinly sliced
2 slices smoked bacon, chopped

DIRECTIONS

Sprinkle the chicken drumsticks with herbs de Provence, salt and pepper; then, drizzle them with rice vinegar and olive oil.
Cook in the baking pan at 360 degrees F for 8 to 10 minutes.
Pause the Air Fryer; stir in the remaining ingredients and continue to cook for 15 minutes longer; make sure to check them periodically. Bon appétit!

110. Must-Serve Turkey Breasts with Parsley

(Ready in about 25 minutes + marinating time | Servings 2)

Per serving: 345 Calories; 18.2g Fat; 1.8g Carbs; 40.9g Protein; 0.7g Sugars; 0.1g Fiber

INGREDIENTS

1/2 tablespoon minced fresh parsley
1 ½ tablespoons Worcestershire sauce
Sea salt flakes and cracked black peppercorns, to savor
1 ½ tablespoons olive oil

1/3 turkey breasts, halved
1 ½ tablespoons rice vinegar
1/2 teaspoon marjoram

DIRECTIONS

Set the Air Fryer to cook at 395 degrees. In a bowl, mix all ingredients together; make sure to coat turkey breast well.
Set aside to marinate for at least 3 hours.
Roast each turkey piece for 23 minutes; make sure to pause the machine and flip once to roast evenly. Bon appétit!

111. Homemade Turkey Sausage with Cauliflower

(Ready in about 45 minutes | Servings 4)

Per serving: 289 Calories; 25.4g Fat; 3.2g Carbs; 11.9g Protein; 1g Sugars; 1.1g Fiber

INGREDIENTS

1 pound ground turkey
1 teaspoon garlic pepper
1 teaspoon garlic powder
1/3 teaspoon dried oregano
1/2 teaspoon salt

1/3 cup onions, chopped
1/2 head cauliflower, broken into florets
1/3 teaspoon dried basil
1/2 teaspoon dried thyme, chopped

DIRECTIONS

In a mixing bowl, thoroughly combine the ground turkey, garlic pepper, garlic powder, oregano, salt, and onion; stir well to combine. Spritz a nonstick skillet with pan spray; form the mixture into 4 sausages.

Then, cook the sausage over medium heat until they are no longer pink, approximately 12 minutes.

Arrange the cauliflower florets at the bottom of a baking dish. Sprinkle with thyme and basil; spritz with pan spray. Top with the turkey sausages.

Roast for 28 minutes at 375 degrees F, turning once halfway through. Eat warm.

112. Turkey with Indian Mint Sauce

(Ready in about 35 minutes + marinating time | Servings 4)

Per serving: 325 Calories; 5.1g Fat;19.6g Carbs; 21.9g Protein; 6.2g Sugars; 0.1g Fiber

INGREDIENTS

1 1/2 pounds turkey breast, quartered
1/2 teaspoon hot paprika
1/2 cup dry sherry
1 teaspoon kosher salt
1/3 teaspoon shallot powder
2 cloves garlic, peeled and halved

Freshly cracked pink or green peppercorns, to taste
For the Indian Mint Sauce:
1/3 cup sour cream
1 ½ tablespoons fresh roughly chopped mint
1 cup plain yogurt

DIRECTIONS

Firstly, rub the garlic halves evenly over the surface of the turkey breast.

Add the dry sherry, shallot powder, hot paprika, salt, and cracked peppercorns. Allow it to marinate in your refrigerator for at least 1½ hours.

Set your air fryer to cook at 365 degrees F. Roast the turkey for 32 minutes, turning halfway through; roast in batches.

Meanwhile, prepare your sauce by mixing all the ingredients. Serve warm the roasted turkey with the sauce. Bon appétit!

113. Spicy Cajun Roasted Turkey

(Ready in about 35 minutes | Servings 4)

Per serving: 426 Calories; 15.4g Fat; 12.4g Carbs; 51g Protein; 6.1g Sugars; 1.3g Fiber

INGREDIENTS

2 pounds turkey thighs, skinless and boneless
1 red onion, sliced
2 bell peppers, deveined and sliced
1 habanero pepper, deveined and minced

1 carrot, sliced
1 tablespoon Cajun seasoning mix
1 tablespoon fish sauce
2 cups chicken broth

DIRECTIONS

Preheat your Air Fryer to 360 degrees F. Now, spritz the bottom and sides of the casserole dish with a nonstick cooking spray.

Arrange the turkey thighs in the casserole dish. Add the onion, pepper, and carrot. Sprinkle with Cajun seasoning.

Afterwards, add the fish sauce and chicken broth. Cook in the preheated Air Fryer for 30 minutes. Serve warm and enjoy!

114. Chicken Sausage, Cauliflower and Ham Gratin

(Ready in about 45 minutes | Servings 4)

Per serving: 443 Calories; 26.1g Fat; 9.3g Carbs; 41g Protein; 2.9g Sugars; 2.1g Fiber

INGREDIENTS

1/2 pound chicken sausages, smoked
1/2 pound ham, sliced
6 ounces cauliflower rice
2 garlic cloves, minced

8 ounces spinach
1/2 cup Ricotta cheese
1/2 cup Asiago cheese, grated
4 eggs

1/2 cup yogurt
1/2 cup milk
Salt and ground black pepper, to taste
1 teaspoon smoked paprika

DIRECTIONS

Start by preheating your Air Fryer to 380 degrees F. Cook the sausages and ham for 10 minutes; set aside.
Meanwhile, in a preheated saucepan, cook the cauliflower and garlic for 4 minutes, stirring frequently; remove from the heat, add the spinach and cover with the lid.
Allow the spinach to wilt completely. Transfer the sautéed mixture to a baking pan. Add the reserved sausage and ham.
In a mixing dish, thoroughly combine the cheese, eggs, yogurt, milk, salt, pepper, and paprika. Pour the cheese mixture over the hash browns in the pan.
Place the baking pan in the cooking basket and cook approximately 30 minutes or until everything is thoroughly cooked. Bon appétit!

115. Marinated Chicken Drumettes with Asparagus

(Ready in about 30 minutes + marinating time | Servings 6)

Per serving: 356 Calories; 22.1g Fat; 7.8g Carbs; 31.4g Protein; 4.1g Sugars; 2.8g Fiber

INGREDIENTS

6 chicken drumettes
1 ½ pounds asparagus, ends trimmed
Marinade:
3 tablespoons canola oil
3 tablespoons soy sauce

3 tablespoons lime juice
3 heaping tablespoons shallots, minced
1 heaping teaspoon fresh garlic, minced

1 (1-inch) piece fresh ginger, peeled and minced
1 teaspoon Creole seasoning
Coarse sea salt and ground black pepper, to taste

DIRECTIONS

In a ceramic bowl, mix all ingredients for the marinade. Add the chicken drumettes and let them marinate at least 5 hours in the refrigerator.
Now, drain the chicken drumettes and discard the marinade.
Cook in the preheated Air Fryer at 370 degrees F for 11 minutes. Turn the chicken drumettes over and cook for a further 11 minutes.
While the chicken drumettes are cooking, add the reserved marinade to the preheated skillet.
Add the asparagus and cook for approximately 5 minutes or until cooked through. Serve with the air-fried chicken and enjoy!

116. Mediterranean-Style Duck with Gravy

(Ready in about 25 minutes | Servings 4)

Per serving: 281 Calories; 12.5g Fat; 7.2g Carbs; 31.3g Protein; 2.4g Sugars; 1.1g Fiber

INGREDIENTS

1 ½ pounds smoked duck breasts, boneless
1 tablespoon yellow mustard
2 tablespoons ketchup, low-carb
8 pearl onions peeled

5 ounces chicken broth
2 egg yolks, whisked
1 teaspoon rosemary, finely chopped

DIRECTIONS

Cook the smoked duck breasts in the preheated Air Fryer at 365 degrees F for 15 minutes.
Smear the mustard and ketchup on the duck breast. Top with pearl onions. Cook for a further 7 minutes or until the skin of the duck breast looks crispy and golden brown.
Slice the duck breasts and reserve. Drain off the duck fat from the pan.
Then, add the reserved 1 tablespoon of duck fat to the pan and warm it over medium heat; add chicken broth and bring to a boil.
Gently fold in the whisked egg yolks and rosemary. Reduce the heat to low and cook until the gravy has thickened slightly. Spoon the warm gravy over the reserved duck breasts. Enjoy!

117. Roast Turkey Breast with Celery

(Ready in about 50 minutes | Servings 6)

Per serving: 316 Calories; 14.2g Fat; 2g Carbs; 41.4g Protein; 0.8g Sugars; 0.5g Fiber

INGREDIENTS

2 ½ pounds turkey breasts
1 tablespoon fresh rosemary, chopped
1 teaspoon sea salt

1/2 teaspoon ground black pepper
1 onion, chopped
1 celery stalk, chopped

DIRECTIONS

Start by preheating your Air Fryer to 360 degrees F. Spritz the sides and bottom of the cooking basket with a nonstick cooking spray. Place the turkey in the cooking basket. Add the rosemary, salt, and black pepper. Cook for 30 minutes in the preheated Air Fryer. Add the onion and celery and cook an additional 15 minutes. Bon appétit!

118. Chicken with Cauliflower and Pecorino Romano

(Ready in about 30 minutes | Servings 4)

Per serving: 388 Calories; 18.9g Fat; 5.6g Carbs; 47.3g Protein; 1.3g Sugars; 1.7g Fiber

INGREDIENTS

2 pounds chicken legs
2 tablespoons olive oil
1 teaspoon sea salt
1/2 teaspoon ground black pepper
1 teaspoon smoked paprika
1 teaspoon dried marjoram

1 (1-pound) head cauliflower, broken into small florets
2 garlic cloves, minced
1/3 cup Pecorino Romano cheese, freshly grated
1/2 teaspoon dried thyme
Salt, to taste

DIRECTIONS

Toss the chicken legs with the olive oil, salt, black pepper, paprika, and marjoram.
Cook in the preheated Air Fryer at 380 degrees F for 11 minutes. Flip the chicken legs and cook for a further 5 minutes.
Toss the cauliflower florets with garlic, cheese, thyme, and salt.
Increase the temperature to 400 degrees F; add the cauliflower florets and cook for 12 more minutes. Serve warm.

119. Chicken Tenders with Parmesan and Lime

(Ready in about 20 minutes | Servings 6)

Per serving: 327 Calories; 18.2g Fat; 3.2g Carbs; 36.1g Protein; 0.8g Sugars; 0.4g Fiber

INGREDIENTS

1 lime
2 pounds chicken tenderloins, cut up
1/2 cup pork rinds, crushed
1/2 cup Parmesan cheese, grated
1 tablespoon olive oil

Sea salt and ground black pepper, to taste
1 teaspoon cayenne pepper
1/3 teaspoon ground cumin
1 teaspoon chili powder
1 egg

DIRECTIONS

Squeeze the lime juice all over the chicken.
Spritz the cooking basket with a nonstick cooking spray.
In a mixing bowl, thoroughly combine the pork rinds, Parmesan, olive oil, salt, black pepper, cayenne pepper, cumin, and chili powder.
In another shallow bowl, whisk the egg until well beaten. Dip the chicken tenders in the egg, then in pork rind mixture.
Transfer the breaded chicken to the prepared cooking basket. Cook in the preheated Air Fryer at 380 degrees F for 12 minutes.
Turn them over halfway through the cooking time. Work in batches. Serve immediately.

120. Authentic Mexican Mole

(Ready in about 35 minutes | Servings 4)

Per serving: 550 Calories; 27.5g Fat; 9.6g Carbs; 61.2g Protein; 2.8g Sugars; 3.7g Fiber

INGREDIENTS

8 chicken thighs, skinless, bone-in
1 tablespoon peanut oil
Sea salt and ground black pepper, to taste
Mole sauce:
1 tablespoon peanut oil

1 onion, chopped
1 ounce dried negro chiles, stemmed, seeded, and chopped
2 garlic cloves, peeled and halved
1 large-sized fresh tomatoes, pureed
1 ½ ounces sugar-free bakers' choco-

late, chopped
1 teaspoon dried Mexican oregano
1/2 teaspoon ground cumin
1 teaspoon coriander seeds
A pinch of ground cloves
1/4 cup almonds, slivered and toasted

DIRECTIONS

Start by preheating your Air Fryer to 380 degrees F. Toss the chicken thighs with the peanut oil, salt, and black pepper.
Cook in the preheated Air Fryer for 12 minutes; flip them and cook an additional 10 minutes; reserve.
To make the sauce, heat 1 tablespoon of peanut oil in a saucepan over medium-high heat. Now, sauté the onion, chiles and garlic until fragrant or about 2 minutes.
Next, stir in the tomatoes, chocolate, oregano, cumin, coriander seeds, and cloves. Let it simmer until the sauce has slightly thickened.
Add the reserved chicken to the baking pan; add the sauce and cook in the preheated Air Fryer at 360 degrees F for 10 minutes or until thoroughly warmed.
Serve garnished with slivered almonds. Enjoy!

121. Spicy and Cheesy Turkey Meatloaf

(Ready in about 55 minutes | Servings 6)

Per serving: 455 Calories; 25.7g Fat; 7.8g Carbs; 45.9g Protein; 4.3g Sugars; 1.1g Fiber

INGREDIENTS

2 pounds turkey breasts, ground
1/2 pound Cheddar cheese, cubed
1/2 cup turkey stock
1/3 teaspoon hot paprika
3 eggs, lightly beaten

1 ½ tablespoon olive oil
2 cloves garlic, pressed
1 ½ teaspoons dried rosemary
1/2 cup yellow onion, chopped
1/3 cup ground almonds

1/2 teaspoon black pepper
A few dashes of Tabasco sauce
1 teaspoon seasoned salt
1/2 cup tomato sauce

DIRECTIONS

Heat the olive oil in a medium-sized saucepan that is placed over a moderate flame; now, sauté the onions, garlic, and dried rosemary until just tender, or about 3 to 4 minutes.
In the meantime, set the Air Fryer to cook at 385 degrees F.
Place all the ingredients, minus the tomato sauce, in a mixing dish together with the sautéed mixture; thoroughly mix to combine.
Shape into meatloaf and top with the tomato sauce. Air-fry for 47 minutes. Bon appétit!

122. Kung Pao Chicken

(Ready in about 50 minutes | Servings 4)

Per serving: 358 Calories; 21.1g Fat; 3.5g Carbs; 36.6g Protein; 2.4g Sugars; 0.2g Fiber

INGREDIENTS

1 ½ pounds chicken breast, halved
1 tablespoon lemon juice
2 tablespoons mirin
1/4 cup milk

2 tablespoons soy sauce
1 tablespoon olive oil
1 teaspoon ginger, peeled and grated
2 garlic cloves, minced

1/2 teaspoon salt
1/2 teaspoon Szechuan pepper
1/2 teaspoon xanthan gum

DIRECTIONS

In a large ceramic dish, place the chicken, lemon juice, mirin, milk, soy sauce, olive oil, ginger, and garlic. Let it marinate for 30 minutes in your refrigerator.
Spritz the sides and bottom of the cooking basket with a nonstick cooking spray. Arrange the chicken in the cooking basket and cook at 370 degrees F for 10 minutes.
Turn over the chicken, baste with the reserved marinade and cook for 4 minutes longer. Taste for doneness, season with salt and pepper, and reserve.
Add the marinade to the preheated skillet over medium heat; add in xanthan gum. Let it cook for 5 to 6 minutes until the sauce thickens.
Spoon the sauce over the reserved chicken and serve immediately.

PORK

123. Boozy Pork Loin Chops

(Ready in about 22 minutes | Servings 6)

Per serving: 393 Calories; 15.4g Fat; 2.6g Carbs; 56g Protein; 0.2g Sugars; 0.2g Fiber

INGREDIENTS

2 tablespoons vermouth
6 center-cut loin pork chops
1/2 tablespoon fresh basil, minced

1/3 teaspoon freshly ground black pepper, or more to taste
2 tablespoons whole grain mustard
1 teaspoon fine kosher salt

DIRECTIONS

Toss pork chops with other ingredients until they are well coated on both sides.
Air-fry your chops for 18 minutes at 405 degrees F, turning once or twice.
Mound your favorite salad on a serving plate; top with pork chops and enjoy.

124. Pork Sausage with Mashed Cauliflower

(Ready in about 30 minutes | Servings 6)

Per serving: 506 Calories; 42g Fat; 5.6g Carbs; 23.8g Protein; 1.8g Sugars; 1.6g Fiber

INGREDIENTS

1 pound cauliflower, chopped
1/2 teaspoon tarragon
1/3 cup Colby cheese
1/2 teaspoon ground black pepper
1/2 onion, peeled and sliced

1 teaspoon cumin powder
1/2 teaspoon sea salt
3 beaten eggs
6 pork sausages, chopped

DIRECTIONS

Boil the cauliflower until tender. Then, purée the cauliflower in your blender. Transfer to a mixing dish along with the other ingredients.
Divide the prepared mixture among six lightly greased rame-kins; now, place ramekins in your air fryer.
Bake in the preheated Air Fryer for 27 minutes at 365 degrees F. Eat warm.

125. Farmhouse Pork with Vegetables

(Ready in about 50 minutes | Servings 6)

Per serving: 589 Calories; 60.7g Fat; 2.5g Carbs; 11.9g Protein; 1.1g Sugars; 0.5g Fiber

INGREDIENTS

1 ½ pounds pork belly
2 bell peppers, sliced
2 cloves garlic, finely minced
4 green onions, quartered, white and green parts
1/4 cup cooking wine

Kosher salt and ground black pepper, to taste
1 teaspoon cayenne pepper
1 tablespoon coriander
1 teaspoon celery seeds

DIRECTIONS

Blanch the pork belly in boiling water for approximately 15 minutes. Then, cut it into chunks.
Arrange the pork chunks, bell peppers, garlic, and green onions in the Air Fryer basket. Drizzle everything with cooking wine of your choice.
Sprinkle with salt, black pepper, cayenne pepper, fresh coriander, and celery seeds. Toss to coat well.
Roast in the preheated Air Fryer at 330 degrees F for 30 minutes.
Serve on individual serving plates. Bon appétit!

126. Spicy Pork Meatballs

(Ready in about 20 minutes | Servings 4)

Per serving: 354 Calories; 23.6g Fat; 3.8g Carbs; 30g Protein; 0.9g Sugars; 1g Fiber

INGREDIENTS

1 pound ground pork
1 cup scallions, finely chopped
2 cloves garlic, finely minced
1 ½ tablespoons Worcester sauce

1 tablespoon oyster sauce
1 teaspoon turmeric powder
1/2 teaspoon freshly grated ginger root
1 small sliced red chili, for garnish

DIRECTIONS

Mix all of the above ingredients, apart from the red chili. Knead with your hands to ensure an even mixture.
Roll into equal balls and transfer them to the Air Fryer cooking basket.
Set the timer for 15 minutes and push the power button. Air-fry at 350 degrees F. Sprinkle with sliced red chili; serve immediately with your favorite sauce for dipping. Enjoy!

127. 30-Minute Hoisin Pork Loin Steak

(Ready in about 30 minutes | Servings 4)

Per serving: 219 Calories; 8.1g Fat; 19.5g Carbs; 17.1g Protein; 14.5g Sugars; 1g Fiber

INGREDIENTS

2 tablespoons dry white wine
1/3 cup hoisin sauce
2 teaspoons smoked cayenne pepper
3 garlic cloves, pressed

1/2 pound pork loin steak, cut into strips
3 teaspoons fresh lime juice
Salt and ground black pepper, to taste

DIRECTIONS

Start by preheating your Air Fryer to 395 degrees F.
Toss the pork with other ingredients; let it marinate at least 20 minutes in a fridge.
Then, air-fry the pork strips for 5 minutes. Bon appétit!

128. Pork Kebabs with Serrano Pepper

(Ready in about 22 minutes | Servings 3)

Per serving: 413 Calories; 32.3g Fat; 3.4g Carbs; 26.3g Protein; 1.6g Sugars; 1g Fiber

INGREDIENTS

2 tablespoons tomato puree
1/2 fresh serrano, minced
1/3 teaspoon paprika
1 pound pork, ground

1/2 cup green onions, finely chopped
3 cloves garlic, peeled and finely minced
1 teaspoon ground black pepper, or more to taste
1 teaspoon salt, or more to taste

DIRECTIONS

Thoroughly combine all ingredients in a mixing dish. Then, form your mixture into sausage shapes.
Cook for 18 minutes at 355 degrees F. Mound salad on a serving platter, top with air-fried kebabs and serve warm. Bon appétit!

129. Pork Kebab with Creamy Dill Sauce

(Ready in about 25 minutes | Servings 4)

Per serving: 407 Calories; 28.5g Fat; 3.4g Carbs; 32.9g Protein; 1.3g Sugars; 0.6g Fiber

INGREDIENTS

2 teaspoons olive oil
1/2 pound ground pork
1/2 pound ground beef
1 egg, whisked
Sea salt and ground black pepper, to taste
1 teaspoon paprika
2 garlic cloves, minced
1 teaspoon dried marjoram
1 teaspoon mustard seeds

1/2 teaspoon celery seeds
Yogurt Sauce:
2 tablespoons olive oil
2 tablespoons fresh lemon juice
Sea salt, to taste
1/4 teaspoon red pepper flakes, crushed
1/2 cup   full-fat yogurt
1 teaspoon dried dill weed

DIRECTIONS

Spritz the sides and bottom of the cooking basket with 2 teaspoons of olive oil.

In a mixing dish, thoroughly combine the ground pork, beef, egg, salt, black pepper, paprika, garlic, marjoram, mustard seeds, and celery seeds.

Form the mixture into kebabs and transfer them to the greased cooking basket. Cook at 365 degrees F for 11 to 12 minutes, turning them over once or twice.

In the meantime, mix all the sauce ingredients and place in the refrigerator until ready to serve. Serve the pork kebabs with the yogurt sauce on the side. Enjoy!

130. Bacon-Wrapped Hot Dogs

(Ready in about 25 minutes | Servings 5)

Per serving: 297 Calories; 26.1g Fat; 9.3g Carbs; 7.1g Protein; 3.2g Sugars; 1.1g Fiber

INGREDIENTS

10 thin slices of bacon
5 pork hot dogs, halved
1 teaspoon cayenne pepper

Sauce:
1/4 cup mayo
4 tablespoons ketchup, low-carb
1 teaspoon rice vinegar
1 teaspoon chili powder

DIRECTIONS

Lay the slices of bacon on your working surface. Place a hot dog on one end of each slice; sprinkle with cayenne pepper and roll them over. Cook in the preheated Air Fryer at 390 degrees F for 10 to 12 minutes.

Whisk all ingredients for the sauce in a mixing bowl and store in your refrigerator, covered, until ready to serve.

Serve bacon-wrapped hot dogs with the sauce on the side. Enjoy!

131. Cheesy Ground Pork Casserole

(Ready in about 25 minutes | Servings 4)

Per serving: 449 Calories; 23g Fat; 5.6g Carbs; 54g Protein; 3.2g Sugars; 0.8g Fiber

INGREDIENTS

1 pound lean ground pork
1/2 pound ground beef
1/4 cup tomato puree
Sea salt and ground black pepper, to taste
1 teaspoon smoked paprika
1/2 teaspoon dried oregano

1 teaspoon dried basil
1 teaspoon dried rosemary
2 eggs
1 cup Cottage cheese, crumbled, at room temperature
1/2 cup Cotija cheese, shredded

DIRECTIONS

Lightly grease a casserole dish with a nonstick cooking oil. Add the ground meat to the bottom of your casserole dish.

Add the tomato puree. Sprinkle with salt, black pepper, paprika, oregano, basil, and rosemary.

In a mixing bowl, whisk the egg with cheese. Place on top of the ground meat mixture. Place a piece of foil on top.

Bake in the preheated Air Fryer at 350 degrees F for 10 minutes; remove the foil and cook an additional 6 minutes. Bon appétit!

132. Spicy Pork with Herbs and Candy Onions

(Ready in about 1 hour | Servings 4)

Per serving: 444 Calories; 12.8g Fat; 8.8g Carbs; 67g Protein; 6.8g Sugars; 1.3g Fiber

INGREDIENTS

1 rosemary sprig, chopped
1 thyme sprig, chopped
1 teaspoon dried sage, crushed
Sea salt and ground black pepper, to taste
1 teaspoon cayenne pepper

2 teaspoons sesame oil
2 pounds pork leg roast, scored
1/2 pound candy onions, peeled
2 chili peppers, minced
4 cloves garlic, finely chopped

DIRECTIONS

Start by preheating your Air Fryer to 400 degrees F.
Then, mix the seasonings with the sesame oil.
Rub the seasoning mixture all over the pork leg. Cook in the preheated Air Fryer for 40 minutes.
Add the candy onions, peppers and garlic and cook an additional 12 minutes. Slice the pork leg. Afterwards, spoon the pan juices over the meat and serve with the candy onions. Bon appétit!

133. Pork Steak with Mustard and Herbs

(Ready in about 20 minutes | Servings 2)

Per serving: 402 Calories; 14.6g Fat; 0.1g Carbs; 67.2g Protein; 0g Sugars; 0.8g Fiber

INGREDIENTS

1 pound porterhouse steak, cut meat from bones in 2 pieces
1/2 teaspoon ground black pepper
1 teaspoon cayenne pepper
1/2 teaspoon salt
1 teaspoon garlic powder

1/2 teaspoon dried thyme
1/2 teaspoon dried marjoram
1 teaspoon Dijon mustard
1 tablespoon butter, melted

DIRECTIONS

Sprinkle the porterhouse steak with all the seasonings.
Spread the mustard and butter evenly over the meat.
Cook in the preheated Air Fryer at 390 degrees F for 12 to 14 minutes.
Taste for doneness with a meat thermometer and serve immediately.

134. Parmesan-Crusted Pork Cutlets

(Ready in about 1 hour 20 minutes | Servings 2)

Per serving: 450 Calories; 26.4g Fat; 8.9g Carbs; 41.2g Protein; 2.6g Sugars; 2.4g Fiber

INGREDIENTS

1 cup water
1 cup red wine
1 tablespoon sea salt
2 pork cutlets
1/4 cup almond meal
1/4 cup flaxseed meal
1/2 teaspoon baking powder

1 teaspoon shallot powder
1/2 teaspoon porcini powder
Sea salt and ground black pepper, to taste
1 egg
1/4 cup yogurt
1 teaspoon brown mustard
1/3 cup parmesan cheese, grated

DIRECTIONS

In a large ceramic dish, combine the water, wine and salt. Add the pork cutlets and put for 1 hour in the refrigerator.
In a shallow bowl, mix the almond meal, flaxseed meal, baking powder, shallot powder, porcini powder, salt, and ground pepper. In another bowl, whisk the eggs with yogurt and mustard.
In a third bowl, place the grated parmesan cheese.
Dip the pork cutlets in the seasoned flour mixture and toss evenly; then, in the egg mixture. Finally, roll them over the grated parmesan cheese.
Spritz the bottom of the cooking basket with cooking oil. Add the breaded pork cutlets and cook at 395 degrees F and for 10 minutes.
Flip and cook for 5 minutes more on the other side. Serve warm.

135. Spicy and Creamy Pork Gratin

(Ready in about 25 minutes | Servings 4)

Per serving: 433 Calories; 20.4g Fat; 2.6g Carbs; 56.5g Protein; 0.3g Sugars; 0.3g Fiber

INGREDIENTS

2 tablespoons olive oil

2 pounds pork tenderloin, cut into serving-size pieces

1 teaspoon coarse sea salt

1/2 teaspoon freshly ground pepper

1/4 teaspoon chili powder

1 teaspoon dried marjoram

1 tablespoon mustard

1 cup Ricotta cheese

1 ½ cups chicken broth

DIRECTIONS

Start by preheating your Air Fryer to 350 degrees F.

Heat the olive oil in a pan over medium-high heat. Once hot, cook the pork for 6 to 7 minutes, flipping it to ensure even cooking.

Arrange the pork in a lightly greased casserole dish. Season with salt, black pepper, chili powder, and marjoram.

In a mixing dish, thoroughly combine the mustard, cheese, and chicken broth. Pour the mixture over the pork chops in the casserole dish.

Bake for another 15 minutes or until bubbly and heated through. Bon appétit!

136. Easy Cheeseburger Meatballs

(Ready in about 15 minutes | Servings 3)

Per serving: 539 Calories; 43g Fat; 3g Carbs; 32g Protein; 0.3g Sugars; 0.1g Fiber

INGREDIENTS

1 pound ground pork

1 tablespoon coconut aminos

1 teaspoon garlic, minced

2 tablespoons spring onions, finely chopped

1/2 cup pork rinds

1/2 cup parmesan cheese, preferably freshly grated

DIRECTIONS

Combine the ground pork, coconut aminos, garlic, and spring onions in a mixing dish. Mix until everything is well incorporated. Form the mixture into small meatballs.

In a shallow bowl, mix the pork rinds and grated parmesan cheese. Roll the meatballs over the parmesan mixture.

Cook at 380 degrees F for 3 minutes; shake the basket and cook an additional 4 minutes or until meatballs are browned on all sides. Bon appétit!

137. Aromatic Pork Tenderloin with Herbs

(Ready in about 20 minutes + marinating time | Servings 4)

Per serving: 168 Calories; 4.1g Fat; 1.4g Carbs; 29.9g Protein; 0.0g Sugars; 0.3g Fiber

INGREDIENTS

1 pound pork tenderloin

4-5 garlic cloves, peeled and halved

1 teaspoon kosher salt

1/3 teaspoon ground black pepper

1 teaspoon dried basil

1/2 teaspoon dried oregano

1/2 teaspoon dried rosemary

1/2 teaspoon dried marjoram

2 tablespoons cooking wine

DIRECTIONS

Rub the pork with garlic halves; add the seasoning and drizzle with the cooking wine. Then, cut slits completely through pork tenderloin. Tuck the remaining garlic into the slits.

Wrap the pork tenderloin with foil; let it marinate overnight.

Roast at 360 degrees F for 15 to 17 minutes. Serve warm with roasted potatoes. Bon appétit!

138. Family Pork Loin Roast

(Ready in about 55 minutes | Servings 6)

Per serving: 278 Calories; 16.0g Fat; 0.3g Carbs; 31.2g Protein; 0.0g Sugars; 0.2g Fiber

INGREDIENTS

1 ½ pounds boneless pork loin roast, washed
1 teaspoon mustard seeds
1 teaspoon garlic powder
1 teaspoon porcini powder
1 teaspoon shallot powder

3/4 teaspoon sea salt flakes
1 teaspoon red pepper flakes, crushed
2 dried sprigs thyme, crushed
2 tablespoons lime juice

DIRECTIONS

Firstly, score the meat using a small knife; make sure to not cut too deep.
In a small-sized mixing dish, combine all seasonings in the order listed above; mix to combine well.
Massage the spice mix into the pork meat to evenly distribute. Drizzle with lemon juice.
Then, set your Air Fryer to cook at 360 degrees F. Place the pork in the Air Fryer basket; roast for 25 to 30 minutes. Pause the machine, check for doneness and cook for 25 minutes more.

139. Classic Smoked Pork Chops

(Ready in about 25 minutes | Servings 6)

Per serving: 332 Calories; 17g Fat; 0.8g Carbs; 40.8g Protein; 0g Sugars; 0.2g Fiber

INGREDIENTS

6 pork chops
Hickory-smoked salt, to savor
Ground black pepper, to savor
1 teaspoon onion powder

1/2 teaspoon garlic powder
1/2 teaspoon cayenne pepper
1/3 cup almond meal

DIRECTIONS

Simply place all of the above ingredients into a zip-top plastic bag; shake them up to coat well.
Spritz the chops with a pan spray (canola spray works well here) and transfer them to the Air Fryer cooking basket.
Roast them for 20 minutes at 375 degrees F. Serve with sautéed vegetables. Bon appétit!

140. Traditional Walliser Schnitzel

(Ready in about 15 minutes | Servings 2)

Per serving: 495 Calories; 34.1g Fat; 2.4g Carbs; 42g Protein; 0.9g Sugars; 0.4g Fiber

INGREDIENTS

1/3 tablespoon cider vinegar
1/3 teaspoon ground black pepper
1 teaspoon garlic salt
1/2 teaspoon mustard
1/2 heaping tablespoon fresh parsley

1/2 cup pork rinds
2 eggs, beaten
1/2 teaspoon fennel seed
2 pork schnitzel, halved

DIRECTIONS

Blitz the vinegar, black pepper, garlic salt, mustard, fennel seeds, fresh parsley and pork rinds in your food processor until uniform and smooth.
Dump the blended mixture into a shallow bowl. Add the beaten egg to another shallow bowl.
Coat the pork schnitzel with the beaten egg; then, dredge them in the herb mixture.
Cook in the preheated Air Fryer at 355 degrees F for about 14 minutes. Bon appétit!

141. Bolognese Sauce with a Twist

(Ready in about 19 minutes | Servings 4)

Per serving: 490 Calories; 37.3g Fat; 6.2g Carbs; 29g Protein; 3.2g Sugars; 1.2g Fiber

INGREDIENTS

1 teaspoon kosher salt
1/3 teaspoon cayenne pepper
1½ pounds ground pork
1/3 cup tomato paste
3 cloves garlic, minced

1/2 medium-sized white onion, peeled and chopped
1/3 tablespoon fresh cilantro, chopped
1/2 tablespoon extra-virgin olive oil
1/3 teaspoon freshly cracked black pepper
1/2 teaspoon grated fresh ginger

DIRECTIONS

Begin by preheating your Air Fryer to 395 degrees F.
Then, thoroughly combine all the ingredients until the mixture is uniform.
Transfer the meat mixture to the Air Fryer baking dish and cook for about 14 minutes. Serve with zucchini noodles and enjoy.

142. Bacon with Shallot and Greens

(Ready in about 10 minutes | Servings 2)

Per serving: 259 Calories; 16.4g Fat; 9.7g Carbs; 18.5g Protein; 2.7g Sugars; 4.5g Fiber

INGREDIENTS

7 ounces mixed greens
8 thick slices pork bacon

2 shallots, peeled and diced
Nonstick cooking spray

DIRECTIONS

Begin by preheating the air fryer to 345 degrees F.
Now, add the shallot and bacon to the Air Fryer cooking basket; set the timer for 2 minutes. Spritz with a nonstick cooking spray.
After that, pause the Air Fryer; throw in the mixed greens; give it a good stir and cook an additional 5 minutes. Serve warm.

143. Sausage Meatballs with Parmesan and Marinara Sauce

(Ready in about 20 minutes | Servings 4)

Per serving: 409 Calories; 33.7g Fat; 7.4g Carbs; 17.1g Protein; 1.5g Sugars; 0.9g Fiber

INGREDIENTS

1 pound pork sausage meat
1 shallot, finely chopped
2 garlic cloves, finely minced
1/2 teaspoon fine sea salt

1/4 teaspoon ground black pepper, or more to taste
3/4 teaspoon paprika
1/2 cup parmesan cheese, preferably freshly grated
1/2 jar marinara sauce

DIRECTIONS

Mix all of the above ingredients, except the marinara sauce, in a large-sized dish, until everything is well incorporated.
Shape into meatballs. Air-fry them at 360 degrees F for 10 minutes; pause the Air Fryer, shake them up and cook for additional 6 minutes or until the balls are no longer pink in the middle.
Meanwhile, heat the marinara sauce over a medium flame. Serve the pork sausage meatballs with marinara sauce. Bon appétit!

144. Pork Butt with Herb-Garlic Sauce

(Ready in about 35 minutes + marinating time | Servings 4)

Per serving: 422 Calories; 30.9g Fat; 2.7g Carbs; 30.8g Protein; 0.8g Sugars; 0.7g Fiber

INGREDIENTS

1 pound pork butt, cut into pieces 2-inches long
1 teaspoon golden flaxseed meal
1 egg white, well whisked
Salt and ground black pepper, to taste
1 tablespoon olive oil
1 tablespoon coconut aminos
1 teaspoon lemon juice, preferably freshly squeezed

For the Coriander-Garlic Sauce:
3 garlic cloves, peeled
1/3 cup fresh parsley leaves
1/3 cup fresh coriander leaves
1/2 tablespoon salt
1 teaspoon lemon juice
1/3 cup extra-virgin olive oil

DIRECTIONS

Combine the pork strips with the flaxseed meal, egg white, salt, pepper, olive oil, coconut aminos, and lemon juice. Cover and refrigerate for 30 to 45 minutes.

After that, spritz the pork strips with a nonstick cooking spray.

Set your Air Fryer to cook at 380 degrees F. Press the power button and air-fry for 15 minutes; pause the machine, shake the basket and cook for 15 more minutes.

Meanwhile, puree the garlic in a food processor until finely minced. Now, puree the parsley, coriander, salt, and lemon juice. With the machine running, carefully pour in the olive oil.

Serve the pork with well-chilled sauce with and enjoy!

145. Pork Ribs with Red Wine Sauce

(Ready in about 25 minutes + marinating time | Servings 4)

Per serving: 438 Calories; 27.3g Fat; 3.3g Carbs; 32.2g Protein; 1.1g Sugars; 0.3g Fiber

INGREDIENTS

For the Pork Ribs:
1 ½ pounds pork ribs
2 tablespoons olive oil
1/2 teaspoon freshly cracked black peppercorns

1/2 teaspoon Hickory-smoked salt
1 tablespoon Dijon mustard
2 tablespoons coconut aminos
2 tablespoons lime juice
1 clove garlic, minced

For the Red Wine Sauce:
1 ½ cups beef stock
1 cup red wine
1 teaspoon balsamic vinegar
1/4 teaspoon salt

DIRECTIONS

Place all ingredients for the pork ribs in a large-sized mixing dish. Cover and marinate in your refrigerator overnight or at least 3 hours.

Air-fry the pork ribs for 10 minutes at 320 degrees F.

Meanwhile, make the sauce. Add a beef stock to a deep pan that is preheated over a moderate flame; boil until it is reduced by half.

Add the remaining ingredients and increase the temperature to high heat. Let it cook for further 10 minutes or until your sauce is reduced by half.

Serve the pork ribs with red wine sauce. Bon appétit!

146. Italian-Style Pork Loin Roast

(Ready in about 50 minutes | Servings 3)

Per serving: 300 Calories; 9g Fat; 1.5g Carbs; 33.8g Protein; 0.3g Sugars; 0.5g Fiber

INGREDIENTS

1 teaspoon Celtic sea salt
1/2 teaspoon black pepper, freshly cracked
1/4 cup red wine
2 tablespoons mustard

2 garlic cloves, minced
1 pound pork top loin
1 tablespoon Italian herb seasoning blend

DIRECTIONS

In a ceramic bowl, mix the salt, black pepper, red wine, mustard, and garlic. Add the pork top loin and let it marinate at least 30 minutes.

Spritz the sides and bottom of the cooking basket with a nonstick cooking spray.

Place the pork top loin in the basket; sprinkle with the Italian herb seasoning blend.

Cook the pork tenderloin at 370 degrees F for 10 minutes. Flip halfway through, spraying with cooking oil and cook for 5 to 6 minutes more. Serve immediately.

147. Ground Pork, Peppers and Cheese Casserole

(Ready in about 50 minutes | Servings 4)

Per serving: 505 Calories; 39.4g Fat; 9.9g Carbs; 28g Protein; 5.1g Sugars; 1.8g Fiber

INGREDIENTS

2 chili peppers
1 red bell pepper
2 tablespoons olive oil
1 large-sized shallot, chopped
1 pound ground pork
2 garlic cloves, minced
2 ripe tomatoes, pureed

1 teaspoon dried marjoram
1/2 teaspoon mustard seeds
1/2 teaspoon celery seeds
1 teaspoon Mexican oregano
1 tablespoon fish sauce
2 tablespoons fresh coriander, chopped
Salt and ground black pepper, to taste

2 cups water
1 tablespoon chicken bouillon granules
2 tablespoons sherry wine
1 cup Mexican cheese blend

DIRECTIONS

Roast the peppers in the preheated Air Fryer at 395 degrees F for 10 minutes, flipping them halfway through cook time.

Let them steam for 10 minutes; then, peel the skin and discard the stems and seeds. Slice the peppers into halves.

Heat the olive oil in a baking pan at 380 degrees F for 2 minutes; add the shallots and cook for 4 minutes. Add the ground pork and garlic; cook for a further 4 to 5 minutes.

After that, stir in the tomatoes, marjoram, mustard seeds, celery seeds, oregano, fish sauce, coriander, salt, and pepper. Add a layer of sliced peppers to the baking pan.

Mix the water with the chicken bouillon granules and sherry wine. Add the mixture to the baking pan.

Cook in the preheated Air Fryer at 395 degrees F for 10 minutes. Top with cheese and bake an additional 5 minutes until the cheese has melted. Serve immediately.

148. German Sausage with Sauerkraut

(Ready in about 35 minutes | Servings 4)

Per serving: 453 Calories; 42.6g Fat; 6.1g Carbs; 17.2g Protein; 2.1g Sugars; 3g Fiber

INGREDIENTS

4 pork sausages, smoked
2 tablespoons canola oil
2 garlic cloves, minced
1 pound sauerkraut

1 teaspoon cayenne pepper
1/2 teaspoon black peppercorns
2 bay leaves

DIRECTIONS

Start by preheating your Air Fryer to 360 degrees F.

Prick holes into the sausages using a fork and transfer them to the cooking basket. Cook approximately 14 minutes, shaking the basket a couple of times. Set aside.

Now, heat the canola oil in a baking pan at 380 degrees F. Add the garlic and cook for 1 minute. Immediately stir in the sauerkraut, cayenne pepper, peppercorns, and bay leaves.

Let it cook for 15 minutes, stirring every 5 minutes. Serve in individual bowls with warm sausages on the side!

149. Pork Sirloin with Greek Tzatziki Sauce

(Ready in about 55 minutes | Servings 4)

Per serving: 560 Calories; 30.1g Fat; 4.9g Carbs; 64.1g Protein; 1.6g Sugars; 1.5g Fiber

INGREDIENTS

Greek Pork:
2 pounds pork sirloin roast
Salt and black pepper, to taste
1 teaspoon smoked paprika
1/2 teaspoon mustard seeds
1/2 teaspoon celery seeds
1 teaspoon fennel seeds
1 teaspoon Ancho chili powder

1 teaspoon turmeric powder
1/2 teaspoon ground ginger
2 tablespoons olive oil
2 cloves garlic, finely chopped
Tzatziki:
1/2 cucumber, finely chopped and squeezed

1 cup full-fat Greek yogurt
1 garlic clove, minced
1 tablespoon extra virgin olive oil
1 teaspoon balsamic vinegar
1 teaspoon minced fresh dill
A pinch of salt

DIRECTIONS

Toss all ingredients for Greek pork in a large mixing bowl. Toss until the meat is well coated.

Cook in the preheated Air Fryer at 360 degrees F for 30 minutes; turn over and cook another 20 minutes.

Meanwhile, prepare the tzatziki by mixing all the tzatziki ingredients. Place in your refrigerator until ready to use.

Serve the pork sirloin roast with the chilled tzatziki on the side. Enjoy!

150. Spanish Pinchos Morunos

(Ready in about 25 minutes + marinating time | Servings 4)

Per serving: 432 Calories; 23g Fat; 3.4g Carbs; 49.4g Protein; 0.4g Sugars; 0.7g Fiber

INGREDIENTS

2 pounds center cut loin chop, cut into bite-sized pieces
1 teaspoon oregano
1/2 teaspoon ground turmeric
1/2 teaspoon ground coriander
1 teaspoon ground cumin
2 teaspoons sweet Spanish paprika

Sea salt and freshly ground black pepper, to taste
2 garlic cloves, minced
2 tablespoons extra virgin olive oil
1/4 cup dry red wine
1 lemon, 1/2 juiced 1/2 wedges

DIRECTIONS

Mix all ingredients, except the lemon wedges, in a large ceramic dish. Allow it to marinate for 2 hours in your refrigerator.
Discard the marinade. Now, thread the pork pieces on to skewers and place them in the cooking basket.
Cook in the preheated Air Fryer at 360 degrees F for 15 to 17 minutes, shaking the basket every 5 minutes. Work in batches.
Serve immediately garnished with lemon wedges. Bon appétit!

151. Pork with Padrón Peppers and Green Olives

(Ready in about 30 minutes | Servings 4)

Per serving: 536 Calories; 29.5g Fat; 5.9g Carbs; 59g Protein; 2.9g Sugars; 1.3g Fiber

INGREDIENTS

1 tablespoon olive oil
8 ounces Padrón peppers
2 pounds pork loin, sliced
1 teaspoon Celtic salt

1 teaspoon paprika
1 heaped tablespoon capers, drained
8 green olives, pitted and halved

DIRECTIONS

Drizzle olive oil all over the Padrón peppers; cook them in the preheated Air Fryer at 400 degrees F for 10 minutes, turning occasionally, until well blistered all over and tender-crisp.
Then, turn the temperature to 360 degrees F.
Season the pork loin with salt and paprika. Add the capers and cook for 16 minutes, turning them over halfway through the cooking time.
Serve with olives and the reserved Padrón peppers. Bon appétit!

152. Meatballs with Herbs and Mozzarella

(Ready in about 20 minutes | Servings 4)

Per serving: 311 Calories; 19.5g Fat; 3.5g Carbs; 30.1g Protein; 1.3g Sugars; 1.1g Fiber

INGREDIENTS

1/2 pound ground pork
1/2 pound ground beef
1 shallot, chopped
2 garlic cloves, minced
1 tablespoon coriander, chopped
1 teaspoon fresh mint, minced

Sea salt and ground black pepper, to taste
1/2 teaspoon mustard seeds
1 teaspoon fennel seeds
1 teaspoon ground cumin
1 cup mozzarella, sliced

DIRECTIONS

In a mixing bowl, combine all ingredients, except the mozzarella.
Shape the mixture into balls and transfer them to a lightly greased cooking basket.
Cook the meatballs in the preheated Air Fryer at 380 degrees for 10 minutes. Check the meatballs halfway through the cooking time.
Top with sliced mozzarella and bake for 3 minutes more. To serve, arrange on a nice serving platter. Bon appétit!

153. Rustic Pork and Mushroom Cheeseburgers

(Ready in about 30 minutes | Servings 4)

Per serving: 399 Calories; 29.7g Fat; 8.7g Carbs; 24.3g Protein; 4.6g Sugars; 1.5g Fiber

INGREDIENTS

1 tablespoon canola oil
1 onion, chopped
2 garlic cloves, minced
1 pound ground pork
1/2 pound brown mushrooms, chopped

Salt and black pepper, to taste
1 teaspoon cayenne pepper
1/2 teaspoon dried rosemary
1/2 teaspoon dried dill
4 slices Cheddar cheese

DIRECTIONS

Start by preheating your Air Fryer to 370 degrees F.

In a mixing bowl, thoroughly combine the oil, onions, garlic, ground pork, mushrooms, salt, black pepper, cayenne pepper, rosemary, and dill.

Shape the meat mixture into four patties.

Spritz the bottom of the cooking basket with cooking spray. Cook the meatballs in the preheated Air Fryer at 370 degrees for 20 minutes, flipping them halfway through cooking.

Top the warm patties with cheese and serve. Enjoy!

154. Sherry-Braised Ribs with Grape Tomatoes

(Ready in about 35 minutes | Servings 2)

Per serving: 341 Calories; 11.1g Fat; 6.3g Carbs; 51g Protein; 3.8g Sugars; 1.8g Fiber

INGREDIENTS

1 rack ribs, cut in half to fit the Air Fryer
1/4 cup sherry wine
2 tablespoons coconut aminos
1 tablespoon Dijon mustard

Sea salt and ground black pepper, to taste
1 cup grape tomatoes
1 teaspoon dried rosemary

DIRECTIONS

Toss the pork ribs with sherry wine, coconut aminos, mustard, salt, and black pepper.

Add the ribs to the lightly greased cooking basket. Cook in the preheated Air Fryer at 370 degrees F for 25 minutes.

Turn the ribs over, add the tomatoes and rosemary; cook an additional 5 minutes. Serve immediately.

155. Cheesy Stuffed Peppers with Ground Pork

(Ready in about 30 minutes | Servings 3)

Per serving: 425 Calories; 25.9g Fat; 9.5g Carbs; 38.3g Protein; 5.2g Sugars; 2.2g Fiber

INGREDIENTS

3 bell peppers, stems and seeds removed
1 tablespoon olive oil
3 scallions, chopped
1 teaspoon fresh garlic, minced
12 ounces lean pork, ground

1/2 teaspoon sea salt
1/2 teaspoon black pepper
1 tablespoon fish sauce
2 ripe tomatoes, pureed
3 ounces Monterey Jack cheese, grated

DIRECTIONS

Cook the peppers in boiling salted water for 4 minutes

In a nonstick skillet, heat the olive oil over medium heat. Then, sauté the scallions and garlic until tender and fragrant.

Stir in the ground pork and continue sautéing until the pork has browned; drain off the excess fat.

Add the salt, black pepper, fish sauce, and 1 pureed tomato; give it a good stir.

Divide the filling among the bell peppers. Arrange the peppers in a baking dish lightly greased with cooking oil. Place the remaining tomato puree around the peppers.

Bake in the preheated Air Fryer at 380 degrees F for 13 minutes. Top with grated cheese and bake another 6 minutes. Serve warm and enjoy!

156. Mexican Salsa Boston Butt

(Ready in about 35 minutes | Servings 4)

Per serving: 374 Calories; 24.1g Fat; 8.6g Carbs; 29.9g Protein; 4.7g Sugars; 1.9g Fiber

INGREDIENTS

1 pound Boston butt, thinly sliced across the grain into 2-inch-long strips
1/2 teaspoon red pepper flakes, crushed

Sea salt and ground black pepper, to taste
1/2 pound tomatillos, chopped
1 small-sized onion, chopped
2 chili peppers, chopped

2 cloves garlic
2 tablespoons fresh cilantro, chopped
1 tablespoon olive oil
1 teaspoon sea salt

DIRECTIONS

Rub the Boston butt with red pepper, salt, and black pepper. Spritz the bottom of the cooking basket with a nonstick cooking spray.
Roast the Boston butt in the preheated Air Fryer at 390 degrees F for 10 minutes. Shake the basket and cook another 10 minutes.
While the pork is roasting, make the salsa.
Blend the remaining ingredients until smooth and uniform. Transfer the mixture to a saucepan and add 1 cup of water.
Bring to a boil; reduce the heat and simmer for 8 to 12 minutes. Serve the roasted pork with the salsa verde on the side. Enjoy!

157. Pork with Buttery Broccoli

(Ready in about 30 minutes | Servings 4)

Per serving: 346 Calories; 18.1g Fat; 9.4g Carbs; 36.2g Protein; 2.1g Sugars; 3.1g Fiber

INGREDIENTS

1 ½ pounds blade steaks skinless, boneless
Kosher salt and ground black pepper, to taste
2 garlic cloves, crushed
2 tablespoons coconut aminos
1 tablespoon oyster sauce

2 tablespoon lemon juice
1 pound broccoli, broken into florets
2 tablespoons butter, melted
1 teaspoon dried dill weed
2 tablespoons sunflower seeds, lightly toasted

DIRECTIONS

Start by preheating your Air Fryer to 385 degrees F. Spritz the bottom and sides of the cooking basket with cooking spray.
Now, season the pork with salt and black pepper. Add the garlic, coconut aminos, oyster sauce, and lemon juice.
Cook for 20 minutes; turning over halfway through the cooking time.
Toss the broccoli with the melted butter and dill. Add the broccoli to the cooking basket and cook at 400 degrees F for 6 minutes, shaking the basket periodically.
Serve the warm pork with broccoli and garnish with sunflower seeds. Bon appétit!

158. Sloppy Joes with a Twist

(Ready in about 45 minutes | Servings 4)

Per serving: 571 Calories; 46.1g Fat; 8.3g Carbs; 31.1g Protein; 2.7g Sugars; 2.9g Fiber

INGREDIENTS

1 tablespoon olive oil
1 shallot, chopped
2 garlic cloves, minced
1 bell pepper, chopped
1 pound ground pork
1 ripe medium-sized tomato, pureed

1 tablespoon poultry seasoning blend
Dash ground allspice
Keto Buns:
1/3 cup ricotta cheese, crumbled
2/3 cup part skim mozzarella cheese, shredded

1 egg
1/3 cup coconut flour
1/2 cup almond flour
1 teaspoon baking soda
1 ½ tablespoons plain whey protein isolate

DIRECTIONS

Start by preheating your Air Fryer to 390 degrees F. Heat the olive oil for a few minutes.
Once hot, sauté the shallots until just tender. Add the garlic and bell pepper; cook for 4 minutes more or until they are aromatic.
Add the ground pork and cook for 5 minutes more, crumbling with a fork. Next step, stir in the pureed tomatoes and spices. Decrease the temperature to 365 degrees F and cook another 10 minutes. Reserve.
To make the keto buns, microwave the cheese for 1 minute 30 seconds, stirring twice. Add the cheese to the bowl of a food processor and blend well. Fold in the egg and mix again.
Add in the flour, baking soda, and plain whey protein isolate; blend again. Scrape the batter onto the center of a lightly greased cling film.
Form the dough into a disk and transfer to your freezer to cool; cut into 4 pieces and transfer to a parchment-lined baking pan (make sure to grease your hands). Bake in the preheated oven at 400 degrees F for about 14 minutes.
Spoon the meat mixture into keto buns and transfer them to the cooking basket. Cook for 7 minutes or until thoroughly warmed.

159. Spicy and Saucy Pork Sirloin

(Ready in about 55 minutes | Servings 3)

Per serving: 426 Calories; 23.6g Fat; 4.1g Carbs; 47.4g Protein; 1.8g Sugars; 1.4g Fiber

INGREDIENTS

2 teaspoons peanut oil

1 ½ pounds pork sirloin

Coarse sea salt and ground black pepper, to taste

1 tablespoon smoked paprika

1/4 cup prepared salsa sauce

DIRECTIONS

Start by preheating your Air Fryer to 360 degrees F.

Drizzle the oil all over the pork sirloin. Sprinkle with salt, black pepper, and paprika.

Cook for 50 minutes in the preheated Air Fryer.

Remove the roast from the Air Fryer and shred with two forks. Mix in the salsa sauce. Enjoy!

160. French-Style Smothered Pork Chops

(Ready in about 20 minutes | Servings 4)

Per serving: 307 Calories; 7.5g Fat; 1.7g Carbs; 33.9g Protein; 0.9g Sugars; 0.4g Fiber

INGREDIENTS

2 tablespoons coconut aminos

2 tablespoons French wine

2 tablespoons rice vinegar

1 pound pork loin center rib chops, bone-in

1 teaspoon Herbes de Provence

Celtic salt and ground black pepper, to taste

1 tablespoon Dijon mustard

DIRECTIONS

Thoroughly combine the coconut aminos, wine, and vinegar; add the pork and let it marinate for 1 hour in the refrigerator.

Sprinkle the pork chops with Herbes de Provence, salt, and black pepper. Spread the mustard, all over the pork chops.

Cook in the preheated Air Fryer at 400 degrees F for 12 minutes. Serve warm with mashed potatoes if desired.

161. Authentic Pakistani Seekh Kebabs

(Ready in about 25 minutes | Servings 3)

Per serving: 456 Calories; 34.7g Fat; 5.1g Carbs; 28.1g Protein; 1.5g Sugars; 0.6g Fiber

INGREDIENTS

1 pound lean pork, ground

1 onion, chopped

1 garlic clove, smashed

1 Thai bird chili, deveined and finely chopped

1 teaspoon mustard

1 teaspoon coriander seed, ground

1/2 teaspoon cumin powder

Salt and ground black pepper, to taste

6 tablespoons parmesan cheese, grated

DIRECTIONS

Mix all ingredients using your hands. Knead until everything is well incorporated.

Shape the meat mixture around flat skewers (sausage shapes).

Cook at 365 degrees F for 11 to 12 minutes, turning them over once or twice. Work in batches. Serve!

162. Spicy Pork Sausage with Eggs

(Ready in about 24 minutes | Servings 6)

Per serving: 468 Calories; 39g Fat; 3.6g Carbs; 22.6g Protein; 1.3g Sugars; 0.7g Fiber

INGREDIENTS

1 green bell pepper, seeded and thinly sliced
6 medium-sized eggs
1 Habanero pepper, seeded and minced
1/2 teaspoon sea salt
2 teaspoons fennel seeds

1 red bell pepper, seeded and thinly sliced
1 teaspoon tarragon
1/2 teaspoon freshly cracked black pepper
6 pork sausages

DIRECTIONS

Place the sausages and all peppers in the Air Fryer cooking basket. Cook at 335 degrees F for 9 minutes.
Divide the eggs among 6 ramekins; sprinkle each egg with the seasonings.
Cook for 11 more minutes at 395 degrees F. Serve warm with sausages. Bon appétit!

163. Pork Tenderloin with Garden Vegetables

(Ready in about 20 minutes | Servings 2)

Per serving: 268 Calories; 5.7g Fat; 3.5g Carbs; 48.1g Protein; 1.6g Sugars; 0.8g Fiber

INGREDIENTS

½ cup cream of onion soup
½ bell pepper, seeded and diced
Fine sea salt and black pepper, to taste
1/3 cup celery, chopped

1/2 pound pork tenderloin, diced
1/3 cup onions, chopped
2 teaspoons cayenne pepper
2 garlic cloves, halved

DIRECTIONS

Begin by preheating your air fryer to 385 degrees F.
Add all ingredients to a baking dish that is previously greased with a thin layer of canola oil; cook about 5 minutes.
Gently stir the ingredients and cook an additional 12 minutes. Bon appétit!

164. Peppery Pork Roast with Herbs

(Ready in about 30 minutes | Servings 6)

Per serving: 241 Calories; 14.4g Fat; 5.3g Carbs; 22.2g Protein; 3.3g Sugars; 0.8g Fiber

INGREDIENTS

1 tablespoon olive oil
1 pound pork loin
1 teaspoon dried basil
1/2 teaspoon dried oregano
1/4 teaspoon crushed red pepper flakes
1 teaspoon dried thyme
1/4 teaspoon freshly grated nutmeg
Sea salt flakes and freshly ground black pepper, to taste

1 Pimento chili pepper, deveined and chopped
1 Yellow wax pepper, deveined and chopped
1 bell pepper, deveined and chopped
1 tablespoon peanut butter
1/4 cup beef broth
1/2 tablespoon whole-grain mustard
1 bay leaf

DIRECTIONS

Lightly grease the inside of an Air Fryer baking dish with a thin layer of olive oil. Then, cut 8 slit down the center of pork (about 3x3").
Sprinkle with the seasonings and massage them into the meat to evenly distribute
Then, tuck peppers into the slits and transfer the meat to the Air Fryer baking dish. Scatter remaining peppers around the roast.
In a mixing dish, whisk the peanut butter, beef broth, and mustard; now, pour broth mixture around the roast.
Add the bay leaf and roast the meat for 25 minutes at 390 degrees F; turn the pork over halfway through the roasting time. Bon appétit!

165. Pork Sausage Meatloaf with Veggies

(Ready in about 30 minutes | Servings 6)

Per serving: 282 Calories; 19.2g Fat; 9.2g Carbs; 18.3g Protein; 5.1g Sugars; 1g Fiber

INGREDIENTS

Non-stick cooking spray
1 shallot, finely chopped
1 rib celery, finely chopped
2 gloves garlic, minced
1 tablespoon Worcestershire sauce
3/4 pound spicy ground pork sausage
1/4 pound ground turkey

2 sprigs rosemary, leaves only, crushed
1/4 cup minced fresh parsley
1 egg, lightly whisked
3 tablespoons fresh panko
Salt and freshly ground pepper, to your liking
1/3 cup tomato paste

DIRECTIONS

Spritz a cast-iron skillet with a cooking spray. Then, sauté the shallots, celery and garlic until just tender and fragrant.
Now, add Worcestershire sauce and both kinds of meat to the sautéed mixture. Remove from the heat. Add the rosemary, parsley, egg, fresh panko, salt, and pepper; mix to combine well.
Transfer the mixture to the baking pan and shape into a loaf. Cover the prepared meatloaf with tomato paste.
Air-fry at 390 degrees F for 25 minutes or until thoroughly warmed.

166. Egg and Sausage Ramekins Breakfast

(Ready in about 20 minutes | Servings 5)

Per serving: 385 Calories; 32.4g Fat; 1.77g Carbs; 20.7g Protein; 1.1g Sugars; 0.1g Fiber

INGREDIENTS

1/2 teaspoon ground black pepper, or more to taste
1/2 teaspoon mustard seeds
10 slices of bacon
1/3 teaspoon fennel seeds

5 eggs
10 pork sausages
1/3 teaspoon kosher salt

DIRECTIONS

Divide the sausages and bacon among five ramekins; crack an egg into each ramekin. Sprinkle with seasonings.
Cook for 18 minutes at 345 degrees F or until your eggs reach desired texture.
Serve warm with some extra Dijon mustard and spicy tomato ketchup. Bon appétit!

167. Pork Chops Romano

(Ready in about 1 hour 12 minutes | Servings 4)

Per serving: 466 Calories; 26.5g Fat; 2.9g Carbs; 51.4g Protein; 1.5g Sugars; 0.2g Fiber

INGREDIENTS

3 eggs, well-beaten
1 cup Romano cheese, grated
2 teaspoons mustard powder
1 ½ tablespoons olive oil
1/2 tablespoon soy sauce
2 tablespoons Worcestershire sauce

½ teaspoon dried rosemary
4 large-sized pork chops
½ teaspoon dried thyme
2 teaspoons fennel seeds
Salt and freshly cracked black pepper, to taste
1 teaspoon red pepper flakes, crushed

DIRECTIONS

Add the pork chops along with olive oil, soy sauce, Worcestershire sauce, and seasonings to a resealable plastic bag. Allow pork chops to marinate for 50 minutes in your refrigerator.
Next step, dip the pork chops into the beaten eggs; then, coat the pork chops with Romano cheese on both sides. Press the breading firmly into the pork chops.
Cook in the Air Fryer for 18 minutes at 405 degrees F, turning once. Bon appétit!

168. Rich Meatball and Mushroom Cassoulet

(Ready in about 41 minutes | Servings 4)

Per serving: 317 Calories; 21.2g Fat; 5.3g Carbs; 27.1g Protein; 1.7g Sugars; 1.1g Fiber

INGREDIENTS

1/2 cup celery, peeled and grated
1 ½ cup mushrooms, sliced
1/2 cup heavy cream
1/2 cup Monterey Jack cheese, preferably freshly grated
Meatballs:
2 tablespoons pork rinds
12 ounces lean ground pork
1 teaspoon saffron

2 teaspoons fennel seeds
1 medium-sized lees, finely chopped
1/teaspoon dried dill weed
2 small-sized egg
1/2 teaspoon cumin
½ teaspoon fine sea salt
Freshly ground black pepper, to taste

DIRECTIONS

Begin by preheating the Air Fryer to 400 degrees F.
In a bowl, mix the ingredients for the meatballs. Shape the mixture into mini meatballs.
In an Air Fryer baking dish, toss the celery and mushrooms with the cream; cook for 23 minutes in the preheated Air Fryer.
Pause the machine and place the reserved meatballs in a single layer on top of the celery/mushroom mixture.
Top with the grated Monterey Jack cheese; bake for 9 minutes longer. Serve warm.

169. Mouthwatering Pork Medallions with Creole mustard

(Ready in about 25 minutes | Servings 4)

Per serving: 292 Calories; 18.2g Fat; 0.9g Carbs; 29g Protein; 0.1g Sugars; 0.4g Fiber

INGREDIENTS

1 pound pork medallions, trimmed and sliced into thick medallions
2 tablespoons Creole mustard
½ tablespoon apple cider vinegar
1 ½ tablespoons extra-virgin olive oil

2 teaspoon cumin seeds, ground
½ teaspoon seasoned salt
1/3 teaspoon freshly cracked black peppercorns, or multi-color peppercorns

DIRECTIONS

Toss the pork medallions with all the other items until well coated. Cook in your Air Fryer for 13 minutes at 365 degrees F.
Check for doneness and cook for 4 to 5 minutes longer as needed.
To finish, mound the wilted kale onto a serving plate. Top with the beef medallions and serve immediately.

170. Spicy Bacon-Pork Pops

(Ready in about 30 minutes + marinating time | Servings 6)

Per serving: 572 Calories; 41.1g Fat; 8.9g Carbs; 41.6g Protein; 5.4g Sugars; 1.8g Fiber

INGREDIENTS

1 cup cream of celery soup
1 (13.5-ounce) can coconut milk, unsweetened
2 tablespoons tamari sauce
1 teaspoon yellow mustard
Salt and freshly ground white pepper, to taste
1/2 teaspoon cayenne pepper

1/2 teaspoon chili powder
1 teaspoon curry powder
2 pounds pork tenderloin, cut into bite-sized cubes
4 ounces bacon, cut into pieces
12 bamboo skewers, soaked in water

DIRECTIONS

In a large pot, bring the cream of the celery soup, coconut milk, tamari sauce, mustard, salt, white pepper, cayenne pepper, chili powder, and curry powder to a boil.
Then, reduce the heat to simmer; cook until the sauce is heated through, about 13 minutes.
Add the pork, gently stir, and place in your refrigerator for 2 hours.
Thread the pork onto the skewers, alternating the cubes of meat with the pieces of bacon.
Preheat your Air Fryer to 370 degrees F. Cook for 15 minutes, turning over a couple of times. Bon appétit!

171. Classic Ribs with Bell Peppers

(Ready in about 55 minutes | Servings 4)

Per serving: 406 Calories; 25.4g Fat; 10g Carbs; 49g Protein; 4.6g Sugars; 1.6g Fiber

INGREDIENTS

1 pound St. Louis-style pork spareribs, individually cut
1 teaspoon seasoned salt
1/2 teaspoon ground black pepper
1 tablespoon sweet paprika

1/2 teaspoon mustard powder
2 tablespoons sesame oil
4 bell pepper, seeded

DIRECTIONS

Toss and rub the spices all over the pork ribs; drizzle with 1 tablespoon of sesame oil.

Cook the pork ribs at 360 degrees F for 15 minutes; flip the ribs and cook an additional 20 minutes or until they are tender inside and crisp on the outside.

Toss the peppers with the remaining 1 tablespoon of oil; season to taste and cook in the preheated Air Fryer at 390 degrees F for 15 minutes. Serve the warm spareribs with the roasted peppers on the side. Enjoy!

172. Spicy Pork Curry

(Ready in about 35 minutes | Servings 4)

Per serving: 396 Calories; 20.1g Fat; 4.9g Carbs; 44.2g Protein; 3.6g Sugars; 1.1g Fiber

INGREDIENTS

2 cardamom pods, only the seeds, crushed
1 teaspoon fennel seeds
1 teaspoon cumin seeds
1 teaspoon coriander seeds
2 teaspoons peanut oil

2 scallions, chopped
2 garlic cloves, smashed
2 jalapeno peppers, minced
1/2 teaspoon ginger, freshly grated
1 pound pork loin, cut into bite-sized cubes

1 cup coconut milk
1 cup chicken broth
1 teaspoon turmeric powder
1 tablespoon tamarind paste
1 tablespoon fresh lime juice

DIRECTIONS

Place the cardamom, fennel, cumin, and coriander seeds in a nonstick skillet over medium-high heat. Stir for 6 minutes until the spices become aromatic and start to brown. Stir frequently to prevent the spices from burning. Set aside.

Preheat your Air Fryer to 370 degrees F. Then, in a baking pan, heat the peanut oil for 2 minutes. Once hot, sauté the scallions for 2 to 3 minutes until tender.

Stir in the garlic, peppers, and ginger; cook an additional minute, stirring frequently. Next, cook the pork for 3 to 4 minutes.

Pour in the coconut milk and broth. Add the reserved seeds, turmeric, and tamarind paste. Let it cook for 15 minutes in the preheated Air Fryer. Divide between individual bowls; drizzle fresh lime juice over the top and serve immediately.

173. Nana's Pork Chops with Cilantro

(Ready in about 22 minutes | Servings 6)

Per serving: 390 Calories; 21.3g Fat; 1g Carbs; 42g Protein; 0.3g Sugars; 0.2g Fiber

INGREDIENTS

1/3 cup pork rinds
Roughly chopped fresh cilantro, to taste
2 teaspoons Cajun seasonings
Nonstick cooking spray
2 eggs, beaten

3 tablespoons almond meal
1 teaspoon seasoned salt
Garlic & onion spice blend, to taste
6 pork chops
1/3 teaspoon freshly cracked black pepper

DIRECTIONS

Coat the pork chops with Cajun seasonings, salt, pepper, and the spice blend on all sides.

Then, add the almond meal to a plate. In a shallow dish, whisk the egg until pale and smooth. Place the pork rinds in the third bowl.

Dredge each pork piece in the almond meal; then, coat them with the egg; finally, coat them with the pork rinds. Spritz them with cooking spray on both sides.

Now, air-fry pork chops for about 18 minutes at 345 degrees F; make sure to taste for doneness after first 12 minutes of cooking. Lastly, garnish with fresh cilantro. Bon appétit!

174. Paprika Burgers with Blue Cheese

(Ready in about 44 minutes | Servings 6)

Per serving: 493 Calories; 38.6g Fat; 4.1g Carbs; 30.1g Protein; 1.4g Sugars; 0.8g Fiber

INGREDIENTS

1 cup blue cheese, sliced
2 teaspoons dried basil
1 teaspoon smoked paprika
2 pounds ground pork
2 tablespoons tomato puree

2 small-sized onions, peeled and chopped
1/2 teaspoon ground black pepper
3 garlic cloves, minced
1 teaspoon fine sea salt

DIRECTIONS

Start by preheating your Air Fryer to 385 degrees F.
In a mixing dish, combine the pork, onion, garlic, tomato puree, and seasonings; mix to combine well.
Form the pork mixture into six patties; cook the burgers for 23 minutes. Pause the machine, turn the temperature to 365 degrees F and cook for 18 more minutes.
Place the prepared burgers on a serving platter; top with blue cheese and serve warm.

175. Tangy Pork Chops with Vermouth

(Ready in about 34 minutes | Servings 5)

Per serving: 400 Calories; 23g Fat; 4.1g Carbs; 40.5g Protein; 1.5g Sugars; 0.4g Fiber

INGREDIENTS

5 pork chops
1/3 cup vermouth
1/2 teaspoon paprika
2 sprigs thyme, only leaves, crushed
1/2 teaspoon dried oregano
Fresh parsley, to serve

1 teaspoon garlic salt
½ lemon, cut into wedges
1 teaspoon freshly cracked black pepper
3 tablespoons lemon juice
3 cloves garlic, minced
2 tablespoons canola oil

DIRECTIONS

Firstly, heat the canola oil in a sauté pan over a moderate heat. Now, sweat the garlic until just fragrant.
Remove the pan from the heat and pour in the lemon juice and vermouth. Now, throw in the seasonings. Dump the sauce into a baking dish, along with the pork chops.
Tuck the lemon wedges among the pork chops and air-fry for 27 minutes at 345 degrees F. Bon appétit!

176. French-Style Pork and Pepper Meatloaf

(Ready in about 35 minutes | Servings 4)

Per serving: 417 Calories; 27.1g Fat; 7.6g Carbs; 33.9g Protein; 2g Sugars; 0.9g Fiber

INGREDIENTS

1 pound pork, ground
1/2 cup parmesan cheese, grated
1 ½ tablespoons green garlic, minced
1½ tablespoon fresh cilantro, minced
1/2 tablespoon fish sauce
1/3 teaspoon dried basil

1 leek, chopped
1 serrano pepper, chopped
2 tablespoons tomato puree
1/2 teaspoons dried thyme
Salt and ground black pepper, to taste

DIRECTIONS

Add all ingredients to a large-sized mixing dish and combine everything using your hands.
Then, form a meatloaf using a spatula.
Bake for 23 minutes at 365 degrees F. Afterward, allow your meatloaf to rest for 10 minutes before slicing and serving. Bon appétit!

177. Ham and Kale Egg Cups

(Ready in about 20 minutes | Servings 2)

Per serving: 398 Calories; 17.8g Fat; 3g Carbs; 61g Protein; 0.9g Sugars; 1.1g Fiber

INGREDIENTS

2 eggs

1/4 teaspoon dried or fresh marjoram

2 teaspoons chili powder

1/3 teaspoon kosher salt

½ cup steamed kale

1/4 teaspoon dried or fresh rosemary

4 pork ham slices

1/3 teaspoon ground black pepper, or more to taste

DIRECTIONS

Divide the kale and ham among 2 ramekins; crack an egg into each ramekin. Sprinkle with seasonings.

Cook for 15 minutes at 335 degrees F or until your eggs reach desired texture.

Serve warm with spicy tomato ketchup and pickles. Bon appétit!

178. Spicy Ground Pork Omelet with Cream Cheese

(Ready in about 20 minutes | Servings 2)

Per serving: 438 Calories; 22.2g Fat; 4.7g Carbs; 28.2g Protein; 5.2g Sugars; 0.7g Fiber

INGREDIENTS

4 garlic cloves, peeled and minced

1/2 tablespoon fresh basil, chopped

1/3 pound ground pork

1/3 teaspoon ground black pepper

1/2 small-sized onion, peeled and finely chopped

1 1/2 tablespoons olive oil

3 medium-sized eggs, beaten

1/2 jalapeno pepper, seeded and chopped

4 tablespoons cream cheese

1/3 teaspoon salt

DIRECTIONS

In a nonstick skillet that is preheated over a moderate flame, heat the oil; then, sweat the onion, garlic and ground pork in the hot oil.

Spritz an Air Fryer baking dish with a cooking spray.

Throw in the sautéed mixture, followed by the remaining ingredients.

Bake at 325 degrees F approximately 15 minutes. Serve with the salad of choice. Bon appétit!

179. Pork Belly with Lime Aromatics

(Ready in about 1 hour 15 minutes + marinating time | Servings 4)

Per serving: 590 Calories; 60.1g Fat; 0.5g Carbs; 10.6g Protein; 0.1g Sugars; 0.5g Fiber

INGREDIENTS

1 pound pork belly

2 garlic cloves, halved

1 teaspoon shallot powder

1 teaspoon sea salt

1 teaspoon dried basil

1 teaspoon dried oregano

1 teaspoon dried thyme

1 teaspoon dried marjoram

1 teaspoon ground black pepper

1 lime, juiced

DIRECTIONS

Blanch the pork belly in a pot of boiling water for 10 to 13 minutes.

Pat it dry with a kitchen towel. Now, poke holes all over the skin by using a fork.

Then, mix the remaining ingredients to make the rub. Massage the rub all over the pork belly. Drizzle lime juice all over the meat; place the pork belly in the refrigerator for 3 hours.

Preheat your Air Fryer to 320 degrees F. Cook the pork belly for 35 minutes.

Turn up the temperature to 360 degrees F and continue cooking for 20 minutes longer. Serve warm. Bon appétit!

180. Mexican Stuffed Peppers with Pork and Cheese

(Ready in about 30 minutes | Servings 3)

Per serving: 425 Calories; 25.9g Fat; 9.5g Carbs; 38.3g Protein; 5.2g Sugars; 2.2g Fiber

INGREDIENTS

3 bell peppers, stems and seeds removed

1 tablespoon canola oil

1/2 cup onions, chopped

1 teaspoon fresh garlic, minced

1 Mexican chili pepper, finely chopped

1 pound lean pork, ground

1/2 teaspoon sea salt

1/2 teaspoon black pepper

1 tablespoon Mexican oregano

1 ripe tomato, pureed

3 ounces Cotija cheese, grated

DIRECTIONS

Cook the peppers in boiling salted water for 4 minutes

In a nonstick skillet, heat the canola oil over medium heat. Then, sauté the onions, garlic and Mexican chili pepper until tender and fragrant.

Stir in the ground pork and continue sautéing until the pork has browned; drain off the excess fat.

Add the salt, black pepper, Mexican oregano, and pureed tomato; give it a good stir.

Divide the filling among the bell peppers. Arrange the peppers in a baking dish lightly greased with cooking oil.

Bake in the preheated Air Fryer at 380 degrees F for 13 minutes. Top with grated Cotija cheese and bake another 6 minutes. Serve warm and enjoy!

181. Italian Twisted Pork Chops

(Ready in about 20 minutes | Servings 3)

Per serving: 517 Calories; 19.3g Fat; 7.3g Carbs; 62g Protein; 3.5g Sugars; 2.2g Fiber

INGREDIENTS

1/4 cup balsamic vinegar

3 center-cut loin pork chops

1/4 cup almond meal

2 tablespoons golden flaxseed meal

1 teaspoon turmeric powder

1 egg

1 teaspoon mustard

Kosher salt, to taste

1/4 teaspoon freshly ground black pepper

1/2 cup pork rinds, crushed

1/2 teaspoon garlic powder

1 teaspoon shallot powder

DIRECTIONS

Drizzle the balsamic vinegar over pork chops and spread to evenly coat.

Place the almond meal, flaxseed meal, and turmeric in a shallow bowl. In another bowl, whisk the eggs, mustard, salt, and black pepper. In the third bowl, mix the pork rinds with the garlic powder and shallot powder.

Preheat your Air Fryer to 390 degrees F. Dredge the pork chops in the almond meal mixture, then in the egg, followed by the pork rind mixture.

Cook the pork chops for 7 minutes per side, spraying with cooking oil. Bon appétit!

182. Herby Pork with Celery Chips

(Ready in about 1 hour 15 minutes | Servings 4)

Per serving: 442 Calories; 25.8g Fat; 5.5g Carbs; 44g Protein; 2.2g Sugars; 2.3g Fiber

INGREDIENTS

1 tablespoon peanut oil

1 ½ pounds pork loin, cut into 4 pieces

Coarse sea salt and ground black pepper, to taste

1/2 teaspoon onion powder

1 teaspoon garlic powder

1/2 teaspoon cayenne pepper

1/2 teaspoon dried rosemary

1/2 teaspoon dried basil

1/2 teaspoon dried oregano

1 pound celery, cut into matchsticks

1 tablespoon coconut oil, melted

DIRECTIONS

Drizzle 1 tablespoon of peanut oil all over the pork loin. Season with salt, black pepper, onion powder, garlic powder, cayenne pepper, rosemary, basil, and oregano.

Cook in the preheated Air Fryer at 360 degrees F for 55 minutes; make sure to turn the pork over every 15 minutes to ensure even cooking. Test for doneness with a meat thermometer.

Toss the carrots with melted coconut oil; season to taste and cook in the preheated Air Fryer at 380 degrees F for 15 minutes.

Serve the warm pork loin with the carrots on the side. Enjoy!

183. Favorite Taco Casserole

(Ready in about 45 minutes | Servings 4)

Per serving: 601 Calories; 49g Fat; 8.2g Carbs; 32.5g Protein; 3.3g Sugars; 1.1g Fiber

INGREDIENTS

1 tablespoon olive oil
1 pound pork, ground
1 tablespoon taco seasoning mix
Sea salt and ground black pepper, to taste
1 medium-sized leek, sliced

1 teaspoon fresh garlic, minced
1/2 cup celery, trimmed and sliced
1 (2-ounce) jar pimiento, drained and chopped
1 can (10 ¾-ounces) condensed cream of mushroom soup

1 cup water
1/2 cup Mexican beer
1/2 cup cream cheese, grated
1 cup Mexican cheese, shredded
1 tablespoon fresh cilantro, chopped

DIRECTIONS

Start by preheating your Air Fryer to 320 degrees F.

Add the olive oil to a baking dish and heat for 1 to 2 minutes. Add the pork, taco seasoning mix, salt, pepper and cook for 6 minutes, crumbling with a fork.

Add the leeks and cook for 4 to 5 minutes, stirring occasionally.

Add the garlic, celery, pimiento, mushroom soup, water, beer, and cream cheese. Gently stir to combine.

Turn the temperature to 370 degrees F.

Top with Mexican cheese. Place the baking dish in the cooking basket and cook approximately 30 minutes or until everything is thoroughly cooked.

Serve garnished with fresh cilantro. Bon appétit!

184. Chinese-Style Pork Shoulder

(Ready in about 25 minutes + marinating time | Servings 3)

Per serving: 353 Calories; 19.6g Fat; 13.5g Carbs; 29.2g Protein; 12.2g Sugars; 0.2g Fiber

INGREDIENTS

2 tablespoons coconut aminos
2 tablespoons Shaoxing wine
2 garlic cloves, minced

1 teaspoon fresh ginger, minced
1 tablespoon cilantro stems and leaves, finely chopped

1 pound boneless pork shoulder
2 tablespoons sesame oil

DIRECTIONS

In a large-sized ceramic dish, thoroughly combine the coconut aminos, Shaoxing wine, garlic, ginger, and cilantro; add the pork shoulder and allow it to marinate for 2 hours in the refrigerator.

Then, grease the cooking basket with sesame oil. Place the pork shoulder in the cooking basket; reserve the marinade.

Cook in the preheated Air Fryer at 395 degrees F for 14 to 17 minutes, flipping and basting with the marinade halfway through. Let it rest for 5 to 6 minutes before slicing and serving.

While the pork is roasting, cook the marinade in a preheated skillet over medium heat; cook until it has thickened.

Brush the pork shoulder with the sauce and enjoy!

185. Cheesy Mini Meatloaves

(Ready in about 50 minutes | Servings 4)

Per serving: 535 Calories; 37.4g Fat; 4.8g Carbs; 42.1g Protein; 2.1g Sugars; 1.2g Fiber

INGREDIENTS

1 pound ground pork
1/2 pound ground beef
1 package onion soup mix
1/2 cup Romano cheese, grated
2 eggs

1 bell pepper, chopped
1 serrano pepper, minced
2 scallions, chopped
2 cloves garlic, finely chopped
Sea salt and black pepper, to your liking

Glaze:
1/2 cup tomato paste
1 tablespoon brown mustard
1 teaspoon smoked paprika

DIRECTIONS

In a large mixing bowl, thoroughly combine all ingredients for meatloaves. Mix with your hands until everything is well incorporated.

Then, shape the mixture into four mini loaves. Transfer them to the cooking basket previously generously greased with cooking oil.

Cook in the preheated Air Fryer at 385 degrees F approximately 43 minutes.

Mix all ingredients for the glaze. Spread the glaze over mini meatloaves and cook for another 6 minutes. Bon appétit!

BEEF

186. Smoked Beef Burgers

(Ready in about 20 minutes | Servings 4)

Per serving: 167 Calories; 5.5g Fat; 1.4g Carbs; 26.4g Protein; 0g Sugars; 0.4g Fiber

INGREDIENTS

1 ¼ pounds lean ground beef
1 tablespoon soy sauce
1 teaspoon Dijon mustard
A few dashes of liquid smoke
1 teaspoon shallot powder
1 clove garlic, minced

1/2 teaspoon cumin powder
1/4 cup scallions, minced
1/3 teaspoon sea salt flakes
1/3 teaspoon freshly cracked mixed peppercorns
1 teaspoon celery seeds
1 teaspoon parsley flakes

DIRECTIONS

Mix all of the above ingredients in a bowl; knead until everything is well incorporated.
Shape the mixture into four patties. Next, make a shallow dip in the center of each patty to prevent them puffing up during air-frying.
Spritz the patties on all sides using a non-stick cooking spray. Cook approximately 12 minutes at 360 degrees F.
Check for doneness – an instant read thermometer should read 160 degrees F. Bon appétit!

187. Spicy Holiday Roast Beef

(Ready in about 50 minutes | Servings 8)

Per serving: 243 Calories; 10.6g Fat; 0.4g Carbs; 34.5g Protein; 0g Sugars; 0.4g Fiber

INGREDIENTS

2 pounds roast beef, at room temperature
2 tablespoons extra-virgin olive oil
1 teaspoon sea salt flakes
1 teaspoon black pepper, preferably freshly ground

1 teaspoon smoked paprika
A few dashes of liquid smoke
2 jalapeño peppers, thinly sliced

DIRECTIONS

Start by preheating the Air Fryer to 330 degrees F.
Then, pat the roast dry using kitchen towels. Rub with extra-virgin olive oil and all seasonings along with liquid smoke.
Roast for 30 minutes in the preheated Air Fryer; then, pause the machine and turn the roast over; roast for additional 15 minutes.
Check for doneness using a meat thermometer and serve sprinkled with sliced jalapeños. Bon appétit!

188. Rich Beef and Sausage Meatloaf

(Ready in about 30 minutes | Servings 4)

Per serving: 206 Calories; 7.9g Fat; 15.9g Carbs; 17.6g Protein; 0.8g Sugars; 0.4g Fiber

INGREDIENTS

3/4 pound ground chuck
1/4 pound ground pork sausage
1 cup shallot, finely chopped
2 eggs, well beaten
3 tablespoons plain milk
1 tablespoon oyster sauce

1 teaspoon porcini mushrooms
1/2 teaspoon cumin powder
1 teaspoon garlic paste
1 tablespoon fresh parsley
Seasoned salt and crushed red pepper flakes, to taste
1 cup parmesan cheese, grated

DIRECTIONS

Simply place all ingredients in a large-sized mixing dish; mix until everything is thoroughly combined.
Press the meatloaf mixture into the Air Fryer baking dish; set your Air Fryer to cook at 360 degrees F for 25 minutes. Press the power button and cook until heated through.
Check for doneness and serve with your favorite wine!

189. Japanese Miso Steak

(Ready in about 15 minutes + marinating time | Servings 4)

Per serving: 367 Calories; 15.1g Fat; 6.4g Carbs; 48.6g Protein; 3.4g Sugars; 0.3g Fiber

INGREDIENTS

1 ¼ pounds flank steak
1 ½ tablespoons sake
1 tablespoon brown miso paste

2 garlic cloves, pressed
1 tablespoon olive oil

DIRECTIONS

Place all the ingredients in a sealable food bag; shake until completely coated and place in your refrigerator for at least 1 hour. Then, spritz the steak with a non-stick cooking spray; make sure to coat on all sides. Place the steak in the Air Fryer baking pan. Set your Air Fryer to cook at 400 degrees F. Roast for 12 minutes, flipping twice. Serve immediately.

190. Classic Keto Cheeseburgers

(Ready in about 15 minutes | Servings 4)

Per serving: 271 Calories; 13.3g Fat; 21.9g Carbs; 15.3g Protein; 2.9g Sugars; 0.2g Fiber

INGREDIENTS

1 ½ pounds ground chuck
1 envelope onion soup mix
Kosher salt and freshly ground black pepper, to taste

1 teaspoon paprika
4 slices Monterey-Jack cheese

DIRECTIONS

In a mixing dish, thoroughly combine ground chuck, onion soup mix, salt, black pepper, and paprika.
Then, set your Air Fryer to cook at 385 degrees F. Shape the mixture into 4 patties. Air-fry them for 10 minutes.
Next step, place the slices of cheese on the top of the warm burgers. Air-fry for one minute more.
Serve with mustard and pickled salad of choice. Bon appétit!

191. Beef Steaks with Mediterranean Herbs

(Ready in about 25 minutes | Servings 4)

Per serving: 445 Calories; 23.7g Fat; 11.3g Carbs; 51.1g Protein; 10.3g Sugars; 0.7g Fiber

INGREDIENTS

2 tablespoons soy sauce
3 heaping tablespoons fresh chives
2 tablespoons olive oil
3 tablespoons dry white wine
4 small-sized beef steaks

2 teaspoons smoked cayenne pepper
1/2 teaspoon dried basil
1/2 teaspoon dried rosemary
1 teaspoon freshly ground pepper
1 teaspoon sea salt, or more to taste

DIRECTIONS

Firstly, coat the steaks with the cayenne pepper, black pepper, salt, basil, and rosemary.
Drizzle the steaks with olive oil, white wine, soy sauce, and honey.
Finally, roast in an Air Fryer basket for 20 minutes at 335 degrees F. Serve garnished with fresh chives. Bon appétit!

192. Japanese Beef with Broccoli

(Ready in about 60 minutes | Servings 4)

Per serving: 220 Calories; 12.4g Fat; 8.3g Carbs; 19.8g Protein; 4.4g Sugars; 1.4g Fiber

INGREDIENTS

½ had broccoli, broken into florets
1/3 cup keto teriyaki marinade
Fine sea salt and ground black pepper, to taste

½ pound rump steak
2 red capsicums, sliced
1 ½ teaspoons sesame oil

DIRECTIONS

Add rump roast and teriyaki marinade to a mixing dish; stir to coat. Let it marinate for about 40 minutes.
Then, roast in the preheated Air Fryer for 13 minutes at 395 degrees F. Stir halfway through cooking time.
Meanwhile, sauté the broccoli in the hot sesame oil along with sliced capsicum; cook until tender and season with salt and pepper to savor.
Place the prepared rump steak on a serving platter and serve garnished with sautéed broccoli. Bon appétit!

193. The Best Minute Steaks

(Ready in about 15 minutes + marinating time | Servings 4)

Per serving: 296 Calories; 14g Fat; 6.7g Carbs; 36.5g Protein; 0.6g Sugars; 0.3g Fiber

INGREDIENTS

1 1/2 tablespoons extra-virgin olive oil
1/2 cup herb vinegar
1/3 teaspoon celery seed
4 minute steaks

1 teaspoon salt
2 teaspoons cayenne pepper
1/3 teaspoon ground black pepper, or to taste

DIRECTIONS

Toss all ingredients in a mixing dish. Cover the dish and marinate the steaks in the refrigerator for about 3 hours.
Finally, cook minute steaks for 13 minutes at 355 degrees F. Eat warm with your favorite salad and French fries. Bon appétit!

194. Almond and Caraway Crust Steak

(Ready in about 16 minutes | Servings 4)

Per serving: 474 Calories; 22.1g Fat; 8.7g Carbs; 54.7g Protein; 1.6g Sugars; 0.6g Fiber

INGREDIENTS

1/3 cup almond flour
2 eggs
2 teaspoons caraway seeds
4 beef steaks

2 teaspoons garlic powder
1 tablespoon melted butter
Fine sea salt and cayenne pepper, to taste

DIRECTIONS

Generously coat steaks with garlic powder, caraway seeds, salt, and cayenne pepper.
In a mixing dish, thoroughly combine melted butter with seasoned crumbs. In another bowl, beat the eggs until they're well whisked.
First, coat steaks with the beaten egg; then, coat beef steaks with the buttered crumb mixture.
Place the steaks in the Air Fryer cooking basket; cook for 10 minutes at 355 degrees F. Bon appétit!

195. Spicy Mexican Beef with Cotija Cheese

(Ready in about 20 minutes | Servings 6)

Per serving: 397 Calories; 23g Fat; 3.5g Carbs; 41.2g Protein; 0.4g Sugars; 0g Fiber

INGREDIENTS

3 eggs, whisked
1/3 cup finely grated cotija cheese
1 cup parmesan cheese
6 minute steaks

2 tablespoons Mexican spice blend
1 ½ tablespoons olive oil
Fine sea salt and ground black pepper, to taste

DIRECTIONS

Begin by sprinkling minute steaks with Mexican spice blend, salt and pepper.
Take a mixing dish and thoroughly combine the oil, cotija cheese, and parmesan cheese. In a separate mixing dish, beat the eggs.
Firstly, dip minute steaks in the egg; then, dip them in the cheese mixture.
Air-fry for 15 minutes at 345 degrees F; work in batches. Bon appétit!

196. Top Chuck with Mustard and Herbs

(Ready in about 1 hour | Servings 3)

Per serving: 406 Calories; 24.1g Fat; 0.3g Carbs; 44.1g Protein; 0g Sugars; 0.7g Fiber

INGREDIENTS

1 ½ pounds top chuck
2 teaspoons olive oil
1 tablespoon Dijon mustard
Sea salt and ground black pepper, to taste

1 teaspoon dried marjoram
1 teaspoon dried thyme
1/2 teaspoon fennel seeds

DIRECTIONS

Start by preheating your Air Fryer to 380 degrees F
Add all ingredients in a Ziploc bag; shake to mix well. Next, spritz the bottom of the Air Fryer basket with cooking spray.
Place the beef in the cooking basket and cook for 50 minutes, turning every 10 to 15 minutes.
Let it rest for 5 to 7 minutes before slicing and serving. Enjoy!

197. Mediterranean Herbed Beef with Zucchini

(Ready in about 20 minutes | Servings 4)

Per serving: 396 Calories; 20.4g Fat; 3.5g Carbs; 47.8g Protein; 0.1g Sugars; 1.5g Fiber

INGREDIENTS

1 ½ pounds beef steak
1 pound zucchini
1 teaspoon dried rosemary
1 teaspoon dried basil

1 teaspoon dried oregano
2 tablespoons extra-virgin olive oil
2 tablespoons fresh chives, chopped

DIRECTIONS

Start by preheating your Air Fryer to 400 degrees F.
Toss the steak and zucchini with the spices and olive oil. Transfer to the cooking basket and cook for 6 minutes.
Now, shale the basket and cook another 6 minutes. Serve immediately garnished with fresh chives. Enjoy!

198. Italian Peperonata with a Twist

(Ready in about 35 minutes | Servings 4)

Per serving: 563 Calories; 41.5g Fat; 10.6g Carbs; 35.6g Protein; 7.9g Sugars; 1g Fiber

INGREDIENTS

2 teaspoons canola oil
2 bell peppers, sliced
1 green bell pepper, sliced
1 serrano pepper, sliced
1 shallot, sliced
Sea salt and pepper, to taste

1/2 dried thyme
1 teaspoon dried rosemary
1/2 teaspoon mustard seeds
1 teaspoon fennel seeds
2 pounds thin beef parboiled sausage

DIRECTIONS

Brush the sides and bottom of the cooking basket with 1 teaspoon of canola oil. Add the peppers and shallot to the cooking basket.
Toss them with the spices and cook at 390 degrees F for 15 minutes, shaking the basket occasionally. Reserve.
Turn the temperature to 380 degrees F
Then, add the remaining 1 teaspoon of oil. Once hot, add the sausage and cook in the preheated Air Frye for 15 minutes, flipping them halfway through the cooking time.
Serve with reserved pepper mixture. Bon appétit!

199. Buttery Tender New York Strip

(Ready in about 20 minutes | Servings 4)

Per serving: 439 Calories; 27.4g Fat; 1.3g Carbs; 48.3g Protein; 0.6g Sugars; 0.3g Fiber

INGREDIENTS

1 tablespoon peanut oil
2 pounds New York Strip
1 teaspoon cayenne pepper

Sea salt and freshly cracked black pepper, to taste
1/2 stick butter, softened
1 teaspoon whole-grain mustard

DIRECTIONS

Rub the peanut oil all over the steak; season with cayenne pepper, salt, and black pepper.
Cook in the preheated Air Fryer at 400 degrees F for 7 minutes; turn over and cook an additional 7 minutes.
Meanwhile, prepare the mustard butter by whisking the butter, whole-grain mustard, and honey.
Serve the roasted New York Strip dolloped with the mustard butter. Bon appétit!

200. Ribeye Steak with Classis Garlic Mayonnaise

(Ready in about 20 minutes | Servings 3)

Per serving: 437 Calories; 24.8g Fat; 1.8g Carbs; 51g Protein; 0.1g Sugars; 0.6g Fiber

INGREDIENTS

1 ½ pounds ribeye, bone-in
1 tablespoon butter, room temperature
Salt, to taste
1/2 teaspoon crushed black pepper
1/2 teaspoon dried dill
1/2 teaspoon cayenne pepper

1/2 teaspoon garlic powder
1/2 teaspoon onion powder
1 teaspoon ground coriander
3 tablespoons mayonnaise
1 teaspoon garlic, minced

DIRECTIONS

Start by preheating your Air Fryer to 400 degrees F.
Pat dry the ribeye and rub it with softened butter on all sides. Sprinkle with seasonings and transfer to the cooking basket.
Cook in the preheated Air Fryer for 15 minutes, flipping them halfway through the cooking time.
In the meantime, simply mix the mayonnaise with garlic and place in the refrigerator until ready to serve. Bon appétit!

201. Beef Sausage Mélange with Greens

(Ready in about 40 minutes | Servings 2)

Per serving: 565 Calories; 47.1g Fat; 14.3g Carbs; 20.6g Protein; 5.2g Sugars; 0.6g Fiber

INGREDIENTS

1 tablespoon lard, melted
1 shallot, chopped
1 bell pepper, chopped
2 red chilies, finely chopped
1 teaspoon ginger-garlic paste
Sea salt, to taste

1/4 teaspoon ground black pepper
4 beef good quality sausages, thinly sliced
2 teaspoons smoked paprika
1 cup beef bone broth
1/2 cup tomato puree
2 handfuls spring greens, shredded

DIRECTIONS

Melt the lard in a Dutch oven over medium-high flame; sauté the shallots and peppers about 4 minutes or until fragrant.
Add the ginger-garlic paste and cook an additional minute. Season with salt and black pepper and transfer to a lightly greased baking pan.
Then, brown the sausages, stirring occasionally, working in batches. Add to the baking pan.
Add the smoked paprika, broth, and tomato puree. Lower the pan onto the Air Fryer basket. Bake at 325 degrees F for 30 minutes.
Stir in the spring greens and cook for 5 minutes more or until they wilt. Serve over the hot rice if desired. Bon appétit!

202. Keto Wiener Schnitzel

(Ready in about 20 minutes | Servings 2)

Per serving: 540 Calories; 33.6g Fat; 1.8g Carbs; 59g Protein; 0.7g Sugars; 0.6g Fiber

INGREDIENTS

1 egg, beaten
1/2 teaspoon ground black pepper
1 teaspoon paprika
1/2 teaspoon coarse sea salt

1 tablespoon ghee, melted
1/2 cup Romano cheese, grated
2 beef schnitzel

DIRECTIONS

Start by preheating your Air Fryer to 360 degrees F.
In a shallow bowl, whisk the egg with black pepper, paprika, and salt.
Thoroughly combine the ghee with the Romano cheese in another shallow bowl. Using a meat mallet, pound the schnitzel to 1/4-inch thick.
Dip the schnitzel into the egg mixture; then, roll the schnitzel over the Romano cheese mixture until coated on all sides.
Cook for 13 minutes in the preheated Air Fryer. Bon appétit!

203. Short Ribs in Spicy Red Sauce

(Ready in about 20 minutes + marinating time | Servings 4)

Per serving: 397 Calories; 15.7g Fat; 4.9g Carbs; 35.2g Protein; 2g Sugars; 1.2g Fiber

INGREDIENTS

1 ½ pounds short ribs
1 cup red wine
1 lemon, juiced
1 teaspoon fresh ginger, grated
1 teaspoon salt
1 teaspoon black pepper

1 teaspoon paprika
1 teaspoon chipotle chili powder
1 cup tomato paste
1 teaspoon garlic powder
1 teaspoon cumin

DIRECTIONS

In a ceramic bowl, place the beef ribs, wine, lemon juice, ginger, salt, black pepper, paprika, and chipotle chili powder. Cover and let it marinate for 3 hours in the refrigerator.
Discard the marinade and add the short ribs to the Air Fryer basket. Cook in the preheated Air fry at 380 degrees F for 10 minutes, turning them over halfway through the cooking time.
In the meantime, heat the saucepan over medium heat; add the reserved marinade and stir in the tomato paste, garlic powder, and cumin. Cook until the sauce has thickened slightly.
Pour the sauce over the warm ribs and serve immediately. Bon appétit!

204. Moroccan Beef Kebab

(Ready in about 30 minutes | Servings 4)

Per serving: 354 Calories; 15.5g Fat; 6g Carbs; 49g Protein; 2.6g Sugars; 1.6g Fiber

INGREDIENTS

1/2 cup leeks, chopped
2 garlic cloves, smashed
2 pounds ground chuck
Salt, to taste
1/4 teaspoon ground black pepper, or more to taste
1 teaspoon cayenne pepper

1/2 teaspoon ground sumac
3 saffron threads
2 tablespoons loosely packed fresh continental parsley leaves
4 tablespoons tahini sauce
4 ounces baby arugula
1 tomato, cut into slices

DIRECTIONS

In a bowl, mix the chopped leeks, garlic, ground chuck, and spices; knead with your hands until everything is well incorporated.
Now, mound the beef mixture around a wooden skewer into a pointed-ended sausage.
Cook in the preheated Air Fryer at 360 degrees F for 25 minutes.
Serve your kebab with the tahini sauce baby arugula and tomato. Enjoy!

205. Thai Curried Meatballs

(Ready in about 20 minutes | Servings 4)

Per serving: 242 Calories; 10.5g Fat; 0.2g Carbs; 34.4g Protein; 0g Sugars; 0.4g Fiber

INGREDIENTS

1 pound ground beef
1 teaspoon red Thai curry paste
1/2 lime, rind and juice

1 teaspoon Thai seasoning blend
2 teaspoons lemongrass, finely chopped
1 tablespoon sesame oil

DIRECTIONS

Thoroughly combine all ingredients in a mixing dish.
Shape into 24 meatballs and place them into the Air Fryer cooking basket. Cook at 380 degrees F for 10 minutes; pause the machine and cook for a further 5 minutes, or until cooked through.
Serve accompanied by the dipping sauce. Bon appétit!

206. Herb-Crusted Filet Mignon

(Ready in about 20 minutes | Servings 4)

Per serving: 315 Calories; 20g Fat; 3.5g Carbs; 29.8g Protein; 0.4g Sugars; 0.4g Fiber

INGREDIENTS

1 pound filet mignon
Sea salt and ground black pepper, to your liking
1/2 teaspoon cayenne pepper
1 teaspoon dried basil
1 teaspoon dried rosemary

1 teaspoon dried thyme
1 tablespoon sesame oil
1 small-sized egg, well-whisked
1/2 cup parmesan cheese, grated

DIRECTIONS

Season the filet mignon with salt, black pepper, cayenne pepper, basil, rosemary, and thyme. Brush with sesame oil.
Put the egg in a shallow plate. Now, place the parmesan cheese in another plate.
Coat the filet mignon with the egg; then, lay it into the parmesan cheese. Set your Air Fryer to cook at 360 degrees F.
Cook for 10 to 13 minutes or until golden. Serve with mixed salad leaves and enjoy!

207. Balsamic London Broil with Garlic

(Ready in about 30 minutes + marinating time | Servings 8)

Per serving: 257 Calories; 9.2g Fat; 0.1g Carbs; 41.0g Protein; 0.4g Sugars; 0.2g Fiber

INGREDIENTS

2 pounds London broil
3 large garlic cloves, minced
3 tablespoons balsamic vinegar
3 tablespoons whole-grain mustard

2 tablespoons olive oil
Sea salt and ground black pepper, to taste
1/2 teaspoon dried hot red pepper flakes

DIRECTIONS

Score both sides of the cleaned London broil.

Thoroughly combine the remaining ingredients; massage this mixture into the meat to coat it on all sides. Let it marinate for at least 3 hours. Set the Air Fryer to cook at 400 degrees F; Then cook the London broil for 15 minutes. Flip it over and cook another 10 to 12 minutes. Bon appétit!

208. Favorite Beef Stroganoff

(Ready in about 20 minutes + marinating time | Servings 4)

Per serving: 418 Calories; 25.8g Fat; 9g Carbs; 32.6g Protein; 1.4g Sugars; 1g Fiber

INGREDIENTS

1 ¼ pounds beef sirloin steak, cut into small-sized strips
1/4 cup balsamic vinegar
1 tablespoon brown mustard
1 tablespoon butter
1 cup beef broth
1 cup leek, chopped

2 cloves garlic, crushed
1 teaspoon cayenne pepper
Sea salt flakes and crushed red pepper, to taste
1 cup sour cream
2 ½ tablespoons tomato paste

DIRECTIONS

Place the beef along with the balsamic vinegar and the mustard in a mixing dish; cover and marinate in your refrigerator for about 1 hour. Butter the inside of a baking dish and put the beef into the dish.

Add the broth, leeks and garlic. Cook at 380 degrees for 8 minutes. Pause the machine and add the cayenne pepper, salt, red pepper, sour cream and tomato paste; cook for additional 7 minutes.

Bon appétit!

209. Shoulder Steak with Herbs and Brussels Sprouts

(Ready in about 30 minutes + marinating time | Servings 4)

Per serving: 302 Calories; 14.2g Fat; 6.5g Carbs; 36.6g Protein; 1.6g Sugars; 2.8g Fiber

INGREDIENTS

1 pound beef chuck shoulder steak
2 tablespoons vegetable oil
1 tablespoon red wine vinegar
1 teaspoon fine sea salt
1/2 teaspoon ground black pepper
1 teaspoon smoked paprika

1 teaspoon onion powder
1/2 teaspoon garlic powder
1/2 pound Brussels sprouts, cleaned and halved
1/2 teaspoon fennel seeds
1 teaspoon dried basil
1 teaspoon dried sage

DIRECTIONS

Firstly, marinate the beef with vegetable oil, wine vinegar, salt, black pepper, paprika, onion powder, and garlic powder. Rub the marinade into the meat and let it stay at least for 3 hours.

Air fry at 390 degrees F for 10 minutes. Pause the machine and add the prepared Brussels sprouts; sprinkle them with fennel seeds, basil, and sage.

Turn the machine to 380 degrees F; press the power button and cook for 5 more minutes. Pause the machine, stir and cook for further 10 minutes.

Next, remove the meat from the cooking basket and cook the vegetables a few minutes more if needed and according to your taste. Serve with your favorite mayo sauce.

210. Shallot and Celery Steak

(Ready in about 17 minutes | Servings 6)

Per serving: 368 Calories; 13.3g Fat; 8.3g Carbs; 50.1g Protein; 0.6g Sugars; 0.8g Fiber

INGREDIENTS

1/3 cup cream of shallot soup

2 sprigs fresh rosemary, chopped

1 cup celery, sliced

1/2 cup tomatoes, crushed

2 sprigs fresh thyme, chopped

1 teaspoon kosher salt

4 tablespoons dry white wine

1 teaspoon ground black pepper, or to taste

6 lean steaks, cut into strips

3 shallots, peeled and cut into wedges

1/2 teaspoon cayenne pepper

DIRECTIONS

Add all ingredients to an Air Fryer baking tray; then, cook for 13 minutes at 395 degrees F.

Work in batches; pause the machine once or twice to shake your food. Bon appétit!

211. Tender and Creamy Beef with Sage

(Ready in about 13 minutes | Servings 2)

Per serving: 428 Calories; 20.1g Fat; 6.7g Carbs; 50.1g Protein; 0.9g Sugars; 1.3g Fiber

INGREDIENTS

1/3 cup sour cream

½ cup green onion, chopped

1 tablespoon mayonnaise

3 cloves garlic, smashed

1 pound beef flank steak, trimmed and cubed

2 tablespoons fresh sage, minced

½ teaspoon salt

1/3 teaspoon black pepper, or to taste

DIRECTIONS

Season your meat with salt and pepper; arrange beef cubes on the bottom of a baking dish that fits in your air fryer.

Stir in green onions and garlic; air-fry for about 7 minutes at 385 degrees F.

Once your beef starts to tender, add the cream, mayonnaise, and sage; air-fry an additional 8 minutes. Bon appétit!

212. Bavarian Beef Schnitzel

(Ready in about 13 minutes | Servings 2)

Per serving: 524 Calories; 31.3g Fat; 5.3g Carbs; 56.1g Protein; 1.6g Sugars; 0.6g Fiber

INGREDIENTS

2 medium-sized eggs

1 teaspoon cayenne pepper, or more to taste

1/4 cup coconut flour

1/4 cup parmesan cheese

1/3 freshly ground black pepper, or more to taste

Wedges of 1 fresh lemon, to serve

2 beef schnitzels

1 teaspoon fine sea salt

1 ½ tablespoons canola oil

DIRECTIONS

Season beef schnitzel with salt, cayenne pepper, and ground black pepper.

In a mixing dish, whisk the oil with coconut flour and parmesan cheese. In another bowl, whisk the eggs until pale and frothy.

Firstly, coat beef schnitzels with the whisked eggs; then, coat it with the parmesan mixture.

Air-fry for 10 minutes at 355 degrees F. Serve warm, garnished with lemon wedges and enjoy!

213. Mexican Chili Beef Sausage Meatballs

(Ready in about 25 minutes | Servings 4)

Per serving: 441 Calories; 37g Fat; 6.5g Carbs; 17.6g Protein; 2.4g Sugars; 2.4g Fiber

INGREDIENTS

1 cup green onion, finely minced

1/2 teaspoon parsley flakes

2 teaspoons onion flakes

1 pound chili sausage, crumbled

2 tablespoons flaxseed meal

3 cloves garlic, finely minced

1 teaspoon Mexican oregano

1 tablespoon poblano pepper, chopped

Fine sea salt and ground black pepper, to taste

½ tablespoon fresh chopped sage

DIRECTIONS

Mix all ingredients in a bowl until the mixture has a uniform consistency.

Roll into bite-sized balls and transfer them to a baking dish.

Cook in the preheated Air Fryer at 345 degrees for 18 minutes. Serve on wooden sticks and enjoy!

214. BBQ Skirt Steak

(Ready in about 20 minutes + marinating time | Servings 5)

Per serving: 401 Calories; 21g Fat; 1.7g Carbs; 51g Protein; 3.3g Sugars; 1g Fiber; 0.4g Fiber

INGREDIENTS

2 pounds skirt steak

2 tablespoons tomato paste

1 tablespoon olive oil

1 tablespoon coconut aminos

1/4 cup rice vinegar

1 tablespoon fish sauce

Sea salt, to taste

1/2 teaspoon dried dill

1/2 teaspoon dried rosemary

1/4 teaspoon black pepper, freshly cracked

DIRECTIONS

Place all ingredients in a large ceramic dish; let it marinate for 3 hours in your refrigerator.

Coat the sides and bottom of the Air Fryer with cooking spray.

Add your steak to the cooking basket; reserve the marinade. Cook the skirt steak in the preheated Air Fryer at 400 degrees F for 12 minutes, turning over a couple of times, basting with the reserved marinade.

Bon appétit!

215. Beef Sausage and Vegetable Bowl

(Ready in about 35 minutes | Servings 4)

Per serving: 490 Calories; 42g Fat; 8.7g Carbs; 18.2g Protein; 4.3g Sugars; 2g Fiber

INGREDIENTS

4 bell peppers

2 tablespoons canola oil

2 medium-sized tomatoes, halved

4 spring onions

4 beef sausages

1 tablespoon mustard

DIRECTIONS

Start by preheating your Air Fryer to 400 degrees F.

Add the bell peppers to the cooking basket. Drizzle 1 tablespoon of canola oil all over the bell peppers.

Cook for 5 minutes. Turn the temperature down to 350 degrees F. Add the tomatoes and spring onions to the cooking basket and cook an additional 10 minutes.

Reserve your vegetables.

Then, add the sausages to the cooking basket. Drizzle with the remaining tablespoon of canola oil.

Cook in the preheated Air Fryer at 380 degrees F for 15 minutes, flipping them halfway through the cooking time.

Serve sausages with the air-fried vegetables and mustard; serve.

216. Grilled Mayo Short Loin Steak

(Ready in about 20 minutes | Servings 4)

Per serving: 620 Calories; 50g Fat; 2.7g Carbs; 39.7g Protein; 1.2g Sugars; 0.3g Fiber

INGREDIENTS

1 cup mayonnaise

1 tablespoon fresh rosemary, finely chopped

2 tablespoons Worcestershire sauce

Sea salt, to taste

1/2 teaspoon ground black pepper

1 teaspoon smoked paprika

1 teaspoon garlic, minced

1 ½ pounds short loin steak

DIRECTIONS

Combine the mayonnaise, rosemary, Worcestershire sauce, salt, pepper, paprika, and garlic; mix to combine well.

Now, brush the mayonnaise mixture over both sides of the steak. Lower the steak onto the grill pan.

Grill in the preheated Air Fryer at 390 degrees F for 8 minutes. Turn the steaks over and grill an additional 7 minutes.

Check for doneness with a meat thermometer. Serve warm and enjoy!

217. Beef Fajita Keto Burrito

(Ready in about 20 minutes | Servings 4)

Per serving: 365 Calories; 20g Fat; 7.8g Carbs; 40.1g Protein; 2.8g Sugars; 3.7g Fiber

INGREDIENTS

1 pound rump steak

1 teaspoon garlic powder

1/2 teaspoon onion powder

1/2 teaspoon cayenne pepper

1 teaspoon piri piri powder

1 teaspoon Mexican oregano

Salt and ground black pepper, to taste

1 cup Mexican cheese blend

1 head romaine lettuce, separated into leaves

DIRECTIONS

Toss the rump steak with the garlic powder, onion powder, cayenne pepper, piri piri powder, Mexican oregano, salt, and black pepper.

Cook in the preheated Air Fryer at 390 degrees F for 10 minutes. Slice against the grain into thin strips. Add the cheese blend and cook for 2 minutes more.

Spoon the beef mixture onto romaine lettuce leaves; roll up burrito-style and serve.

218. Wine Marinated Flank Steak

(Ready in about 20 minutes + marinating time | Servings 4)

Per serving: 312 Calories; 15.5g Fat; 2.5g Carbs; 36.8g Protein; 1.9g Sugars; 0.2g Fiber

INGREDIENTS

1 ½ pounds flank steak

1/2 cup red wine

1/2 cup apple cider vinegar

2 tablespoons soy sauce

Salt, to taste

1/2 teaspoon ground black pepper

1/2 teaspoon red pepper flakes, crushed

1/2 teaspoon dried basil

1 teaspoon thyme

DIRECTIONS

Add all ingredients to a large ceramic bowl. Cover and let it marinate for 3 hours in your refrigerator.

Transfer the flank steak to the Air Fryer basket that is previously greased with nonstick cooking oil.

Cook in the preheated Air Fryer at 400 degrees F for 12 minutes, flipping over halfway through the cooking time. Bon appétit!

219. Classic Cube Steak with Sauce

(Ready in about 20 minutes | Servings 4)

Per serving: 469 Calories; 30.4g Fat; 0.6g Carbs; 46g Protein; 0g Sugars; 0.4g Fiber

INGREDIENTS

1 ½ pounds cube steak
Salt, to taste
1/4 teaspoon ground black pepper, or more to taste
4 ounces butter
2 garlic cloves, finely chopped

2 scallions, finely chopped
2 tablespoon fresh parsley, finely chopped
1 tablespoon fresh horseradish, grated
1 teaspoon cayenne pepper

DIRECTIONS

Pat dry the cube steak and season it with salt and black pepper. Spritz the Air Fryer basket with cooking oil. Add the meat to the basket. Cook in the preheated Air Fryer at 400 degrees F for 14 minutes.

Meanwhile, melt the butter in a skillet over a moderate heat. Add the remaining ingredients and simmer until the sauce has thickened and reduced slightly.

Top the warm cube steaks with Cowboy sauce and serve immediately.

220. Tangy and Saucy Beef Fingers

(Ready in about 20 minutes + marinating time | Servings 4)

Per serving: 475 Calories; 26.3g Fat; 7.9g Carbs; 45g Protein; 1.1g Sugars; 0.6g Fiber

INGREDIENTS

1 ½ pounds sirloin steak
1/4 cup red wine
1/4 cup fresh lime juice
1 teaspoon garlic powder
1 teaspoon shallot powder
1 teaspoon celery seeds

1 teaspoon mustard seeds
Coarse sea salt and ground black pepper, to taste
1 teaspoon red pepper flakes
2 eggs, lightly whisked
1 cup parmesan cheese
1 teaspoon paprika

DIRECTIONS

Place the steak, red wine, lime juice, garlic powder, shallot powder, celery seeds, mustard seeds, salt, black pepper, and red pepper in a large ceramic bowl; let it marinate for 3 hours.

Tenderize the cube steak by pounding with a mallet; cut into 1-inch strips.

In a shallow bowl, whisk the eggs. In another bowl, mix the parmesan cheese and paprika.

Dip the beef pieces into the whisked eggs and coat on all sides. Now, dredge the beef pieces in the parmesan mixture.

Cook at 400 degrees F for 14 minutes, flipping halfway through the cooking time.

Meanwhile, make the sauce by heating the reserved marinade in a saucepan over medium heat; let it simmer until thoroughly warmed.

Serve the steak fingers with the sauce on the side. Enjoy!

221. Spicy T-Bone Steak with Aromatics

(Ready in about 20 minutes | Servings 3)

Per serving: 428 Calories; 24.6g Fat; 7.1g Carbs; 43.7g Protein; 3.6g Sugars; 1.5g Fiber

INGREDIENTS

1 pound T-bone steak
4 garlic cloves, halved
2 tablespoons olive oil
1/4 cup tamari sauce
4 tablespoons tomato paste

1 teaspoon Sriracha sauce
2 tablespoons white vinegar
1 teaspoon dried rosemary
1/2 teaspoon dried basil
2 heaping tablespoons cilantro, chopped

DIRECTIONS

Rub the garlic halves all over the T-bone steak.

Drizzle the oil all over the steak and transfer it to the grill pan; grill the steak in the preheated Air Fryer at 400 degrees F for 10 minutes.

Meanwhile, whisk the tamari sauce, tomato paste, Sriracha, vinegar, rosemary, and basil. Cook an additional 5 minutes

Serve garnished with fresh cilantro. Bon appétit!

222. Saucy Lemony Beef Steaks

(Ready in about 25 minutes | Servings 2)

Per serving: 456 Calories; 20g Fat; 3.4g Carbs; 48g Protein; 1.1g Sugars; 1g Fiber

INGREDIENTS

1 pound beef steaks
4 tablespoons white wine
2 teaspoons crushed coriander seeds
½ teaspoon fennel seeds
1/3 cup beef broth

2 tablespoons lemon zest, grated
2 tablespoons canola oil
1/2 lemon, cut into wedges
Salt flakes and freshly ground black pepper, to taste

DIRECTIONS

Heat the oil in a saucepan over a moderate flame. Then, cook the garlic for 1 minute, or until just fragrant.

Remove the pan from the heat; add the beef broth, wine, lemon zest, coriander seeds, fennel, salt flakes, and freshly ground black. Pour the mixture into a baking dish.

Add beef steaks to the baking dish; toss to coat well. Now, tuck the lemon wedges among the beef steaks.

Bake for 18 minutes at 335 degrees F. Serve warm.

223. Beef Chops with English Mustard and Coriander

(Ready in about 35 minutes | Servings 3)

Per serving: 402 Calories; 44.5g Fat; 2g Carbs; 31.9g Protein; 0.4g Sugars; 0.6g Fiber

INGREDIENTS

1 ½ teaspoon English mustard
3 boneless beef chops
1/3 teaspoon garlic pepper
2 teaspoons oregano, dried
2 tablespoons vegetable oil

1 ½ tablespoons fresh coriander, chopped
1/2 teaspoon onion powder
1/2 teaspoon basil, dried
Grated rind of 1/2 small-sized lime
1/2 teaspoon fine sea salt

DIRECTIONS

Firstly, make the rub for the beef chops by mixing all the ingredients, except the chops and the new potatoes.

Now, evenly spread the beef chops with the English mustard rub.

Then, arrange the new potatoes in the bottom of the air fryer cooking basket. Top them with the prepared beef chops.

Roast for about 27 minutes at 365 degrees F, turning halfway through. Serve on individual plates with a keto salad on the side, if desired.

224. Beef with Green Parmesan Salad

(Ready in about 15 minutes | Servings 2)

Per serving: 206 Calories; 18g Fat; 1.7g Carbs; 9.8g Protein; 0.4g Sugars; 1.5g Fiber

INGREDIENTS

1/2 cup vegetable stock
1/3 cup scallions, chopped
1 cloves garlic, minced
2 beef chops
½ tablespoon melted butter
Table salt and ground black pepper, to savor
For the Salad:

1 ½ tablespoons freshly grated Parmesan
1 tablespoon apple cider vinegar
2 tablespoons extra-virgin olive oil
2 cups very finely chopped or slivered curly kale
1/3 teaspoon ground black pepper, or more to taste
1 teaspoon table salt

DIRECTIONS

Take an oven safe dish and toss beef chops with salt, pepper, butter, scallions, and garlic; pour in the stock; gently stir to coat.

Now, roast your chops at 395 degrees F for 12 to 14 minutes.

Meanwhile, make the parmesan-kale salad by mixing all salad components. Serve warm beef chops with the prepared kale salad.

225. Beer-Braised Beef with Leeks

(Ready in about 20 minutes + marinating time | Servings 4)

Per serving: 339 Calories; 15.4g Fat; 6g Carbs; 39.3g Protein; 0.9g Sugars; 0.5g Fiber

INGREDIENTS

1 ½ pounds short loin
2 tablespoons olive oil
2-3 cloves garlic, finely minced
1 cup leeks, sliced
1 bottle beer

1 rosemary sprig
2 thyme sprigs
1 teaspoon mustard seeds
1 bay leaf

DIRECTIONS

Pat the beef dry; then, tenderize the beef with a meat mallet to soften the fibers. Place it in a large-sized mixing dish.
Add the remaining ingredients; toss to coat well and let it marinate for at least 1 hour.
Cook about 7 minutes at 395 degrees F; after that, pause the Air Fryer. Flip the meat over and cook for another 8 minutes, or until it's done.

226. Teriyaki Steak with Fresh Herbs

(Ready in about 40 minutes | Servings 4)

Per serving: 297 Calories; 17.6g Fat; 7.6g Carbs; 25.1g Protein; 5.1g Sugars; 0.8g Fiber

INGREDIENTS

2 heaping tablespoons fresh parsley, roughly chopped
1 pound beef rump steaks
2 heaping tablespoons fresh chives, roughly chopped
Salt and black pepper (or mixed peppercorns), to savor
For the Sauce:
1/4 cup rice vinegar

1 tablespoon fresh ginger, grated
1 ½ tablespoons mirin
3 garlic cloves, minced
2 tablespoon rice bran oil
1/3 cup soy sauce
A few drops of liquid Stevia

DIRECTIONS

Firstly, steam the beef rump steaks for 8 minutes (use the method of steaming that you prefer). Season the beef with salt and black pepper; scatter the chopped parsley and chives over the top.
Roast the beef rump steaks in an Air Fryer basket for 28 minutes at 345 degrees, turning halfway through.
While the beef is cooking, combine the ingredients for the teriyaki sauce in a sauté pan. Then, let it simmer over low heat until it has thickened.
Toss the beef with the teriyaki sauce until it is well covered and serve. Enjoy!

227. Korean Beef Bulgogi Burgers

(Ready in about 20 minutes | Servings 4)

Per serving: 377 Calories; 19.3g Fat; 2.4g Carbs; 45.9g Protein; 0.7g Sugars; 0.8g Fiber

INGREDIENTS

1 ½ pounds ground beef
1 teaspoon garlic, minced
2 tablespoons scallions, chopped
Sea salt and cracked black pepper, to taste
1 teaspoon Gochugaru (Korean chili powder)
1/2 teaspoon dried marjoram

1 teaspoon dried thyme
1 teaspoon mustard seeds
1/2 teaspoon shallot powder
1/2 teaspoon cumin powder
1/2 teaspoon paprika
1 tablespoon liquid smoke flavoring

DIRECTIONS

In a mixing bowl, thoroughly combine all ingredients until well combined.
Shape into four patties and spritz them with cooking oil on both sides. Bake at 357 degrees F for 18 minutes, flipping over halfway through the cooking time.
Serve warm. Bon appétit!

228. Beef, Pearl Onions and Cauliflower

(Ready in about 20 minutes + marinating time | Servings 4)

Per serving: 298 Calories; 13.8g Fat; 7.4g Carbs; 37g Protein; 3.1g Sugars; 2g Fiber

INGREDIENTS

1 ½ pounds New York strip, cut into strips
1 (1-pound) head cauliflower, broken into florets
1 cup pearl onion, sliced
Marinade:
1 tablespoon olive oil

2 cloves garlic, minced
1 teaspoon of ground ginger
1/4 cup tomato paste
1/2 cup red wine

DIRECTIONS

Mix all ingredients for the marinade. Add the beef to the marinade and let it sit in your refrigerator for 1 hour.
Preheat your Air Fryer to 400 degrees F. Transfer the meat to the Air Fryer basket. Add the cauliflower and onions.
Drizzle a few tablespoons of marinade all over the meat and vegetables. Cook for 12 minutes, shaking the basket halfway through the cooking time. Serve warm.

229. Asian-Style Round Steak

(Ready in about 40 minutes + marinating time | Servings 4)

Per serving: 418 Calories; 12.2g Fat; 4.8g Carbs; 68.2g Protein; 2.3g Sugars; 0.8g Fiber

INGREDIENTS

2 pounds top round steak, cut into bite-sized strips
2 garlic cloves, sliced
1 teaspoon dried marjoram
1/4 cup red wine
1 tablespoon tamari sauce

Salt and black pepper, to taste
1 tablespoon olive oil
1 red onion, sliced
2 bell peppers, sliced
1 celery stalk, sliced

DIRECTIONS

Place the top round, garlic, marjoram, red wine, tamari sauce, salt and pepper in a bowl, cover and let it marinate for 1 hour.
Preheat your Air Fryer to 390 degrees F and add the oil.
Once hot, discard the marinade and cook the beef for 15 minutes. Add the onion, peppers, carrot, and garlic and continue cooking until tender about 15 minutes more.
Open the Air Fryer every 5 minutes and baste the meat with the remaining marinade. Serve immediately.

230. Easy Marinated London Broil

(Ready in about 30 minutes + marinating time | Servings 4)

Per serving: 517 Calories; 24.1g Fat; 5g Carbs; 70g Protein; 2.4g Sugars; 0.7g Fiber

INGREDIENTS

For the marinade:
2 tablespoons Worcestershire sauce
2 garlic cloves, minced
1 tablespoon oil
2 tablespoons rice vinegar

London Broil:
2 pounds London broil
2 tablespoons tomato paste
Sea salt and cracked black pepper, to taste
1 tablespoon mustard

DIRECTIONS

Combine all the marinade ingredients in a mixing bowl; add the London boil to the bowl. Cover and let it marinate for 3 hours.
Preheat the Air Fryer to 400 degrees F. Spritz the Air Fryer grill pan with cooking oil.
Grill the marinated London broil in the preheated Air Fryer for 18 minutes. Turn London broil over, top with the tomato paste, salt, black pepper, and mustard.
Continue to grill an additional 10 minutes. Serve immediately.

231. Filet Mignon with Chili Peanut Sauce

(Ready in about 25 minutes + marinating time | Servings 4)

Per serving: 420 Calories; 22.1g Fat; 6.5g Carbs; 50g Protein; 3.7g Sugars; 1g Fiber

INGREDIENTS

2 pounds filet mignon, sliced into bite-sized strips
1 tablespoon oyster sauce
2 tablespoons sesame oil
2 tablespoons tamari sauce
1 tablespoon ginger-garlic paste
1 tablespoon mustard

1 teaspoon chili powder
1/4 cup peanut butter
2 tablespoons lime juice
1 teaspoon red pepper flakes
2 tablespoons water

DIRECTIONS

Place the beef strips, oyster sauce, sesame oil, tamari sauce, ginger-garlic paste, mustard, and chili powder in a large ceramic dish. Cover and allow it to marinate for 2 hours in your refrigerator.
Cook in the preheated Air Fryer at 400 degrees F for 18 minutes, shaking the basket occasionally.
Mix the peanut butter with lime juice, red pepper flakes, and water. Spoon the sauce onto the air fried beef strips and serve warm.

232. Beef Sausage with Grilled Broccoli

(Ready in about 25 minutes | Servings 4)

Per serving: 477 Calories; 43.2g Fat; 7.3g Carbs; 15.9g Protein; 0.7g Sugars; 3.6g Fiber

INGREDIENTS

1 pound beef Vienna sausage
1/2 cup mayonnaise
1 teaspoon yellow mustard
1 tablespoon fresh lemon juice

1 teaspoon garlic powder
1/4 teaspoon black pepper
1 pound broccoli

DIRECTIONS

Start by preheating your Air Fryer to 380 degrees F. Spritz the grill pan with cooking oil.
Cut the sausages into serving sized pieces. Cook the sausages for 15 minutes, shaking the basket occasionally to get all sides browned. Set aside.
In the meantime, whisk the mayonnaise with mustard, lemon juice, garlic powder, and black pepper. Toss the broccoli with the mayo mixture.
Turn up temperature to 400 degrees F. Cook broccoli for 6 minutes, turning halfway through the cooking time.
Serve the sausage with the grilled broccoli on the side. Bon appétit!

233. Rich Meatloaf with Mustard and Peppers

(Ready in about 35 minutes | Servings 5)

Per serving: 398 Calories; 26.4g Fat; 9g Carbs; 31.2g Protein; 4.3g Sugars; 1.6g Fiber

INGREDIENTS

1 pound beef, ground
1/2 pound veal, ground
1 egg
4 tablespoons vegetable juice
1/2 cup pork rinds
2 bell peppers, chopped

1 onion, chopped
2 garlic cloves, minced
2 tablespoons tomato paste
2 tablespoons soy sauce
1 (1-ounce) package ranch dressing mix

Sea salt, to taste
1/2 teaspoon ground black pepper, to taste
7 ounces tomato puree
1 tablespoon Dijon mustard

DIRECTIONS

Start by preheating your Air Fryer to 330 degrees F.
In a mixing bowl, thoroughly combine the ground beef, veal, egg, vegetable juice, pork rinds, bell peppers, onion, garlic, tomato paste, soy sauce, ranch dressing mix, salt, and ground black pepper.
Mix until everything is well incorporated and press into a lightly greased meatloaf pan.
Cook approximately 25 minutes in the preheated Air Fryer. Whisk the tomato puree with the mustard and spread the topping over the top of your meatloaf.
Continue to cook 2 minutes more. Let it stand on a cooling rack for 6 minutes before slicing and serving. Enjoy!

234. Smoked Sausage and Bacon Shashlik

(Ready in about 20 minutes | Servings 4)

Per serving: 422 Calories; 36g Fat; 6.9g Carbs; 16.8g Protein; 2.6g Sugars; 0.7g Fiber

INGREDIENTS

1 pound smoked Polish beef sausage, sliced
1 tablespoon mustard
1 tablespoon olive oil

2 tablespoons Worcestershire sauce
2 bell peppers, sliced
Salt and ground black pepper, to taste

DIRECTIONS

Toss the sausage with the mustard, olive, and Worcestershire sauce. Thread sausage and peppers onto skewers.
Sprinkle with salt and black pepper.
Cook in the preheated Air Fryer at 360 degrees F for 11 minutes. Brush the skewers with the reserved marinade. Bon appétit!

235. Spicy Paprika Steak

(Ready in about 20 minutes | Servings 2)

Per serving: 450 Calories; 25.6g Fat; 3.4g Carbs; 50.8g Protein; 0.3g Sugars; 1.3g Fiber

INGREDIENTS

1/2 Ancho chili pepper, soaked in hot water before using
1 tablespoon brandy
2 teaspoons smoked paprika
1 1/2 tablespoons olive oil

2 beef steaks
Kosher salt, to taste
1 teaspoon ground allspice
3 cloves garlic, sliced

DIRECTIONS

Sprinkle the beef steaks with salt, paprika, and allspice. Add the steak to a baking dish that fits your fryer. Scatter the sliced garlic over the top.
Now, drizzle it with brandy and olive oil; spread minced Ancho chili pepper over the top.
Bake at 385 degrees F for 14 minutes, turning halfway through. Serve warm.

236. Steak with Cascabel-Garlic Sauce

(Ready in about 20 minutes | Servings 4)

Per serving: 329 Calories; 17.6g Fat; 2.8g Carbs; 37g Protein; 0.9g Sugars; 0.6g Fiber

INGREDIENTS

2 teaspoons brown mustard
2 tablespoons mayonnaise
1 ½ pounds beef flank steak, trimmed and cubed
2 teaspoons minced cascabel
½ cup scallions, finely chopped
1/3 cup Crème fraîche

2 teaspoons cumin seeds
3 cloves garlic, pressed
Pink peppercorns to taste, freshly cracked
1 teaspoon fine table salt
1/3 teaspoon black pepper, preferably freshly ground

DIRECTIONS

Firstly, fry the cumin seeds just about 1 minute or until they pop.
After that, season your beef flank steak with fine table salt, black pepper and the fried cumin seeds; arrange the seasoned beef cubes on the bottom of your baking dish that fits in the air fryer.
Throw in the minced cascabel, garlic, and scallions; air-fry approximately 8 minutes at 390 degrees F.
Once the beef cubes start to tender, add your favorite mayo, Crème fraîche, freshly cracked pink peppercorns and mustard; air-fry 7 minutes longer. Serve over hot wild rice. Bon appétit!

237. Grandma's Meatballs with Spicy Sauce

(Ready in about 20 minutes | Servings 4)

Per serving: 360 Calories; 27.3g Fat; 7.6g Carbs; 20.3g Protein; 4g Sugars; 1.2g Fiber

INGREDIENTS

4 tablespoons pork rinds
1/3 cup green onion
1 pound beef sausage meat
3 garlic cloves, minced
1/3 teaspoon ground black pepper
Sea salt, to taste
For the sauce:

2 tablespoons Worcestershire sauce
1/3 yellow onion, minced
Dash of Tabasco sauce
1/3 cup tomato paste
1 teaspoon cumin powder
1/2 tablespoon balsamic vinegar

DIRECTIONS

Knead all of the above ingredients until everything is well incorporated.

Roll into balls and cook in the preheated Air Fryer at 365 degrees for 13 minutes.

In the meantime, in a saucepan, cook the ingredients for the sauce until thoroughly warmed. Serve your meatballs with the tomato sauce and enjoy!

238. Marinated Cajun Beef

(Ready in about 1 hour 5 minutes | Servings 2)

Per serving: 483 Calories; 25.3g Fat; 6.5g Carbs; 52.3g Protein; 1.6g Sugars; 1.4g Fiber

INGREDIENTS

1/3 cup beef broth
2 tablespoons Cajun seasoning, crushed
1/2 teaspoon garlic powder
3/4 pound beef tenderloins
½ tablespoon pear cider vinegar

1/3 teaspoon cayenne pepper
1 ½ tablespoon olive oil
1/2 teaspoon freshly ground black pepper
1 teaspoon salt

DIRECTIONS

Firstly, coat the beef tenderloins with salt, cayenne pepper, and black pepper.

Mix the remaining items in a medium-sized bowl; let the meat marinate for 40 minutes in this mixture.

Roast the beef for about 22 minutes at 385 degrees F, turning it halfway through the cooking time. Bon appétit!

239. Christmas Filet Mignon Steak

(Ready in about 25 minutes | Servings 6)

Per serving: 452 Calories; 36.2g Fat; 0.8g Carbs; 29.6g Protein; 0.6g Sugars; 0.1g Fiber

INGREDIENTS

1/3 stick butter, at room temperature
1/2 cup heavy cream
1/2 medium-sized garlic bulb, peeled and pressed
6 filet mignon steaks

2 teaspoons mixed peppercorns, freshly cracked
1 ½ tablespoons apple cider
A dash of hot sauce
1 ½ teaspoons sea salt flakes

DIRECTIONS

Season the mignon steaks with the cracked peppercorns and salt flakes. Roast the mignon steaks in the preheated Air Fryer for 24 minutes at 385 degrees F, turning once. Check for doneness and set aside, keeping it warm.

In a small nonstick saucepan that is placed over a moderate flame, mash the garlic to a smooth paste. Whisk in the rest of the above ingredients. Whisk constantly until it has a uniform consistency.

To finish, lay the filet mignon steaks on serving plates; spoon a little sauce onto each filet mignon. Bon appétit!

240. Chinese-Style Spicy and Herby Beef

(Ready in about 24 minutes | Servings 4)

Per serving: 354 Calories; 26.4g Fat; 1.8g Carbs; 25.1g Protein; 0.3g Sugars; 0.3g Fiber

INGREDIENTS

1 pound flank steak, cut into small pieces
1 teaspoon fresh sage leaves, minced
1/3 cup olive oil
3 teaspoons sesame oil
3 tablespoons Shaoxing wine
2 tablespoons tamari

1 teaspoon hot sauce
1/8 teaspoon xanthum gum
1 teaspoon seasoned salt
3 cloves garlic, minced
1 teaspoon fresh rosemary leaves, finely minced
1/2 teaspoon freshly cracked black pepper

DIRECTIONS

Warm the oil in a sauté pan over a moderate heat. Now, sauté the garlic until just tender and fragrant.
Now, add the remaining ingredients. Toss to coat well.
Then, roast for about 18 minutes at 345 degrees F. Check doneness and serve warm.

241. Irish Whisky Steak

(Ready in about 25 minutes + marinating time | Servings 6)

Per serving: 260 Calories; 13.7g Fat; 1.8g Carbs; 31.5g Protein; 1.2g Sugars; 0.1g Fiber

INGREDIENTS

2 pounds sirloin steaks
1 ½tablespoons tamari sauce
1/3 teaspoon cayenne pepper
1/3 teaspoon ground ginger

2 garlic cloves, thinly sliced
2 tablespoons Irish whiskey
2 tablespoons olive oil
Fine sea salt, to taste

DIRECTIONS

Firstly, add all the ingredients, minus the olive oil and the steak, to a resealable plastic bag.
Throw in the steak and let it marinate for a couple of hours. After that, drizzle the sirloin steaks with 2 tablespoons olive oil.
Roast for approximately 22 minutes at 395 degrees F, turning it halfway through the time. Bon appétit!

242. Greek Souvlaki with Eggplant

(Ready in about 1 hour 30 minutes | Servings 4)

Per serving: 372 Calories; 21.2g Fat; 9.2g Carbs; 36.3g Protein; 3.6g Sugars; 2.7g Fiber

INGREDIENTS

1 ½ pounds beef stew meat cubes
1/4 cup mayonnaise
1/4 cup sour cream
1 tablespoon yellow mustard

1 tablespoon Worcestershire sauce
1 cup pearl onions
1 small-sized eggplant, 1 ½-inch cubes
Sea salt and ground black pepper, to taste

DIRECTIONS

In a mixing bowl, toss all ingredients until everything is well coated.
Place in your refrigerator, cover, and let it marinate for 1 hour.
Soak wooden skewers in water for 15 minutes
Thread the beef cubes, pearl onions and eggplant onto skewers. Cook in preheated Air Fryer at 395 degrees F for 12 minutes, flipping halfway through the cooking time. Serve warm.

243. Sirloin Steak with Cremini Mushroom Sauce

(Ready in about 20 minutes | Servings 5)

Per serving: 349 Calories; 16.2g Fat; 7.4g Carbs; 42.9g Protein; 2.6g Sugars; 1.4g Fiber

INGREDIENTS

2 tablespoons butter
2 pounds sirloin, cut into four pieces
Salt and cracked black pepper, to taste
1 teaspoon cayenne pepper
1/2 teaspoon dried rosemary
1/2 teaspoon dried dill

1/4 teaspoon dried thyme
1 pound Cremini mushrooms, sliced
1 cup sour cream
1 teaspoon mustard
1/2 teaspoon curry powder

DIRECTIONS

Start by preheating your Air Fryer to 396 degrees F. Grease a baking pan with butter.
Add the sirloin, salt, black pepper, cayenne pepper, rosemary, dill, and thyme to the baking pan. Cook for 9 minutes.
Next, stir in the mushrooms, sour cream, mustard, and curry powder. Continue to cook another 5 minutes or until everything is heated through.
Spoon onto individual serving plates. Bon appétit!

244. Spicy Meatloaf with Peppers and Parmesan Cheese

(Ready in about 35 minutes | Servings 4)

Per serving: 415 Calories; 32.2g Fat; 4.4g Carbs; 25.3g Protein; 1.5g Sugars; 2.1g Fiber

INGREDIENTS

1/2 pound beef sausage, crumbled
1/2 pound ground beef
1/4 cup pork rinds
2 tablespoons Parmesan, preferably freshly grated
1 shallot, finely chopped

2 garlic cloves, minced
Sea salt and ground black pepper, to taste
1 red bell pepper, finely chopped
1 serrano pepper, finely chopped

DIRECTIONS

Start by preheating your Air Fryer to 390 degrees F.
Mix all ingredients in a bowl. Knead until everything is well incorporated.
Shape the mixture into a meatloaf and place in the baking pan that is previously greased with cooking oil.
Cook for 24 minutes in the preheated Air Fryer.
Let it stand on a cooling rack for 6 minutes before slicing and serving. Enjoy!

245. Seekh Kebab with Yogurt Sauce

(Ready in about 25 minutes | Servings 4)

Per serving: 530 Calories; 31.1g Fat; 9.3g Carbs; 49.3g Protein; 6.1g Sugars; 1.1g Fiber

INGREDIENTS

1 ½ pounds ground chuck
1 egg
1 medium-sized leek, chopped
2 garlic cloves, smashed
2 tablespoons fresh parsley, chopped
1 teaspoon fresh rosemary, chopped
Sea salt, to taste
1/2 teaspoon ground black pepper
1/2 teaspoon chili powder

1 teaspoon garam masala
1 teaspoon ginger paste
1/2 teaspoon ground cumin
Raita Sauce:
1 small-sized cucumber, grated and squeezed
A pinch of salt
1 cup full-fat yogurt
1/4 cup fresh cilantro, coarsely chopped

DIRECTIONS

Combine all ingredients until everything is well incorporated. Press the meat mixture into a baking pan.
Cook in the preheated Air Fryer at 360 degrees F for 15 minutes. Taste for doneness with a meat thermometer.
Meanwhile, mix all ingredients for the sauce. Serve the warm meatloaf with the sauce on the side. Enjoy!

246. Hungarian Beef Goulash

(Ready in about 1 hour 10 minutes | Servings 4)

Per serving: 306 Calories; 16.1g Fat; 8.8g Carbs; 39.6g Protein; 3.6g Sugars; 1.8g Fiber

INGREDIENTS

Sea salt and cracked black pepper, to taste
1 teaspoon Hungarian paprika
1 ½ pounds beef chuck roast, boneless, cut into bite-sized cubes
2 teaspoons sunflower oil
1 medium-sized leek, chopped
2 garlic cloves, minced
2 bay leaves

1 teaspoon caraway seeds.
2 cups roasted vegetable broth
1 ripe tomato, pureed
2 tablespoons red wine
2 bell peppers, chopped
1 celery stalk, peeled and diced

DIRECTIONS

Add the salt, black pepper, Hungarian paprika, and beef to a resealable bag; shake to coat well.
Heat the oil in a Dutch oven over medium-high flame; sauté the leeks, garlic, bay leaves, and caraway seeds about 4 minutes or until fragrant. Transfer to a lightly greased baking pan.
Then, brown the beef, stirring occasionally, working in batches. Add to the baking pan.
Add the vegetable broth, tomato, and red wine. Lower the pan onto the Air Fryer basket. Bake at 325 degrees F for 40 minutes.
Add the bell peppers and celery. Cook an additional 20 minutes. Serve immediately and enjoy!

247. Cajun Steak with Spicy Green Beans

(Ready in about 25 minutes | Servings 4)

Per serving: 379 Calories; 18.1g Fat; 5.3g Carbs; 49g Protein; 1.9g Sugars; 2g Fiber

INGREDIENTS

2 garlic cloves, smashed
2 teaspoons sunflower oil
1/2 teaspoon cayenne pepper
1 tablespoon Cajun seasoning

1 ½ pounds blade steak
2 cups green beans
1/2 teaspoon Tabasco pepper sauce
Sea salt and ground black pepper, to taste

DIRECTIONS

Start by preheating your Air Fryer to 330 degrees F.
Mix the garlic, oil, cayenne pepper, and Cajun seasoning to make a paste. Rub it over both sides of the blade steak.
Cook for 13 minutes in the preheated Air Fryer. Now, flip the steak and cook an additional 8 minutes.
Heat the green beans in a saucepan. Add a few tablespoons of water, Tabasco, salt, and black pepper; heat until it wilts or about 10 minutes.
Serve the roasted blade steak with green beans on the side. Bon appétit!

248. Saucy Beef with Cotija Cheese

(Ready in about 27 minutes | Servings 3)

Per serving: 589 Calories; 47g Fat; 6.3g Carbs; 33.1g Protein; 2.5g Sugars; 2g Fiber

INGREDIENTS

2 ounces Cotija cheese, cut into sticks
2 teaspoons paprika
2 teaspoons dried thyme
1/2 cup shallots, peeled and chopped
3 beef tenderloins, cut in half lengthwise
2 teaspoons dried basil

1/3 cup homemade bone stock
2 tablespoon olive oil
3 cloves garlic, minced
1 ½ cups tomato puree, no sugar added
1 teaspoon ground black pepper, or more to taste
1 teaspoon fine sea salt, or more to taste

DIRECTIONS

Firstly, season the beef tenderloin with the salt, ground black pepper, and paprika; place a piece of the Cotija cheese in the middle.
Now, tie each tenderloin with a kitchen string; drizzle with olive oil and reserve.
Stir the garlic, shallots, bone stock, tomato puree into an oven safe bowl; cook in the preheated Air Fryer at 375 degrees F for 7 minutes.
Add the reserved beef along with basil and thyme. Set the timer for 14 minutes. Eat warm and enjoy!

249. Beef Sausage and Vegetable Medley

(Ready in about 25 minutes | Servings 4)

Per serving: 428 Calories; 35g Fat; 8.1g Carbs; 18.9g Protein; 2.7g Sugars; 2g Fiber

INGREDIENTS

1 pound beef sausage
2 red bell peppers, cut lengthwise
1 poblano pepper, minced
1 sprig rosemary, chopped
2 shallots, cut into wedges

2 garlic cloves, minced
1/2 pound broccoli, cut into chunks
½ celery stalk, sliced
½ teaspoon caraway seeds
1 teaspoon salt

DIRECTIONS

Place all the ingredients on the bottom of the Air Fryer basket. Toss until everything is well combined.
Roast for approximately 32 minutes at 385 degrees F, stirring once halfway through. Serve warm on a serving platter.

250. Winter Beef with Garlic-Mayo Sauce

(Ready in about 1 hour 22 minutes | Servings 4)

Per serving: 296 Calories; 14.6g Fat; 6.2g Carbs; 36g Protein; 0.5g Sugars; 0.5g Fiber

INGREDIENTS

1½ pounds beef, cubed
½ cup full fat sour cream
1/2 cup white wine
2 teaspoons dried rosemary
1½ tablespoon herb vinegar
1 teaspoon sweet paprika

3 cloves garlic, minced
2 tablespoons extra-virgin olive oil
2 teaspoons dried basil
1 tablespoon mayonnaise
Salt and ground black pepper, to taste

DIRECTIONS

In a large-sized mixing bowl, whisk together the oil, wine, and beef. Now, stir in the seasonings and herb vinegar. Cover and marinate at least 50 minutes.
Then, preheat your Air Fryer to 375 degrees F. Roast the marinated beef for about 18 minutes, turning halfway through.
Meanwhile, make the sauce by mixing the sour cream with the mayonnaise and garlic. Serve the warm beef with the garlic sauce and enjoy!

251. Easy Beef Medallions with Parsley and Peppers

(Ready in about 30 minutes | Servings 4)

Per serving: 335 Calories; 17.4g Fat; 6.1g Carbs; 36.8g Protein; 2.5g Sugars; 1.7g Fiber

INGREDIENTS

2 tablespoons olive oil
2 small bunch parsley, roughly chopped
1 ½ pounds beef medallions
3 bell peppers, seeded and sliced

2 sprigs thyme
1 sprig rosemary
Umami dust seasoning, to taste
Salt and ground black pepper, to taste

DIRECTIONS

Firstly, arrange the vegetables on the bottom of the air fry Air Fryer basket; add seasonings and drizzle with olive oil. Roast for 8 minutes and pause the machine.
Now, place beef medallions on top of the vegetables.
Roast for 18 minutes longer at 375 degrees, stirring once halfway through. To serve, sprinkle with umami dust seasoning and enjoy!

252. Tuscan Beef with Herb Vinegar

(Ready in about 20 minutes | Servings 3)

Per serving: 492 Calories; 40.1g Fat; 4.2g Carbs; 25.9g Protein; 1.1g Sugars; 0.7g Fiber

INGREDIENTS

3 sprigs fresh thyme, chopped
1/3 cup herb vinegar
2 teaspoons Tuscan seasoning
3 beef chops
2 teaspoons garlic powder
Kosher salt and ground black pepper, to taste

DIRECTIONS

Toss the beef chops with the other ingredients.
Roast at 395 degrees F for 16 minutes, turning once or twice. Afterward, taste for doneness, add the seasonings and serve warm. Bon appétit!

FISH & SEAFOOD

253. Snapper Fillets with Nutty Tomato Sauce

(Ready in about 20 minutes | Servings 4)

Per serving: 491 Calories; 38.2g Fat; 7.5g Carbs; 29g Protein; 1.1g Sugars; 3.3g Fiber

INGREDIENTS

4 skin-on snapper fillets
Sea salt and ground pepper, to taste
1/2 cup parmesan cheese, grated
2 tablespoons fresh cilantro, chopped
1/2 cup coconut flour
2 tablespoon flaxseed meal
2 medium-sized eggs
For the Almond sauce:

1/4 cup almonds
2 garlic cloves, pressed
1 cup tomato paste
1 teaspoon dried dill weed
1/2 teaspoon salt
1/4 teaspoon freshly ground mixed peppercorns
1/4 cup olive oil

DIRECTIONS

Season fish fillets with sea salt and pepper.
In a shallow plate, thoroughly combine the parmesan cheese and fresh chopped cilantro.
In another shallow plate, whisk the eggs until frothy. Place the coconut flour and flaxseed meal in a third plate.
Dip the fish fillets in the flour, then in the egg; afterward, coat them with the parmesan mixture. Set the Air Fryer to cook at 390 degrees F; air fry for 14 to 16 minutes or until crisp.
To make the sauce, chop the almonds in a food processor. Add the remaining sauce ingredients, but not the olive oil.
Blitz for 30 seconds; then, slowly and gradually pour in the oil; process until smooth and even. Serve the sauce with the prepared snapper fillets. Bon appétit!

254. Cod Fillets with Garlic and Herbs

(Ready in about 15 minutes | Servings 4)

Per serving: 181 Calories; 8.1g Fat; 3.0g Carbs; 23.8g Protein; 1.1g Sugars; 0.8g Fiber

INGREDIENTS

4 cod fillets
1/4 teaspoon fine sea salt
1/4 teaspoon ground black pepper, or more to taste
1 teaspoon cayenne pepper
1/2 cup non-dairy milk

1/2 cup fresh Italian parsley, coarsely chopped
1 teaspoon dried basil
1/2 teaspoon dried oregano
1 Italian pepper, chopped
4 garlic cloves, minced

DIRECTIONS

Coat the inside of a baking dish with a thin layer of vegetable oil.
Season the cod fillets with salt, pepper, and cayenne pepper.
Next, puree the remaining ingredients in your food processor. Toss the fish fillets with this mixture.
Set the Air Fryer to cook at 380 degrees F. Cook for 10 to 12 minutes or until the cod flakes easily. Bon appétit!

255. Halibut Steaks with Vermouth and Herbs

(Ready in about 15 minutes | Servings 4)

Per serving: 304 Calories; 20.7g Fat; 8.8g Carbs; 22.1g Protein; 8.7g Sugars; 0.6g Fiber

INGREDIENTS

1 pound halibut steaks
Salt and pepper, to your liking
1 teaspoon dried basil
2 tablespoons honey
1/4 cup vegetable oil

2 ½ tablespoons Worcester sauce
1 tablespoon freshly squeezed lemon juice
2 tablespoons vermouth
1 tablespoon fresh parsley leaves, coarsely chopped

DIRECTIONS

Place all the ingredients in a large-sized mixing dish. Gently stir to coat the fish evenly.
Set your Air Fryer to cook at 390 degrees F; roast for 5 minutes. Pause the machine and flip the fish over.
Then, cook for another 5 minutes; check for doneness and cook for a few more minutes as needed. Bon appétit!

256. Classic Parmesan Fish Fillets

(Ready in about 15 minutes | Servings 4)

Per serving: 297 Calories; 7.7g Fat; 5.4g Carbs; 37.5g Protein; 0.8g Sugars; 0.2g Fiber

INGREDIENTS

1 cup parmesan, grated
1 teaspoon garlic powder
1/2 teaspoon shallot powder
1 egg, well whisked

4 white fish fillets
Salt and ground black pepper, to taste
Fresh Italian parsley, to serve

DIRECTIONS

Place the parmesan cheese in a shallow bowl.
In another bowl, combine the garlic powder, shallot powder, and the beaten egg.
Generously season the fish fillets with salt and pepper. Dip each fillet into the beaten egg.
Then, roll the fillets over the parmesan mixture. Set your Air Fryer to cook at 370 degrees F. Air-fry for 10 to 12 minutes.
Serve garnished with fresh parsley and enjoy!

257. Italian Sardinas Fritas

(Ready in about 1 hour 15 minutes | Servings 4)

Per serving: 437 Calories; 26.2g Fat; 3.5g Carbs; 42.5g Protein; 1.7g Sugars; 0.5g Fiber

INGREDIENTS

1 ½ pounds sardines, cleaned and rinsed
Salt and ground black pepper, to savor
1 tablespoon Italian seasoning mix

1 tablespoon lemon juice
1 tablespoon soy sauce
2 tablespoons olive oil

DIRECTIONS

Firstly, pat the sardines dry with a kitchen towel. Add salt, black pepper, Italian seasoning mix, lemon juice, soy sauce, and olive oil; marinate them for 30 minutes.
Air-fry the sardines at 350 degrees F for approximately 5 minutes. Increase the temperature to 385 degrees F and air-fry them for further 7 to 8 minutes.
Then, place the sardines in a nice serving platter. Bon appétit!

258. Aromatic Shrimp with Herbs

(Ready in about 40 minutes | Servings 4)

Per serving: 261 Calories; 9.6g Fat; 1g Carbs; 39.9g Protein; 0g Sugars; 0.2g Fiber

INGREDIENTS

1/2 tablespoon fresh basil leaves, chopped
1 ½ pounds shrimp, shelled and deveined
1 ½ tablespoons olive oil
3 cloves garlic, minced

1 teaspoon smoked cayenne pepper
1/2 teaspoon fresh mint, roughly chopped
½ teaspoon ginger, freshly grated
1 teaspoon sea salt

DIRECTIONS

Firstly, set your Air Fryer to cook at 395 degrees F.
In a mixing dish, combine all of the above items; toss until everything is well combined and let it stand for about 28 minutes.
Air-fry for 3 to 4 minutes. Bon appétit!

259. Shrimp with Garlic and Goat Cheese

(Ready in about 10 minutes | Servings 2)

Per serving: 547 Calories; 31.3g Fat; 4.2g Carbs; 62g Protein; 2.8g Sugars; 0.2g Fiber

INGREDIENTS

1/2 tablespoon fresh parsley, roughly chopped

1 ½ tablespoons balsamic vinegar

Sea salt flakes, to taste

1 pound shrimp, deveined

1 tablespoon coconut aminos

1 teaspoon Dijon mustard

1/2 teaspoon garlic powder

1 ½ tablespoons olive oil

1/2 teaspoon smoked cayenne pepper

Salt and ground black peppercorns, to savor

1 cup goat cheese, shredded

DIRECTIONS

Set the Air Fryer to cook at 385 degrees F.

In a bowl, thoroughly combine all ingredients, except for cheese.

Dump the shrimp into the cooking basket; air-fry for 7 to 8 minutes. Bon appétit!

260. Spicy Tuna Casserole

(Ready in about 20 minutes | Servings 4)

Per serving: 268 Calories; 15.8g Fat; 3.2g Carbs; 27.7g Protein; 1.7g Sugars; 0.3g Fiber

INGREDIENTS

5 eggs, beaten

1/2 chili pepper, deveined and finely minced

1 ½ tablespoons sour cream

1/3 teaspoon dried oregano

1/2 tablespoon sesame oil

1/3 cup yellow onions, chopped

2 cups canned tuna

1/2 bell pepper, deveined and chopped

1/3 teaspoon dried basil

Fine sea salt and ground black pepper, to taste

DIRECTIONS

Warm sesame oil in a nonstick skillet that is preheated over a moderate flame. Then, sweat the onions and peppers for 4 minutes, or until they are just fragrant.

Add chopped canned tuna and stir until heated through.

Meanwhile, lightly grease a baking dish with a pan spray. Throw in sautéed tuna/pepper mix. Add the remaining ingredients in the order listed above.

Bake for 12 minutes at 325 degrees F. Eat warm garnished with Tabasco sauce if desired.

261. Curried Halibut Fillets

(Ready in about 20 minutes | Servings 4)

Per serving: 237 Calories; 17.7g Fat; 5g Carbs; 14.4g Protein; 0.7g Sugars; 0.4g Fiber

INGREDIENTS

2 medium-sized halibut fillets

1 teaspoon curry powder

1/2 teaspoon ground coriander

Kosher salt and freshly cracked mixed peppercorns, to taste

1 ½ tablespoons olive oil

1/2 cup parmesan cheese, grated

2 eggs

1/2 teaspoon hot paprika

A few drizzles of tabasco sauce

DIRECTIONS

Set your Air Fryer to cook at 365 degrees F.

Then, grab two mixing bowls. In the first bowl, combine the parmesan cheese with olive oil.

In another shallow bowl, thoroughly whisk the egg. Next step, evenly drizzle the halibut fillets with Tabasco sauce; add hot paprika, curry, coriander, salt, and cracked mixed peppercorns.

Dip each fish fillet into the whisked egg; now, roll it over the parmesan mix.

Place in a single layer in the Air Fryer cooking basket. Cook for 10 minutes, working in batches. Serve over creamed salad if desired. Bon appétit!

262. Chipotle Salmon Fish Cakes

(Ready in about 2 hours 15 minutes | Servings 4)

Per serving: 401 Calories; 19.4g Fat; 2g Carbs; 53g Protein; 0.9g Sugars; 0.5g Fiber

INGREDIENTS

1/2 teaspoon chipotle powder
1/2 teaspoon butter, at room temperature
1/3 teaspoon smoked cayenne pepper
1/2 teaspoon dried parsley flakes
1/3 teaspoon ground black pepper
1 pound salmon, chopped into 1/2 inch pieces

1 1/2 tablespoons milk
1/2 white onion, peeled and finely chopped
1 teaspoon fine sea salt
2 tablespoons coconut flour
2 tablespoons parmesan cheese, grated

DIRECTIONS

Place all ingredients in a large-sized mixing dish.
Shape into cakes and roll each cake over seasoned breadcrumbs. After that, refrigerate for about 2 hours.
Then, set your Air Fryer to cook at 395 degrees F for 13 minutes.
Serve warm with a dollop of sour cream if desired. Bon appétit!

263. Mediterranean Grilled Scallops

(Ready in about 2 hour 12 minutes | Servings 2)

Per serving: 179 Calories; 10.7g Fat; 7g Carbs; 14g Protein; 1.3g Sugars; 0.8g Fiber

INGREDIENTS

1 1/2 tablespoons coconut aminos
1 tablespoon Mediterranean seasoning mix
1/3 cup shallots, chopped
1/2 tablespoon balsamic vinegar
1 1/2 tablespoons olive oil

1 clove garlic, chopped
1/2 teaspoon ginger, grated
1 pound scallops, cleaned
Belgian endive, for garnish

DIRECTIONS

In a small-sized sauté pan that is placed over a moderate flame, simmer all ingredients, minus scallops and Belgian endive. Allow this mixture to cool down completely.
After that, add the scallops and let them marinate for at least 2 hours in the refrigerator.
Arrange the scallops in a single layer in the Air Fryer grill pan. Spritz with a cooking oil. Air-fry at 345 degrees for 10 minutes, turning halfway through.
Serve immediately with Belgian endive. Bon appétit!

264. Herbed Tuna with Red Onions

(Ready in about 20 minutes | Servings 4)

Per serving: 487 Calories; 19g Fat; 7g Carbs; 68g Protein; 2.8g Sugars; 1.4g Fiber

INGREDIENTS

4 tuna steaks
1/2 pound red onions
4 teaspoons olive oil
1 teaspoon dried rosemary
1 teaspoon dried marjoram

1 tablespoon cayenne pepper
1/2 teaspoon sea salt
1/2 teaspoon black pepper, preferably freshly cracked
1 lemon, sliced

DIRECTIONS

Place the tuna steaks in the lightly greased cooking basket. Top with the pearl onions; add the olive oil, rosemary, marjoram, cayenne pepper, salt, and black pepper.
Bake in the preheated Air Fryer at 400 degrees F for 9 to 10 minutes. Work in two batches.
Serve warm with lemon slices and enjoy!

265. Fried Haddock Fillets

(Ready in about 20 minutes | Servings 2)

Per serving: 434 Calories; 26.3g Fat; 4.3g Carbs; 43g Protein; 0.3g Sugars; 0.2g Fiber

INGREDIENTS

2 haddock fillets
1/2 cup parmesan cheese, freshly grated
1 teaspoon dried parsley flakes
1 egg, beaten

1/2 teaspoon coarse sea salt
1/4 teaspoon ground black pepper
1/4 teaspoon cayenne pepper
2 tablespoons olive oil

DIRECTIONS

Start by preheating your Air Fryer to 360 degrees F. Pat dry the haddock fillets and set aside.
In a shallow bowl, thoroughly combine the parmesan and parsley flakes. Mix until everything is well incorporated.
In a separate shallow bowl, whisk the egg with salt, black pepper, and cayenne pepper.
Dip the haddock fillets into the egg. Then, dip the fillets into the parmesan mixture until well coated on all sides.
Drizzle the olive oil all over the fish fillets. Lower the coated fillets into the lightly greased Air Fryer basket. Cook for 11 to 13 minutes. Bon appétit!

266. Summer Shrimp Skewers

(Ready in about 15 minutes + marinating time | Servings 4)

Per serving: 228 Calories; 7.2g Fat; 4.9g Carbs; 25.5g Protein; 1.7g Sugars; 0.3g Fiber

INGREDIENTS

1 ½ pounds shrimp
1/4 cup vermouth
2 cloves garlic, crushed
Kosher salt, to taste

1/4 teaspoon black pepper, freshly ground
2 tablespoons olive oil
8 skewers, soaked in water for 30 minutes
1 lemon, cut into wedges

DIRECTIONS

Add the shrimp, vermouth, garlic, salt, black pepper, and olive oil in a ceramic bowl; let it sit for 1 hour in your refrigerator.
Discard the marinade and toss the shrimp with flour. Thread on to skewers and transfer to the lightly greased cooking basket.
Cook at 400 degrees F for 5 minutes, tossing halfway through. Serve with lemon wedges. Bon appétit!

267. Lobster Tails with Olives and Butter

(Ready in about 20 minutes | Servings 5)

Per serving: 189 Calories; 6.9g Fat; 1.8g Carbs; 30.4g Protein; 0.5g Sugars; 0.3g Fiber

INGREDIENTS

2 pounds fresh lobster tails, cleaned and halved, in shells
2 tablespoons butter, melted
1 teaspoon onion powder
1 teaspoon cayenne pepper

Salt and ground black pepper, to taste
2 garlic cloves, minced
1 cup green olives

DIRECTIONS

In a plastic closeable bag, thoroughly combine all ingredients; shake to combine well.
Transfer the coated lobster tails to the greased cooking basket.
Cook in the preheated Air Fryer at 390 degrees for 6 to 7 minutes, shaking the basket halfway through. Work in batches.
Serve with green olives and enjoy!

268. Piri Piri King Prawns

(Ready in about 10 minutes | Servings 2)

Per serving: 220 Calories; 9.7g Fat; 15.1g Carbs; 17.6g Protein; 2.2g Sugars; 1.1g Fiber

INGREDIENTS

12 king prawns, rinsed
1 tablespoon coconut oil
1/2 teaspoon piri piri powder
Salt and ground black pepper, to taste

1 teaspoon garlic paste
1 teaspoon onion powder
1/2 teaspoon cumin powder
1 teaspoon curry powder

DIRECTIONS

In a mixing bowl, toss all ingredient until the prawns are well coated on all sides.
Cook in the preheated Air Fryer at 360 degrees F for 4 minutes. Shake the basket and cook for 4 minutes more.
Serve over hot rice if desired. Bon appétit!

269. Tuna Patties with Cheese Sauce

(Ready in about 2 hours 20 minutes | Servings 4)

Per serving: 309 Calories; 15.3g Fat; 7.8g Carbs; 31.2g Protein; 1g Sugars; 0.3g Fiber

INGREDIENTS

1 pound canned tuna, drained
1 egg, whisked
1 garlic clove, minced
2 tablespoons shallots, minced
1 cup Romano cheese, grated
Sea salt and ground black pepper, to taste

1 tablespoon sesame oil
Cheese Sauce:
1 tablespoon butter
1 cup beer
2 tablespoons Colby cheese, grated

DIRECTIONS

In a mixing bowl, thoroughly combine the tuna, egg, garlic, shallots, Romano cheese, salt, and black pepper. Shape the tuna mixture into four patties and place in your refrigerator for 2 hours.
Brush the patties with sesame oil on both sides. Cook in the preheated Air Fryer at 360 degrees F for 14 minutes.
In the meantime, melt the butter in a pan over a moderate heat. Add the beer and whisk until it starts bubbling.
Now, stir in the grated cheese and cook for 3 to 4 minutes longer or until the cheese has melted. Spoon the sauce over the fish cake burgers and serve immediately.

270. Snapper Fillets with Thai Sauce

(Ready in about 30 minutes + marinating time | Servings 2)

Per serving: 420 Calories; 24g Fat; 4.5g Carbs; 48.4g Protein; 2.4g Sugars; 1.4g Fiber

INGREDIENTS

1/2 cup full-fat coconut milk
2 tablespoons lemon juice
1 teaspoon fresh ginger, grated

2 snapper fillets
1 tablespoon olive oil
Salt and white pepper, to taste

DIRECTIONS

Place the milk, lemon juice, and ginger in a glass bowl; add fish and let it marinate for 1 hour.
Removed the fish from the milk mixture and place in the Air Fryer basket. Drizzle olive oil all over the fish fillets.
Cook in the preheated Air Fryer at 390 degrees F for 15 minutes.
Meanwhile, heat the milk mixture over medium-high heat; bring to a rapid boil, stirring continuously. Reduce to simmer and add the salt, and pepper; continue to cook 12 minutes more.
Spoon the sauce over the warm snapper fillets and serve immediately. Bon appétit!

271. Spicy Shrimp Kebab

(Ready in about 25 minutes | Servings 4)

Per serving: 247 Calories; 8.4g Fat; 6g Carbs; 36.4g Protein; 3.5g Sugars; 1.8g Fiber

INGREDIENTS

1 ½ pounds jumbo shrimp, cleaned, shelled and deveined
1 pound cherry tomatoes
2 tablespoons butter, melted
1 tablespoons Sriracha sauce
Sea salt and ground black pepper, to taste

1/2 teaspoon dried oregano
1/2 teaspoon dried basil
1 teaspoon dried parsley flakes
1/2 teaspoon marjoram
1/2 teaspoon mustard seeds

DIRECTIONS

Toss all ingredients in a mixing bowl until the shrimp and tomatoes are covered on all sides.
Soak the wooden skewers in water for 15 minutes.
Thread the jumbo shrimp and cherry tomatoes onto skewers. Cook in the preheated Air Fryer at 400 degrees F for 5 minutes, working with batches. Bon appétit!

272. Crumbed Fish Fillets with Tarragon

(Ready in about 25 minutes | Servings 4)

Per serving: 305 Calories; 17.7g Fat; 6.3g Carbs; 27.2g Protein; 0.3g Sugars; 0.1g Fiber

INGREDIENTS

2 eggs, beaten
1/2 teaspoon tarragon
4 fish fillets, halved
2 tablespoons dry white wine

1/3 cup parmesan cheese, grated
1 teaspoon seasoned salt
1/3 teaspoon mixed peppercorns
1/2 teaspoon fennel seed

DIRECTIONS

Add the parmesan cheese, salt, peppercorns, fennel seeds, and tarragon to your food processor; blitz for about 20 seconds.
Drizzle fish fillets with dry white wine. Dump the egg into a shallow dish.
Now, coat the fish fillets with the beaten egg on all sides; then, coat them with the seasoned cracker mix.
Air-fry at 345 degrees F for about 17 minutes. Bon appétit!

273. Smoked and Creamed White Fish

(Ready in about 20 minutes | Servings 4)

Per serving: 249 Calories; 22.1g Fat; 7.6g Carbs; 5.3g Protein; 3.1g Sugars; 0.7g Fiber

INGREDIENTS

1/2 tablespoon yogurt
1/3 cup spring garlic, finely chopped
Fresh chopped chives, for garnish
3 eggs, beaten
1/2 teaspoon dried dill weed
1 teaspoon dried rosemary
1/3 cup scallions, chopped

1/3 cup smoked white fish, chopped
1 ½ tablespoons crème fraîche
1 teaspoon kosher salt
1 teaspoon dried marjoram
1/3 teaspoon ground black pepper, or more to taste
Cooking spray

DIRECTIONS

Firstly, spritz four oven safe ramekins with cooking spray. Then, divide smoked whitefish, spring garlic, and scallions among greased ramekins.
Crack an egg into each ramekin; add the crème, yogurt and all seasonings.
Now, air-fry approximately 13 minutes at 355 degrees F. Taste for doneness and eat warm garnished with fresh chives. Bon appétit!

274. Parmesan and Paprika Baked Tilapia

(Ready in about 20 minutes | Servings 6)

Per serving: 294 Calories; 16.1g Fat; 2.7g Carbs; 35.9g Protein; 0.1g Sugars; 0.2g Fiber

INGREDIENTS

1 cup parmesan cheese, grated
1 teaspoon paprika
1 teaspoon dried dill weed
2 pounds tilapia fillets

1/3 cup mayonnaise
1/2 tablespoon lime juice
Salt and ground black pepper, to taste

DIRECTIONS

Mix the mayonnaise, parmesan, paprika, salt, black pepper, and dill weed until everything is thoroughly combined.
Then, drizzle tilapia fillets with the lime juice.
Cover each fish fillet with Parmesan/mayo mixture; roll them in parmesan/paprika mixture. Bake at 335 for about 10 minutes. Eat warm and enjoy!

275. Tangy Cod Fillets

(Ready in about 20 minutes | Servings 2)

Per serving: 291 Calories; 11.1g Fat; 2.7g Carbs; 41.6g Protein; 1.2g Sugars; 0.5g Fiber

INGREDIENTS

1 ½ tablespoons sesame oil
1/2 heaping teaspoon dried parsley flakes
1/3 teaspoon fresh lemon zest, finely grated
2 medium-sized cod fillets

1 teaspoon sea salt flakes
A pinch of salt and pepper
1/3 teaspoon ground black pepper, or more to savor
1/2 tablespoon fresh lemon juice

DIRECTIONS

Set the Air Fryer to cook at 375 degrees F. Season each cod fillet with sea salt flakes, black pepper and dried parsley flakes. Now, drizzle them with sesame oil.
Place the seasoned cod fillets in a single layer at the bottom of the cooking basket; air-fry approximately 10 minutes.
While the fillets are cooking, prepare the sauce by mixing the other ingredients. Serve cod fillets on four individual plates garnished with the creamy citrus sauce. Bon appétit!

276. Fish and Cauliflower Cakes

(Ready in about 2 hours 20 minutes | Servings 4)

Per serving: 285 Calories; 15.1g Fat; 4.3g Carbs; 31.1g Protein; 1.6g Sugars; 1.3g Fiber

INGREDIENTS

1/2 pound cauliflower florets
1/2 teaspoon English mustard
2 tablespoons butter, room temperature
1/2 tablespoon cilantro, minced

2 tablespoons sour cream
2 ½ cups cooked white fish
Salt and freshly cracked black pepper, to savor

DIRECTIONS

Boil the cauliflower until tender. Then, purée the cauliflower in your blender. Transfer to a mixing dish.
Now, stir in the fish, cilantro, salt, and black pepper.
Add the sour cream, English mustard, and butter; mix until everything's well incorporated. Using your hands, shape into patties.
Place in the refrigerator for about 2 hours. Cook for 13 minutes at 395 degrees F. Serve with some extra English mustard.

277. Marinated Scallops with Butter and Beer

(Ready in about 1 hour 10 minutes | Servings 4)

Per serving: 471 Calories; 27.3g Fat; 1.9g Carbs; 54g Protein; 0.2g Sugars; 0.1g Fiber

INGREDIENTS

2 pounds sea scallops
1/2 cup beer
4 tablespoons butter

2 sprigs rosemary, only leaves
Sea salt and freshly cracked black pepper, to taste

DIRECTIONS

In a ceramic dish, mix the sea scallops with beer; let it marinate for 1 hour.
Meanwhile, preheat your Air Fryer to 400 degrees F. Melt the butter and add the rosemary leaves. Stir for a few minutes.
Discard the marinade and transfer the sea scallops to the Air Fryer basket. Season with salt and black pepper.
Cook the scallops in the preheated Air Fryer for 7 minutes, shaking the basket halfway through the cooking time. Work in batches.
Bon appétit!

278. Cheesy Fish Gratin

(Ready in about 30 minutes | Servings 4)

Per serving: 335 Calories; 18.1g Fat; 7.8g Carbs; 33.7g Protein; 2.6g Sugars; 0.6g Fiber

INGREDIENTS

1 tablespoon avocado oil
1 pound hake fillets
1 teaspoon garlic powder
Sea salt and ground white pepper, to taste
2 tablespoons shallots, chopped
1 bell pepper, seeded and chopped

1/2 cup Cottage cheese
1/2 cup sour cream
1 egg, well whisked
1 teaspoon yellow mustard
1 tablespoon lime juice
1/2 cup Swiss cheese, shredded

DIRECTIONS

Brush the bottom and sides of a casserole dish with avocado oil. Add the hake fillets to the casserole dish and sprinkle with garlic powder, salt, and pepper.
Add the chopped shallots and bell peppers.
In a mixing bowl, thoroughly combine the Cottage cheese, sour cream, egg, mustard, and lime juice. Pour the mixture over fish and spread evenly.
Cook in the preheated Air Fryer at 370 degrees F for 10 minutes.
Top with the Swiss cheese and cook an additional 7 minutes. Let it rest for 10 minutes before slicing and serving. Bon appétit!

279. Fijan Coconut Fish

(Ready in about 20 minutes + marinating time | Servings 2)

Per serving: 426 Calories; 21.5g Fat; 9.4g Carbs; 50.2g Protein; 5g Sugars; 3.4g Fiber

INGREDIENTS

1 cup coconut milk
2 tablespoons lime juice
2 tablespoons Shoyu sauce
Salt and white pepper, to taste
1 teaspoon turmeric powder

1/2 teaspoon ginger powder
1/2 Thai Bird's Eye chili, seeded and finely chopped
1 pound tilapia
2 tablespoons olive oil

DIRECTIONS

In a mixing bowl, thoroughly combine the coconut milk with the lime juice, Shoyu sauce, salt, pepper, turmeric, ginger, and chili pepper.
Add tilapia and let it marinate for 1 hour.
Brush the Air Fryer basket with olive oil. Discard the marinade and place the tilapia fillets in the Air Fryer basket.
Cook the tilapia in the preheated Air Fryer at 400 degrees F for 6 minutes; turn them over and cook for 6 minutes more. Work in batches.
Serve with some extra lime wedges if desired. Enjoy!

280. Sole Fish and Cauliflower Fritters

(Ready in about 30 minutes | Servings 2)

Per serving: 322 Calories; 14g Fat; 27.4g Carbs; 22.1g Protein; 4.2g Sugars; 3.5g Fiber

INGREDIENTS

1/2 pound sole fillets
1/2 pound mashed cauliflower
1 egg, well beaten
1/2 cup red onion, chopped
2 garlic cloves, minced
2 tablespoons fresh parsley, chopped

1 bell pepper, finely chopped
1/2 teaspoon scotch bonnet pepper, minced
1 tablespoon olive oil
1 tablespoon coconut aminos
1/2 teaspoon paprika
Salt and white pepper, to taste

DIRECTIONS

Start by preheating your Air Fryer to 395 degrees F. Spritz the sides and bottom of the cooking basket with cooking spray.
Cook the sole fillets in the preheated Air Fryer for 10 minutes, flipping them halfway through the cooking time.
In a mixing bowl, mash the sole fillets into flakes. Stir in the remaining ingredients. Shape the fish mixture into patties.
Bake in the preheated Air Fryer at 390 degrees F for 14 minutes, flipping them halfway through the cooking time. Bon appétit!

281. French-Style Sea Bass

(Ready in about 15 minutes | Servings 2)

Per serving: 384 Calories; 28.5g Fat; 3.5g Carbs; 27.6g Protein; 1g Sugars; 1g Fiber

INGREDIENTS

1 tablespoon olive oil
2 sea bass fillets
Sauce:
1/2 cup mayonnaise

1 tablespoon capers, drained and chopped
1 tablespoon gherkins, drained and chopped
2 tablespoons scallions, finely chopped
2 tablespoons lemon juice

DIRECTIONS

Start by preheating your Air Fryer to 395 degrees F. Drizzle olive oil all over the fish fillets.
Cook the sea bass in the preheated Air Fryer for 10 minutes, flipping them halfway through the cooking time.
Meanwhile, make the sauce by whisking the remaining ingredients until everything is well incorporated. Place in the refrigerator until ready to serve. Bon appétit!

282. Asian-Style Salmon Burgers

(Ready in about 15 minutes | Servings 4)

Per serving: 301 Calories; 15.1g Fat; 5.6g Carbs; 33.1g Protein; 1.4g Sugars; 0.2g Fiber

INGREDIENTS

1 pound salmon
1 egg
1 garlic clove, minced
2 green onions, minced
1 cup parmesan cheese

Sauce:
1 teaspoon rice wine
1 ½ tablespoons soy sauce
A pinch of salt
1 teaspoon gochugaru (Korean red chili pepper flakes)

DIRECTIONS

Start by preheating your Air Fryer to 380 degrees F. Spritz the Air Fryer basket with cooking oil.
Mix the salmon, egg, garlic, green onions, and parmesan cheese in a bowl; knead with your hands until everything is well incorporated.
Shape the mixture into equally sized patties. Transfer your patties to the Air Fryer basket.
Cook the fish patties for 10 minutes, turning them over halfway through.
Meanwhile, make the sauce by whisking all ingredients. Serve the warm fish patties with the sauce on the side.

283. Crusted Flounder Fillets

(Ready in about 20 minutes | Servings 2)

Per serving: 325 Calories; 18.3g Fat; 6.1g Carbs; 34.4g Protein; 2.2g Sugars; 1.7g Fiber

INGREDIENTS

2 flounder fillets

1 egg

1/2 teaspoon Worcestershire sauce

1/4 cup coconut flour

1/4 cup almond flour

1/2 teaspoon lemon pepper

1/2 teaspoon coarse sea salt

1/4 teaspoon chili powder

DIRECTIONS

Rinse and pat dry the flounder fillets.

Whisk the egg and Worcestershire sauce in a shallow bowl. In a separate bowl, mix the coconut flour, almond flour, lemon pepper, salt, and chili powder.

Then, dip the fillets into the egg mixture. Lastly, coat the fish fillets with the coconut flour mixture until they are coated on all sides.

Spritz with cooking spray and transfer to the Air Fryer basket. Cook at 390 degrees for 7 minutes.

Turn them over, spritz with cooking spray on the other side, and cook another 5 minutes. Bon appétit!

284. Pecan Crusted Tilapia

(Ready in about 20 minutes | Servings 5)

Per serving: 264 Calories; 17.1g Fat; 3.9g Carbs; 25.5g Protein; 1g Sugars; 2g Fiber

INGREDIENTS

2 tablespoons ground flaxseeds

1 teaspoon paprika

Sea salt and white pepper, to taste

1 teaspoon garlic paste

2 tablespoons extra-virgin olive oil

1/2 cup pecans, ground

5 tilapia fillets, slice into halves

DIRECTIONS

Combine the ground flaxseeds, paprika, salt, white pepper, garlic paste, olive oil, and ground pecans in a Ziploc bag. Add the fish fillets and shake to coat well.

Spritz the Air Fryer basket with cooking spray. Cook in the preheated Air Fryer at 400 degrees F for 10 minutes; turn them over and cook for 6 minutes more. Work in batches.

Serve with lemon wedges, if desired. Enjoy!

285. Grilled Salmon with Butter and Wine

(Ready in about 45 minutes | Servings 4)

Per serving: 516 Calories; 25.6g Fat; 2.4g Carbs; 65.7g Protein; 0.7g Sugars; 0.5g Fiber

INGREDIENTS

2 cloves garlic, minced

4 tablespoons butter, melted

Sea salt and ground black pepper, to taste

1 teaspoon smoked paprika

1/2 teaspoon onion powder

1 tablespoon lime juice

1/4 cup dry white wine

4 salmon steaks

DIRECTIONS

Place all ingredients in a large ceramic dish. Cover and let it marinate for 30 minutes in the refrigerator.

Arrange the salmon steaks on the grill pan. Bake at 390 degrees for 5 minutes, or until the salmon steaks are easily flaked with a fork.

Flip the fish steaks, baste with the reserved marinade, and cook another 5 minutes. Bon appétit!

286. Garlicky Grilled Shrimp

(Ready in about 35 minutes | Servings 4)

Per serving: 188 Calories; 8.9g Fat; 3.5g Carbs; 23.1g Protein; 0g Sugars; 0.5g Fiber

INGREDIENTS

18 shrimps, shelled and deveined
2 tablespoons freshly squeezed lemon juice
1/2 teaspoon hot paprika
1/2 teaspoon salt
1 teaspoon lemon-pepper seasoning

2 tablespoons extra-virgin olive oil
2 garlic cloves, peeled and minced
1 teaspoon onion powder
1/4 teaspoon cumin powder
1/2 cup fresh parsley, coarsely chopped

DIRECTIONS

Place all the ingredients in a mixing dish; gently stir, cover and let it marinate for 30 minutes in the refrigerator.
Air-fry in the preheated Air Fryer at 400 degrees F for 5 minutes or until the shrimps turn pink. Bon appétit!

287. Tilapia with Cheesy Caper Sauce

(Ready in about 15 minutes | Servings 4)

Per serving: 253 Calories; 13.1g Fat; 3.5g Carbs; 21.5g Protein; 0.6g Sugars; 0.1g Fiber

INGREDIENTS

4 tilapia fillets
1 tablespoon extra-virgin olive oil
Celery salt, to taste
Freshly cracked pink peppercorns, to taste
For the Creamy Caper Sauce:

1/2 cup crème fraîche
2 tablespoons mayonnaise
1/4 cup Cottage cheese, at room temperature
1 tablespoon capers, finely chopped

DIRECTIONS

Toss the tilapia fillets with olive oil, celery salt, and cracked peppercorns until they are well coated.
Place the fillets in a single layer at the bottom of the Air Fryer cooking basket. Air-fry at 360 degrees F for about 12 minutes; turn them over once during cooking.
Meanwhile, prepare the sauce by mixing the remaining items.
Lastly, garnish air-fried tilapia fillets with the sauce and serve immediately!

288. Japanese Flounder with Chives

(Ready in about 15 minutes + marinating time | Servings 4)

Per serving: 288 Calories; 18.3g Fat; 5.1g Carbs; 19.8g Protein; 3.2g Sugars; 0.4g Fiber

INGREDIENTS

4 flounder fillets
Sea salt and freshly cracked mixed peppercorns, to taste
1 ½ tablespoons dark sesame oil
2 tablespoons sake

1/4 cup soy sauce
1 tablespoon grated lemon rind
2 garlic cloves, minced
2 tablespoons chopped chives, to serve

DIRECTIONS

Place all the ingredients, without the chives, in a large-sized mixing dish. Cover and allow it to marinate for about 2 hours in your fridge.
Remove the fish from the marinade and cook in the Air Fryer cooking basket at 360 degrees F for 10 to 12 minutes; flip once during cooking.
Pour the remaining marinade into a pan that is preheated over a medium-low heat; let it simmer, stirring continuously, until it has thickened.
Pour the prepared glaze over flounder and serve garnished with fresh chives.

289. Garlic Lemony Shrimp

(Ready in about 10 minutes | Servings 4)

Per serving: 224 Calories; 14.1g Fat; 2g Carbs; 23.1g Protein; 0.7g Sugars; 0.3g Fiber

INGREDIENTS

1 teaspoon crushed red pepper flakes, or more to taste
2 cloves garlic, finely minced
Garlic pepper, to savor
1 ½ tablespoons fresh parsley, roughly chopped

1 pound shrimps, deveined
1 ½ tablespoons lemon juice
4 tablespoons olive oil
Sea salt flakes, to taste

DIRECTIONS

Set the air fryer to cook at 385 degrees F.
In a bowl, thoroughly combine all the ingredients, coating the shrimps on all sides.
Dump the shrimps into the cooking basket; air-fry for 7 to 8 minutes in the grill pan. Bon appétit!

290. Dilled Crab and Cauliflower Cakes

(Ready in about 20 minutes | Servings 4)

Per serving: 184 Calories; 11.6g Fat; 3.2g Carbs; 16.2g Protein; 1.5g Sugars; 1.4g Fiber

INGREDIENTS

1 ½ tablespoons mayonnaise
1/2 teaspoon whole-grain mustard
2 eggs, well beaten
1/3 teaspoon ground black pepper
1/2 pound cup mashed cauliflower

1/2 teaspoon dried dill weed
1/2 pound crabmeat
A pinch of salt
1 ½ tablespoons softened butter

DIRECTIONS

Mix all the ingredients thoroughly. Shape into 4 patties.
Then, spritz your patties with cooking oil.
Air-fry at 365 degrees F for 12 minutes, turning halfway through. Serve over boiled potatoes. Bon appétit!

291. Rockfish with Greek Avocado Cream

(Ready in about 15 minutes + marinating time | Servings 4)

Per serving: 347 Calories; 25.7g Fat; 6.9g Carbs; 22.7g Protein; 2.3g Sugars; 3.4g Fiber

INGREDIENTS

For the Fish Fillets:
1 1/2 tablespoons balsamic vinegar
1/2 cup vegetable broth
1/3 teaspoon shallot powder
1 tablespoon soy sauce
4 Rockfish fillets
1 teaspoon ground black pepper
1 ½ tablespoons olive oil
Fine sea salt, to taste
1/3 teaspoon garlic powder

For the Avocado Cream:
2 tablespoons Greek-style yogurt
1 clove garlic, peeled and minced
1 teaspoon ground black pepper
1/2 tablespoon olive oil
1/3 cup vegetable broth
1 avocado
1/2 teaspoon lime juice
1/3 teaspoon fine sea salt

DIRECTIONS

In a bowl, wash and pat the fillets dry using some paper towels. Add all the seasonings. In another bowl, stir in the remaining ingredients for the fish fillets.
Add the seasoned fish fillets; cover and let the fillets marinate in your refrigerator at least 3 hours.
Then, set your Air Fryer to cook at 325 degrees F. Cook marinated rockfish fillets in the air fryer grill basket for 9 minutes.
In the meantime, prepare the avocado sauce by mixing all the ingredients with an immersion blender or regular blender. Serve the rockfish fillets topped with the avocado sauce. Enjoy!

292. Salmon with Cilantro and Citrus Sauce

(Ready in about 50 minutes | Servings 4)

Per serving: 304 Calories; 15.2g Fat; 1.7g Carbs; 38.1g Protein; 0.5g Sugars; 0.1g Fiber

INGREDIENTS

1 ½ pounds salmon steak
½ teaspoon grated lemon zest
Freshly cracked mixed peppercorns, to taste
1/3 cup lemon juice

Fresh chopped chives, for garnish
1/2 cup dry white wine
1/2 teaspoon fresh cilantro, chopped
Fine sea salt, to taste

DIRECTIONS

To prepare the marinade, place all ingredients, except for salmon steak and chives, in a deep pan. Bring to a boil over medium-high flame until it has reduced by half. Allow it to cool down.

After that, allow salmon steak to marinate in the refrigerator approximately 40 minutes. Discard the marinade and transfer the fish steak to the preheated Air Fryer.

Air-fry at 400 degrees F for 9 to10 minutes. To finish, brush hot fish steaks with the reserved marinade, garnish with fresh chopped chives, and serve right away!

293. Cod Fillets with Lemon and Mustard

(Ready in about 20 minutes | Servings 2)

Per serving: 501 Calories; 35.2g Fat; 32.4g Carbs; 30.9g Protein; 6.2g Sugars; 1.1g Fiber

INGREDIENTS

2 medium-sized cod fillets
1/2 tablespoon fresh lemon juice
1 ½ tablespoons olive oil
1/2 tablespoon whole-grain mustard

Sea salt and ground black pepper, to savor
1/2 cup coconut flour
2 eggs

DIRECTIONS

Set your Air Fryer to cook at 355 degrees F. Thoroughly combine olive oil and coconut flour in a shallow bowl.

In another shallow bowl, whisk the egg. Drizzle each cod fillet with lemon juice and spread with mustard. Then, sprinkle each fillet with salt and ground black pepper.

Dip each fish fillet into the whisked egg; now, roll it in the olive oil/breadcrumb mix.

Place in a single layer in the Air Fryer cooking basket. Cook for 10 minutes, working in batches, turning once or twice. Serve with potato salad. Bon appétit!

294. Mediterranean Crab Cakes with Capers

(Ready in about 20 minutes | Servings 5)

Per serving: 392Calories; 11.3g Fat; 49g Carbs; 23.1g Protein; 0.2g Sugars; 0.3g Fiber

INGREDIENTS

1/3 teaspoon ground black pepper
1/2 tablespoon nonpareil capers
3 eggs, well whisked
½ teaspoon dried dill weed
1 1/2 tablespoons softened butter

1/2 teaspoon whole-grain mustard
1 1/2 pound backfin blue crabmeat
1 cup Romano cheese, grated
2 ½ tablespoons mayonnaise
A pinch of salt

DIRECTIONS

Mix all the ingredients thoroughly. Shape into 4 balls and press each ball to form the cakes.

Then, spritz your cakes with cooking oil.

Air-fry at 365 degrees F for 12 minutes, turning halfway through. Bon appétit!

295. Classic Coconut Shrimp

(Ready in about 25 minutes | Servings 4)

Per serving: 346 Calories; 12.6g Fat; 8.7g Carbs; 52.2g Protein; 1.2g Sugars; 6.1g Fiber

INGREDIENTS

1/3 teaspoon paprika
3 egg whites
1/3 cup unsweetened coconut, shredded
1 teaspoon salt
12 large shrimps, peeled and de-veined

1/2 cup flaxseed meal
Lime slices, for garnish
A pinch of ground allspice
Grated zest of 1/2 small-sized lime

DIRECTIONS

Set up a dredging station with three mixing bowls. Dump the flaxseed meal into the first bowl. Beat the eggs whites in another bowl.
In the third bowl, combine the coconut, lime zest, allspice, salt and paprika. Set the Air Fryer to cook at 395 degrees F.
Dredge your shrimps in the flaxseed mixture; then, coat them with egg whites on all sides; lastly, press them into the coconut mixture.
Make sure to coat well.
Spritz each shrimp on all sides with cooking oil. Air-fry for 7 to 8 minutes, working in two batches.
Turn the temperature to 335 degrees F. Air-fry an additional 3 minutes. Serve with lime slices on a nice serving platter. Bon appétit!

296. Fish Fingers with Dijon Mayo Sauce

(Ready in about 15 minutes | Servings 4)

Per serving: 460 Calories; 37.4g Fat; 4.1g Carbs; 26g Protein; 0.9g Sugars; 1.1g Fiber

INGREDIENTS

For the Fish:
1 pound white fish, cut into strips
1 ½ tablespoons olive oil
1/2 teaspoon garlic salt
1 teaspoon red pepper flakes, crushed
1/2 teaspoon dried dill weed
1/2 cup coconut flour

1/2 cup parmesan cheese, grated
2 medium-sized eggs, well whisked
For the Dijon Sauce:
1 ½ tablespoons Dijon mustard
1/2 cup mayonnaise
1/2 teaspoon lemon juice, freshly squeezed

DIRECTIONS

Rub the fish strips with olive oil, salt, red pepper and dill weed. Then, prepare three shallow bowls.
Put the coconut flour into the first bowl. In another shallow bowl, place the eggs; in the third one, the parmesan cheese.
Meanwhile, preheat your machine to cook at 385 degrees F. Cover the fish strips with the coconut flour, and then with the eggs; finally, roll each fish piece over the parmesan cheese.
Air-fry for 5 minutes, then pause the machine, flip them over and cook for another 5 minutes or until cooked through.
In the meantime, make the sauce by mixing together all the sauce ingredients. Serve as a dipping sauce and enjoy!

297. Curried Fish Patties with Green Beans

(Ready in about 1 hour 20 minutes | Servings 4)

Per serving: 231 Calories; 12.5g Fat; 6.1g Carbs; 23.2g Protein; 2.6g Sugars; 2g Fiber

INGREDIENTS

1 pound whitefish fillets, minced
1/2 pound green beans, finely chopped
1/2 cup scallions, chopped
1 chili pepper, deveined and minced
1 tablespoon red curry paste
1 tablespoon fish sauce

2 tablespoons apple cider vinegar
1 teaspoon water
Sea salt flakes, to taste
1/2 teaspoon cracked black peppercorns
2 tablespoons butter, at room temperature
1/2 teaspoon lemon

DIRECTIONS

Add all ingredients in the order listed above to the mixing dish. Mix to combine well using a spatula or your hands.
Form into small cakes and chill for 1 hour. Place a piece of aluminum foil over the cooking basket. Place the cakes on foil.
Cook at 390 degrees F for 10 minutes; pause the machine, flip each fish cake over and air-fry for additional 5 minutes. Mound a cucumber relish onto the plates; add the fish cakes and serve warm.

298. Filipino Fried Bangus

(Ready in about 10 minutes + marinating time | Servings 4)

Per serving: 243 Calories; 14.4g Fat; 2.1g Carbs; 24.7g Protein; 1.2g Sugars; 0.1g Fiber

INGREDIENTS

A belly of 2 milkfish, deboned and sliced into 4 portions
3/4 teaspoon salt
1/4 teaspoon ground black pepper
1/4 teaspoon cumin powder
2 tablespoons calamansi juice
2 lemongrass, trimmed and cut crosswise into small pieces

1/2 cup rice wine
2 tablespoons fish sauce (Patis)
1 teaspoon garlic powder
1/2 cup chicken broth
2 tablespoons olive oil

DIRECTIONS

Firstly, pat the fish dry using kitchen towels. Put the fish into a large-sized mixing dish; add the remaining ingredients and marinate for 3 hours in the refrigerator.

Cook the fish steaks on an Air Fryer grill basket at 340 degrees F for 5 minutes.

Pause the machine, flip the steaks over and set the timer for 4 more minutes. Cook until the color turns medium brown. Serve over mashed cauliflower and enjoy!

299. Grilled Fish and Celery Burgers

(Ready in about 10 minutes + chilling time | Servings 4)

Per serving: 241 Calories; 11.5g Fat; 2.3g Carbs; 29.9g Protein; 0.2g Sugars; 0.3g Fiber

INGREDIENTS

2 cans canned tuna fish
2 celery stalks, trimmed and finely chopped
1 egg, whisked
1/2 cup parmesan cheese, grated

1 teaspoon whole-grain mustard
1/2 teaspoon sea salt
1/4 teaspoon freshly cracked black peppercorns
1 teaspoon paprika

DIRECTIONS

Mix all of the above ingredients in the order listed above; mix to combine well and shape into four cakes; chill for 50 minutes.

Place on an Air Fryer grill pan. Spritz each cake with a non-stick cooking spray, covering all sides.

Grill at 360 degrees F for 5 minutes; then, pause the machine, flip the cakes over and set the timer for another 3 minutes. Serve over mashed potatoes.

300. Fried Shrimp with Chipotle Sauce

(Ready in about 10 minutes | Servings 4)

Per serving: 288 Calories; 11.2g Fat; 0.2g Carbs; 45.1g Protein; 0g Sugars; 0.1g Fiber

INGREDIENTS

12 jumbo shrimp
1/2 teaspoon garlic salt
1/4 teaspoon freshly cracked mixed peppercorns
For the Sauce:
1 teaspoon Dijon mustard

4 tablespoons mayonnaise
1 teaspoon lemon rind, grated
1 teaspoon chipotle powder
1/2 teaspoon cumin powder

DIRECTIONS

Season your shrimp with garlic salt and cracked peppercorns.

Now, air-fry them in the cooking basket at 395 degrees F for 5 minutes. After that, pause the machine. Flip them over and set the timer for 2 more minutes.

Meanwhile, mix all ingredients for the sauce; whisk to combine well. Serve with the warm shrimps. Bon appétit!

301. Cajun Fish Fritters

(Ready in about 30 minutes | Servings 4)

Per serving: 478 Calories; 30.1g Fat; 27.2g Carbs; 23.8g Protein; 2g Sugars; 0.1g Fiber

INGREDIENTS

2 catfish fillets
1 cup parmesan cheese
3 ounces butter
1 teaspoon baking powder

1 teaspoon baking soda
1/2 cup buttermilk
1 teaspoon Cajun seasoning
1 cup Swiss cheese, shredded

DIRECTIONS

Bring a pot of salted water to a boil. Boil the fish fillets for 5 minutes or until it is opaque. Flake the fish into small pieces. Mix the remaining ingredients in a bowl; add the fish and mix until well combined. Shape the fish mixture into 12 patties. Cook in the preheated Air Fryer at 380 degrees F for 15 minutes. Work in batches. Enjoy!

302. Paprika Crab Burgers

(Ready in about 2 hours 20 minutes | Servings 3)

Per serving: 279 Calories; 15.4g Fat; 5.7g Carbs; 28.3g Protein; 0.5g Sugars; 0.6g Fiber

INGREDIENTS

2 eggs, beaten
1 shallot, chopped
2 garlic cloves, crushed
1 tablespoon olive oil
1 teaspoon yellow mustard
1 teaspoon fresh cilantro, chopped

10 ounces crab meat
1 teaspoon smoked paprika
1/2 teaspoon ground black pepper
Sea salt, to taste
3/4 cup parmesan cheese

DIRECTIONS

In a mixing bowl, thoroughly combine the eggs, shallot, garlic, olive oil, mustard, cilantro, crab meat, paprika, black pepper, and salt. Mix until well combined.

Shape the mixture into 6 patties. Roll the crab patties over grated parmesan cheese, coating well on all sides. Place in your refrigerator for 2 hours.

Spritz the crab patties with cooking oil on both sides. Cook in the preheated Air Fryer at 360 degrees F for 14 minutes. Serve on dinner rolls if desired. Bon appétit!

303. Greek-Style Monkfish with Vegetables

(Ready in about 20 minutes | Servings 2)

Per serving: 292 Calories; 19.1g Fat; 9.1g Carbs; 22.2g Protein; 2.9g Sugars; 2.6g Fiber

INGREDIENTS

2 teaspoons olive oil
1 cup celery, sliced
2 bell peppers, sliced
1 teaspoon dried thyme
1/2 teaspoon dried marjoram
1/2 teaspoon dried rosemary

2 monkfish fillets
1 tablespoon soy sauce
2 tablespoons lime juice
Coarse salt and ground black pepper, to taste
1 teaspoon cayenne pepper
1/2 cup Kalamata olives, pitted and sliced

DIRECTIONS

In a nonstick skillet, heat the olive oil for 1 minute. Once hot, sauté the celery and peppers until tender, about 4 minutes. Sprinkle with thyme, marjoram, and rosemary and set aside.

Toss the fish fillets with the soy sauce, lime juice, salt, black pepper, and cayenne pepper. Place the fish fillets in a lightly greased cooking basket and bake at 390 degrees F for 8 minutes.

Turn them over, add the olives, and cook an additional 4 minutes. Serve with the sautéed vegetables on the side. Bon appétit!

304. Summer Fish Packets

(Ready in about 20 minutes | Servings 2)

Per serving: 329 Calories; 9.8g Fat; 12.7g Carbs; 46.7g Protein; 5.4g Sugars; 0.8g Fiber

INGREDIENTS

2 snapper fillets
1 shallot, peeled and sliced
2 garlic cloves, halved
1 bell pepper, sliced
1 small-sized serrano pepper, sliced
1 tomato, sliced

1 tablespoon olive oil
1/4 teaspoon freshly ground black pepper
1/2 teaspoon paprika
Sea salt, to taste
2 bay leaves

DIRECTIONS

Place two parchment sheets on a working surface. Place the fish in the center of one side of the parchment paper.
Top with the shallot, garlic, peppers, and tomato. Drizzle olive oil over the fish and vegetables. Season with black pepper, paprika, and salt. Add the bay leaves.
Fold over the other half of the parchment. Now, fold the paper around the edges tightly and create a half moon shape, sealing the fish inside.
Cook in the preheated Air Fryer at 390 degrees F for 15 minutes. Serve warm.

305. Fish Cakes with Horseradish Sauce

(Ready in about 20 minutes | Servings 4)

Per serving: 532 Calories; 38.2g Fat; 3.3g Carbs; 28g Protein; 1.3g Sugars; 0.6g Fiber

INGREDIENTS

Halibut Cakes:
1 pound halibut
2 tablespoons olive oil
1/2 teaspoon cayenne pepper
1/4 teaspoon black pepper

Salt, to taste
2 tablespoons cilantro, chopped
1 shallot, chopped
2 garlic cloves, minced
1 cup Romano cheese, grated

1 egg, whisked
1 tablespoon Worcestershire sauce
Mayo Sauce:
1 teaspoon horseradish, grated
1/2 cup mayonnaise

DIRECTIONS

Start by preheating your Air Fryer to 380 degrees F. Spritz the Air Fryer basket with cooking oil.
Mix all ingredients for the halibut cakes in a bowl; knead with your hands until everything is well incorporated.
Shape the mixture into equally sized patties. Transfer your patties to the Air Fryer basket. Cook the fish patties for 10 minutes, turning them over halfway through.
Mix the horseradish and mayonnaise. Serve the halibut cakes with the horseradish mayo. Bon appétit!

306. Zingy Dilled Salmon

(Ready in about 20 minutes + marinating time | Servings 2)

Per serving: 476 Calories; 16.8g Fat; 3.2g Carbs; 46.7g Protein; 0.8g Sugars; 0.4g Fiber

INGREDIENTS

2 salmon steaks
Coarse sea salt, to taste
1/4 teaspoon freshly ground black pepper, or more to taste
1 tablespoon sesame oil
Zest of 1 lemon

1 tablespoon fresh lemon juice
1 teaspoon garlic, minced
1/2 teaspoon smoked cayenne pepper
1/2 teaspoon dried dill

DIRECTIONS

Preheat your Air Fryer to 380 degrees F. Pat dry the salmon steaks with a kitchen towel.
In a ceramic dish, combine the remaining ingredients until everything is well whisked.
Add the salmon steaks to the ceramic dish and let them sit in the refrigerator for 1 hour. Now, place the salmon steaks in the cooking basket. Reserve the marinade.
Cook for 12 minutes, flipping halfway through the cooking time.
Meanwhile, cook the marinade in a small sauté pan over a moderate flame. Cook until the sauce has thickened.
Pour the sauce over the steaks and serve. Bon appétit!

307. Italian Shrimp Scampi

(Ready in about 20 minutes | Servings 4)

Per serving: 300 Calories; 11.3g Fat; 6.5g Carbs; 43.7g Protein; 0.8g Sugars; 1.2g Fiber

INGREDIENTS

2 egg whites
1/2 cup coconut flour
1 cup Parmigiano-Reggiano, grated
1/2 teaspoon celery seeds
1/2 teaspoon porcini powder
1/2 teaspoon onion powder

1 teaspoon garlic powder
1/2 teaspoon dried rosemary
1/2 teaspoon sea salt
1/2 teaspoon ground black pepper
1 ½ pounds shrimp, deveined

DIRECTIONS

Whisk the egg with coconut flour and Parmigiano-Reggiano. Add in seasonings and mix to combine well.
Dip your shrimp in the batter. Roll until they are covered on all sides.
Cook in the preheated Air Fryer at 390 degrees F for 5 to 7 minutes or until golden brown. Work in batches. Serve with lemon wedges if desired.

308. Red Hot Chili Fish Curry

(Ready in about 25 minutes | Servings 4)

Per serving: 298 Calories; 19.8g Fat; 5.4g Carbs; 23.3g Protein; 4.7g Sugars; 0.7g Fiber

INGREDIENTS

2 tablespoons sunflower oil
1 pound fish, chopped
2 red chilies, chopped
1 tablespoon coriander powder
1 teaspoon red curry paste
1 cup coconut milk

Salt and white pepper, to taste
1/2 teaspoon fenugreek seeds
1 shallot, minced
1 garlic clove, minced
1 ripe tomato, pureed

DIRECTIONS

Preheat your Air Fryer to 380 degrees F; brush the cooking basket with 1 tablespoon of sunflower oil.
Cook your fish for 10 minutes on both sides. Transfer to the baking pan that is previously greased with the remaining tablespoon of sunflower oil.
Add the remaining ingredients and reduce the heat to 350 degrees F. Continue to cook an additional 10 to 12 minutes or until everything is heated through. Enjoy!

309. Cod with Avocado Mayo Sauce

(Ready in about 20 minutes | Servings 2)

Per serving: 344 Calories; 24.7g Fat; 7.8g Carbs; 24.1g Protein; 0.8g Sugars; 3.7g Fiber

INGREDIENTS

2 cod fish fillets
1 egg
Sea salt, to taste
2 teaspoons olive oil
1/2 avocado, peeled, pitted, and mashed
1 tablespoon mayonnaise
3 tablespoons sour cream

1/2 teaspoon yellow mustard
1 teaspoon lemon juice
1 garlic clove, minced
1/4 teaspoon black pepper
1/4 teaspoon salt
1/4 teaspoon hot pepper sauce

DIRECTIONS

Start by preheating your Air Fryer to 360 degrees F. Spritz the Air Fryer basket with cooking oil.
Pat dry the fish fillets with a kitchen towel. Beat the egg in a shallow bowl. Add in the salt and olive oil.
Dip the fish into the egg mixture, making sure to coat thoroughly. Cook in the preheated Air Fryer approximately 12 minutes.
Meanwhile, make the avocado sauce by mixing the remaining ingredients in a bowl. Place in your refrigerator until ready to serve.
Serve the fish fillets with chilled avocado sauce on the side. Bon appétit!

310. Pollock with Kalamata Olives and Capers

(Ready in about 20 minutes | Servings 3)

Per serving: 480 Calories; 32.7g Fat; 6.9g Carbs; 45.9g Protein; 3.5g Sugars; 2g Fiber

INGREDIENTS

2 tablespoons olive oil
1 red onion, sliced
2 cloves garlic, chopped
1 Florina pepper, deveined and minced

3 pollock fillets, skinless
2 ripe tomatoes, diced
12 Kalamata olives, pitted and chopped
2 tablespoons capers

1 teaspoon oregano
1 teaspoon rosemary
Sea salt, to taste
1/2 cup white wine

DIRECTIONS

Start by preheating your Air Fryer to 360 degrees F. Heat the oil in a baking pan. Once hot, sauté the onion, garlic, and pepper for 2 to 3 minutes or until fragrant.

Add the fish fillets to the baking pan. Top with the tomatoes, olives, and capers. Sprinkle with the oregano, rosemary, and salt. Pour in white wine and transfer to the cooking basket.

Turn the temperature to 395 degrees F and bake for 10 minutes. Taste for seasoning and serve on individual plates, garnished with some extra Mediterranean herbs if desired. Enjoy!

311. Hake Fillets with Classic Garlic Sauce

(Ready in about 20 minutes | Servings 3)

Per serving: 565 Calories; 39.9g Fat; 6.6g Carbs; 42.1g Protein; 0.7g Sugars; 0.2g Fiber

INGREDIENTS

3 hake fillets
6 tablespoons mayonnaise
1 teaspoon Dijon mustard
1 tablespoon fresh lime juice
1 cup parmesan cheese, grated

Salt, to taste
1/4 teaspoon ground black pepper, or more to taste
Garlic Sauce
1/4 cup Greek-style yogurt

2 tablespoons olive oil
2 cloves garlic, minced
1/2 teaspoon tarragon leaves, minced

DIRECTIONS

Pat dry the hake fillets with a kitchen towel.

In a shallow bowl, whisk together the mayonnaise, mustard, and lime juice. In another shallow bowl, thoroughly combine the parmesan cheese with salt, and black pepper.

Dip the fish fillets in the mayo mixture; then, press them over the parmesan mixture.

Spritz the Air Fryer grill pan with non-stick cooking spray. Grill in the preheated Air Fry at 395 degrees F for 10 minutes, flipping halfway through the cooking time.

Meanwhile, make the sauce by whisking all the ingredients. Serve warm fish fillets with the sauce on the side. Bon appétit!

312. Saucy Swordfish Steaks with Roasted Peppers

(Ready in about 30 minutes | Servings 3)

Per serving: 460 Calories; 17.1g Fat; 5.1g Carbs; 66g Protein; 2.3g Sugars; 0.8g Fiber

INGREDIENTS

3 bell peppers
3 swordfish steaks
1 tablespoon butter, melted
2 garlic cloves, minced

Sea salt and freshly ground black pepper, to taste
1/2 teaspoon cayenne pepper
1/2 teaspoon ginger powder

DIRECTIONS

Start by preheating your Air Fryer to 400 degrees F. Brush the Air Fryer basket lightly with cooking oil.

Then, roast the bell peppers for 5 minutes. Give the peppers a half turn; place them back in the cooking basket and roast for another 5 minutes. Turn them one more time and roast until the skin is charred and soft or 5 more minutes. Peel the peppers and set aside.

Then, add the swordfish steaks to the lightly greased cooking basket and cook at 400 degrees F for 10 minutes.

Meanwhile, melt the butter in a small saucepan. Cook the garlic until fragrant and add the salt, pepper, cayenne pepper, and ginger powder. Cook until everything is thoroughly heated.

Plate the peeled peppers and the roasted swordfish; spoon the sauce over them and serve warm.

313. Restaurant-Style Flounder Cutlets

(Ready in about 15 minutes | Servings 2)

Per serving: 425 Calories; 26.3g Fat; 7.1g Carbs; 37.6g Protein; 0.1g Sugars; 0g Fiber

INGREDIENTS

1 egg
1 cup Pecorino Romano cheese, grated
Sea salt and white pepper, to taste

1/2 teaspoon cayenne pepper
1 teaspoon dried parsley flakes
2 flounder fillets

DIRECTIONS

To make a breading station, whisk the egg until frothy.
In another bowl, mix Pecorino Romano cheese, and spices.
Dip the fish in the egg mixture and turn to coat evenly; then, dredge in the cracker crumb mixture, turning a couple of times to coat evenly.
Cook in the preheated Air Fryer at 390 degrees F for 5 minutes; turn them over and cook another 5 minutes. Enjoy!

314. Tuna au Gratin with Herbs

(Ready in about 20 minutes | Servings 4)

Per serving: 313 Calories; 15.5g Fat; 7.9g Carbs; 34.2g Protein; 1.7g Sugars; 0.8g Fiber

INGREDIENTS

1 tablespoon butter, melted
1 medium-sized leek, thinly sliced
1 tablespoon chicken stock
1 tablespoon dry white wine
1 pound tuna
1/2 teaspoon red pepper flakes, crushed

Sea salt and ground black pepper, to taste
1/2 teaspoon dried rosemary
1/2 teaspoon dried basil
1/2 teaspoon dried thyme
2 small ripe tomatoes, pureed
1 cup Parmesan cheese, grated

DIRECTIONS

Melt 1/2 tablespoon of butter in a sauté pan over medium-high heat. Now, cook the leek and garlic until tender and aromatic. Add the stock and wine to deglaze the pan.
Preheat your Air Fryer to 370 degrees F.
Grease a casserole dish with the remaining 1/2 tablespoon of melted butter. Place the fish in the casserole dish. Add the seasonings. Top with the sautéed leek mixture.
Add the tomato puree. Cook for 10 minutes in the preheated Air Fryer. Top with grated Parmesan cheese; cook an additional 7 minutes until the crumbs are golden. Bon appétit!

EGGS & DAIRY

315. Omelet with Mushrooms and Peppers

(Ready in about 20 minutes | Servings 2)

Per serving: 272 Calories; 19.1g Fat; 8.1g Carbs; 18.3g Protein; 4.5g Sugars; 1.9g Fiber

INGREDIENTS

1 tablespoon olive oil
1/2 cup scallions, chopped
1 bell pepper, seeded and thinly sliced
6 ounces button mushrooms, thinly sliced

4 eggs
2 tablespoons milk
Sea salt and freshly ground black pepper, to taste
1 tablespoon fresh chives, for serving

DIRECTIONS

Heat the olive oil in a skillet over medium-high heat. Now, sauté the scallions and peppers until aromatic.
Add the mushrooms and continue to cook an additional 3 minutes or until tender. Reserve.
Generously grease a baking pan with nonstick cooking spray.
Then, whisk the eggs, milk, salt, and black pepper. Spoon into the prepared baking pan.
Cook in the preheated Air Fryer at 360 F for 4 minutes. Flip and cook for a further 3 minutes.
Place the reserved mushroom filling on one side of the omelet. Fold your omelet in half and slide onto a serving plate. Serve immediately garnished with fresh chives. Bon appétit!

316. Italian Creamy Frittata with Kale

(Ready in about 20 minutes | Servings 3)

Per serving: 289 Calories; 19.6g Fat; 9.2g Carbs; 19.9g Protein; 5g Sugars; 2.1g Fiber

INGREDIENTS

1 yellow onion, finely chopped
6 ounces wild mushrooms, sliced
6 eggs
1/4 cup double cream
1/2 teaspoon cayenne pepper

Sea salt and ground black pepper, to taste
1 tablespoon butter, melted
2 tablespoons fresh Italian parsley, chopped
2 cups kale, chopped
1/2 cup mozzarella, shredded

DIRECTIONS

Begin by preheating the Air Fryer to 360 degrees F. Spritz the sides and bottom of a baking pan with cooking oil.
Add the onions and wild mushrooms, and cook in the preheated Air Fryer at 360 degrees F for 4 to 5 minutes.
In a mixing dish, whisk the eggs and double cream until pale. Add the spices, butter, parsley, and kale; stir until everything is well incorporated.
Pour the mixture into the baking pan with the mushrooms.
Top with the cheese. Cook in the preheated Air Fryer for 10 minutes. Serve immediately and enjoy!

317. Double Cheese Crêpes

(Ready in about 35 minutes | Servings 3)

Per serving: 301 Calories; 22.4g Fat; 7.1g Carbs; 18.1g Protein; 2.4g Sugars; 1.9g Fiber

INGREDIENTS

1/4 cup coconut flour
1 tablespoon psyllium husk
2 eggs, beaten
3 egg whites, beaten
1/4 teaspoon allspice
1/2 teaspoon salt

1 teaspoon cream of tartar
3/4 cup milk
1/2 cup ricotta cheese
1/2 cup Parmigiano-Reggiano cheese, preferably freshly grated
1 cup marinara sauce

DIRECTIONS

Mix the coconut flour, psyllium husk, eggs, allspice, salt, and cream of tartar in a large bowl. Gradually add the milk and ricotta cheese, whisking continuously, until well combined.
Let it stand for 20 minutes.
Spritz the Air Fryer baking pan with cooking spray. Pour the batter into the prepared pan.
Cook at 230 degrees F for 3 minutes. Flip and cook until browned in spots, 2 to 3 minutes longer.
Repeat with the remaining batter. Serve with Parmigiano-Reggiano cheese and marinara sauce. Bon appétit!

318. Eggs Florentine with Spinach

(Ready in about 20 minutes | Servings 2)

Per serving: 243 Calories; 20.1g Fat; 3.7g Carbs; 12.3g Protein; 1.2g Sugars; 1.2g Fiber

INGREDIENTS

2 tablespoons ghee, melted
2 cups baby spinach, torn into small pieces
2 tablespoons shallots, chopped
1/4 teaspoon red pepper flakes

Salt, to taste
1 tablespoon fresh thyme leaves, roughly chopped
4 eggs

DIRECTIONS

Start by preheating your Air Fryer to 350 degrees F. Brush the sides and bottom of a gratin dish with the melted ghee.
Put the spinach and shallots into the bottom of the gratin dish. Season with red pepper, salt, and fresh thyme.
Make four indents for the eggs; crack one egg into each indent. Bake for 12 minutes, rotating the pan once or twice to ensure even cooking.
Enjoy!

319. Spicy Peppery Egg Salad

(Ready in about 20 minutes + chilling time | Servings 3)

Per serving: 401 Calories; 35.2g Fat; 6.5g Carbs; 12.4g Protein; 3.4g Sugars; 1.1g Fiber

INGREDIENTS

6 eggs
1 teaspoon mustard
1/2 cup mayonnaise
1 tablespoon white vinegar
1 habanero pepper, minced

1 red bell pepper, seeded and sliced
1 green bell pepper, seeded and sliced
1 shallot, sliced
Sea salt and ground black pepper, to taste

DIRECTIONS

Place the wire rack in the Air Fryer basket; lower the eggs onto the wire rack.
Cook at 270 degrees F for 15 minutes.
Transfer them to an ice-cold water bath to stop the cooking. Peel the eggs under cold running water; coarsely chop the hard-boiled eggs and set aside.
Toss with the remaining ingredients and serve well chilled. Bon appétit!

320. Muffins with Brown Mushrooms

(Ready in about 25 minutes | Servings 6)

Per serving: 227 Calories; 17.5g Fat; 5.7g Carbs; 12.2g Protein; 3.5g Sugars; 0.5g Fiber

INGREDIENTS

2 tablespoons butter, melted
1 yellow onion, chopped
2 garlic cloves, minced
1 cup brown mushrooms, sliced

Sea salt and ground black pepper, to taste
1 teaspoon fresh basil
8 eggs, lightly whisked
6 ounces goat cheese, crumbled

DIRECTIONS

Start by preheating your Air Fryer to 330 degrees F. Now, spritz a 6-tin muffin tin with cooking spray.
Melt the butter in a heavy-bottomed skillet over medium-high heat. Sauté the onions, garlic, and mushrooms until just tender and fragrant.
Add the salt, black pepper, and basil and remove from heat. Divide out the sautéed mixture into the muffin tin.
Pour the whisked eggs on top and top with the goat cheese. Bake for 20 minutes rotating the pan halfway through the cooking time. Bon appétit!

321. Spicy Eggs with Sausage and Swiss Cheese

(Ready in about 25 minutes | Servings 6)

Per serving: 289 Calories; 17.5g Fat; 4g Carbs; 26.6g Protein; 1.7g Sugars; 0.5g Fiber

INGREDIENTS

1 teaspoon lard
1/2 pound turkey sausage
6 eggs
1 scallion, chopped
1 garlic clove, minced

1 bell pepper, seeded and chopped
1 chili pepper, seeded and chopped
Sea salt and ground black pepper, to taste
1/2 cup Swiss cheese, shredded

DIRECTIONS

Start by preheating your Air Fryer to 330 degrees F. Now, spritz 4 silicone molds with cooking spray.
Melt the lard in a saucepan over medium-high heat. Now, cook the sausage for 5 minutes or until no longer pink.
Coarsely chop the sausage; add the eggs, scallions, garlic, peppers, salt, and black pepper. Divide the egg mixture between the silicone molds. Top with the shredded cheese.
Bake in the preheated Air Fryer at 340 degrees F for 15 minutes, checking halfway through the cooking time to ensure even cooking. Enjoy!

322. Western Eggs with Ham and Cheese

(Ready in about 20 minutes | Servings 4)

Per serving: 243 Calories; 14.6g Fat; 7.2g Carbs; 19.1g Protein; 4.4g Sugars; 0.6g Fiber

INGREDIENTS

6 eggs
1/2 cup milk
2 ounces cream cheese, softened
Sea salt, to your liking
1/4 teaspoon ground black pepper

1/4 teaspoon paprika
6 ounces cooked ham, diced
1 onion, chopped
1/2 cup cheddar cheese, shredded

DIRECTIONS

Begin by preheating the Air Fryer to 360 degrees F. Spritz the sides and bottom of a baking pan with cooking oil.
In a mixing dish, whisk the eggs, milk, and cream cheese until pale. Add the spices, ham, and onion; stir until everything is well incorporated.
Pour the mixture into the baking pan; top with the cheddar cheese.
Bake in the preheated Air Fryer for 12 minutes. Serve warm and enjoy!

323. Egg Salad with Asparagus and Spinach

(Ready in about 25 minutes + chilling time | Servings 4)

Per serving: 348 Calories; 30.4g Fat; 7.3g Carbs; 12.4g Protein; 3.4g Sugars; 2.9g Fiber

INGREDIENTS

4 eggs
1 pound asparagus, chopped
2 cup baby spinach
1/2 cup mayonnaise

1 teaspoon mustard
1 teaspoon fresh lemon juice
Sea salt and ground black pepper, to taste

DIRECTIONS

Place the wire rack in the Air Fryer basket; lower the eggs onto the wire rack.
Cook at 270 degrees F for 15 minutes.
Transfer them to an ice-cold water bath to stop the cooking. Peel the eggs under cold running water; coarsely chop the hard-boiled eggs and set aside.
Increase the temperature to 400 degrees F. Place your asparagus in the lightly greased Air Fryer basket.
Cook for 5 minutes or until tender. Place in a nice salad bowl. Add the baby spinach.
In a mixing dish, thoroughly combine the remaining ingredients. Drizzle this dressing over the asparagus in the salad bowl and top with the chopped eggs. Bon appétit!

324. Scrambled Egg Muffins with Cheese

(Ready in about 20 minutes | Servings 6)

Per serving: 234 Calories; 15.7g Fat; 5.3g Carbs; 17.6g Protein; 0.9g Sugars; 0.4g Fiber

INGREDIENTS

6 ounces smoked turkey sausage, chopped
6 eggs, lightly beaten
2 tablespoons shallots, finely chopped
2 garlic cloves, minced

Sea salt and ground black pepper, to taste
1 teaspoon cayenne pepper
6 ounces Monterey Jack cheese, shredded

DIRECTIONS

Simply combine the sausage, eggs, shallots, garlic, salt, black pepper, and cayenne pepper in a mixing dish. Mix to combine well.
Spoon the mixture into 6 standard-size muffin cups with paper liners.
Bake in the preheated Air Fryer at 340 degrees F for 8 minutes. Top with the cheese and bake an additional 8 minutes. Enjoy!

325. Frittata with Porcini Mushrooms

(Ready in about 40 minutes | Servings 4)

Per serving: 242 Calories; 16g Fat; 5.2g Carbs; 17.2g Protein; 2.8g Sugars; 1.3g Fiber

INGREDIENTS

3 cups Porcini mushrooms, thinly sliced
1 tablespoon melted butter
1 shallot, peeled and slice into thin rounds
1 garlic cloves, peeled and finely minced
1 lemon grass, cut into 1-inch pieces
1/3 teaspoon table salt

8 eggs
1/2 teaspoon ground black pepper, preferably freshly ground
1 teaspoon cumin powder
1/3 teaspoon dried or fresh dill weed
1/2 cup goat cheese, crumbled

DIRECTIONS

Melt the butter in a nonstick skillet that is placed over medium heat. Sauté the shallot, garlic, thinly sliced Porcini mushrooms, and lemon grass over a moderate heat until they have softened. Now, reserve the sautéed mixture.
Preheat your Air Fryer to 335 degrees F. Then, in a mixing bowl, beat the eggs until frothy. Now, add the seasonings and mix to combine well.
Coat the sides and bottom of a baking dish with a thin layer of vegetable spray. Pour the egg/seasoning mixture into the baking dish; throw in the onion/mushroom sauté. Top with the crumbled goat cheese.
Place the baking dish in the Air Fryer cooking basket. Cook for about 32 minutes or until your frittata is set. Enjoy!

326. Vegetarian Tofu Scramble

(Ready in about 15 minutes | Servings 2)

Per serving: 232 Calories; 16.6g Fat; 5.8g Carbs; 19.9g Protein; 1.2g Sugars; 2g Fiber

INGREDIENTS

1/2 teaspoon fresh lemon juice
1 teaspoon coarse salt
1 teaspoon coarse ground black pepper
4 ounces fresh spinach, chopped

1 tablespoon butter, melted
1/3 cup fresh basil, roughly chopped
1/2 teaspoon fresh lemon juice
13 ounces soft silken tofu, drained

DIRECTIONS

Add the tofu and olive oil to a baking dish.
Cook for 9 minutes at 272 degrees F.
Add the other ingredients and cook another 5 minutes. Serve warm.

327. Baked Eggs with Linguica Sausage

(Ready in about 18 minutes | Servings 2)

Per serving: 544 Calories; 45.1g Fat; 8.2g Carbs; 24.4g Protein; 4.2g Sugars; 0.9g Fiber

INGREDIENTS

1/2 cup Cheddar cheese, shredded
4 eggs
2 ounces Linguica (Portuguese pork sausage), chopped
1/2 onion, peeled and chopped
2 tablespoons olive oil

1/2 teaspoon rosemary, chopped
½ teaspoon marjoram
1/4 cup sour cream
Sea salt and freshly ground black pepper, to taste
½ teaspoon fresh sage, chopped

DIRECTIONS

Lightly grease 2 oven safe ramekins with olive oil. Now, divide the sausage and onions among these ramekins.
Crack an egg into each ramekin; add the remaining items, minus the cheese. Air-fry at 355 degrees F approximately 13 minutes.
Immediately top with Cheddar cheese, serve, and enjoy.

328. Mediterranean Eggs with Spinach and Tomato

(Ready in about 15 minutes | Servings 2)

Per serving: 274 Calories; 23.2g Fat; 5.7g Carbs; 13.7g Protein; 2.6g Sugars; 2.6g Fiber

INGREDIENTS

2 tablespoons olive oil, melted
4 eggs, whisked
5 ounces fresh spinach, chopped
1 medium-sized tomato, chopped

1 teaspoon fresh lemon juice
1/2 teaspoon coarse salt
1/2 teaspoon ground black pepper
1/2 cup of fresh basil, roughly chopped

DIRECTIONS

Add the olive oil to an Air Fryer baking pan. Make sure to tilt the pan to spread the oil evenly.
Simply combine the remaining ingredients, except for the basil leaves; whisk well until everything is well incorporated.
Cook in the preheated Air Fryer for 8 to 12 minutes at 280 degrees F. Garnish with fresh basil leaves. Serve warm with a dollop of sour cream if desired.

329. Broccoli Bites with Cheese Sauce

(Ready in about 20 minutes | Servings 6)

Per serving: 176 Calories; 13g Fat; 9.8g Carbs; 7.2g Protein; 3.6g Sugars; 3.3g Fiber

INGREDIENTS

For the Broccoli Bites:
1 medium-sized head broccoli, broken into florets
1/2 teaspoon lemon zest, freshly grated
1/3 teaspoon fine sea salt
1/2 teaspoon hot paprika
1 teaspoon shallot powder
1 teaspoon porcini powder
1/2 teaspoon granulated garlic

1/3 teaspoon celery seeds
1 ½ tablespoons olive oil
For the Cheese Sauce:
2 tablespoons butter
1 tablespoon golden flaxseed meal
1 cup milk
1/2 cup blue cheese

DIRECTIONS

Toss all the ingredients for the broccoli bites in a mixing bowl, covering the broccoli florets on all sides.
Cook them in the preheated Air Fryer at 360 degrees for 13 to 15 minutes.
In the meantime, melt the butter over a medium heat; stir in the golden flaxseed meal and let cook for 1 min or so.
Gradually pour in the milk, stirring constantly, until the mixture is smooth. Bring it to a simmer and stir in the cheese. Cook until the sauce has thickened slightly.
Pause your Air Fryer, mix the broccoli with the prepared sauce and cook for further 3 minutes. Bon appétit!

330. Party Mozzarella Stick

(Ready in about 40 minutes | Servings 4)

Per serving: 492 Calories; 34.7g Fat; 9.1g Carbs; 35.1g Protein; 1.7g Sugars; 2.3g Fiber

INGREDIENTS

12 ounces mozzarella cheese strings
2 eggs
2 tablepsoons flaxseed meal
1/4 cup almond flour

1/2 cup parmesan cheese finely grated
1 teaspoon garlic powder
1 teaspoon dried oregano
1/2 cup salsa, preferably homemade

DIRECTIONS

Set up your breading station. Put the eggs in a shallow bowl; in another bowl, mix the flaxseed meal, almond flour, parmesan cheese, garlic powder, and oregano.
Dip the mozzarella sticks in the egg, then in the parmesan mixture, then in the egg and parmesan mixture again.
Place in your freezer for 30 minutes.
Place the breaded cheese sticks in the lightly greased Air Fryer basket. Cook at 380 degrees F for 6 minutes.
Serve with salsa on the side and enjoy!

331. Stuffed Mushrooms with Cheese

(Ready in about 15 minutes | Servings 5)

Per serving: 188 Calories; 15.7g Fat; 4.4g Carbs; 8.4g Protein; 1.6g Sugars; 0.8g Fiber

INGREDIENTS

1/2 cup parmesan cheese, grated
2 cloves garlic, pressed
2 tablespoons fresh coriander, chopped
1/3 teaspoon kosher salt
1/2 teaspoon crushed red pepper flakes
1 ½ tablespoons olive oil

20 medium-sized mushrooms, cut off the stems
1/2 cup Gorgonzola cheese, grated
1/4 cup low-fat mayonnaise
1 teaspoon prepared horseradish, well-drained
1 tablespoon fresh parsley, finely chopped

DIRECTIONS

Mix the parmesan cheese together with the garlic, coriander, salt, red pepper, and the olive oil; mix to combine well.
Stuff the mushroom caps with the parmesan filling. Top with grated Gorgonzola.
Place the mushrooms in the Air Fryer grill pan and slide them into the machine. Grill them at 380 degrees F for 8 to 12 minutes or until the stuffing is warmed through.
Meanwhile, prepare the horseradish mayo by mixing the mayonnaise, horseradish and parsley. Serve with the warm fried mushrooms. Enjoy!

332. Cheesy Cauliflower Balls

(Ready in about 26 minutes | Servings 4)

Per serving: 157 Calories; 11.3g Fat; 7.9g Carbs; 7.1g Protein; 2.7g Sugars; 1.4g Fiber

INGREDIENTS

4 ounces cauliflower florets
1/2 cup roasted vegetable stock
1 egg, beaten
1 cup white mushrooms, finely chopped
1/2 cup parmesan cheese, grated
3 garlic cloves, peeled and minced
1/2 yellow onion, finely chopped

1/3 teaspoon ground black pepper, or more to taste
1 ½ bell peppers, seeded minced
1/2 chipotle pepper, seeded and minced
1/2 cup Colby cheese, grated
1 ½ tablespoons canola oil
Sea salt, to savor

DIRECTIONS

Blitz the cauliflower florets in your food processor until they're crumbled (it is the size of rice).
Heat a saucepan over a moderate heat; now, heat the oil and sweat the garlic, onions, bell pepper, cauli rice, and chipotle pepper until tender.
Throw in the mushrooms and fry until they are fragrant and the liquid has almost evaporated.
Add in the stock; boil for 18 minutes. Now, add the cheese and spices; mix to combine.
Allow the mixture to cool completely. Shape the mixture into balls. Dip the balls in the beaten egg; then, roll them over the grated parmesan.
Air-fry these balls for 6 minutes at 400 degrees F. Serve with marinara sauce and enjoy!

333. Greek Frittata with Feta Cheese

(Ready in about 10 minutes | Servings 4)

Per serving: 221 Calories; 10.7g Fat; 2.1g Carbs; 27g Protein; 1.1g Sugars; 0.3g Fiber

INGREDIENTS

1/3 cup Feta cheese, crumbled

1 teaspoon dried rosemary

2 tablespoons fish sauce

1 ½ cup cooked chicken breasts, boneless and shredded

1/2 teaspoon coriander sprig, finely chopped

6 medium-sized whisked eggs

1/3 teaspoon ground white pepper

1 cup fresh chives, chopped

1/2 teaspoon garlic paste

Fine sea salt, to taste

Nonstick cooking spray

DIRECTIONS

Grab a baking dish that fit in your Air Fryer.

Lightly coat the inside of the baking dish with a nonstick cooking spray of choice. Stir in all ingredients, minus feta cheese. Stir to combine well.

Set your Air Fryer to cook at 335 degrees for 8 minutes; check for doneness. Scatter crumbled feta over the top and eat immediately!

334. Turkey with Cheese and Pasilla Peppers

(Ready in about 30 minutes | Servings 2)

Per serving: 504 Calories; 37.8g Fat; 6.5g Carbs; 33.9g Protein; 0.4g Sugars; 1g Fiber

INGREDIENTS

1/2 cup Parmesan cheese, shredded

1/2 pound turkey breasts, cut into four pieces

1/3 cup mayonnaise

1 ½ tablespoons sour cream

1 dried Pasilla peppers

1 teaspoon onion salt

1/3 teaspoon mixed peppercorns, freshly cracked

DIRECTIONS

In a shallow bowl, mix Parmesan cheese, onion salt, and the cracked mixed peppercorns together.

In a food processor, blitz the mayonnaise, along with the cream and dried Pasilla peppers until there are no lumps.

Coat the turkey breasts with this mixture, ensuring that all sides are covered.

Then, coat each piece of turkey in the Parmesan mixture. Now, preheat the Air Fryer to 365 degrees F; cook for 28 minutes until thoroughly cooked.

335. Baked Denver Omelet with Sausage

(Ready in about 14 minutes | Servings 5)

Per serving: 323 Calories; 18.6g Fat; 2.7g Carbs; 34.1g Protein; 1.4g Sugars; 0.4g Fiber

INGREDIENTS

3 pork sausages, chopped

8 well-beaten eggs

1 ½ bell peppers, seeded and chopped

1 teaspoon smoked cayenne pepper

2 tablespoons Fontina cheese

1/2 teaspoon tarragon

1/2 teaspoon ground black pepper

1 teaspoon salt

DIRECTIONS

In a cast-iron skillet, sweat the bell peppers together with the chopped pork sausages until the peppers are fragrant and the sausage begins to release liquid.

Lightly grease the inside of a baking dish with pan spray.

Throw all of the above ingredients into the prepared baking dish, including the sautéed mixture; stir to combine.

Bake at 345 degrees F approximately 9 minutes. Serve right away with the salad of choice.

336. Baked Eggs with Beef and Tomato

(Ready in about 20 minutes | Servings 4)

Per serving: 236 Calories; 13.7g Fat; 4.1g Carbs; 23.8g Protein; 1.0g Sugars; 0.8g Fiber

INGREDIENTS

Non-stick cooking spray
1/2 pound leftover beef, coarsely chopped
2 garlic cloves, pressed
1 cup kale, torn into pieces and wilted
1 tomato, chopped

4 eggs, beaten
4 tablespoons heavy cream
1/2 teaspoon turmeric powder
Salt and ground black pepper, to your liking
1/8 teaspoon ground allspice

DIRECTIONS

Spritz the inside of four ramekins with a cooking spray.
Divide all of the above ingredients among the prepared ramekins. Stir until everything is well combined.
Air-fry at 360 degrees F for 16 minutes; check with a wooden stick and return the eggs to the Air Fryer for a few more minutes as needed.
Serve immediately.

337. Cheese Balls with Spinach

(Ready in about 15 minutes | Servings 4)

Per serving: 314 Calories; 24.1g Fat; 5.7g Carbs; 11.3g Protein; 1.1g Sugars; 4.1g Fiber

INGREDIENTS

1/4 cup milk
2 eggs
1 cup cheese
2 cups spinach, torn into pieces

1/3 cup flaxseed meal
1/2 teaspoon baking powder
2 tablespoons canola oil
Salt and ground black pepper, to taste

DIRECTIONS

Add all the ingredients to a food processor or blender; then, puree the ingredients until it becomes dough.
Next, roll the dough into small balls. Preheat your air fryer to 310 degrees F.
Cook the balls in your Air Fryer for about 12 minutes or until they are crispy. Bon appétit!

338. Double Cheese Mushroom Balls

(Ready in about 30 minutes | Servings 4)

Per serving: 305 Calories; 25.1g Fat; 7.9g Carbs; 11.7g Protein; 3.2g Sugars; 1.1g Fiber

INGREDIENTS

1 ½ tablespoons olive oil
4 ounces cauliflower florets
3 garlic cloves, peeled and minced
1/2 yellow onion, finely chopped
1 small-sized red chili pepper, seeded and minced
1/2 cup roasted vegetable stock

2 cups white mushrooms, finely chopped
Sea salt and ground black pepper, or more to taste
1/2 cup Swiss cheese, grated
1/4 cup pork rinds
1 egg, beaten
1/4 cup Romano cheese, grated

DIRECTIONS

Blitz the cauliflower florets in your food processor until they're crumbled (it is the size of rice).
Heat a saucepan over a moderate heat; now, heat the oil and sweat the cauliflower. garlic, onions, and chili pepper until tender.
Throw in the mushrooms and fry until they are fragrant and the liquid has almost evaporated.
Add the vegetable stock and boil for 18 minutes. Now, add the salt, black pepper, Swiss cheese pork rinds, and beaten egg; mix to combine.
Allow the mixture to cool completely. Shape the mixture into balls. Dip the balls in the grated Romano cheese. Air-fry the balls for 7 minutes at 400 degrees F. Bon appétit!

339. Greek Omelet with Halloumi Cheese

(Ready in about 17 minutes | Servings 2)

Per serving: 278 Calories; 18.5g Fat; 7.6g Carbs; 20.4g Protein; 3.4g Sugars; 1.1g Fiber

INGREDIENTS

1/2 cup Halloumi cheese, sliced
2 teaspoons garlic paste
2 teaspoons fresh chopped rosemary
4well-whisked eggs

2 bell peppers, seeded and chopped
1 ½ tablespoons fresh basil, chopped
3 tablespoons onions, chopped
Fine sea salt and ground black pepper, to taste

DIRECTIONS

Spritz your baking dish with a canola cooking spray.
Throw in all ingredients and stir until everything is well incorporated.
Bake for about 15 minutes at 325 degrees F. Eat warm.

340. Parmesan Broccoli Fritters

(Ready in about 30 minutes | Servings 6)

Per serving: 204 Calories; 14g Fat; 4.4g Carbs; 14.5g Protein; 0.9g Sugars; 1.1g Fiber

INGREDIENTS

1 1/2 cups Monterey Jack cheese
1 teaspoon dried dill weed
1/3 teaspoon ground black pepper
3 eggs, whisked

1 teaspoon cayenne pepper
1/2 teaspoon kosher salt
2 ½ cups broccoli florets
1/2 cup Parmesan cheese

DIRECTIONS

Blitz the broccoli florets in a food processor until finely crumbed. Then, combine the broccoli with the rest of the above ingredients.
Roll the mixture into small balls; place the balls in the fridge for approximately half an hour.
Preheat your Air Fryer to 335 degrees F and set the timer to 14 minutes; cook until broccoli croquettes are browned and serve warm.

341. Celery and Bacon Cakes

(Ready in about 25 minutes | Servings 4)

Per serving: 238 Calories; 20g Fat; 2.9g Carbs; 10.9g Protein; 0.7g Sugars; 0.5g Fiber

INGREDIENTS

2 eggs, lightly beaten
1/3 teaspoon freshly cracked black pepper
1 cup Colby cheese, grated
1/2 tablespoon fresh dill, finely chopped
1/2 tablespoon garlic paste

1/3 cup onion, finely chopped
1/3 cup bacon, chopped
2 teaspoons fine sea salt
2 medium-sized celery stalks, trimmed and grated
1/3 teaspoon baking powder

DIRECTIONS

Place the celery on a paper towel and squeeze them to remove the excess liquid.
Combine the vegetables with the other ingredients in the order listed above. Shape the balls using 1 tablespoon of the vegetable mixture.
Then, gently flatten each ball with your palm or a wide spatula. Spritz the croquettes with a nonstick cooking oil.
Bake the vegetable cakes in a single layer for 17 minutes at 318 degrees F. Serve warm with sour cream.

342. Omelet with Smoked Tofu and Veggies

(Ready in about 20 minutes | Servings 2)

Per serving: 298 Calories; 18.5g Fat; 6.6g Carbs; 26.3g Protein; 2.5g Sugars; 1.9g Fiber

INGREDIENTS

2 eggs, beaten

1/3 cup cherry tomatoes, chopped

1 bell pepper, seeded and chopped

1/3 teaspoon freshly ground black pepper

1/2 purple onion, peeled and sliced

1 teaspoon smoked cayenne pepper

5 medium-sized eggs, well-beaten

1/3 cup smoked tofu, crumbled

1 teaspoon seasoned salt

1 1/2 tablespoons fresh chives, chopped

DIRECTIONS

Brush a baking dish with a spray coating.

Throw all ingredients, minus fresh chives, into the baking dish; give it a good stir.

Cook about 15 minutes at 325 degrees F. Garnish with fresh chopped chives. Bon appétit!

343. Cauliflower and Manchego Croquettes

(Ready in about 15 minutes | Servings 4)

Per serving: 200 Calories; 15.7g Fat; 6.9g Carbs; 9.4g Protein; 2.4g Sugars; 2.7g Fiber

INGREDIENTS

1 cup Manchego cheese, shredded

1 teaspoon paprika

1 teaspoon freshly ground black pepper

1/2 tablespoon fine sea salt

1/2 cup scallions, finely chopped

1 pound cauliflower florets

2 tablespoons canola oil

2 teaspoons dried basil

DIRECTIONS

Blitz the cauliflower florets in a food processor until finely crumbed. Then, combine the broccoli with the rest of the above ingredients.

Then, shape the balls using your hands. Now, flatten the balls to make the patties.

Next, cook your patties at 360 degrees F approximately 10 minutes. Bon appétit!

344. Gruyère Stuffed Mushrooms

(Ready in about 19 minutes | Servings 3)

Per serving: 186 Calories; 13.7g Fat; 4g Carbs; 13.2g Protein; 1.6g Sugars; 1.1g Fiber

INGREDIENTS

2 garlic cloves, minced

1 teaspoon ground black pepper, or more to taste

1/2 teaspoon paprika

1 teaspoon dried parsley flakes

1½ tablespoons fresh mint, chopped

1 teaspoon salt, or more to taste

1 cup Gruyère cheese, shredded

9 large mushrooms, cleaned, stalks removed

DIRECTIONS

Mix all of the above ingredients, minus the mushrooms, in a mixing bowl to prepare the filling.

Then, stuff the mushrooms with the prepared filling.

Air-fry stuffed mushrooms at 375 degrees F for about 12 minutes. Taste for doneness and serve at room temperature as an appetizer.

345. Double Cheese Asparagus Casserole

(Ready in about 27 minutes | Servings 2)

Per serving: 198 Calories; 12.7g Fat; 6.8g Carbs; 13.6g Protein; 3.5g Sugars; 1.7g Fiber

INGREDIENTS

1 cup cauliflower rice
1/3 cup milk
1/3 cup Colby cheese, grated
1 1/2 cups white mushrooms, sliced
2 asparagus spears, chopped

1 teaspoon table salt, or to taste
2 well-beaten eggs
1/3 teaspoon smoked cayenne pepper
1 teaspoon ground black pepper, or to taste
1/3 teaspoon dried rosemary, crushed

DIRECTIONS

Throw the cauliflower rice into the baking dish.
In a mixing dish, thoroughly combine the eggs and milk. Stir in 1/2 of cheese; add the seasonings. Pour 3/4 of egg/cheese mixture over the bread cubes in the baking dish; press gently using a wide spatula.
Now, top with the mushrooms and chopped asparagus. Pour the remaining egg/cheese mixture over the top; make sure to spread it evenly.
Top with the remaining Colby cheese and bake for 20 minutes at 325 degrees F.

346. Winter Baked Eggs with Italian Sausage

(Ready in about 30 minutes | Servings 4)

Per serving: 555 Calories; 36g Fat; 9.5g Carbs; 23.3g Protein; 2.5g Sugars; 2.1g Fiber

INGREDIENTS

1 pound Italian sausage
2 sprigs rosemary
1 celery, sliced
1/2 pound broccoli, cut into small florets
2 sprigs thyme
1 bell pepper, trimmed and cut into matchsticks

2 garlic cloves, smashed
2 tablespoons extra-virgin olive oil
1 leek, cut into halves lengthwise
A pinch of grated nutmeg
Salt and black pepper, to taste
4 whole eggs

DIRECTIONS

Arrange vegetables on the bottom of the Air Fryer baking dish.
Sprinkle with the seasonings and top with the sausage.
Roast approximately 20 minutes at 375 degrees F, stirring occasionally. Top with eggs and reduce the temperature to 330 degrees F.
Bake an additional 5 to 6 minutes. Bon appétit!

347. Breakfast Pizza Cups

(Ready in about 30 minutes | Servings 4)

Per serving: 291 Calories; 18.8g Fat; 7g Carbs; 22.4g Protein; 4.6g Sugars; 0.6g Fiber

INGREDIENTS

12 slices pepperoni, 2-inch
2 tablespoons butter, melted
4 eggs, beaten
1/4 teaspoon ground black pepper

Salt, to taste
4 slices smoked ham, chopped
1 cup mozzarella cheese, shredded
4 tablespoons ketchup

DIRECTIONS

Start by preheating your Air Fryer to 350 degrees F. Now, lightly grease a muffin tin with nonstick spray.
Place pepperoni into a mini muffin pan. In a mixing bowl, thoroughly combine the remaining ingredients.
Bake in the preheated Air Fryer for 20 minutes until a toothpick inserted comes out clean. Let it cool for 5 minutes before removing to a serving platter.
Bon appétit!

348. Easy Frittata with Chicken Sausage

(Ready in about 15 minutes | Servings 2)

Per serving: 528 Calories; 42g Fat; 5.6g Carbs; 26.2g Protein; 2.6g Sugars; 0.8g Fiber

INGREDIENTS

1 tablespoon olive oil
2 chicken sausages, sliced
4 eggs
1 garlic clove, minced

1/2 yellow onion, chopped
Sea salt and ground black pepper, to taste
4 tablespoons Monterey-Jack cheese
1 tablespoon fresh parsley leaves, chopped

DIRECTIONS

Grease the sides and bottom of a baking pan with olive oil.

Add the sausages and cook in the preheated Air Fryer at 360 degrees F for 4 to 5 minutes.

In a mixing dish, whisk the eggs with garlic and onion. Season with salt and black pepper.

Pour the mixture over sausages. Top with cheese. Cook in the preheated Air Fryer at 360 degrees F for another 6 minutes.

Serve immediately with fresh parsley leaves. Bon appétit!

349. Eggs with Turkey Bacon and Green Onions

(Ready in about 25 minutes | Servings 4)

Per serving: 390 Calories; 32.3g Fat; 5.6g Carbs; 18.1g Protein; 4g Sugars; 0.8g Fiber

INGREDIENTS

1/2 pound turkey bacon
4 eggs
1/3 cup milk
2 tablespoons yogurt

1/2 teaspoon sea salt
1 bell pepper, finely chopped
2 green onions, finely chopped
1/2 cup Colby cheese, shredded

DIRECTIONS

Place the turkey bacon in the cooking basket.

Cook at 360 degrees F for 9 to 11 minutes. Work in batches. Reserve the fried bacon.

In a mixing bowl, thoroughly whisk the eggs with milk and yogurt. Add salt, bell pepper, and green onions.

Brush the sides and bottom of the baking pan with the reserved 1 teaspoon of bacon grease.

Pour the egg mixture into the baking pan. Cook at 355 degrees F about 5 minutes. Top with shredded Colby cheese and cook for 5 to 6 minutes more.

Serve the scrambled eggs with the reserved bacon and enjoy!

350. Filipino Ground Meat Omelet (Tortang Giniling)

(Ready in about 20 minutes | Servings 3)

Per serving: 508 Calories; 33.2g Fat; 5.7g Carbs; 44.3g Protein; 3.2g Sugars; 0.7g Fiber

INGREDIENTS

1 teaspoon lard
2/3 pound ground beef
1/4 teaspoon chili powder
1/2 teaspoon ground bay leaf
1/2 teaspoon ground pepper
Sea salt, to taste

1 green bell pepper, seeded and chopped
1 red bell pepper, seeded and chopped
6 eggs
1/3 cup double cream
1/2 cup Colby cheese, shredded
1 tomato, sliced

DIRECTIONS

Melt the lard in a cast-iron skillet over medium-high heat. Add the ground beef and cook for 4 minutes until no longer pink, crumbling with a spatula.

Add the ground beef mixture, along with the spices to the baking pan. Now, add the bell peppers.

In a mixing bowl, whisk the eggs with double cream. Spoon the mixture over the meat and peppers in the pan.

Cook in the preheated Air Fryer at 355 degrees F for 10 minutes.

Top with the cheese and tomato slices. Continue to cook for 5 minutes more or until the eggs are golden and the cheese has melted.

351. Cod and Shallot Frittata

(Ready in about 20 minutes | Servings 3)

Per serving: 216 Calories; 10g Fat; 5.2g Carbs; 24.4g Protein; 3.4g Sugars; 0.4g Fiber

INGREDIENTS

2 cod fillets
6 eggs
1/2 cup milk
1 shallot, chopped

2 garlic cloves, minced
Sea salt and ground black pepper, to taste
1/2 teaspoon red pepper flakes, crushed

DIRECTIONS

Bring a pot of salted water to a boil. Boil the cod fillets for 5 minutes or until it is opaque. Flake the fish into bite-sized pieces.
In a mixing bowl, whisk the eggs and milk. Stir in the shallots, garlic, salt, black pepper, and red pepper flakes. Stir in the reserved fish.
Pour the mixture into the lightly greased baking pan.
Cook in the preheated Air Fryer at 360 degrees F for 9 minutes, flipping over halfway through. Bon appétit!

352. Keto Rolls with Halibut and Eggs

(Ready in about 25 minutes | Servings 4)

Per serving: 434 Calories; 22.1g Fat; 6.5g Carbs; 46g Protein; 1.8g Sugars; 0.4g Fiber

INGREDIENTS

4 keto rolls
1 pound smoked halibut, chopped
4 eggs

1 teaspoon dried thyme
1 teaspoon dried basil
Salt and black pepper, to taste

DIRECTIONS

Cut off the top of each keto roll; then, scoop out the insides to make the shells.
Lay the prepared keto roll shells in the lightly greased cooking basket.
Spritz with cooking oil; add the halibut. Crack an egg into each keto roll shell; sprinkle with thyme, basil, salt, and black pepper.
Bake in the preheated Air Fryer at 325 degrees F for 20 minutes. Bon appétit!

353. Steak Fingers with Mushrooms and Swiss Cheese

(Ready in about 25 minutes | Servings 4)

Per serving: 373 Calories; 20.7g Fat; 8.2g Carbs; 41.5g Protein; 3.4g Sugars; 1.2g Fiber

INGREDIENTS

2 eggs, beaten
4 tablespoons yogurt
1 cup parmesan cheese, grated
1 teaspoon dry mesquite flavored seasoning mix
Coarse salt and ground black pepper, to taste

1/2 teaspoon onion powder
1 pound cube steak, cut into 3 inch long strips
1 pound button mushrooms
1 cup Swiss cheese, shredded

DIRECTIONS

In a shallow bowl, beat the eggs and yogurt. In a resealable bag, mix the parmesan cheese, mesquite seasoning, salt, pepper, and onion powder.
Dip the steak pieces in the egg mixture; then, place in the bag, and shake to coat on all sides.
Cook at 400 degrees F for 14 minutes, flipping halfway through the cooking time.
Add the mushrooms to the lightly greased cooking basket. Top with shredded Swiss cheese.
Bake in the preheated Air Fryer at 400 degrees F for 5 minutes. Serve with the beef nuggets. Bon appétit!

354. Parmesan-Crusted Fish Fingers

(Ready in about 20 minutes | Servings 4)

Per serving: 468 Calories; 12.7g Fat; 45.6g Carbs; 41.9g Protein; 1.4g Sugars; 0.8g Fiber

INGREDIENTS

1 ½ pounds tilapia pieces (fingers)
1/2 cup coconut flour
2 eggs
1 tablespoon yellow mustard
1 cup parmesan cheese, grated

1 teaspoon garlic powder
1 teaspoon onion powder
Sea salt and ground black pepper, to taste
1/2 teaspoon celery powder
2 tablespoons peanut oil

DIRECTIONS

Pat dry the fish fingers with a kitchen towel.

To make a breading station, place the coconut flour in a shallow dish. In a separate dish, whisk the eggs with mustard.

In a third bowl, mix parmesan cheese with the remaining ingredients.

Dredge the fish fingers in the flour, shaking the excess into the bowl; dip in the egg mixture and turn to coat evenly; then, dredge in the parmesan mixture, turning a couple of times to coat evenly.

Cook in the preheated Air Fryer at 390 degrees F for 5 minutes; turn them over and cook another 5 minutes. Enjoy!

355. Onion Rings with Mayo Dip

(Ready in about 25 minutes | Servings 3)

Per serving: 264 Calories; 22.3g Fat; 9.2g Carbs; 8.1g Protein; 3g Sugars; 2.2g Fiber

INGREDIENTS

1 large onion
1/2 cup almond flour
1 teaspoon salt
1/2 teaspoon ground black pepper
1 teaspoon cayenne pepper
1/2 teaspoon dried thyme

1/2 teaspoon dried oregano
1/2 teaspoon ground cumin
2 eggs
4 tablespoons milk
Mayo Dip:
3 tablespoons mayonnaise

3 tablespoons sour cream
1 tablespoon horseradish, drained
Kosher salt and freshly ground black pepper, to taste

DIRECTIONS

Cut off the top 1/2 inch of the Vidalia onion; peel your onion and place it cut-side down. Starting 1/2 inch from the root, cut the onion in half. Make a second cut that splits each half in two. You will have 4 quarters held together by the root.

Repeat these cuts, splitting the 4 quarters to yield eighths; then, you should split them again until you have 16 evenly spaced cuts. Turn the onion over and gently separate the outer pieces using your fingers.

In a mixing bowl, thoroughly combine the almond flour and spices. In a separate bowl, whisk the eggs and milk. Dip the onion into the egg mixture, followed by the almond flour mixture.

Spritz the onion with cooking spray and transfer to the lightly greased cooking basket. Cook for 370 degrees F for 12 to 15 minutes.

Meanwhile, make the mayo dip by whisking the remaining ingredients. Serve and enjoy!

356. Deviled Eggs with Pickle Relish

(Ready in about 20 minutes | Servings 3)

Per serving: 261 Calories; 19.2g Fat; 5.5g Carbs; 15.5g Protein; 4.1g Sugars; 0.2g Fiber

INGREDIENTS

5 eggs
2 tablespoons mayonnaise
2 tablespoons pickle relish

Sea salt, to taste
1/2 teaspoon mixed peppercorns, crushed

DIRECTIONS

Place the wire rack in the Air Fryer basket; lower the eggs onto the wire rack.

Cook at 270 degrees F for 15 minutes.

Transfer them to an ice-cold water bath to stop the cooking. Peel the eggs under cold running water; slice them into halves.

Mash the egg yolks with the mayo, sweet pickle relish, and salt; spoon yolk mixture into egg whites. Arrange on a nice serving platter and garnish with the mixed peppercorns. Bon appétit!

357. Cheese Sticks with Ketchup

(Ready in about 15 minutes | Servings 4)

Per serving: 218 Calories; 10.7g Fat; 6.2g Carbs; 25.8g Protein; 1.7g Sugars; 2.2g Fiber

INGREDIENTS

1/4 cup coconut flour
1/4 cup almond flour
2 eggs
1/2 cup parmesan cheese, grated

1 tablespoon Cajun seasonings
8 cheese sticks, kid-friendly
1/4 cup ketchup, low-carb

DIRECTIONS

To begin, set up your breading station. Place the flour in a shallow dish. In a separate dish, whisk the eggs.
Finally, mix the parmesan cheese and Cajun seasoning in a third dish.
Start by dredging the cheese sticks in the flour; then, dip them into the egg. Press the cheese sticks into the parmesan mixture, coating evenly.
Place the breaded cheese sticks in the lightly greased Air Fryer basket. Cook at 380 degrees F for 6 minutes.
Serve with ketchup and enjoy!

358. Italian-Style Broccoli Balls with Cheese

(Ready in about 25 minutes | Servings 4)

Per serving: 357 Calories; 25.2g Fat; 7g Carbs; 25.5g Protein; 1.6g Sugars; 1.6g Fiber

INGREDIENTS

1/2 pound broccoli
1/2 pound Romano cheese, grated
2 garlic cloves, minced
1 shallot, chopped
4 eggs, beaten

2 tablespoons butter, at room temperature
1/2 teaspoon paprika
1/4 teaspoon dried basil
Sea salt and ground black pepper, to taste

DIRECTIONS

Add the broccoli to your food processor and pulse until the consistency resembles rice.
Stir in the remaining ingredients; mix until everything is well combined. Shape the mixture into bite-sized balls and transfer them to the lightly greased cooking basket.
Cook in the preheated Air Fryer at 375 degrees F for 16 minutes, shaking halfway through the cooking time. Serve with cocktail sticks and tomato ketchup on the side.

359. Italian Cheese Chips

(Ready in about 15 minutes | Servings 4)

Per serving: 231 Calories; 16.5g Fat; 6.4g Carbs; 14g Protein; 1.4g Sugars; 0.7g Fiber

INGREDIENTS

1 cup Parmesan cheese, shredded
1 cup Cheddar cheese, shredded

1 teaspoon Italian seasoning
1/2 cup marinara sauce

DIRECTIONS

Start by preheating your Air Fryer to 350 degrees F. Place a piece of parchment paper in the cooking basket.
Mix the cheese with the Italian seasoning.
Add about 1 tablespoon of the cheese mixture (per crisp) to the basket, making sure they are not touching. Bake for 6 minutes or until browned to your liking.
Work in batches and place them on a large tray to cool slightly. Serve with the marinara sauce. Bon appétit!

360. Cheesy Zucchini with Queso Añejo

(Ready in about 25 minutes | Servings 4)

Per serving: 231 Calories; 16.8g Fat; 6.8g Carbs; 13.4g Protein; 1.2g Sugars; 1g Fiber

INGREDIENTS

1 large-sized zucchini, thinly sliced
1/4 cup almond flour
1 cup parmesan cheese

1 egg, whisked
1/2 cup Queso Añejo, grated
Salt and cracked pepper, to taste

DIRECTIONS

Pat dry the zucchini slices with a kitchen towel.

Mix the remaining ingredients in a shallow bowl; mix until everything is well combined. Dip each zucchini slice in the prepared batter.

Cook in the preheated Air Fryer at 400 degrees F for 12 minutes, shaking the basket halfway through the cooking time.

Work in batches until the zucchini slices are crispy and golden brown. Enjoy!

361. Egg Breakfast Muffins

(Ready in about 20 minutes | Servings 4)

Per serving: 309 Calories; 26.1g Fat; 8.3g Carbs; 10.1g Protein; 6.2g Sugars; 0.7g Fiber

INGREDIENTS

1/2 cup almond flour
1 teaspoon baking powder
1 tablespoon granulated sweetener of choice
4 eggs

1 teaspoon cinnamon powder
1 teaspoon vanilla paste
1/4 cup coconut oil
4 tablespoons peanut butter

DIRECTIONS

Start by preheating your Air Fryer to 330 degrees F. Now, spritz the silicone muffin tins with cooking spray.

Thoroughly combine all ingredients in a mixing dish. Fill the muffin cups with batter.

Cook in the preheated Air Fryer approximately 13 minutes. Check with a toothpick; when the toothpick comes out clean, your muffins are done.

Place on a rack to cool slightly before removing from the muffin tins. Enjoy!

362. Japanese Fried Rice with Eggs

(Ready in about 30 minutes | Servings 2)

Per serving: 257 Calories; 19.2g Fat; 7.7g Carbs; 12g Protein; 3.1g Sugars; 2.5g Fiber

INGREDIENTS

2 cups cauliflower rice
2 teaspoons sesame oil
Sea salt and freshly ground black pepper, to your liking
2 eggs, beaten

2 scallions, white and green parts separated, chopped
1 tablespoon Shoyu sauce
1 tablespoon sake
2 tablespoons Kewpie Japanese mayonnaise

DIRECTIONS

Thoroughly combine the cauliflower rice, sesame oil, salt, and pepper in a baking dish.

Cook at 340 degrees F about 13 minutes, stirring halfway through the cooking time.

Pour the eggs over the cauliflower rice and continue to cook about 5 minutes. Next, add the scallions and stir to combine. Continue to cook 2 to 3 minutes longer or until everything is heated through.

Meanwhile, make the sauce by whisking the Shoyu sauce, sake, and Japanese mayonnaise in a mixing bowl.

Divide the fried cauliflower rice between individual bowls and serve with the prepared sauce. Enjoy!

363. Frittata with Turkey Breasts and Cottage Cheese

(Ready in about 50 minutes | Servings 4)

Per serving: 327 Calories; 13.4g Fat; 3.5g Carbs; 45.4g Protein; 2.3g Sugars; 0.4g Fiber

INGREDIENTS

1 tablespoon olive oil
1 pound turkey breasts, slices
6 large-sized eggs
3 tablespoons Greek yogurt
3 tablespoons Cottage cheese, crumbled

1/4 teaspoon ground black pepper
1/4 teaspoon red pepper flakes, crushed
Himalayan salt, to taste
1 red bell pepper, seeded and sliced
1 green bell pepper, seeded and sliced

DIRECTIONS

Grease the cooking basket with olive oil. Add the turkey and cook in the preheated Air Fryer at 350 degrees F for 30 minutes, flipping them over halfway through. Cut into bite-sized strips and reserve.

Now, beat the eggs with Greek yogurt, cheese, black pepper, red pepper, and salt. Add the bell peppers to a baking pan that is previously lightly greased with a cooking spray.

Add the turkey strips; pour the egg mixture over all ingredients.

Bake in the preheated Air Fryer at 360 degrees F for 15 minutes. Serve right away!

364. Cheddar Cheese and Pastrami Casserole

(Ready in about 20 minutes | Servings 2)

Per serving: 427 Calories; 31.4g Fat; 6.7g Carbs; 30.4g Protein; 3.8g Sugars; 0.6g Fiber

INGREDIENTS

4 eggs
1 bell pepper, chopped
2 spring onions, chopped
1 cup pastrami, sliced

1/4 cup Greek-style yogurt
1/2 cup Cheddar cheese, grated
Sea salt, to taste
1/4 teaspoon ground black pepper

DIRECTIONS

Start by preheating your Air Fryer to 330 degrees F. Spritz the baking pan with cooking oil.

Then, thoroughly combine all ingredients and pour the mixture into the prepared baking pan.

Cook for 7 to 9 minutes or until the eggs have set. Place on a cooling rack and let it sit for 10 minutes before slicing and serving.

365. Breakfast Eggs and Seafood Casserole

(Ready in about 30 minutes | Servings 2)

Per serving: 414 Calories; 23.4g Fat; 11.6g Carbs; 38.8g Protein; 7.2g Sugars; 1.2g Fiber

INGREDIENTS

1 tablespoon olive oil
2 garlic cloves, minced
1 small yellow onion, chopped
1/4 pound tilapia pieces
1/4 pound rockfish pieces

1/2 teaspoon dried basil
Salt and white pepper, to taste
4 eggs, lightly beaten
1 tablespoon dry sherry
4 tablespoons cheese, shredded

DIRECTIONS

Start by preheating your Air Fryer to 350 degrees F; add the olive oil to a baking pan. Once hot, cook the garlic and onion for 2 minutes or until fragrant.

Add the fish, basil, salt, and pepper. In a mixing dish, thoroughly combine the eggs with sherry and cheese. Pour the mixture into the baking pan.

Cook at 360 degrees F approximately 20 minutes. Bon appétit!

366. Snapper with Gruyere Cheese

(Ready in about 25 minutes | Servings 4)

Per serving: 406 Calories; 19.9g Fat; 9.3g Carbs; 46.4g Protein; 4.5g Sugars; 1g Fiber

INGREDIENTS

2 tablespoons olive oil
1 shallot, thinly sliced
2 garlic cloves, minced
1 ½ pounds snapper fillets
Sea salt and ground black pepper, to taste

1 teaspoon cayenne pepper
1/2 teaspoon dried basil
1/2 cup tomato puree
1/2 cup white wine
1 cup Gruyere cheese, shredded

DIRECTIONS

Heat 1 tablespoon of olive oil in a saucepan over medium-high heat. Now, cook the shallot and garlic until tender and aromatic.
Preheat your Air Fryer to 370 degrees F.
Grease a casserole dish with 1 tablespoon of olive oil. Place the snapper fillet in the casserole dish. Season with salt, black pepper, and cayenne pepper. Add the sautéed shallot mixture.
Add the basil, tomato puree and wine to the casserole dish. Cook for 10 minutes in the preheated Air Fryer.
Top with the shredded cheese and cook an additional 7 minutes. Serve immediately.

367. Two Cheese and Shrimp Dip

(Ready in about 25 minutes | Servings 8)

Per serving: 135 Calories; 9.7g Fat; 3.3g Carbs; 8.7g Protein; 1g Sugars; 2.7g Fiber

INGREDIENTS

2 teaspoons butter, melted
8 ounces shrimp, peeled and deveined
2 garlic cloves, minced
1/4 cup chicken stock
2 tablespoons fresh lemon juice
Salt and ground black pepper, to taste

1/2 teaspoon red pepper flakes
4 ounces cream cheese, at room temperature
1/2 cup sour cream
4 tablespoons mayonnaise
1/4 cup mozzarella cheese, shredded

DIRECTIONS

Start by preheating the Air Fryer to 395 degrees F. Grease the sides and bottom of a baking dish with the melted butter.
Place the shrimp, garlic, chicken stock, lemon juice, salt, black pepper, and red pepper flakes in the baking dish.
Transfer the baking dish to the cooking basket and bake for 10 minutes. Add the mixture to your food processor; pulse until the coarsely is chopped.
Add the cream cheese, sour cream, and mayonnaise. Top with the mozzarella cheese and bake in the preheated Air Fryer at 360 degrees F for 6 to 7 minutes or until the cheese is bubbling.
Serve immediately with breadsticks if desired. Bon appétit!

368. Baked Eggs with Cheese and Cauli Rice

(Ready in about 30 minutes | Servings 4)

Per serving: 433 Calories; 34g Fat; 9.3g Carbs; 22.4g Protein; 3g Sugars; 2.7g Fiber

INGREDIENTS

1 pound cauliflower rice
1 onion, diced
6 slices bacon, precooked
1 tablespoon butter, melted

Sea salt and ground black pepper, to taste
6 eggs
1 cup cheddar cheese, shredded

DIRECTIONS

Place the cauliflower rice and onion in a lightly greased casserole dish. Add the bacon and the reserved quinoa. Drizzle the melted butter over cauliflower rice and sprinkle with salt and pepper.
Bake in the preheated Air Fryer at 390 degrees F for 10 minutes.
Turn the temperature down to 350 degrees F.
Make six indents for the eggs; crack one egg into each indent. Bake for 10 minutes, rotating the pan once or twice to ensure even cooking.
Top with cheese and bake for a further 5 minutes. Enjoy!

369. Spicy Omelet with Ground Chicken

(Ready in about 15 minutes | Servings 2)

Per serving: 246 Calories; 13.0g Fat; 3.5g Carbs; 28.1g Protein; 1.3g Sugars; 1.2g Fiber

INGREDIENTS

4 eggs, whisked
4 ounces ground chicken
1/2 cup scallions, finely chopped
2 cloves garlic, finely minced
1/2 teaspoon salt

1/2 teaspoon ground black pepper
1/2 teaspoon paprika
1 teaspoon dried thyme
A dash of hot sauce

DIRECTIONS

Thoroughly combine all the ingredients in a mixing dish. Now, scrape the egg mixture into two oven safe ramekins that are previously greased with a thin layer of the vegetable oil.

Set your machine to cook at 350 degrees F; air-fry for 13 minutes or until thoroughly cooked. Serve immediately.

370. Za'atar Eggs with Chicken and Provolone cheese

(Ready in about 20 minutes | Servings 2)

Per serving: 440 Calories; 28.5g Fat; 8.7g Carbs; 36.9g Protein; 5.2g Sugars; 1.5g Fiber

INGREDIENTS

1/3 cup milk
1 1/2 Roma tomato, chopped
1/3 cup Provolone cheese, grated
1 teaspoon freshly cracked pink peppercorns
3 eggs

1 teaspoon Za'atar
½ chicken breast, cooked
1 teaspoon fine sea salt
1 teaspoon freshly cracked pink peppercorns

DIRECTIONS

Preheat your air fryer to cook at 365 degrees F. In a medium-sized mixing dish, whisk the eggs together with the milk, Za'atar, sea salt, and cracked pink peppercorns.

Spritz the ramekins with cooking oil; divide the prepared egg mixture among the greased ramekins.

Shred the chicken with two forks or a stand mixer. Add the shredded chicken to the ramekins, followed by the tomato and the cheese.

To finish, air-fry for 18 minutes or until it is done. Bon appétit!

371. Keto Brioche with Caciocavallo

(Ready in about 15 minutes | Servings 6)

Per serving: 546 Calories; 32.9g Fat; 9.2g Carbs; 52.1g Protein; 1.1g Sugars; 1.6g Fiber

INGREDIENTS

1/2 cup ricotta cheese, crumbled
1 cup part skim mozzarella cheese, shredded
1 egg
1/2 cup coconut flour
1/2 cup almond flour
1 teaspoon baking soda
2 tablespoons plain whey protein isolate
3 tablespoons sesame oil

2 teaspoons dried thyme
1 ½ cups Caciocavallo, grated
1 cup leftover chicken, shredded
3 eggs
1 teaspoon kosher salt
1 teaspoon freshly cracked black pepper, or more to taste
1/3 teaspoon gremolata

DIRECTIONS

To make the keto brioche, microwave the cheese for 1 minute 30 seconds, stirring twice. Add the cheese to the bowl of a food processor and blend well. Fold in the egg and mix again.

Add in the flour, baking soda, and plain whey protein isolate; blend again. Scrape the batter onto the center of a lightly greased cling film. Form the dough into a disk and transfer to your freezer to cool; cut into 6 pieces and transfer to a parchment-lined baking pan (make sure to grease your hands).

Firstly, slice off the top of each brioche; then, scoop out the insides.

Brush each brioche with sesame oil. Add the remaining ingredients in the order listed above.

Place the prepared brioche onto the bottom of the cooking basket. Bake for 7 minutes at 345 degrees F. Bon appétit!

372. Double Cheese Stuffed Chicken

(Ready in about 30 minutes | Servings 6)

Per serving: 398 Calories; 21.1g Fat; 4.1g Carbs; 45.4g Protein; 0.5g Sugars; 0.9g Fiber

INGREDIENTS

2 eggs, well-whisked

1 cup grated parmesan cheese

1 1/2 tablespoons extra-virgin olive oil

1 ½ tablespoons fresh chives, chopped

3 chicken breasts, halved lengthwise

1 ½ cup mozzarella cheese

2 teaspoons sweet paprika

1/2 teaspoon whole grain mustard

1/2 teaspoon cumin powder

1/3 teaspoon fine sea salt

1/3 cup fresh cilantro, chopped

1/3 teaspoon freshly ground black pepper, or more to taste

DIRECTIONS

Flatten out each piece of the chicken breast using a rolling pin. Then, grab three mixing dishes.

In the first one, combine mozzarella cheese with the cilantro, fresh chives, cumin, and mustard.

In another mixing dish, whisk the eggs together with the sweet paprika. In the third dish, combine the salt, black pepper, and parmesan cheese.

Spread the cheese mixture over each piece of chicken. Repeat with the remaining pieces of the chicken breasts; now, roll them up.

Coat each chicken roll with the whisked egg; dredge each chicken roll into the parmesan mixture. Lower the rolls onto the Air Fryer cooking basket. Drizzle extra-virgin olive oil over all rolls.

Air fry at 345 degrees F for 28 minutes, working in batches. Serve warm, garnished with sour cream if desired.

373. Spring Frittata with Chicken and Goat Cheese

(Ready in about 10 minutes | Servings 4)

Per serving: 321 Calories; 17.7g Fat; 1.3g Carbs; 36.5g Protein; 0.7g Sugars; 0.3g Fiber

INGREDIENTS

1 cup goat cheese, crumbled

1 teaspoon dried rosemary

2 cups cooked chicken breasts, boneless and shredded

1/4 teaspoon mustard seeds

1 teaspoon red pepper flakes , crushed

5 medium-sized whisked eggs

1/3 teaspoon ground white pepper

1/2 cup green onions, chopped

1 green garlic stalk, chopped

Fine sea salt, to taste

Nonstick cooking spray

DIRECTIONS

Grab a baking dish that fit in your Air Fryer.

Lightly coat the inside of the baking dish with a nonstick cooking spray of choice. Stir in all ingredients, minus cheese. Stir to combine well.

Set your machine to cook at 335 degrees for 8 minutes; check for doneness. Scatter crumbled goat cheese over the top and eat immediately!

374. Cottage Cheese Stuffed Chicken Rolls

(Ready in about 20 minutes | Servings 2)

Per serving: 424 Calories; 24.5g Fat; 7.5g Carbs; 43.4g Protein; 5.3g Sugars; 0.1g Fiber

INGREDIENTS

1/2 cup Cottage cheese

2 eggs, beaten

2 medium-sized chicken breasts, halved

2 tablespoons fresh coriander, chopped

1 teaspoon fine sea salt

1/2 cup parmesan cheese, grated

1/3 teaspoon freshly ground black pepper, to savor

3 cloves garlic, finely minced

DIRECTIONS

Firstly, flatten out the chicken breast using a meat tenderizer.

In a medium-sized mixing dish, combine the Cottage cheese with the garlic, coriander, salt, and black pepper.

Spread 1/3 of the mixture over the first chicken breast. Repeat with the remaining ingredients. Roll the chicken around the filling; make sure to secure with toothpicks.

Now, whisk the egg in a shallow bowl. In another shallow bowl, combine the salt, ground black pepper, and parmesan cheese.

Coat the chicken breasts with the whisked egg; now, roll them in the parmesan cheese.

Cook in the air fryer cooking basket at 365 degrees F for 22 minutes. Serve immediately.

375. Masala-Style Baked Eggs

(Ready in about 25 minutes | Servings 6)

Per serving: 377 Calories; 15.2g Fat; 2.4g Carbs; 54.5g Protein; 0.6g Sugars; 0.6g Fiber

INGREDIENTS

6 medium-sized eggs, beaten
1 teaspoon garam masala
1 cup scallions, finely chopped
3 cloves garlic, finely minced
2 cups leftover chicken, shredded
2 tablespoons sesame oil

Hot sauce, for drizzling
1 teaspoon turmeric
1 teaspoon mixed peppercorns, freshly cracked
1 teaspoon kosher salt
1/3 teaspoon smoked paprika

DIRECTIONS

Warm sesame oil in a sauté pan over a moderate flame; then, sauté the scallions together with garlic until just fragrant; it takes about 5 minutes. Now, throw in leftover chicken and stir until thoroughly warmed.
In a medium-sized bowl or a measuring cup, thoroughly combine the eggs with all seasonings.
Then, coat the inside of six oven safe ramekins with a nonstick cooking spray. Divide the egg/chicken mixture among your ramekins.
Air-fry approximately 18 minutes at 355 degrees F. Drizzle with hot sauce and eat warm.

376. Fluffy Omelet with Leftover Beef

(Ready in about 20 minutes | Servings 4)

Per serving: 305 Calories; 19.7g Fat; 5g Carbs; 26.2g Protein; 1.7g Sugars; 0.4g Fiber

INGREDIENTS

Non-stick cooking spray
1/2 pound leftover beef, coarsely chopped
2 garlic cloves, pressed
1 cup kale, torn into pieces and wilted
1 bell pepper, chopped

6 eggs, beaten
6 tablespoons sour cream
1/2 teaspoon turmeric powder
1 teaspoon red pepper flakes
Salt and ground black pepper, to your liking

DIRECTIONS

Spritz the inside of four ramekins with a cooking spray.
Divide all of the above ingredients among the prepared ramekins. Stir until everything is well combined.
Air-fry at 360 degrees F for 16 minutes; check with a wooden stick and return the eggs to the Air Fryer for a few more minutes as needed.
Serve immediately.

377. Hearty Southwestern Cheeseburger Frittata

(Ready in about 30 minutes | Servings 2)

Per serving: 511 Calories; 35.8g Fat; 5.1g Carbs; 40g Protein; 2.1g Sugars; 1.1g Fiber

INGREDIENTS

3 tablespoons goat cheese, crumbled
2 cups lean ground beef
1 ½ tablespoons olive oil
½ teaspoon dried marjoram
2 eggs

½ onion, peeled and chopped
½ teaspoon paprika
½ teaspoon kosher salt
1 teaspoon ground black pepper

DIRECTIONS

Set your air fryer to cook at 345 degrees F.
Melt the oil in a skillet over a moderate flame; then, sweat the onion until it has softened. Add ground beef and cook until browned; crumble with a fork and set aside, keeping it warm.
Whisk the eggs with all the seasonings.
Spritz the inside of a baking dish with a pan spray. Pour the beaten egg mixture into the baking dish, followed by the reserved beef/onion mixture. Top with the crumbled goat cheese.
Bake for about 27 minutes or until a tester comes out clean and dry when stuck in the center of the frittata. Bon appétit!

378. Italian Eggs with Smoked Salmon

(Ready in about 25 minutes | Servings 4)

Per serving: 310 Calories; 17.2g Fat; 2.1g Carbs; 33.2g Protein; 1.7g Sugars; 0.2g Fiber

INGREDIENTS

1/3 cup Asiago cheese, grated
1/3 teaspoon dried dill weed
1/2 tomato, chopped
6 eggs
1/3 cup milk

Pan spray
1 cup smoked salmon, chopped
Fine sea salt and freshly cracked black pepper, to taste
1/3 teaspoon smoked cayenne pepper

DIRECTIONS

Set your air fryer to cook at 365 degrees F. In a mixing bowl, whisk the eggs, milk, smoked cayenne pepper, salt, black pepper, and dill weed.
Lightly grease 4 ramekins with pan spray of choice; divide the egg/milk mixture among the prepared ramekins.
Add the salmon and tomato; top with the grated Asiago cheese. Finally, air-fry for 16 minutes. Bon appétit!

379. Breakfast Eggs with Swiss Chard and Ham

(Ready in about 20 minutes | Servings 2)

Per serving: 417 Calories; 17.8g Fat; 3g Carbs; 61g Protein; 0.9g Sugars; 1.3g Fiber

INGREDIENTS

2 eggs
1/4 teaspoon dried or fresh marjoram
2 teaspoons chili powder
1/3 teaspoon kosher salt

1/2 cup steamed Swiss Chard
1/4 teaspoon dried or fresh rosemary
4 pork ham slices
1/3 teaspoon ground black pepper, or more to taste

DIRECTIONS

Divide the Swiss Chard and ham among 2 ramekins; crack an egg into each ramekin. Sprinkle with seasonings.
Cook for 15 minutes at 335 degrees F or until your eggs reach desired texture.
Serve warm with spicy tomato ketchup and pickles. Bon appétit!

380. Decadent Frittata with Roasted Garlic and Sausage

(Ready in about 20 minutes | Servings 6)

Per serving: 291 Calories; 14.1g Fat; 3.5g Carbs; 35.9g Protein; 1.7g Sugars; 0.4g Fiber

INGREDIENTS

6 large-sized eggs
2 tablespoons butter, melted
3 tablespoons cream
1 cup chicken sausage, chopped
2 tablespoons roasted garlic, pressed

1/3 cup goat cheese such as Caprino, crumbled
1 teaspoon smoked cayenne pepper
1 teaspoon freshly ground black pepper
1/2 red onion, peeled and chopped
1 teaspoon fine sea salt

DIRECTIONS

First of all, grease six oven safe ramekins with melted butter. Then, divide roasted garlic and red onion among your ramekins. Add chicken sausage and toss to combine.
Beat the eggs with cream until well combined and pale; sprinkle with cayenne pepper, salt, and black pepper; beat again.
Scrape the mixture into your ramekins and air-fry for about 13 minutes at 355 degrees F.
Top with crumbled cheese and serve immediately.

VEGETARIAN

381. Spicy Braised Vegetables

(Ready in about 25 minutes | Servings 4)

Per serving: 144 Calories; 13.6g Fat; 5.4g Carbs; 1.2g Protein; 1.8g Sugars; 1.2g Fi

INGREDIENTS

1 large-sized zucchini, sliced
1 Serrano pepper, deveined and thinly sliced
2 bell peppers, deveined and thinly sliced

1 celery stalk, cut into matchsticks
1/4 cup olive oil
1/2 teaspoon porcini powder
1/4 teaspoon mustard powder
1/2 teaspoon fennel seeds

1 tablespoon garlic powder
1/2 teaspoon fine sea salt
1/4 teaspoon ground black pepper
1/2 cup tomato puree

DIRECTIONS

Place the sweet potatoes, zucchini, peppers, and the carrot into the Air Fryer cooking basket.

Drizzle with olive oil and toss to coat; cook in the preheated Air Fryer at 350 degrees F for 15 minutes.

While the vegetables are cooking, prepare the sauce by thoroughly whisking the other ingredients, without the tomato ketchup. Lightly grease a baking dish that fits into your machine.

Transfer cooked vegetables to the prepared baking dish; add the sauce and toss to coat well.

Turn the Air Fryer to 390 degrees F and cook the vegetables for 5 more minutes. Bon appétit!

382. Zucchini with Mediterranean Dill Sauce

(Ready in about 1 hour | Servings 4)

Per serving: 184 Calories; 15.4g Fat; 5.5g Carbs; 8.1g Protein; 1g Sugars; 1.6g Fiber

INGREDIENTS

1 pound zucchini, peeled and cubed
2 tablespoons melted butter
1 teaspoon sea salt flakes
1 sprig rosemary, leaves only, crushed
2 sprigs thyme, leaves only, crushed
1/2 teaspoon freshly cracked black peppercorns

For Mediterranean Dipping Sauce:
1/2 cup mascarpone cheese
1/3 cup yogurt
1 tablespoon fresh dill, chopped
1 tablespoon olive oil

DIRECTIONS

Firstly, set your Air Fryer to cook at 350 degrees F. Now, add the potato cubes to the bowl with cold water and soak them approximately for 35 minutes.

After that, dry the potato cubes using a paper towel.

In a mixing dish, thoroughly whisk the melted butter with sea salt flakes, rosemary, thyme, and freshly cracked peppercorns. Rub the potato cubes with this butter/spice mix.

Air-fry the potato cubes in the cooking basket for 18 to 20 minutes or until cooked through; make sure to shake the potatoes to cook them evenly.

Meanwhile, make the Mediterranean dipping sauce by mixing the remaining ingredients. Serve warm potatoes with Mediterranean sauce for dipping and enjoy!

383. Classic Onion Rings

(Ready in about 30 minutes | Servings 8)

Per serving: 179 Calories; 12.3g Fat; 7.1g Carbs; 9.7g Protein; 2.7g Sugars; 1.5g Fiber

INGREDIENTS

2 medium-sized yellow onions, cut into rings
1 cup almond flour
1/2 teaspoon baking soda
1 teaspoon baking powder

1 ½ teaspoons sea salt flakes
2 medium-sized eggs
1 ½ cups plain milk
1 ¼ cups grated parmesan cheese
1/2 teaspoon green peppercorns,

freshly cracked
1/2 teaspoon dried dill weed
1/4 teaspoon paprika

DIRECTIONS

Begin by preheating your Air Fryer to 356 degrees F.

Place the onion rings into the bowl with icy cold water; let them stay 15 to 20 minutes; drain the onion rings and dry them using a kitchen towel.

In a shallow bowl, mix the flour together with baking soda, baking powder and sea salt flakes. Then, coat each onion ring with the flour mixture;

In another shallow bowl, beat the eggs with milk; add the mixture to the remaining flour mixture and whisk well. Dredge the coated onion rings into this batter.

In a third bowl, mix the parmesan cheese, green peppercorns, dill, and paprika. Roll the onion rings over the parmesan cheese mixture, covering well.

Air-fry them in the cooking basket for 8 to 11 minutes or until thoroughly cooked to golden.

384. Cheese Stuffed Zucchini with Scallions

(Ready in about 20 minutes | Servings 4)

Per serving: 199 Calories; 16.4g Fat; 4.5g Carbs; 9.2g Protein; 1.5g Sugars; 0.5g Fiber

INGREDIENTS

1 large zucchini, cut into four pieces
2 tablespoons olive oil
1 cup Ricotta cheese, room temperature
2 tablespoons scallions, chopped
1 heaping tablespoon fresh parsley, roughly chopped

1 heaping tablespoon coriander, minced
2 ounces Cheddar cheese, preferably freshly grated
1 teaspoon celery seeds
1/2 teaspoon salt
1/2 teaspoon garlic pepper

DIRECTIONS

Cook your zucchini in the Air Fryer cooking basket for approximately 10 minutes at 350 degrees F. Check for doneness and cook for 2-3 minutes longer if needed.

Meanwhile, make the stuffing by mixing the other items.

When your zucchini is thoroughly cooked, open them up. Divide the stuffing among all zucchini pieces and bake an additional 5 minutes.

385. Rainbow Omelet with Halloumi Cheese

(Ready in about 15 minutes | Servings 2)

Per serving: 313 Calories; 21.8g Fat; 8.5g Carbs; 21.1g Protein; 4.2g Sugars; 2.1g Fiber

INGREDIENTS

3 tablespoons plain milk
4 eggs, whisked
1 teaspoon melted butter
Kosher salt and freshly ground black pepper, to taste
1 red bell pepper, deveined and chopped

1 yellow bell pepper, deveined and chopped
1 white onion, finely chopped
1/2 cup baby spinach leaves, roughly chopped
1/2 cup Halloumi cheese, shaved

DIRECTIONS

Start with spreading the canola cooking spray onto the Air Fryer baking pan.

Add all of the above ingredients to the baking pan; give them a good stir.

Then, set your machine to cook at 350 degrees F; cook your omelet for 13 minutes. Serve warm and enjoy!

386. Hearty Celery Croquettes with Chive Mayo

(Ready in about 15 minutes | Servings 4)

Per serving: 214 Calories; 18g Fat; 6.8g Carbs; 7g Protein; 0.9g Sugars; 1.6g Fiber

INGREDIENTS

2 medium-sized celery stalks, trimmed and grated
1/2 cup of leek, finely chopped
1 tablespoon garlic paste
1/4 teaspoon freshly cracked black pepper
1 teaspoon fine sea salt
1 tablespoon fresh dill, finely chopped

1 egg, lightly whisked
1/4 cup almond flour
1/2 cup parmesan cheese, freshly grated
1/4 teaspoon baking powder
2 tablespoons fresh chives, chopped
4 tablespoons mayonnaise

DIRECTIONS

Place the celery on a paper towel and squeeze them to remove excess liquid.

Combine the vegetables with the other ingredients, except the chives and mayo. Shape the balls using 1 tablespoon of the vegetable mixture.

Then, gently flatten each ball with your palm or a wide spatula. Spritz the croquettes with a non - stick cooking oil.

Air-fry the vegetable croquettes in a single layer for 6 minutes at 360 degrees F.

Meanwhile, mix fresh chives and mayonnaise. Serve warm croquettes with chive mayo. Bon appétit!

387. Cauliflower and Colby Cheese Fritters

(Ready in about 15 minutes | Servings 8)

Per serving: 274 Calories; 21.2g Fat; 8.7g Carbs; 13.3g Protein; 2.5g Sugars; 2.5g Fiber

INGREDIENTS

2 pounds cauliflower florets
1/2 cup scallions, finely chopped
1/2 teaspoon freshly ground black pepper, or more to taste
1 tablespoon fine sea salt

1/2 teaspoon hot paprika
2 cups Colby cheese, shredded
1 cup parmesan cheese, grated
1/4 cup canola oil

DIRECTIONS

Firstly, boil the cauliflower until fork tender. Drain, peel and mash your cauliflower.
Thoroughly mix the mashed cauliflower with scallions, pepper, salt, paprika, and Colby cheese. Then, shape the balls using your hands. Now, flatten the balls to make the patties.
Roll the patties over grated parmesan cheese. Drizzle canola oil over them.
Next, cook your patties at 360 degrees F approximately 10 minutes, working in batches. Serve with tabasco mayo if desired. Bon appétit!

388. Favorite Broccoli with Garlic Sauce

(Ready in about 19 minutes | Servings 4)

Per serving: 247 Calories; 22.2g Fat; 9.3g Carbs; 4.1g Protein; 2g Sugars; 3g Fiber

INGREDIENTS

2 tablespoons vegetable oil of choice
Kosher salt and freshly ground black pepper, to taste
1 pound broccoli florets

For the Dipping Sauce:
2 teaspoons dried rosemary, crushed
3 garlic cloves, minced
1/3 teaspoon dried marjoram, crushed
1/4 cup sour cream
1/3 cup mayonnaise

DIRECTIONS

Lightly grease your broccoli with a thin layer of vegetable oil. Season with salt and ground black pepper.
Arrange the seasoned broccoli in an Air Fryer cooking basket. Bake at 395 degrees F for 15 minutes, shaking once or twice.
In the meantime, prepare the dipping sauce by mixing all the sauce ingredients. Serve warm broccoli with the dipping sauce and enjoy!

389. Kid-Friendly Zucchini Fries

(Ready in about 20 minutes | Servings 4)

Per serving: 85 Calories; 7.4g Fat; 3.8g Carbs; 3.1g Protein; 0g Sugars; 1.3g Fiber

INGREDIENTS

2 tablespoons olive oil
1/2 teaspoon smoked cayenne pepper
1 large zucchini, peeled and cut into 1/4-inch long slices

1/2 teaspoon shallot powder
1/3 teaspoon freshly ground black pepper, or more to taste
3/4 teaspoon garlic salt

DIRECTIONS

Firstly, preheat your Air Fryer to 360 degrees F.
Then, add the zucchini to a mixing dish; toss them with the other ingredients.
Cook the zucchini fries approximately 14 minutes. Serve with a dipping sauce of choice.

390. Dilled Zucchini and Spinach Croquettes

(Ready in about 9 minutes | Servings 6)

Per serving: 171 Calories; 10.8g Fat; 5.9g Carbs; 13.1g Protein; 0.3g Sugars; 1g Fiber

INGREDIENTS

4 eggs, slightly beaten
1⁄2 cup almond flour
1⁄2 cup goat cheese, crumbled
1 teaspoon fine sea salt
4 garlic cloves, minced

1 cup baby spinach
1⁄2 cup parmesan cheese grated
1/3 teaspoon red pepper flakes
1 pound zucchini, peeled and grated
1/3 teaspoon dried dill weed

DIRECTIONS

Thoroughly combine all ingredients in a bowl. Now, roll the mixture to form small croquettes.
Air fry at 335 degrees F for 7 minutes or until golden. Tate, adjust for seasonings and serve warm.

391. Minty Eggplant and Zucchini Bites

(Ready in about 35 minutes | Servings 8)

Per serving: 110 Calories; 8.3g Fat; 8.8g Carbs; 2.6g Protein; 2.4g Sugars; 2.5g Fiber

INGREDIENTS

2 teaspoons fresh mint leaves, chopped
1 ½ teaspoons red pepper chili flakes
2 tablespoons melted butter

1 pound eggplant, peeled and cubed
1 pound zucchini, peeled and cubed
3 tablespoons olive oil

DIRECTIONS

Toss all of the above ingredients in a large-sized mixing dish.
Roast the eggplant and zucchini bites for 30 minutes at 325 degrees F in your Air Fryer, turning once or twice.
Serve with a homemade dipping sauce.

392. Mom's Veggie Fritters

(Ready in about 30 minutes | Servings 3)

Per serving: 344 Calories; 27g Fat; 9.3g Carbs; 17.4g Protein; 3.1g Sugars; 3.7g Fiber

INGREDIENTS

1 cup celery, chopped
1 cup cauliflower rice
2 garlic cloves, minced
1 shallot, chopped
Sea salt and ground black pepper, to taste

2 tablespoons fresh parsley, chopped
1 egg, well beaten
1 cup Romano cheese, grated
1/2 cup almond flour
1 tablespoon olive oil

DIRECTIONS

Mix the veggies, spices, egg, almond flour, and Romano cheese until everything is well incorporated.
Take 1 tablespoon of the veggie mixture and roll into a ball. Roll the balls onto the dried bread flakes. Brush the veggie balls with olive oil on all sides.
Cook in the preheated Air Fryer at 360 degrees F for 15 minutes or until thoroughly cooked and crispy.
Repeat the process until you run out of ingredients. Bon appétit!

393. Fried Pickles with Dijon Sauce

(Ready in about 15 minutes | Servings 2)

Per serving: 351 Calories; 28g Fat; 7.6g Carbs; 16.1g Protein; 4.8g Sugars; 1.1g Fiber

INGREDIENTS

1 egg, whisked
2 tablespoons buttermilk
1/2 cup Romano cheese, grated
1/2 teaspoon onion powder
1/2 teaspoon garlic powder
1 ½ cups dill pickle chips, pressed dry with kitchen towels

Mayo Sauce:
1/3 cup mayonnaise
1 tablespoon Dijon mustard
1 tablespoon ketchup
1/4 teaspoon ground black pepper

DIRECTIONS

In a shallow bowl, whisk the egg with buttermilk.
In another bowl, mix Romano cheese, onion powder, and garlic powder.
Dredge the pickle chips in the egg mixture, then, in the cheese mixture.
Cook in the preheated Air Fryer at 400 degrees F for 5 minutes; shake the basket and cook for 5 minutes more.
Meanwhile, mix all the sauce ingredients until well combined. Serve the fried pickles with the mayo sauce for dipping.

394. Crispy Green Beans with Pecorino Romano

(Ready in about 15 minutes | Servings 3)

Per serving: 191 Calories; 12.8g Fat; 9.5g Carbs; 11.4g Protein; 2.8g Sugars; 5g Fiber

INGREDIENTS

2 tablespoons buttermilk
1 egg
4 tablespoons almond meal
4 tablespoons golden flaxseed meal

4 tablespoons Pecorino Romano cheese, finely grated
Coarse salt and crushed black pepper, to taste
1 teaspoon smoked paprika
6 ounces green beans, trimmed

DIRECTIONS

In a shallow bowl, whisk together the buttermilk and egg.
In a separate bowl, combine the almond meal, golden flaxseed meal, Pecorino Romano cheese, salt, black pepper, and paprika.
Dip the green beans in the egg mixture, then, in the cheese mixture. Place the green beans in the lightly greased cooking basket.
Cook in the preheated Air Fryer at 390 degrees F for 4 minutes. Shake the basket and cook for a further 3 minutes.
Taste, adjust the seasonings, and serve with the dipping sauce if desired. Bon appétit!

395. Spicy Celery Sticks

(Ready in about 20 minutes | Servings 4)

Per serving: 82 Calories; 6.9g Fat; 4.4g Carbs; 1.1g Protein; 2g Sugars; 2g Fiber

INGREDIENTS

1 pound celery, cut into matchsticks
2 tablespoons peanut oil
1 jalapeño, seeded and minced

1/4 teaspoon dill
1/2 teaspoon basil
Salt and white pepper to taste

DIRECTIONS

Start by preheating your Air Fryer to 380 degrees F.
Toss all ingredients together and place them in the Air Fryer basket.
Cook for 15 minutes, shaking the basket halfway through the cooking time. Transfer to a serving platter and enjoy!

396. The Best Avocado Fries Ever

(Ready in about 50 minutes | Servings 4)

Per serving: 540 Calories; 46.7g Fat; 9.5g Carbs; 22.1g Protein; 1.4g Sugars; 4g Fiber

INGREDIENTS

1/2 head garlic (6-7 cloves)
1/2 cup almond meal
Sea salt and ground black pepper, to taste
2 eggs
1/2 cup parmesan cheese, grated

2 avocados, cut into wedges
Sauce:
1/2 cup mayonnaise
1 teaspoon lemon juice
1 teaspoon mustard

DIRECTIONS

Place the garlic on a piece of aluminum foil and spritz with cooking spray. Wrap the garlic in the foil.
Cook in the preheated Air Fryer at 400 degrees for 12 minutes. Check the garlic, open the top of the foil and continue to cook for 10 minutes more.
Let it cool for 10 to 15 minutes; remove the cloves by squeezing them out of the skins; mash the garlic and reserve.
In a shallow bowl, combine the almond meal, salt, and black pepper. In another shallow dish, whisk the eggs until frothy.
Place the parmesan cheese in a third shallow dish. Dredge the avocado wedges in the almond meal mixture, shaking off the excess. Then, dip in the egg mixture; lastly, dredge in parmesan cheese.
Spritz the avocado wedges with cooking oil on all sides.
Cook in the preheated Air Fryer at 395 degrees F approximately 8 minutes, turning them over halfway through the cooking time.
Meanwhile, combine the sauce ingredients with the smashed roasted garlic. To serve, divide the avocado fries between plates and top with the sauce. Enjoy!

397. Cottage and Mayonnaise Stuffed Peppers

(Ready in about 20 minutes | Servings 2)

Per serving: 312 Calories; 25g Fat; 8.7g Carbs; 12.9g Protein; 5.1g Sugars; 1.1g Fiber

INGREDIENTS

1 red bell pepper, top and seeds removed
1 yellow bell pepper, top and seeds removed
Salt and pepper, to taste

1 cup Cottage cheese
4 tablespoons mayonnaise
2 pickles, chopped

DIRECTIONS

Arrange the peppers in the lightly greased cooking basket. Cook in the preheated Air Fryer at 400 degrees F for 15 minutes, turning them over halfway through the cooking time.
Season with salt and pepper.
Then, in a mixing bowl, combine the cream cheese with the mayonnaise and chopped pickles. Stuff the pepper with the cream cheese mixture and serve. Enjoy!

398. Stuffed Mushrooms with Cheese and Herbs

(Ready in about 15 minutes | Servings 3)

Per serving: 280 Calories; 23.3g Fat; 7.1g Carbs; 12.3g Protein; 3.1g Sugars; 0.9g Fiber

INGREDIENTS

9 large button mushrooms, stems removed
1 tablespoon olive oil
Salt and ground black pepper, to taste
1/2 teaspoon dried rosemary
6 tablespoons Swiss cheese shredded

6 tablespoons Romano cheese, shredded
6 tablespoons cream cheese
1 teaspoon soy sauce
1 teaspoon garlic, minced
3 tablespoons green onions, minced

DIRECTIONS

Brush the mushroom caps with olive oil; sprinkle with salt, pepper, and rosemary.
In a mixing bowl, thoroughly combine the remaining ingredients; mix to combine well and divide the filling mixture among the mushroom caps.
Cook in the preheated Air Fryer at 390 degrees F for 7 minutes.
Let the mushrooms cool slightly before serving. Bon appétit!

399. Mediterranean Vegetable Gratin

(Ready in about 35 minutes | Servings 4)

Per serving: 266 Calories; 22.8g Fat; 8.3g Carbs; 7.4g Protein; 5.1g Sugars; 1.9g Fiber

INGREDIENTS

1 eggplant, peeled and sliced
2 bell peppers, seeded and sliced
1 red onion, sliced
1 teaspoon fresh garlic, minced
4 tablespoons olive oil
1 teaspoon mustard

1 teaspoon dried oregano
1 teaspoon smoked paprika
Salt and ground black pepper, to taste
1 tomato, sliced
6 ounces halloumi cheese, sliced lengthways

DIRECTIONS

Start by preheating your Air Fryer to 370 degrees F. Spritz a baking pan with nonstick cooking spray.

Place the eggplant, peppers, onion, and garlic on the bottom of the baking pan. Add the olive oil, mustard, and spices. Transfer to the cooking basket and cook for 14 minutes.

Top with the tomatoes and cheese; increase the temperature to 390 degrees F and cook for 5 minutes more until bubbling. Let it sit on a cooling rack for 10 minutes before serving.

Bon appétit!

400. Chinese Cabbage Bake

(Ready in about 35 minutes | Servings 4)

Per serving: 489 Calories; 45.1g Fat; 8.9g Carbs; 14.2g Protein; 4.4g Sugars; 3.4g Fiber

INGREDIENTS

1/2 pound Chinese cabbage, roughly chopped
2 bell peppers, seeded and sliced
1 jalapeno pepper, seeded and sliced
1 onion, thickly sliced
2 garlic cloves, sliced
1/2 stick butter

4 tablespoons flaxseed meal
1/2 cup milk
1 cup cream cheese
Sea salt and freshly ground black pepper, to taste
1/2 teaspoon cayenne pepper
1 cup Monterey Jack cheese, shredded

DIRECTIONS

Heat a pan of salted water and bring to a boil. Boil the Chinese cabbage for 2 to 3 minutes. Transfer the Chinese cabbage to cold water to stop the cooking process.

Place the Chinese cabbage in a lightly greased casserole dish. Add the peppers, onion, and garlic.

Next, melt the butter in a saucepan over a moderate heat. Gradually add the flaxseed meal and cook for 2 minutes to form a paste.

Slowly pour in the milk, stirring continuously until a thick sauce forms. Add the cream cheese. Season with the salt, black pepper, and cayenne pepper. Add the mixture to the casserole dish.

Top with the shredded Monterey Jack cheese and bake in the preheated Air Fryer at 390 degrees F for 25 minutes. Serve hot.

401. Crispy Leek Strips

(Ready in about 52 minutes | Servings 6)

Per serving: 114 Calories; 8.7g Fat; 8.4g Carbs; 2.7g Protein; 2.3g Sugars; 2.4g Fiber

INGREDIENTS

1/2 teaspoon porcini powder
1 cup almond flour
1/2 cup coconut flour
1 tablespoon vegetable oil

2 medium-sized leeks, slice into julienne strips
2 large-sized dishes with ice water
2 teaspoons onion powder
Fine sea salt and cayenne pepper, to taste

DIRECTIONS

Allow the leeks to soak in ice water for about 25 minutes; drain well.

Place the flour, salt, cayenne pepper, onions powder, and porcini powder into a resealable bag. Add the leeks and shake to coat well.

Drizzle vegetable oil over the seasoned leeks. Air fry at 390 degrees F for about 18 minutes; turn them halfway through the cooking time.

Serve with homemade mayonnaise or any other sauce for dipping. Enjoy!

402. Mushrooms with Tahini Sauce

(Ready in about 22 minutes | Servings 5)

Per serving: 211 Calories; 17.2g Fat; 9.5g Carbs; 8.2g Protein; 3.2g Sugars; 3.5g Fiber

INGREDIENTS

1/2 cup tahini

1/2 teaspoon turmeric powder

1/3 teaspoon cayenne pepper

2 tablespoons lemon juice, freshly squeezed

1 teaspoon kosher salt

1/3 teaspoon freshly cracked black pepper

1 1/2 tablespoons vermouth

1 ½ tablespoons olive oil

1 ½ pounds Cremini mushrooms

DIRECTIONS

Grab a mixing dish and toss the mushrooms with the olive oil, turmeric powder, salt, black pepper, and cayenne pepper. Cook them in your air fryer for 9 minutes at 355 degrees F.

Pause your Air Fryer, give it a good stir and cook for 10 minutes longer.

Meanwhile, thoroughly combine lemon juice, vermouth, and tahini. Serve warm mushrooms with tahini sauce. Bon appétit!

403. Keto Cauliflower Hash Browns

(Ready in about 23 minutes | Servings 6)

Per serving: 155 Calories; 11.2g Fat; 8.7g Carbs; 5.6g Protein; 2.7g Sugars; 2.1g Fiber

INGREDIENTS

1/2 cup Cheddar cheese, shredded

1 tablespoon soft cheese, at room temperature

1/3 cup almond meal

1 ½ yellow or white medium-sized onion, chopped

5 ounces condensed cream of celery soup

1 tablespoon fresh cilantro, finely minced

1/3 cup sour cream

3 cloves garlic, peeled and finely minced

2 cups cauliflower, grated

1 1/2 tablespoons margarine, melted

Sea salt and freshly ground black pepper, to your liking

Crushed red pepper flakes, to your liking

DIRECTIONS

Grab a large-sized bowl and whisk the celery soup, sour cream, soft cheese, red pepper, salt, and black pepper. Stir in the cauliflower, onion, garlic, cilantro, and Cheddar cheese. Mix until everything is thoroughly combined.

Scrape the mixture into a baking dish that is previously lightly greased.

In another mixing bowl, combine together the almond meal and melted margarine. Spread the mixture evenly over the top of the hash brown mixture.

Bake for 17 minutes at 290 degrees F. Eat warm, garnished with some extra sour cream if desired.

404. Spicy Ricotta Stuffed Mushrooms

(Ready in about 25 minutes | Servings 4)

Per serving: 144 Calories; 8.4g Fat; 7.7g Carbs; 11.4g Protein; 3.1g Sugars; 1.6g Fiber

INGREDIENTS

1 pound small white mushrooms

Sea salt and ground black pepper, to taste

4 tablespoons Ricotta cheese

1/2 teaspoon ancho chili powder

1 teaspoon paprika

1 egg

1/2 cup parmesan cheese, grated

DIRECTIONS

Remove the stems from the mushroom caps and chop them; mix the chopped mushrooms steams with the salt, black pepper, cheese, chili powder, and paprika.

Add in eggs and mix to combine well. Stuff the mushroom caps with the egg/cheese filling.

To with parmesan cheese. Spritz the stuffed mushrooms with cooking spray.

Cook in the preheated Air Fryer at 360 degrees F for 18 minutes. Bon appétit!

405. Cauliflower with Cholula Sauce

(Ready in about 20 minutes | Servings 4)

Per serving: 184 Calories; 15.1g Fat; 9g Carbs; 5.4g Protein; 2.8g Sugars; 5g Fiber

INGREDIENTS

1/2 cup almond flour
2 tablespoons flaxseed meal
1/2 cup water
Salt, to taste
1/2 teaspoon ground black pepper
1/2 teaspoon shallot powder

1/2 teaspoon garlic powder
1/2 teaspoon cayenne pepper
2 tablespoons olive oil
1 pound cauliflower, broken into small florets
1/4 cup Cholula sauce

DIRECTIONS

Start by preheating your Air Fryer to 400 degrees F. Lightly grease a baking pan with cooking spray.
In a mixing bowl, combine the almond flour, flaxseed meal, water, spices, and olive oil. Coat the cauliflower with the prepared batter; arrange the cauliflower on the baking pan.
Then, bake in the preheated Air Fryer for 8 minutes or until golden brown.
Brush the Cholula sauce all over the cauliflower florets and bake an additional 4 to 5 minutes. Bon appétit!

406. Celeriac with Greek Yogurt Dip

(Ready in about 25 minutes | Servings 2)

Per serving: 207 Calories; 17.4g Fat; 9.3g Carbs; 3.6g Protein; 4.1g Sugars; 2.6g Fiber

INGREDIENTS

1/2 pound celeriac, cut into 1 1/2-inch pieces
1 red onion, cut into 1 1/2-inch pieces
1 tablespoon sesame oil
1/2 teaspoon ground black pepper, to taste
1/2 teaspoon sea salt

Spiced Yogurt:
1/4 cup Greek yogurt
2 tablespoons mayonnaise
1/2 teaspoon mustard seeds
1/2 teaspoon chili powder

DIRECTIONS

Place the vegetables in a single layer in the lightly greased cooking basket. Drizzle the sesame oil over vegetables.
Sprinkle with black pepper and sea salt.
Cook at 390 degrees F for 20 minutes, shaking the basket halfway through the cooking time.
Meanwhile, make the sauce by whisking all ingredients. Spoon the sauce over the roasted vegetables. Bon appétit!

407. Tangy Asparagus and Broccoli

(Ready in about 25 minutes | Servings 4)

Per serving: 144 Calories; 9.1g Fat; 7.3g Carbs; 9.6g Protein; 2.6g Sugars; 2.8g Fiber

INGREDIENTS

1/2 pound asparagus, cut into 1 1/2-inch pieces
1/2 pound broccoli, cut into 1 1/2-inch pieces
2 tablespoons peanut oil

Some salt and white pepper, to taste
1/2 cup chicken broth
2 tablespoons apple cider vinegar

DIRECTIONS

Place the vegetables in a single layer in the lightly greased cooking basket. Drizzle the peanut oil over the vegetables.
Sprinkle with salt and white pepper.
Cook at 380 degrees F for 15 minutes, shaking the basket halfway through the cooking time.
Add 1/2 cup of chicken broth to a saucepan; bring to a rapid boil and add the vinegar. Cook for 5 to 7 minutes or until the sauce has reduced by half.
Spoon the sauce over the warm vegetables and serve immediately. Bon appétit!

408. Colorful Vegetable Croquettes

(Ready in about 40 minutes | Servings 4)

Per serving: 280 Calories; 22.5g Fat; 9.8g Carbs; 9.6g Protein; 4g Sugars; 3.2g Fiber

INGREDIENTS

1/2 pound broccoli
4 tablespoons milk
2 tablespoons butter
Salt and black pepper, to taste
1/2 teaspoon cayenne pepper

1/2 cup mushrooms, chopped
1 bell pepper, chopped
1 clove garlic, minced
3 tablespoons scallions, minced
2 tablespoons olive oil

1/2 cup almond flour
1/4 cup coconut flour
2 eggs
1/2 cup parmesan cheese, grated

DIRECTIONS

In a large saucepan, boil the broccoli for 17 to 20 minutes. Drain the broccoli and mash with the milk, butter, salt, black pepper, and cayenne pepper.

Add the mushrooms, bell pepper, garlic, scallions, and olive oil; stir to combine well. Shape the mixture into patties.

In a shallow bowl, place the flour; beat the eggs in another bowl; in a third bowl, place the parmesan cheese.

Dip each patty into the flour, followed by the eggs, and then the parmesan cheese; press to adhere.

Cook in the preheated Air Fryer at 375 degrees F for 16 minutes, shaking halfway through the cooking time. Bon appétit!

409. Vegetable Casserole with Swiss Cheese

(Ready in about 40 minutes | Servings 6)

Per serving: 212 Calories; 13.4g Fat; 9.8g Carbs; 14.1g Protein; 3.3g Sugars; 2.9g Fiber

INGREDIENTS

1 tablespoon olive oil
1 shallot, sliced
2 cloves garlic, minced
1 red bell pepper, seeded and sliced
1 yellow bell pepper, seeded and sliced
1 ½ cups kale

1 pound broccoli florets, steamed
6 eggs
1/2 cup milk
Sea salt and ground black pepper, to your liking
1 cup Swiss cheese, shredded
4 tablespoons Romano cheese, grated

DIRECTIONS

Heat the olive oil in a saucepan over medium-high heat. Sauté the shallot, garlic, and peppers for 2 to 3 minutes. Add the kale and cook until wilted.

Arrange the broccoli florets evenly over the bottom of a lightly greased casserole dish. Spread the sautéed mixture over the top.

In a mixing bowl, thoroughly combine the eggs, milk, salt, pepper, and shredded cheese. Pour the mixture into the casserole dish.

Lastly, top with Romano cheese. Bake at 330 degrees F for 30 minutes or until top is golden brown. Bon appétit!

410. Baby Portabellas with Romano Cheese

(Ready in about 15 minutes | Servings 4)

Per serving: 230 Calories; 15.3g Fat; 9.2g Carbs; 15.1g Protein; 2.8g Sugars; 2.6g Fiber

INGREDIENTS

1 pound baby portabellas
1/2 cup almond meal
2 eggs
2 tablespoons milk
1 cup Romano cheese, grated

Sea salt and ground black pepper
1/2 teaspoon shallot powder
1 teaspoon garlic powder
1/2 teaspoon cumin powder
1/2 teaspoon cayenne pepper

DIRECTIONS

Pat the mushrooms dry with a paper towel.

To begin, set up your breading station. Place the almond meal in a shallow dish. In a separate dish, whisk the eggs with milk.

Finally, place grated Romano cheese and seasonings in the third dish.

Start by dredging the baby portabellas in the almond meal mixture; then, dip them into the egg wash. Press the baby portabellas into Romano cheese, coating evenly.

Spritz the Air Fryer basket with cooking oil. Add the baby portabellas and cook at 400 degrees F for 6 minutes, flipping them halfway through the cooking time. Bon appétit!

411. Fried Spicy Tofu

(Ready in about 55 minutes | Servings 4)

Per serving: 173 Calories; 12.3g Fat; 6.5g Carbs; 12.2g Protein; 1.8g Sugars; 2.1g Fiber

INGREDIENTS

16 ounces firm tofu, pressed and cubed
1 tablespoon vegan oyster sauce
1 tablespoon tamari sauce
1 teaspoon cider vinegar
1 teaspoon pure maple syrup
1 teaspoon sriracha

1/2 teaspoon shallot powder
1/2 teaspoon porcini powder
1 teaspoon garlic powder
1 tablespoon sesame oil
2 tablespoons golden flaxseed meal

DIRECTIONS

Toss the tofu with the oyster sauce, tamari sauce, vinegar, maple syrup, sriracha, shallot powder, porcini powder, garlic powder, and sesame oil. Let it marinate for 30 minutes.
Toss the marinated tofu with the flaxseed meal.
Cook at 360 degrees F for 10 minutes; turn them over and cook for 12 minutes more. Bon appétit!

412. Restaurant-Style Roasted Vegetables

(Ready in about 25 minutes | Servings 4)

Per serving: 43 Calories; 0.4g Fat; 9.6g Carbs; 1.7g Protein; 3.5g Sugars; 2.3g Fiber

INGREDIENTS

1 red bell pepper, seeded and cut into 1/2-inch chunks
1 yellow bell pepper, seeded and cut into 1/2-inch chunks
1 yellow onion, quartered
1 green bell pepper, seeded and cut into 1/2-inch chunks
1 cup broccoli, broken into 1/2-inch florets
1/2 cup parsnip, trimmed and cut into 1/2-inch chunks
2 garlic cloves, minced

Pink Himalayan salt and ground black pepper, to taste
1/2 teaspoon marjoram
1/2 teaspoon dried oregano
1/4 cup dry white wine
1/4 cup vegetable broth
1/2 cup Kalamata olives, pitted and sliced

DIRECTIONS

Arrange your vegetables in a single layer in the baking pan in the order of the rainbow (red, orange, yellow, and green). Scatter the minced garlic around the vegetables.
Season with salt, black pepper, marjoram, and oregano. Drizzle the white wine and vegetable broth over the vegetables.
Roast in the preheated Air Fryer at 390 degrees F for 15 minutes, rotating the pan once or twice.
Scatter the Kalamata olives all over your vegetables and serve warm. Bon appétit!

413. Crispy Shawarma Broccoli

(Ready in about 25 minutes | Servings 4)

Per serving: 107 Calories; 7.6g Fat; 8.7g Carbs; 3.4g Protein; 2g Sugars; 3.3g Fiber

INGREDIENTS

1 pound broccoli, steamed and drained
2 tablespoons canola oil
1 teaspoon cayenne pepper

1 teaspoon sea salt
1 tablespoon Shawarma spice blend

DIRECTIONS

Toss all ingredients in a mixing bowl.
Roast in the preheated Air Fryer at 380 degrees F for 10 minutes, shaking the basket halfway through the cooking time.
Work in batches. Bon appétit!

414. Caribbean Fried Peppers with Tofu

(Ready in about 20 minutes | Servings 2)

Per serving: 265 Calories; 21.5g Fat; 7.8g Carbs; 14.3g Protein; 2.3g Sugars; 2.6g Fiber

INGREDIENTS

2 bell peppers, peeled and cut into slices
6 ounces firm tofu, cut into cubes

2 tablespoons avocado oil
2 teaspoons Caribbean Sorrel Rum Spice Mix

DIRECTIONS

Toss the bell peppers and tofu with the avocado oil and spice mix.
Cook in the preheated Air Fryer at 400 degrees F for 10 minutes, shaking the cooking basket halfway through the cooking time.
Adjust the seasonings to taste and enjoy!

415. Cauliflower with Traditional Buffalo Sauce

(Ready in about 30 minutes | Servings 4)

Per serving: 137 Calories; 10.6g Fat; 9.7g Carbs; 3.9g Protein; 3.5g Sugars; 3g Fiber

INGREDIENTS

1 pound cauliflower florets
1/3 cup coconut flour
Sea salt and cracked black pepper, to taste
1/2 teaspoon cayenne pepper
1/2 teaspoon chili powder
1/2 cup full-fat milk
2 tablespoons tahini

1 tablespoon vegetable oil
2 cloves garlic, minced
2 scotch bonnet peppers, seeded and sliced
1 small-sized onion, minced
1/2 teaspoon salt
1 cup water
2 tablespoons white vinegar

DIRECTIONS

Rinse the cauliflower florets and pat them dry. Spritz the Air Fryer basket with cooking spray.
In a mixing bowl, combine the coconut flour, salt, black pepper, cayenne pepper, and chili powder.
Add the milk and tahini. Stir until a thick batter is formed. Dip the cauliflower florets in the batter.
Cook the cauliflower at 400 degrees F for 16 minutes, turning them over halfway through the cooking time.
Meanwhile, heat the vegetable oil in a saucepan over medium-high heat; then, sauté the garlic, peppers, and onion for a minute or so or until they are fragrant.
Add the remaining ingredients and bring the mixture to a rapid boil. Now, reduce the heat to simmer, and continue cooking for 10 minutes more or until the sauce has reduced by half.
Pour the sauce over the prepared cauliflower and serve. Bon appétit!

416. Vegetable Skewers with Asian-Style Peanut Sauce

(Ready in about 30 minutes | Servings 4)

Per serving: 135 Calories; 10.2g Fat; 8.8g Carbs; 3.7g Protein; 3.7g Sugars; 1.6g Fiber

INGREDIENTS

2 bell peppers, diced into 1-inch pieces
4 pearl onions, halved
8 small button mushrooms, cleaned
2 tablespoons extra-virgin olive oil
Sea salt and ground black pepper, to taste
1 teaspoon red pepper flakes, crushed
1 teaspoon dried rosemary, crushed

1/3 teaspoon granulated garlic
Peanut Sauce:
2 tablespoons peanut butter
1 tablespoon balsamic vinegar
1 tablespoon soy sauce
1/2 teaspoon garlic salt

DIRECTIONS

Soak the wooden skewers in water for 15 minutes.
Thread the vegetables on skewers; drizzle the olive oil all over the vegetable skewers; sprinkle with spices.
Cook in the preheated Air Fryer at 400 degrees F for 13 minutes.
Meanwhile, in a small dish, whisk the peanut butter with the balsamic vinegar, soy sauce, and garlic salt. Serve your skewers with the peanut sauce on the side. Enjoy!

417. Crispy Brussels Sprout Chips

(Ready in about 20 minutes | Servings 2)

Per serving: 64 Calories; 2.6g Fat; 9.1g Carbs; 3.3g Protein; 2.2g Sugars; 4g Fiber

INGREDIENTS

10 Brussels sprouts, separated into leaves
1 teaspoon canola oil

1 teaspoon coarse sea salt
1 teaspoon paprika

DIRECTIONS

Toss all ingredients in the lightly greased Air Fryer basket.
Bake at 380 degrees F for 15 minutes, shaking the basket halfway through the cooking time to ensure even cooking.
Serve and enjoy!

418. Ricotta Cauliflower Fritters

(Ready in about 30 minutes | Servings 4)

Per serving: 290 Calories; 24.6g Fat; 9.5g Carbs; 11.8g Protein; 2.9g Sugars; 4.9g Fiber

INGREDIENTS

1 tablespoon olive oil
1/2 pound cauliflower
1/2 cup Ricotta cheese
1/4 cup ground flaxseed meal
1/4 cup almond flour

1/2 teaspoon baking powder
1/2 onion, chopped
1 garlic clove, minced
Sea salt and ground black pepper, to your liking
1 cup parmesan cheese, grated

DIRECTIONS

Start by preheating your Air Fryer to 400 degrees F.
Drizzle the olive oil all over the cauliflower. Place the cauliflower in the Air Fryer basket and cook approximately 15 minutes, shaking the basket periodically.
Then, mash the cauliflower and combine with the other ingredients. Form the mixture into patties.
Bake in the preheated Air Fryer at 380 degrees F for 14 minutes, flipping them halfway through the cooking time to ensure even cooking.
Bon appétit!

419. Roasted Cauliflower and Broccoli Salad

(Ready in about 20 minutes + chilling time | Servings 4)

Per serving: 151 Calories; 12.1g Fat; 9.5g Carbs; 3.3g Protein; 3.4g Sugars; 3.7g Fiber

INGREDIENTS

1/2 pound cauliflower florets
1/3 pound broccoli florets
Sea salt, to taste
1/2 teaspoon red pepper flakes
2 tablespoons cider vinegar
1 teaspoon Dijon mustard

2 tablespoons extra-virgin olive oil
1 avocado, pitted, peeled and sliced
1 small sized onion, peeled and sliced
1 garlic clove, minced
2 cups arugula
2 tablespoons sesame seeds, lightly toasted

DIRECTIONS

Start by preheating your Air Fryer to 400 degrees F.
Brush the cauliflower and broccoli florets with cooking spray.
Cook for 12 minutes, shaking the cooking basket halfway through the cooking time. Season with salt and red pepper.
In a mixing dish, whisk the vinegar, Dijon mustard, and olive oil. Dress the salad. Add the avocado, onion, garlic, and arugula. Top with sesame seeds.
Bon appétit!

420. Zoodles with Cheese

(Ready in about 30 minutes | Servings 4)

Per serving: 300 Calories; 27.3g Fat; 5.3g Carbs; 11.2g Protein; 1g Sugars; 1.4g Fiber

INGREDIENTS

12 ounces zucchini noodles
2 garlic cloves, minced
1/3 cup butter
2 tablespoons milk
1/2 teaspoon curry powder

1/2 teaspoon mustard powder
1/2 teaspoon celery seeds
Sea salt and white pepper, to taste
1 cup cheddar cheese, grated
1 heaping tablespoon Italian parsley, roughly chopped

DIRECTIONS

Place zucchini noodles in a colander and salt generously. Let them sit for 15 minutes to remove any excess water.
Cook in the preheated Air Fryer at 425 degrees F and fry for 20 minutes or until they have softened.
In a mixing dish, thoroughly combine the remaining ingredients.
Toss the cheese mixture with your zoodles and serve immediately. Bon appétit!

421. Paprika Vegetable Kabobs

(Ready in about 20 minutes | Servings 4)

Per serving: 159 Calories; 13.2g Fat; 8.9g Carbs; 1.1g Protein; 3.2g Sugars; 2.7g Fiber

INGREDIENTS

1 celery, cut into thick slices
1 parsnip, cut into thick slices
1 fennel bulb, diced
1 teaspoon whole grain mustard
2 cloves garlic, pressed
1 red onion, cut into wedges

2 tablespoons dry white wine
1/4 cup sesame oil
1 teaspoon sea salt flakes
1/2 teaspoon ground black pepper
1 teaspoon smoked paprika

DIRECTIONS

Place all of the above ingredients in a mixing dish; toss to coat well. Alternately thread vegetables onto the bamboo skewers.
Cook on the Air Fryer grill pan for 15 minutes at 380 degrees F. Flip them over halfway through the cooking time.
Taste, adjust the seasonings and serve warm.

422. Asian-Style Cauliflower

(Ready in about 25 minutes | Servings 4)

Per serving: 93 Calories; 6.1g Fat; 8.2g Carbs; 2.4g Protein; 2.6g Sugars; 2.2g Fiber

INGREDIENTS

2 cups cauliflower, grated
1 onion, peeled and finely chopped
1 tablespoon sesame oil
1 tablespoon tamari sauce
1 tablespoon sake

2 cloves garlic, peeled and pressed
1 tablespoon ginger, freshly grated
1 tablespoon fresh parsley, finely chopped
1/4 cup of lime juice
2 tablespoons sesame seeds

DIRECTIONS

Combine the cauliflower, onion, sesame oil, tamari sauce, sake, garlic, and the ginger in a mixing dish; stir until everything's well incorporated.
Air-fry at 400 degrees F for 12 minutes.
Pause the Air Fryer. Add the parsley and lemon juice. Turn the machine to cook at 390 degrees F; cook additional 10 minutes.
Meanwhile, toast the sesame seeds in a non-stick skillet; stir them constantly over a medium-low flame. Sprinkle over prepared cauliflower and serve warm.

423. Traditional Indian Bhaji

(Ready in about 40 minutes | Servings 4)

Per serving: 141 Calories; 9.8g Fat; 8.6g Carbs; 6.1g Protein; 3.2g Sugars; 2.9g Fiber

INGREDIENTS

2 eggs, beaten
1/2 cup almond meal
1/2 cup coconut flour
1/2 teaspoon baking powder
1 teaspoon curry paste
1 teaspoon cumin seed

1 teaspoon minced fresh ginger root
Salt and black pepper, to your liking
2 red onions, chopped
1 Indian green chili, pureed
Non-stick cooking spray

DIRECTIONS

Whisk the eggs, almond meal, coconut flour and baking powder in a mixing dish to make a thick batter; add in the cold water if needed.
Add in curry paste, cumin seeds, ginger root, salt, and black pepper.
Now, add onions and chili pepper; mix until everything is well incorporated.
Shape the balls and slightly press them to make the patties. Spritz the patties with cooking oil on all sides.
Place a sheet of aluminum foil in the Air Fryer food basket. Place the fritters on foil.
Then, air-fry them at 360 degrees F for 15 minutes; flip them over, press the power button and cook for another 20 minutes. Serve right away!

424. Roasted Peppers with Greek Mayo Sauce

(Ready in about 35 minutes | Servings 4)

Per serving: 207 Calories; 21.2g Fat; 2.6g Carbs; 0.7g Protein; 1.3g Sugars; 0.4g Fiber

INGREDIENTS

2 bell peppers, cut into strips
1 teaspoon avocado oil
1/2 teaspoon celery salt
1/4 teaspoon red pepper flakes, crushed

1/2 cup mayonnaise
1 clove garlic, minced
1 teaspoon lemon juice

DIRECTIONS

Toss the peppers with avocado oil, celery salt, and red pepper flakes.
Air-fry them at 380 degrees F for 10 minutes. Shake the cooking basket and cook for 20 minutes more.
In the meantime, thoroughly combine the mayonnaise, garlic, and lemon juice.
When the peppers come out of the Air Fryer, check them for doneness. Serve with chilled mayonnaise sauce and enjoy!

425. Vegetable Salsa Wraps

(Ready in about 15 minutes | Servings 4)

Per serving: 115 Calories; 0.2g Fat; 8.9g Carbs; 19.4g Protein; 4.3g Sugars; 2.7g Fiber

INGREDIENTS

1 cup red onion, sliced
1 zucchini, chopped
1 poblano pepper, deveined and finely chopped

1 head lettuce
1/2 cup salsa (homemade or store-bought)
8 ounces mozzarella cheese

DIRECTIONS

Begin by preheating your Air Fryer to 390 degrees F.
Cook red onion, zucchini, and poblano pepper until they are tender and fragrant or about 7 minutes.
Divide the sautéed mixture among lettuce leaves; spoon the salsa over the top. Finish off with mozzarella cheese. Wrap lettuce leaves around the filling. Enjoy!

426. Mediterranean Falafel with Tzatziki

(Ready in about 30 minutes | Servings 4)

Per serving: 131 Calories; 9.6g Fat; 9.4g Carbs; 3.9g Protein; 4.5g Sugars; 2.1g Fiber

INGREDIENTS

For the Falafel:
2 cups cauliflower, grated
1/4 teaspoon baking powder
1/3 cup warm water
1/2 teaspoon salt
1 tablespoon coriander leaves, finely chopped
2 tablespoons fresh lemon juice

Vegan Tzatziki:
1 cup plain Greek yogurt
2 tablespoons lime juice, freshly squeezed
1/4 teaspoon ground black pepper, or more to taste
1/3 teaspoon sea salt flakes
2 tablespoons extra-virgin olive oil
2 tablespoons chopped fresh dill
1 clove garlic, pressed
1/2 fresh cucumber, grated

DIRECTIONS

In a bowl, thoroughly combine all the ingredients for the falafel. Allow the mixture to stay for approximately 10 minutes.
Now, air-fry at 390 degrees F for 15 minutes; make sure to flip them over halfway through the cooking time.
To make Greek tzatziki, blend all ingredients in your food processor.
Serve warm falafel with chilled tzatziki. Enjoy!

427. Veggie Fingers with Monterey Jack Cheese

(Ready in about 20 minutes | Servings 4)

Per serving: 189 Calories; 13.5g Fat; 8.9g Carbs; 9.8g Protein; 1.6g Sugars; 2.3g Fiber

INGREDIENTS

10 ounces cauliflower
1/4 cup almond flour
1 ½ teaspoons soy sauce
Salt and freshly ground black pepper, to taste

1 teaspoon cayenne pepper
1 cup parmesan cheese, grated
3/4 teaspoon dried dill weed
1 tablespoon olive oil

DIRECTIONS

Firstly, pulse the cauliflower in your food processor; transfer them to a bowl and add 1/4 cup almond flour, soy sauce, salt, black pepper, and cayenne pepper.
Roll the mixture into veggie fingers shape. In another bowl, place grated parmesan cheese and dried dill.
Now, coat the veggie fingers with the parmesan mixture, covering completely. Drizzle veggie fingers with olive oil.
Air-fry for 15 minutes at 350 degrees F; turn them over once or twice during the cooking time. Eat with your favorite sauce. Enjoy!

428. Easy Cheddar and Coriander Balls

(Ready in about 30 minutes | Servings 6)

Per serving: 380 Calories; 36.5g Fat; 5.8g Carbs; 9.9g Protein; 0.8g Sugars; 3.9g Fiber

INGREDIENTS

1 cup almond flour
1/4 cup flaxseed meal
A pinch of salt
1/2 cup canola oil
1 cup cheddar cheese, cubed

1/2 cup green coriander, minced
1/4 teaspoon cumin powder
1 teaspoon dried parsley flakes
Water

DIRECTIONS

Firstly, make the dough by mixing the flour, salt, and canola oil; add water and knead it into dough. Let it stay for about 20 minutes.
Divide the dough into equal size balls. Sprinkle cheese cubes with green coriander, cumin powder, and parsley.
Now, press the cheese cubes down into the center of the dough balls. Then, pinch the edges securely to form a ball. Repeat with the rest of the dough.
Lay the balls in the Air Fryer's cooking basket; spritz each ball with a cooking spray, coating on all sides. After that, cook for 8 to 10 minutes, shaking the basket once during the cooking time.
Serve with your favorite sauce for dipping. Bon appétit!

429. Green Beans with Cheese

(Ready in about 1 hour | Servings 3)

Per serving: 454 Calories; 38g Fat; 7.7g Carbs; 22.1g Protein; 3.1g Sugars; 2.3g Fiber

INGREDIENTS

1/2 pound green beans
9 ounces cheddar cheese, sliced
1/4 cup tomato paste, no sugar added
1 tablespoon white vinegar
1 tablespoon mustard
1/4 teaspoon ground black pepper

1/2 teaspoon sea salt
1/4 teaspoon smoked paprika
1/2 teaspoon freshly grated ginger
2 cloves garlic, minced
2 tablespoons olive oil

DIRECTIONS

Toss green beans with the tomato paste, white vinegar, mustard, black pepper, sea salt, paprika, ginger, garlic, and olive oil.
Cook at 390 degrees F for 10 minutes. Top with cheddar cheese and cook an additional 5 minute or until cheese melts.
Serve immediately. Bon appétit!

430. Keto Falafel with Homemade Mayonnaise

(Ready in about 25 minutes | Servings 2)

Per serving: 378 Calories; 36.8g Fat; 9g Carbs; 5.8g Protein; 2.9g Sugars; 3.3g Fiber

INGREDIENTS

Keto Falafel:
1/2 pound cauliflower
1/2 onion, chopped
2 cloves garlic, minced
2 tablespoons fresh cilantro leaves, chopped
1/4 cup almond meal
1/2 teaspoon baking powder
1 teaspoon cumin powder

A pinch of ground cardamom
Sea salt and ground black pepper, to taste
Homemade Mayonnaise:
1 egg yolk
1 tablespoon sour cream
1/4 cup olive oil
1/4 teaspoon salt
1 tablespoon lemon juice

DIRECTIONS

Pulse all the falafel ingredients in your food processor.
Form the falafel mixture into balls and place them in the lightly greased Air Fryer basket.
Cook at 380 degrees F for about 15 minutes, shaking the basket occasionally to ensure even cooking.
In a mixing bowl, place egg yolk and sour cream. Gradually and slowly, pour in your oil while whisking constantly.
Once you reach a thick consistency, add in the salt and lemon juice. Whisk again to combine. Serve falafel with your homemade mayonnaise and enjoy!

431. Rich and Easy Vegetable Croquettes

(Ready in about 15 minutes | Servings 4)

Per serving: 219 Calories; 16.6g Fat; 9.5g Carbs; 10g Protein; 2g Sugars; 3.2g Fiber

INGREDIENTS

1/2 pound broccoli florets
1 tablespoon ground flaxseeds
1 yellow onion, finely chopped
1 bell pepper, seeded and chopped
2 garlic cloves, pressed
1 teaspoon turmeric powder

1/2 teaspoon ground cumin
1/2 cup almond flour
1/2 cup parmesan cheese
2 eggs, whisked
Salt and ground black pepper, to taste
2 tablespoons olive oil

DIRECTIONS

Blanch the broccoli in salted boiling water until al dente, about 3 to 4 minutes. Drain well and transfer to a mixing bowl; mash the broccoli florets with the remaining ingredients.
Form the mixture into patties and place them in the lightly greased Air Fryer basket.
Cook at 400 degrees F for 6 minutes, turning them over halfway through the cooking time; work in batches.
Serve warm with mayonnaise. Enjoy!

432. Rosemary Vegetables Au Gratin

(Ready in about 45 minutes | Servings 4)

Per serving: 157 Calories; 10.3g Fat; 8.7g Carbs; 8.2g Protein; 2g Sugars; 1.4g Fiber

INGREDIENTS

3/4 pound cauliflower, steamed
1 onion, sliced
2 garlic cloves, minced
1 bell pepper, deveined and sliced
2 eggs, beaten

1 cup sour cream
Kosher salt and ground black pepper, to taste
1 teaspoon cayenne pepper
1 tablespoon fresh rosemary

DIRECTIONS

Place your vegetables in the lightly greased casserole dish. In a mixing dish, thoroughly combine the remaining ingredients.
Spoon the cream mixture on top of the vegetables.
Bake in the preheated Air Fryer at 325 degrees F for 20 minutes. Serve warm.

433. Hungarian Pilau with Mushrooms and Herbs

(Ready in about 25 minutes | Servings 4)

Per serving: 198 Calories; 15.1g Fat; 9.8g Carbs; 8.4g Protein; 4.4g Sugars; 2.6g Fiber

INGREDIENTS

1 ½ cups cauliflower rice
3 cups vegetable broth
2 tablespoons olive oil
1 pound fresh porcini mushrooms, sliced
2 tablespoons olive oil
2 garlic cloves

1 onion, chopped
1/4 cup dry vermouth
1 teaspoon dried thyme
1/2 teaspoon dried tarragon
1 teaspoon sweet Hungarian paprika

DIRECTIONS

Thoroughly combine cauliflower rice with the remaining ingredients in a lightly greased baking dish.
Cook in the preheated Air Fryer at 370 degrees for 20 minutes, checking periodically to ensure even cooking.
Serve in individual bowls. Bon appétit!

434. Swiss Cheese and Eggplant Crisps

(Ready in about 45 minutes | Servings 4)

Per serving: 158 Calories; 10.1g Fat; 9.1g Carbs; 9.2g Protein; 2.7g Sugars; 3g Fiber

INGREDIENTS

1/2 pound eggplant, sliced
1/4 cup almond meal
2 tablespoons flaxseed meal

Coarse sea salt and ground black pepper, to taste
1 teaspoon paprika
1 cup parmesan, freshly grated

DIRECTIONS

Toss the eggplant with 1 tablespoon of salt and let it stand for 30 minutes. Drain and rinse well.
Mix the almond meal, flaxseed meal, salt, black pepper, and paprika in a bowl. Then, pour in the water and whisk to combine well.
Then, place parmesan in another shallow bowl.
Dip the eggplant slices in the almond meal mixture, then in parmesan; press to coat on all sides. Transfer to the lightly greased Air Fryer basket.
Cook at 370 degrees F for 6 minutes. Turn each slice over and cook an additional 5 minutes.
Serve garnished with spicy ketchup if desired. Bon appétit!

435. Roasted Pepper Salad with Goat Cheese

(Ready in about 20 minutes + chilling time | Servings 4)

Per serving: 206 Calories; 18.7g Fat; 5.6g Carbs; 4.9g Protein; 0.8g Sugars; 0.9g Fiber

INGREDIENTS

1 yellow bell pepper
1 red bell pepper
1 Serrano pepper
4 tablespoons olive oil
2 tablespoons cider vinegar
2 garlic cloves, peeled and pressed

1 teaspoon cayenne pepper
Sea salt, to taste
1/2 teaspoon mixed peppercorns, freshly crushed
1/2 cup goat cheese, cubed
2 tablespoons fresh Italian parsley leaves, roughly chopped

DIRECTIONS

Start by preheating your Air Fryer to 400 degrees F. Brush the Air Fryer basket lightly with cooking oil.

Then, roast the peppers for 5 minutes. Give the peppers a half turn; place them back in the cooking basket and roast for another 5 minutes. Turn them one more time and roast until the skin is charred and soft or 5 more minutes. Peel the peppers and let them cool to room temperature.

In a small mixing dish, whisk the olive oil, vinegar, garlic, cayenne pepper, salt, and crushed peppercorns. Dress the salad and set aside.

Scatter goat cheese over the peppers and garnish with parsley. Bon appétit!

436. Cauli Rice Salad with Tomatoes

(Ready in about 25 minutes | Servings 4)

Per serving: 100 Calories; 7.1g Fat; 7.9g Carbs; 2.7g Protein; 3.2g Sugars; 2.8g Fiber

INGREDIENTS

1 pound cauliflower rice
2 garlic cloves, pressed
1/3 cup coriander, chopped
1 cup shallots, chopped

4 ounces tomato, sliced
1 cup arugula lettuce, torn into pieces
2 tablespoons apple cider vinegar
Sea salt and ground black pepper, to taste

DIRECTIONS

Put cauliflower rice into the Air Fryer basket. Cook at 375 degrees F for 10 minutes. Shake the basket and continue to cook for 10 minutes more.

Transfer the prepared couscous to a nice salad bowl. Add the remaining ingredients; stir to combine and enjoy!

Bon appétit!

437. Thai Zucchini Balls

(Ready in about 30 minutes | Servings 4)

Per serving: 166 Calories; 13.1g Fat; 9.6g Carbs; 6.2g Protein; 2.1g Sugars; 4.7g Fiber

INGREDIENTS

1 pound zucchini, grated
1 tablespoon orange juice
1/2 teaspoon ground cinnamon
1/4 teaspoon ground cloves

1/2 cup almond meal
1 teaspoon baking powder
1 cup coconut flakes

DIRECTIONS

In a mixing bowl, thoroughly combine all ingredients, except for coconut flakes.

Roll the balls in the coconut flakes.

Bake in the preheated Air Fryer at 360 degrees F for 15 minutes or until thoroughly cooked and crispy.

Repeat the process until you run out of ingredients. Bon appétit!

438. Cheesy Green Beans with Mushrooms and Peppers

(Ready in about 15 minutes | Servings 3)

Per serving: 149 Calories; 8.2g Fat; 9.5g Carbs; 5.9g Protein; 4.3g Sugars; 2.8g Fiber

INGREDIENTS

1 tablespoon extra-virgin olive oil
2 garlic cloves, minced
1/2 cup scallions, chopped
2 cups oyster mushrooms, sliced
2 Italian peppers, deseeded and sliced

1/2 pound green beans, trimmed
1/2 teaspoon mustard seeds
Sea salt and ground black pepper, to taste
1 cup cream cheese

DIRECTIONS

Start by preheating your Air Fryer to 390 degrees F. Heat the oil and sauté the garlic and scallions until tender and fragrant, about 5 minutes. Add the remaining ingredients and stir to combine well.
Increase the temperature to 400 degrees F and cook for a further 5 minutes. Serve warm.

439. Rich Asparagus and Mushroom Patties

(Ready in about 15 minutes | Servings 4)

Per serving: 208 Calories; 15.1g Fat; 9g Carbs; 11.2g Protein; 3.2g Sugars; 2.9g Fiber

INGREDIENTS

3/4 pound asparagus spears
1 tablespoon canola oil
1 teaspoon paprika
Sea salt and freshly ground black pepper, to taste
1 teaspoon garlic powder
3 tablespoons scallions, chopped

1 cup button mushrooms, chopped
1/2 cup parmesan cheese, grated
2 tablespoons flax seeds
2 eggs, beaten
4 tablespoons sour cream, for garnish

DIRECTIONS

Place the asparagus spears in the lightly greased cooking basket. Toss the asparagus with the canola oil, paprika, salt, and black pepper.
Cook in the preheated Air Fryer at 400 degrees F for 5 minutes. Chop the asparagus spears and add the garlic powder, scallions, mushrooms, parmesan, flax seeds, and eggs.
Mix until everything is well incorporated and form the asparagus mixture into patties.
Cook in the preheated Air Fryer at 400 degrees F for 5 minutes, flipping halfway through the cooking time. Serve with well-chilled sour cream. Bon appétit!

440. Vegetable Bake with Cheese and Olives

(Ready in about 25 minutes | Servings 3)

Per serving: 208 Calories; 17.5g Fat; 7.9g Carbs; 7.1g Protein; 3.9g Sugars; 2.7g Fiber

INGREDIENTS

1/2 pound cauliflower, cut into 1-inch florets
1/4 pound zucchini, cut into 1-inch chunks
1 red onion, sliced
2 bell peppers, cut into 1-inch chunks
2 tablespoons extra-virgin olive oil
1 cup dry white wine

1 teaspoon dried rosemary
Sea salt and freshly cracked black pepper, to taste
1/2 teaspoon dried basil
1/2 cup tomato, pureed
1/2 cup cheddar cheese, grated
1 ounce Kalamata olives, pitted and halved

DIRECTIONS

Toss the vegetables with the olive oil, wine, rosemary, salt, black pepper, and basil until well coated.
Add the pureed tomatoes to a lightly greased baking dish; spread to cover the bottom of the baking dish.
Add the vegetables and top with grated cheese. Scatter the Kalamata olives over the top.
Bake in the preheated Air Fryer at 390 degrees F for 20 minutes, rotating the dish halfway through the cooking time. Serve warm and enjoy!

SNACKS & APPETIZERS

441. Must-Serve Thai Prawns

(Ready in about 10 minutes | Servings 4)

Per serving: 259 Calories; 5.8g Fat; 3.4g Carbs; 47.1g Protein; 0.7g Sugars; 1.8g Fil

INGREDIENTS

16 prawns, cleaned and deveined
Salt and ground black pepper, to your liking
1/2 teaspoon cumin powder
1 teaspoon fresh lemon juice
1 medium-sized egg, whisked

1/3 cup of beer
1 teaspoon baking powder
1 tablespoon curry powder
1/2 teaspoon grated fresh ginger
1/2 cup coconut flour

DIRECTIONS

Toss the prawns with salt, pepper, cumin powder, and lemon juice.
In a mixing dish, place the whisked egg, beer, baking powder, curry, and the ginger; mix to combine well.
In another mixing dish, place the coconut flour.
Now, dip the prawns in the beer mixture; roll your prawns over the coconut flour.
Air-fry at 360 degrees F for 5 minutes; turn them over, press the power button again and cook for additional 2 to 3 minutes. Bon appétit!

442. Bacon Wrapped Onion Rings

(Ready in about 30 minutes | Servings 2)

Per serving: 444 Calories; 41.2g Fat; 5.2g Carbs; 13.9g Protein; 2.8g Sugars; 1.4g Fiber

INGREDIENTS

1 onion, cut into 1/2-inch slices
1 teaspoon curry powder
1 teaspoon cayenne pepper

Salt and ground black pepper, to your liking
8 strips bacon
1/4 cup spicy ketchup

DIRECTIONS

Place the onion rings in the bowl with cold water; let them soak approximately 20 minutes; drain the onion rings and pat dry using a kitchen towel.
Sprinkle curry powder, cayenne pepper, salt, and black pepper over onion rings.
Wrap one layer of bacon around onion, trimming any excess. Secure the rings with toothpicks.
Spritz the Air Fryer basket with cooking spray; arrange the breaded onion rings in the Air Fryer basket.
Cook in the preheated Air Fryer at 360 degrees F for 15 minutes, turning them over halfway through the cooking time. Serve with spicy ketchup. Bon appétit!

443. Brussels Sprout Crisps

(Ready in about 20 minutes | Servings 4)

Per serving: 74 Calories; 3.8g Fat; 8.8g Carbs; 3.4g Protein; 2g Sugars; 3.9g Fiber

INGREDIENTS

1 pound Brussels sprouts, ends and yellow leaves removed and halved lengthwise
Salt and black pepper, to taste

1 tablespoon toasted sesame oil
1 teaspoon fennel seeds
Chopped fresh parsley, for garnish

DIRECTIONS

Place the Brussels sprouts, salt, pepper, sesame oil, and fennel seeds in a resealable plastic bag. Seal the bag and shake to coat.
Air-fry at 380 degrees F for 15 minutes or until tender. Make sure to flip them over halfway through the cooking time.
Serve sprinkled with fresh parsley. Bon appétit!

444. Cheesy Eggplant Crisps

(Ready in about 45 minutes | Servings 4)

Per serving: 218 Calories; 19.1g Fat; 9.2g Carbs; 3.6g Protein; 4g Sugars; 4.9g Fiber

INGREDIENTS

1 eggplant, peeled and thinly sliced
Salt
1/2 cup almond meal
1/4 cup canola oil

1/2 cup water
1 teaspoon garlic powder
1/2 teaspoon dried dill weed
1/2 teaspoon ground black pepper, to taste

DIRECTIONS

Salt the eggplant slices and let them stay for about 30 minutes. Squeeze the eggplant slices and rinse them under cold running water.
Toss the eggplant slices with the other ingredients. Cook at 390 degrees F for 13 minutes, working in batches.
Serve with a sauce for dipping. Bon appétit!

445. Crispy Fried Leek with Mustard

(Ready in about 15 minutes | Servings 4)

Per serving: 187 Calories; 13.8g Fat; 8.8g Carbs; 7.7g Protein; 4.6g Sugars; 1.9g Fiber

INGREDIENTS

1 large-sized leek, cut into 1/2-inch wide rings
Salt and pepper, to taste
1 teaspoon mustard
1 cup milk

1 egg
1/2 cup almond flour
1/2 teaspoon baking powder
1/2 cup pork rinds, crushed

DIRECTIONS

Toss your leeks with salt and pepper.
In a mixing bowl, whisk the mustard, milk and egg until frothy and pale.
Now, combine almond flour and baking powder in another mixing bowl. In the third bowl, place the pork rinds.
Coat the leek slices with the almond meal mixture. Dredge the floured leek slices into the milk/egg mixture, coating well. Finally, roll them over the pork rinds.
Air-fry for approximately 10 minutes at 370 degrees F. Bon appétit!

446. Broccoli Melts with Coriander and Cheese

(Ready in about 20 minutes | Servings 6)

Per serving: 322 Calories; 23.8g Fat; 9.2g Carbs; 19.3g Protein; 1.5g Sugars; 2.8g Fiber

INGREDIENTS

2 eggs, well whisked
2 cups Colby cheese, shredded
1/2 cup almond meal
2 tablespoons sesame seeds

Seasoned salt, to taste
1/4 teaspoon ground black pepper, or more to taste
1 head broccoli, grated
1 cup parmesan cheese, grated

DIRECTIONS

Thoroughly combine the eggs, Colby cheese, almond meal, sesame seeds, salt, black pepper, and broccoli to make the consistency of dough.
Chill for 1 hour and shape into small balls; roll the patties over parmesan cheese. Spritz them with cooking oil on all sides.
Cook at 360 degrees F for 10 minutes. Check for doneness and return to the Air Fryer for 8 to 10 more minutes. Serve with a sauce for dipping. Bon appétit!

447. Chicken Wings in Barbecue Sauce

(Ready in about 20 minutes | Servings 6)

Per serving: 219 Calories; 7.8g Fat; 1.3g Carbs; 33.7g Protein; 0.4g Sugars; 0.5g Fiber

INGREDIENTS

For the Sauce:
1 tablespoon yellow mustard
1 tablespoon apple cider vinegar
1 tablespoon olive oil
1/4 cup ketchup, no sugar added
1 garlic clove, minced
Salt and ground black pepper, to your liking

1/8 teaspoon ground allspice
1/4 cup water
For the Wings:
2 pounds chicken wings
1/4 teaspoon celery salt
1/4 cup habanero hot sauce
Chopped fresh parsley, or garnish

DIRECTIONS

In a sauté pan that is preheated over a medium-high flame, place all the ingredients for the sauce and bring it to a boil. Then, reduce the temperature and simmer until it has thickened.

Meanwhile, preheat your Air Fryer to 400 degrees F; cook the chicken wings for 6 minutes; flip them over and cook for additional 6 minutes. Season them with celery salt.

Serve with the prepared sauce and habanero hot sauce, garnished with fresh parsley leaves. Bon appétit!

448. Paprika Bacon Shrimp

(Ready in about 45 minutes | Servings 10)

Per serving: 282 Calories; 22.6g Fat; 1g Carbs; 18.6g Protein; 0.6g Sugars; 0.3g Fiber

INGREDIENTS

1 ¼ pounds shrimp, peeled and deveined
1 teaspoon paprika
1/2 teaspoon ground black pepper
1/2 teaspoon red pepper flakes, crushed
1 tablespoon salt

1 teaspoon chili powder
1 tablespoon shallot powder
1/4 teaspoon cumin powder
1 ¼ pounds thin bacon slices

DIRECTIONS

Toss the shrimps with all the seasoning until they are coated well.

Next, wrap a slice of bacon around the shrimps, securing with a toothpick; repeat with the remaining ingredients; chill for 30 minutes.

Air-fry them at 360 degrees F for 7 to 8 minutes, working in batches. Serve with cocktail sticks if desired. Enjoy!

449. Broccoli and Pecorino Toscano Fat Bombs

(Ready in about 20 minutes | Servings 6)

Per serving: 171 Calories; 12.2g Fat; 7.7g Carbs; 9.1g Protein; 1.5g Sugars; 2g Fiber

INGREDIENTS

1 large-sized head of broccoli, broken into small florets
1/2 teaspoon sea salt
1/4 teaspoon ground black pepper, or more to taste
1 tablespoon Shoyu sauce

1 teaspoon groundnut oil
1 cup bacon bits
1 cup Pecorino Toscano, freshly grated
Paprika, to taste

DIRECTIONS

Add the broccoli florets to boiling water; boil approximately 4 minutes; drain well.

Season with salt and pepper; drizzle with Shoyu sauce and groundnut oil. Mash with a potato masher.

Add the bacon and cheese to the mixture; shape the mixture into bite-sized balls.

Air-fry at 390 degrees F for 10 minutes; shake the Air Fryer basket, push the power button again, and continue to cook for 5 minutes more.

Toss the fried keto bombs with paprika. Bon appétit!

450. Sage Roasted Zucchini Cubes

(Ready in about 20 minutes | Servings 6)

Per serving: 70 Calories; 5.1g Fat; 5.2g Carbs; 3.3g Protein; 0.6g Sugars; 1.7g Fiber

INGREDIENTS

1 ½ pounds zucchini, peeled and cut into 1/2-inch chunks
2 tablespoons melted coconut oil
A pinch of coarse salt
A pinch of pepper

2 tablespoons sage, finely chopped
Zest of 1 small-sized lemon
1/8 teaspoon ground allspice

DIRECTIONS

Toss the squash chunks with the other items.
Roast in the Air Fryer cooking basket at 350 degrees F for 10 minutes.
Pause the machine, and turn the temperature to 400 degrees F; stir and roast for additional 8 minutes. Bon appétit!

451. Brussels Sprouts with Feta Cheese

(Ready in about 20 minutes | Servings 4)

Per serving: 133 Calories; 8.2g Fat; 8.6g Carbs; 8.1g Protein; 3.2g Sugars; 3g Fiber

INGREDIENTS

3/4 pound Brussels sprouts, trimmed and cut off the ends
1 teaspoon kosher salt
1 tablespoon lemon zest

Non-stick cooking spray
1 cup feta cheese, cubed

DIRECTIONS

Firstly, peel the Brussels sprouts using a small paring knife. Toss the leaves with salt and lemon zest; spritz them with a cooking spray, coating all sides.
Bake at 380 degrees for 8 minutes; shake the cooking basket halfway through the cooking time and cook for 7 more minutes.
Make sure to work in batches so everything can cook evenly. Taste and adjust the seasonings. Serve with feta cheese. Bon appétit!

452. Saucy Chicken Wings with Sage

(Ready in about 1 hour 10 minutes | Servings 4)

Per serving: 228 Calories; 6.5g Fat; 1.7g Carbs; 38.4g Protein; 1.1g Sugars; 0.3g Fiber

INGREDIENTS

1/3 cup almond flour
1/3 cup buttermilk
1 ½ pound chicken wings
1 tablespoon tamari sauce
1/3 teaspoon fresh sage

1 teaspoon mustard seeds
1/2 teaspoon garlic paste
1/2 teaspoon freshly ground mixed peppercorns
1/2 teaspoon seasoned salt
2 teaspoons fresh basil

DIRECTIONS

Place the seasonings along with the garlic paste, chicken wings, buttermilk, and tamari sauce in a large-sized mixing dish. Let it soak about 55 minutes; drain the wings.
Dredge the wings in the almond flour and transfer them to the Air Fryer cooking basket.
Air-fry for 16 minutes at 355 degrees F. Serve on a nice serving platter with a dressing on the side. Bon appétit!

453. Crispy Crackling Bites

(Ready in about 50 minutes | Servings 10)

Per serving: 245 Calories; 14.1g Fat; 0g Carbs; 27.6g Protein; 0g Sugars; 0.5g Fiber

INGREDIENTS

1 pound pork rind raw, scored by the butcher
1 tablespoon sea salt
2 tablespoons smoked paprika

DIRECTIONS

Sprinkle and rub salt on the skin side of the pork rind. Allow it to sit for 30 minutes.
Roast at 380 degrees F for 8 minutes; turn them over and cook for a further 8 minutes or until blistered.
Sprinkle the smoked paprika all over the pork crackling and serve. Bon appétit!

454. Roasted Spicy Hot Dogs

(Ready in about 20 minutes | Servings 6)

Per serving: 542 Calories; 47.2g Fat; 5.7g Carbs; 21.1g Protein; 3.6g Sugars; 0.2g Fiber

INGREDIENTS

6 hot dogs
1 tablespoon mustard
6 tablespoons ketchup, no sugar added

DIRECTIONS

Place the hot dogs in the lightly greased Air Fryer basket.
Bake at 380 degrees F for 15 minutes, turning them over halfway through the cooking time to promote even cooking.
Serve on cocktail sticks with the mustard and ketchup. Enjoy!

455. Celery Chips with Harissa Mayonnaise Sauce

(Ready in about 30 minutes | Servings 3)

Per serving: 234 Calories; 23.7g Fat; 4.3g Carbs; 1.3g Protein; 1.9g Sugars; 1.5g Fiber

INGREDIENTS

1/2 pound celery root
2 tablespoons olive oil
Sea salt and ground black pepper, to taste
Harissa Mayo
1/4 cup mayonnaise

2 tablespoons sour cream
1/2 tablespoon harissa paste
1/4 teaspoon ground cumin
Salt, to taste

DIRECTIONS

Cut the celery root into desired size and shape.
Then, preheat your Air Fryer to 400 degrees F. Now, spritz the Air Fryer basket with cooking spray.
Toss the celery chips with the olive oil, salt, and black pepper. Bake in the preheated Air Fryer for 25 to 30 minutes, turning them over every 10 minutes to promote even cooking.
Meanwhile, mix all ingredients for the harissa mayo. Place in your refrigerator until ready to serve. Bon appétit!

456. Glazed Carrot Chips with Cheese

(Ready in about 20 minutes | Servings 3)

Per serving: 122 Calories; 10g Fat; 4.2g Carbs; 4.1g Protein; 0.4g Sugars; 0.6g Fiber

INGREDIENTS

3 carrots, sliced into sticks
1 tablespoon coconut oil
1/3 cup Romano cheese, preferably freshly grated

2 teaspoons granulated garlic
Sea salt and ground black pepper, to taste

DIRECTIONS

Toss all ingredients in a mixing bowl until the carrots are coated on all sides.
Cook at 380 degrees F for 15 minutes, shaking the basket halfway through the cooking time.
Serve with your favorite dipping sauce. Bon appétit!

457. Spinach Melts with Parsley Yogurt Dip

(Ready in about 20 minutes | Servings 4)

Per serving: 301 Calories; 25.2g Fat; 8.5g Carbs; 11.4g Protein; 2.2g Sugars; 3.7g Fiber

INGREDIENTS

Spinach Melts:
2 cups spinach, torn into pieces
1 ½ cups cauliflower
1 tablespoon sesame oil
1/2 cup scallions, chopped
2 garlic cloves, minced
1/2 cup almond flour
1/4 cup coconut flour
1 teaspoon baking powder
1/2 teaspoon sea salt

1/2 teaspoon ground black pepper
1/4 teaspoon dried dill
1/2 teaspoon dried basil
1 cup cheddar cheese, shredded
Parsley Yogurt Dip:
1/2 cup Greek-Style yoghurt
2 tablespoons mayonnaise
2 tablespoons fresh parsley, chopped
1 tablespoon fresh lemon juice
1/2 teaspoon garlic, smashed

DIRECTIONS

Place spinach in a mixing dish; pour in hot water. Drain and rinse well.
Add cauliflower to the steamer basket; steam until the cauliflower is tender about 5 minutes.
Mash the cauliflower; add the remaining ingredients for Spinach Melts and mix to combine well. Shape the mixture into patties and transfer them to the lightly greased cooking basket.
Bake at 330 degrees F for 14 minutes or until thoroughly heated.
Meanwhile, make your dipping sauce by whisking the remaining ingredients. Place in your refrigerator until ready to serve.
Serve the Spinach Melts with the chilled sauce on the side. Enjoy!

458. Indian Onion Rings (Bhaji)

(Ready in about 25 minutes | Servings 4)

Per serving: 197 Calories; 17.2g Fat; 7.4g Carbs; 5g Protein; 2.5g Sugars; 3g Fiber

INGREDIENTS

2 eggs, beaten
2 tablespoons olive oil
2 onions, sliced
1 green chili, deseeded and finely chopped
2 ounces almond flour

1 ounce coconut flour
Salt and black pepper, to taste
1 teaspoon cumin seeds
1/2 teaspoon ground turmeric

DIRECTIONS

Place all ingredients, except for the onions, in a mixing dish; mix to combine well, adding a little water to the mixture.
Once you've got a thick batter, add the onions; stir to coat well.
Cook in the preheated Air Fryer at 370 degrees F for 20 minutes flipping them halfway through the cooking time.
Work in batches and transfer to a serving platter. Enjoy!

459. Country-Style Deviled Eggs

(Ready in about 25 minutes | Servings 3)

Per serving: 417 Calories; 35.5g Fat; 5.2g Carbs; 18.2g Protein; 3.4g Sugars; 0.7g Fiber

INGREDIENTS

6 eggs
6 slices bacon
2 tablespoons mayonnaise
1 teaspoon hot sauce
1/2 teaspoon Worcestershire sauce

2 tablespoons green onions, chopped
1 tablespoon pickle relish
Salt and ground black pepper, to taste
1 teaspoon smoked paprika

DIRECTIONS

Place the wire rack in the Air Fryer basket; lower the eggs onto the wire rack.
Cook at 270 degrees F for 15 minutes.
Transfer them to an ice-cold water bath to stop the cooking. Peel the eggs under cold running water; slice them into halves.
Cook the bacon at 400 degrees F for 3 minutes; flip the bacon over and cook an additional 3 minutes; chop the bacon and reserve.
Mash the egg yolks with the mayo, hot sauce, Worcestershire sauce, green onions, pickle relish, salt, and black pepper; add the reserved bacon and spoon the yolk mixture into the egg whites.
Garnish with smoked paprika. Bon appétit!

460. Chinese-Style Glazed Baby Carrots

(Ready in about 20 minutes | Servings 6)

Per serving: 70 Calories; 4.6g Fat; 7.1g Carbs; 0.7g Protein; 2.8g Sugars; 2.4g Fiber

INGREDIENTS

1 pound baby carrots
2 tablespoons sesame oil
1/2 teaspoon Szechuan pepper
1 teaspoon Wuxiang powder (Five-spice powder)

3-4 drops liquid Stevia
1 large garlic clove, crushed
1 (1-inch) piece fresh ginger root, peeled and grated
2 tablespoons tamari sauce

DIRECTIONS

Start by preheating your Air Fryer to 380 degrees F.
Toss all ingredients together and place them in the Air Fryer basket.
Cook for 15 minutes, shaking the basket halfway through the cooking time. Enjoy!

461. Cocktail Wieners with Spicy Sauce

(Ready in about 20 minutes | Servings 4)

Per serving: 304 Calories; 26.2g Fat; 4.5g Carbs; 12.4g Protein; 1.0g Sugars; 0.4g Fiber

INGREDIENTS

1 pound pork cocktail sausages
For the Sauce:
1/4 cup mayonnaise
1/4 cup cream cheese

1 whole grain mustard
1 teaspoon balsamic vinegar
1 garlic clove, finely minced
1 teaspoon chili powder

DIRECTIONS

Take your sausages, give them a few pricks using a fork and place them on the Air Fryer grill pan.
Set the timer for 15 minutes; after 8 minutes, pause the Air Fryer, turn the sausages over and cook for further 7 minutes.
Check for doneness and take the sausages out of the machine.
In the meantime, thoroughly combine all the ingredients for the sauce. Serve with warm sausages and enjoy!

462. Aromatic Kale Chips

(Ready in about 5 minutes | Servings 4)

Per serving: 91 Calories; 8.8g Fat; 3.2g Carbs; 1g Protein; 0g Sugars; 0.3g Fiber

INGREDIENTS

2 ½ tablespoons olive oil
1 ½ teaspoons garlic powder
1 bunch of kale, torn into small pieces

2 tablespoons lemon juice
1 1/2 teaspoons seasoned salt

DIRECTIONS

Toss your kale with the other ingredients.
Cook at 195 degrees F for 4 to 5 minutes, tossing kale halfway through.
Serve with your favorite dipping sauce.

463. Movie Night Zucchini Fries

(Ready in about 26 minutes | Servings 4)

Per serving: 135 Calories; 7.7g Fat; 8.2g Carbs; 9.2g Protein; 3.9g Sugars; 2.3g Fiber

INGREDIENTS

2 zucchinis, slice into sticks
2 teaspoons shallot powder
1/4 teaspoon dried dill weed
2 teaspoons garlic powder
1/2 cup Parmesan cheese, preferably freshly grated

1/3 teaspoon cayenne pepper
3 egg whites
1/3 cup almond meal
Cooking spray
Salt and ground black pepper, to your liking

DIRECTIONS

Pat the zucchini sticks dry using a kitchen towel.
Grab a mixing bowl and beat the egg whites until pale; then, add all the seasonings in the order listed above and beat again
Take another mixing bowl and mix together almond meal and the Parmesan cheese.
Then, coat the zucchini sticks with the seasoned egg mixture; then, roll them over the parmesan cheese mixture.
Lay the breaded zucchini sticks in a single layer on the tray that is coated lightly with cooking spray.
Bake at 375 degrees F for about 20 minutes until the sticks are golden brown. Serve with your favorite sauce for dipping.

464. Mozzarella, Brie and Artichoke Dip

(Ready in about 22 minutes | Servings 10)

Per serving: 128 Calories; 10.2g Fat; 2.7g Carbs; 7.3g Protein; 0.5g Sugars; 0.7g Fiber

INGREDIENTS

2 cups arugula leaves, torn into pieces
1/3 can artichoke hearts, drained and chopped
1/2 cup Mozzarella cheese, shredded
1/3 cup sour cream
3 cloves garlic, minced
1/3 teaspoon dried basil

1 teaspoon sea salt
7 ounces Brie cheese
1/2 cup mayonnaise
1/3 teaspoon ground black pepper, or more to taste
A pinch of ground allspice

DIRECTIONS

Combine together the Brie cheese, mayonnaise, sour cream, garlic, basil, salt, ground black pepper, and the allspice.
Throw in the artichoke hearts and arugula; gently stir to combine. Transfer the prepared mixture to a baking dish. Now, scatter the Mozzarella cheese evenly over the top.
Bake in your Air Fryer at 325 degrees F for 17 minutes. Serve with keto veggie sticks. Bon appétit!

465. Dad's Boozy Wings

(Ready in about 1 hour 15 minutes | Servings 4)

Per serving: 184 Calories; 9.6g Fat; 5.5g Carbs; 13.7g Protein; 3.5g Sugars; 0.5g Fiber

INGREDIENTS

2 teaspoons coriander seeds

1 ½ tablespoons soy sauce

1/3 cup vermouth

3/4 pound chicken wings

1 ½ tablespoons each fish sauce

2 tablespoons melted butter

1 teaspoon seasoned salt

Freshly ground black pepper, to taste

DIRECTIONS

Rub the chicken wings with the black pepper and seasoned salt; now, add the other ingredients.

Next, soak the chicken wings in this mixture for 55 minutes in the refrigerator.

Air-fry the chicken wings at 365 degrees F for 16 minutes or until warmed through. Bon appétit!

466. Kid-Friendly Cocktail Meatballs

(Ready in about 20 minutes | Servings 8)

Per serving: 350 Calories; 25.1g Fat; 1.2g Carbs; 28.3g Protein; 0.4g Sugars; 0.2g Fiber

INGREDIENTS

½ teaspoon fine sea salt

1 cup Romano cheese, grated

3 cloves garlic, minced

1½ pound ground pork

½ cup scallions, finely chopped

2 eggs, well whisked

1/3 teaspoon cumin powder

2/3 teaspoon ground black pepper, or more to taste

2 teaspoons basil

DIRECTIONS

Simply combine all the ingredients in a large-sized mixing bowl.

Shape into bite-sized balls; cook the meatballs in the air fryer for 18 minutes at 345 degrees F. Serve with some tangy sauce such as marinara sauce if desired. Bon appétit!

467. Mini Cheeseburger Bites

(Ready in about 20 minutes | Servings 4)

Per serving: 469 Calories; 30.1g Fat; 4.5g Carbs; 43.4g Protein; 2.1g Sugars; 1.1g Fiber

INGREDIENTS

1 tablespoon Dijon mustard

2 tablespoons minced scallions

1 pound ground beef

1 ½ teaspoons minced green garlic

1/2 teaspoon cumin

Salt and ground black pepper, to savor

12 cherry tomatoes

12 cubes cheddar cheese

DIRECTIONS

In a large-sized mixing dish, place the mustard, ground beef, cumin, scallions, garlic, salt, and pepper; mix with your hands or a spatula so that everything is evenly coated.

Form into 12 meatballs and cook them in the preheated Air Fryer for 15 minutes at 375 degrees F. Air-fry until they are cooked in the middle.

Thread cherry tomatoes, mini burgers and cheese on cocktail sticks. Bon appétit!

468. Exotic Wings with Thai Chili Sauce

(Ready in about 25 minutes | Servings 6)

Per serving: 169 Calories; 4.4g Fat; 4.6g Carbs; 25.5g Protein; 1.8g Sugars; 1g Fiber

INGREDIENTS

2 ½ tablespoons dry sherry
2 teaspoons ginger powder
1 ½ pound chicken wings
Lime wedges, to serve

2 teaspoons garlic powder
1/3 cup Thai chili sauce
1 teaspoon smoked paprika
Sea salt and ground black pepper, to taste

DIRECTIONS

Toss the chicken wings with the ginger powder, garlic powder, paprika, sea salt, ground black pepper, and dry sherry.
Air-fry the chicken wings for 16 minutes at 365 degrees F or until they are thoroughly heated.
Serve with the Thai chili sauce and the lemon wedges. Bon appétit!

469. Decadent Brie and Pork Meatballs

(Ready in about 25 minutes | Servings 8)

Per serving: 275 Calories; 18.6g Fat; 2.7g Carbs; 22.9g Protein; 1.2g Sugars; 0.4g Fiber

INGREDIENTS

1 teaspoon cayenne pepper
2 teaspoons mustard
2 tablespoons Brie cheese, grated
5 garlic cloves, minced

2 small-sized yellow onions, peeled and chopped
1½ pounds ground pork
Sea salt and freshly ground black pepper, to taste

DIRECTIONS

Mix all of the above ingredients until everything is well incorporated.
Now, form the mixture into balls (the size of golf a ball).
Cook for 17 minutes at 375 degrees F. Serve with your favorite sauce.

470. BBQ Lil Smokies

(Ready in about 20 minutes | Servings 6)

Per serving: 275 Calories; 23.6g Fat; 3.6g Carbs; 11.9g Protein; 1.8g Sugars; 0.9g Fiber

INGREDIENTS

1 pound beef cocktail wieners
10 ounces barbecue sauce, no sugar added

DIRECTIONS

Start by preheating your Air Fryer to 380 degrees F.
Prick holes into your sausages using a fork and transfer them to the baking pan.
Cook for 13 minutes. Spoon the barbecue sauce into the pan and cook an additional 2 minutes.
Serve with toothpicks. Bon appétit!

471. Broccoli Fries with Spicy Dip

(Ready in about 15 minutes | Servings 4)

Per serving: 219 Calories; 19.3g Fat; 8.5g Carbs; 4.9g Protein; 2.8g Sugars; 2.5g Fiber

INGREDIENTS

3/4 pound broccoli florets
1/2 teaspoon onion powder
1 teaspoon granulated garlic
1/2 teaspoon cayenne pepper
Sea salt and ground black pepper, to taste
2 tablespoons sesame oil

4 tablespoons parmesan cheese, preferably freshly grated
Spicy Dip:
1/4 cup mayonnaise
1/4 cup Greek yogurt
1/4 teaspoon Dijon mustard
1 teaspoon hot sauce

DIRECTIONS

Start by preheating the Air Fryer to 400 degrees F.
Blanch the broccoli in salted boiling water until al dente, about 3 to 4 minutes. Drain well and transfer to the lightly greased Air Fryer basket.
Add the onion powder, garlic, cayenne pepper, salt, black pepper, sesame oil, and parmesan cheese.
Cook for 6 minutes, tossing halfway through the cooking time.
Meanwhile, mix all of the spicy dip ingredients. Serve broccoli fries with chilled dipping sauce. Bon appétit!

472. Classic Kale Chips with Tahini

(Ready in about 15 minutes | Servings 4)

Per serving: 170 Calories; 15g Fat; 7.1g Carbs; 4.2g Protein; 0.7g Sugars; 2.7g Fiber

INGREDIENTS

5 cups kale leaves, torn into 1-inch pieces
1 ½ tablespoons sesame oil
1/2 teaspoon shallot powder
1 teaspoon garlic powder
1/4 teaspoon porcini powder

1/2 teaspoon mustard seeds
1 teaspoon salt
1/3 cup tahini (sesame butter)
1 tablespoon fresh lemon juice
2 cloves garlic, minced

DIRECTIONS

Toss the kale with the sesame oil and seasonings.
Bake in the preheated Air Fryer at 350 degrees F for 10 minutes, shaking the cooking basket occasionally.
Bake until the edges are brown. Work in batches.
Meanwhile, make the sauce by whisking all ingredients in a small mixing bowl. Serve and enjoy!

473. Picnic Chicken Nuggets

(Ready in about 20 minutes | Servings 6)

Per serving: 268 Calories; 18.9g Fat; 3.6g Carbs; 20.2g Protein; 1.2g Sugars; 0.9g Fiber

INGREDIENTS

1 pound chicken breasts, slice into tenders
1/2 teaspoon cayenne pepper
Salt and black pepper, to taste
1/4 cup almond meal

1 egg, whisked
1/2 cup parmesan cheese, freshly grated
1/4 cup mayo
1/4 cup barbecue sauce

DIRECTIONS

Pat the chicken tenders dry with a kitchen towel. Season with the cayenne pepper, salt, and black pepper.
Dip the chicken tenders into the almond meal, followed by the egg. Press the chicken tenders into the parmesan cheese, coating evenly.
Place the chicken tenders in the lightly greased Air Fryer basket. Cook at 360 degrees for 9 to 12 minutes, turning them over to cook evenly.
In a mixing bowl, thoroughly combine the mayonnaise with the barbecue sauce. Serve the chicken nuggets with the sauce for dipping. Bon appétit!

474. Twisted Wings with Blue Cheese

(Ready in about 20 minutes | Servings 6)

Per serving: 242 Calories; 12.1g Fat; 1.9g Carbs; 30g Protein; 0.7g Sugars; 0.2g Fiber

INGREDIENTS

1 ½ pounds chicken wings
2 teaspoons sesame oil
Kosher salt and ground black pepper, to taste
2 tablespoons tamari sauce

1 tablespoon rice vinegar
2 garlic cloves, minced
1 cup blue cheese, crumbled

DIRECTIONS

Toss the chicken wings with the sesame oil, salt, and pepper. Add chicken wings to a lightly greased baking pan.
Roast the chicken wings in the preheated Air Fryer at 390 degrees F for 7 minutes. Turn them over once or twice to ensure even cooking.
In a mixing dish, thoroughly combine the tamari sauce, vinegar, garlic, and blue cheese.
Pour the sauce all over the chicken wings; bake an additional 5 minutes. Bon appétit!

475. Herb-Roasted Cauliflower

(Ready in about 20 minutes | Servings 2)

Per serving: 160 Calories; 14g Fat; 7.9g Carbs; 3.1g Protein; 3g Sugars; 3.2g Fiber

INGREDIENTS

3 cups cauliflower florets
2 tablespoons sesame oil
1 teaspoon onion powder
1 teaspoon garlic powder
1 teaspoon thyme

1 teaspoon sage
1 teaspoon rosemary
Sea salt and cracked black pepper, to taste
1 teaspoon paprika

DIRECTIONS

Start by preheating your Air Fryer to 400 degrees F.
Toss the cauliflower with the remaining ingredients; toss to coat well.
Cook for 12 minutes, shaking the cooking basket halfway through the cooking time. They will crisp up as they cool. Bon appétit!

476. Celery Fries with Homemade Aioli

(Ready in about 20 minutes | Servings 4)

Per serving: 172 Calories; 17.2g Fat; 3.4g Carbs; 0.9g Protein; 1.6g Sugars; 1.8g Fiber

INGREDIENTS

1 pound celery, peel long strips
2 tablespoons sesame oil
Sea salt and ground black pepper, to taste
1 teaspoon red pepper flakes, crushed
1/2 teaspoon curry powder
1/2 teaspoon mustard seeds

Spicy Citrus Aioli:
1/4 cup mayonnaise
1 tablespoon fresh lime juice
1 clove garlic, smashed
Salt and black pepper, to taste

DIRECTIONS

Start by preheating the Air Fryer to 380 degrees F.
Toss the parsnip chips with the sesame oil, salt, black pepper, red pepper, curry powder, and mustard seeds.
Cook for 15 minutes, shaking the Air Fryer basket periodically.
Meanwhile, make the sauce by whisking the mayonnaise, lime juice, garlic, salt, and pepper. Place in the refrigerator until ready to use.
Bon appétit!

477. Greek Calamari Appetizer

(Ready in about 20 minutes | Servings 6)

Per serving: 254 Calories; 15.8g Fat; 2.6g Carbs; 25.3g Protein; 1.2g Sugars; 0.1g Fiber

INGREDIENTS

1 ½ pounds calamari tubes, cleaned, cut into rings
Sea salt and ground black pepper, to taste
2 tablespoons lemon juice

1/2 cup almond meal
2 eggs, whisked
1/4 cup buttermilk

DIRECTIONS

Preheat your Air Fryer to 390 degrees F. Rinse the calamari and pat it dry. Season with salt and black pepper. Drizzle lemon juice all over the calamari.

Now, combine the almond meal, eggs, and buttermilk. Dredge the calamari in the batter.

Arrange them in the Air Fryer cooking basket. Spritz with cooking oil and cook for 9 to 12 minutes, shaking the basket occasionally. Work in batches.

Serve with toothpicks. Bon appétit!

478. Asian Teriyaki Chicken

(Ready in about 40 minutes | Servings 6)

Per serving: 301 Calories; 21.3g Fat; 3.9g Carbs; 22.1g Protein; 2.4g Sugars; 0.4g Fiber

INGREDIENTS

1 ½ pounds chicken drumettes
Sea salt and cracked black pepper, to taste
2 tablespoons fresh chives, roughly chopped
Teriyaki Sauce:
1 tablespoon sesame oil
1/4 cup soy sauce

1/2 cup water
1/2 teaspoon Five-spice powder
2 tablespoons rice wine vinegar
1/2 teaspoon fresh ginger, grated
2 cloves garlic, crushed

DIRECTIONS

Start by preheating your Air Fryer to 380 degrees F. Rub the chicken drumettes with salt and cracked black pepper.

Cook in the preheated Air Fryer approximately 15 minutes. Turn them over and cook an additional 7 minutes.

While the chicken drumettes are roasting, combine the sesame oil, soy sauce, water, Five-spice powder, vinegar, ginger, and garlic in a pan over medium heat. Cook for 5 minutes, stirring occasionally.

Now, reduce the heat and let it simmer until the glaze thickens.

After that, brush the glaze all over the chicken drumettes. Air-fry for a further 6 minutes or until the surface is crispy. Serve topped with the remaining glaze and garnished with fresh chives. Bon appétit!

479. Zucchini Chips with Greek Dipping Sauce

(Ready in about 25 minutes | Servings 4)

Per serving: 173 Calories; 14.3g Fat; 4.5g Carbs; 7.5g Protein; 1.1g Sugars; 1.1g Fiber

INGREDIENTS

1/3 cup almond meal
1/2 cup Parmesan cheese, grated
Sea salt and ground black pepper, to taste
1/4 teaspoon oregano
1 medium-sized zucchini, cut into slices
2 tablespoons grapeseed oil

Sauce:
1/2 cup Greek-style yogurt
1 tablespoon fresh cilantro, chopped
1 garlic clove, minced
Freshly ground black pepper, to your liking

DIRECTIONS

In a shallow bowl, thoroughly combine the almond meal, Parmesan, salt, black pepper, and oregano.

Dip the zucchini slices in the prepared batter, pressing to adhere.

Brush with the grapeseed oil and cook in the preheated Air Fryer at 400 degrees F for 12 minutes. Shake the Air Fryer basket periodically to ensure even cooking. Work in batches.

While the chips are baking, whisk the sauce ingredients; place in your refrigerator until ready to serve. Enjoy!

480. Grilled Meatball Kabobs

(Ready in about 20 minutes | Servings 6)

Per serving: 189 Calories; 13g Fat; 3.9g Carbs; 14.1g Protein; 2g Sugars; 0.8g Fiber

INGREDIENTS

1/2 pound ground pork
1/2 pound ground beef
1 teaspoon dried onion flakes
1 teaspoon fresh garlic, minced
1 teaspoon dried parsley flakes

Salt and black pepper, to taste
1 red pepper, 1-inch pieces
1 cup pearl onions
1/2 cup barbecue sauce, no sugar added

DIRECTIONS

Mix the ground meat with the onion flakes, garlic, parsley flakes, salt, and black pepper. Shape the mixture into 1-inch balls.
Thread the meatballs, pearl onions, and peppers alternately onto skewers. Place the skewers on the Air Fryer grill pan.
Microwave the barbecue sauce for 10 seconds.
Cook in the preheated Air Fryer at 380 degrees for 5 minutes. Turn the skewers over halfway through the cooking time. Brush with the sauce and cook for a further 5 minutes. Work in batches.
Serve with the remaining barbecue sauce and enjoy!

481. Batter-Fried Shallots

(Ready in about 25 minutes | Servings 4)

Per serving: 262 Calories; 20.4g Fat; 8.3g Carbs; 10.5g Protein; 2.8g Sugars; 2.3g Fiber

INGREDIENTS

1/2 cup almond flour
2 large-sized eggs
1/2 teaspoon baking powder
2/3 teaspoon red pepper flakes, crushed

1 cup shallots, sliced into rings
1/2 cup beer
1/2 teaspoon fine sea salt
1 cup pork rinds

DIRECTIONS

Start by preheating the Air Fryer for 7 to 10 minutes.
Then, use a medium-sized bowl to combine almond flour with eggs, baking powder, sea salt, beer and crushed red pepper flakes.
Dip shallots rings into the prepared batter; make sure to coat them on all sides. Now, coat them with the pork rinds.
Afterward, cook the shallots approximately 11 minutes at 345 degrees F. Eat warm.

482. Ranch Kale Chips

(Ready in about 7 minutes | Servings 4)

Per serving: 77 Calories; 7g Fat; 3g Carbs; 0.9g Protein; 1.3g Sugars; 1g Fiber

INGREDIENTS

1 1/2 teaspoons Ranch seasoning mix
2 tablespoons sesame oil
Salt and pepper, to taste

3 heads of kale, torn into small pieces
2 tablespoons Worchester sauce

DIRECTIONS

Toss all ingredients together in a mixing bowl.
Then, cook at 195 degrees F for about 4 minutes. Enjoy!

483. Easy Habanero Wings

(Ready in about 25 minutes | Servings 6)

Per serving: 157 Calories; 4.6g Fat; 2.7g Carbs; 25.2g Protein; 1.8g Sugars; 0.1g Fiber

INGREDIENTS

3 cloves garlic, peeled and halved
2 tablespoons habanero hot sauce
1/2 tablespoon soy sauce
1 ½ pounds chicken wings

1 teaspoon garlic salt
1 teaspoon smoked cayenne pepper
1 teaspoon freshly ground black pepper, or to taste

DIRECTIONS

Rub the chicken wings with the garlic. Then, season them with the salt, black pepper, and the smoked cayenne pepper.
Transfer the chicken wings to the food basket; add the soy sauce, habanero hot sauce, and honey; toss to coat on all sides.
Air-fry the chicken wings at 365 degrees F for 16 minutes or until warmed through.

484. Spicy Avocado Fries Wrapped in Bacon

(Ready in about 10 minutes | Servings 5)

Per serving: 202 Calories; 18.7g Fat; 6g Carbs; 4.5g Protein; 0.4g Sugars; 4.3g Fiber

INGREDIENTS

2 teaspoons chili powder
2 avocados, pitted and cut into 10 pieces
1 teaspoon salt

½ teaspoon garlic powder
1 teaspoon ground black pepper
5 rashers back bacon, cut into halves

DIRECTIONS

Lay the bacon rashers on a clean surface; then, place one piece of avocado slice on each bacon slice. Add the salt, black pepper, chili powder, and garlic powder.
Then, wrap the bacon slice around the avocado and repeat with the remaining rolls; secure them with a cocktail sticks or toothpicks.
Preheat your Air Fryer to 370 degrees F; cook in the preheated air fryer for 5 minutes and serve with your favorite sauce for dipping.

485. Mediterranean-Style Cocktail Meatballs

(Ready in about 15 minutes | Servings 4)

Per serving: 435 Calories; 31g Fat; 2.9g Carbs; 33.4g Protein; 0.6g Sugars; 0.7g Fiber

INGREDIENTS

For the Meatballs:
1 1/2 tablespoons melted butter
2 teaspoons red pepper flakes, crushed
½ tablespoon fresh cilantro, finely chopped
2 eggs
2 tablespoons fresh mint leaves, finely chopped
1 teaspoon kosher salt
4 garlic cloves, finely minced
1 pound ground pork
2 tablespoons capers

For Mediterranean Dipping sauce:
1/3 cup black olives, pitted and finely chopped
2 tablespoons fresh Italian parsley
1/2 teaspoon lemon zest
1/3 cup Greek-style yogurt
1/2 teaspoon dill, fresh or dried and chopped
2 tablespoons fresh rosemary

DIRECTIONS

Start by preheating your Air Fryer to 395 degrees F.
In a large-sized mixing dish, place all ingredients for the meatballs; mix to combine well. Shape the mixture into golf ball sized meatballs.
Cook the meatballs for about 9 minutes, working in batches.
In the meantime, make the dipping sauce by thoroughly whisking all the sauce ingredients. Serve warm meatballs with the prepared Mediterranean dipping sauce.

486. Grandma's Spicy Wings

(Ready in about 40 minutes + chilling time | Servings 4)

Per serving: 492 Calories; 10.7g Fat; 1.7g Carbs; 13.1g Protein; 0.2g Sugars; 0.2g Fiber

INGREDIENTS

2 cloves garlic, smashed
3 tablespoons melted butter
Ground black pepper and fine sea salt, to taste

8 chicken wings
A few dashes of hot sauce

DIRECTIONS

First of all, steam chicken wings for 8 minutes; pat them dry and place in the refrigerator for about 55 minutes.
Now, bake in the preheated Air Fryer at 335 degrees F for 28 minutes, turning halfway through. While the chicken wings are cooking, combine the other ingredients to make the sauce.
To finish, toss air fried chicken wings with the sauce and serve immediately.

487. Tangy Parmesan Chicken Meatballs

(Ready in about 15 minutes | Servings 4)

Per serving: 388 Calories; 28.7g Fat; 2.9g Carbs; 28.2g Protein; 0.5g Sugars; 0.3g Fiber

INGREDIENTS

1/2 cup almond flour
2 eggs
1 ½ tablespoons melted butter
1/3 teaspoon mustard seeds
1 pound ground chicken
2 garlic cloves, finely minced

1 teaspoon dried basil
1/2 teaspoon Hungarian paprika
1/3 cup Parmesan cheese, preferably freshly grated
1/2 lime, zested
1 teaspoon fine sea salt
1/3 teaspoon ground black pepper, or more to taste

DIRECTIONS

In a nonstick skillet that is preheated over a moderate flame, place the ground chicken and garlic; cook until the chicken is no longer pink and the garlic is just browned, about 3 minutes.
Throw in the remaining ingredients; shape the mixture into balls (e.g. the size of a golf ball).
Transfer them to the greased Air Fryer cooking basket.
Set your Air Fryer to cook at 385 degrees F; cook for about 8 minutes, or till they're thoroughly heated.

488. Thai Zingy Turkey Bites

(Ready in about 20 minutes | Servings 6)

Per serving: 278 Calories; 17.4g Fat; 4.8g Carbs; 23.7g Protein; 2.1g Sugars; 1.5g Fiber

INGREDIENTS

1 ½ pounds turkey wings, cut into pieces
1 teaspoon ginger-garlic paste
1 ½ tablespoons rice wine
1 ½ tablespoons coconut oil, melted

1/2 palmful minced lemongrass
1 teaspoon cayenne pepper
Sea salt flakes and ground black pepper, to savor
1/3 cup Thai chili sauce

DIRECTIONS

Toss turkey wings with all of the above ingredients.
Air-fry them for 18 minutes at 355 degrees or until they are thoroughly cooked.
Serve with Thai sweet chili sauce and lemon wedges. Bon appétit!

489. Bacon and Onion Fat Bombs

(Ready in about 15 minutes | Servings 6)

Per serving: 298 Calories; 26.5g Fat; 0.8g Carbs; 14g Protein; 0.4g Sugars; 0.1g Fiber

INGREDIENTS

2 onions, sliced
1 cup bacon, finely chopped
1/2 cup Colby cheese, shredded

8 ounces soft cheese
2 ½ tablespoons canola oil
2 eggs

DIRECTIONS

Combine all the ingredients in a mixing dish. Roll the mixture into bite-sized balls.
Air-fry them at 390 degrees F for 5 minutes. Work in batches.
Serve with toothpicks and enjoy!

490. Mexican Zucchini and Bacon Cakes Ole

(Ready in about 22 minutes | Servings 4)

Per serving: 311 Calories; 25.5g Fat; 4.9g Carbs; 17.6g Protein; 0.9g Sugars; 1.6g Fiber

INGREDIENTS

1/3 cup Swiss cheese, grated
1/3 teaspoon fine sea salt
1/3 teaspoon baking powder
1/3 cup scallions, finely chopped
1/2 tablespoon fresh basil, finely chopped
1 zucchini, trimmed and grated
1/2 teaspoon freshly cracked black pepper

1 teaspoon Mexican oregano
1 cup bacon, chopped
1/4 cup almond meal
1/4 cup coconut flour
2 small eggs, lightly beaten
1 cup Cotija cheese, grated

DIRECTIONS

Mix all ingredients, except for Cotija cheese, until everything is well combined.
Then, gently flatten each ball. Spritz the cakes with a nonstick cooking oil.
Bake your cakes for 13 minutes at 305 degrees F; work with batches. Serve warm with tomato ketchup and mayonnaise.

491. Parmigiana Tomato Chips

(Ready in about 15 minutes | Servings 4)

Per serving: 130 Calories; 10.2g Fat; 5.6g Carbs; 4.8g Protein; 2.2g Sugars; 1g Fiber

INGREDIENTS

4 Roma tomatoes, sliced
2 tablespoons olive oil
Sea salt and white pepper, to taste

1 teaspoon Italian seasoning mix
1/2 cup Parmesan cheese, grated

DIRECTIONS

Start by preheating your Air Fryer to 350 degrees F. Generously grease the Air Fryer basket with nonstick cooking oil.
Toss the sliced tomatoes with the remaining ingredients. Transfer them to the cooking basket without overlapping.
Cook in the preheated Air Fryer for 5 minutes. Shake the cooking basket and cook an additional 5 minutes. Work in batches.
Serve with Mediterranean aioli for dipping, if desired. Bon appétit!

492. Bell Pepper Chips

(Ready in about 20 minutes | Servings 4)

Per serving: 164 Calories; 10.2g Fat; 13.1g Carbs; 6.1g Protein; 1.1g Sugars; 1.3g Fiber

INGREDIENTS

1 egg, beaten
1/2 cup parmesan, grated
1 teaspoon sea salt

1/2 teaspoon red pepper flakes, crushed
3/4 pound bell peppers, deveined and cut to 1/4-inch strips
2 tablespoons grapeseed oil

DIRECTIONS

In a mixing bowl, combine together the egg, parmesan, salt, and red pepper flakes; mix to combine well.
Dip bell peppers into the batter and transfer them to the cooking basket. Brush with the grapeseed oil.
Cook in the preheated Air Fryer at 390 degrees F for 4 minutes. Shake the basket and cook for a further 3 minutes. Work in batches.
Taste, adjust the seasonings and serve. Bon appétit!

493. Skinny Spinach Chips

(Ready in about 20 minutes | Servings 3)

Per serving: 128 Calories; 12.3g Fat; 3.1g Carbs; 1.8g Protein; 1.2g Sugars; 1.1g Fiber

INGREDIENTS

3 cups fresh spinach leaves
1 tablespoon extra-virgin olive oil
1 teaspoon sea salt
1/2 teaspoon cayenne pepper
1 teaspoon garlic powder

Chili Yogurt Dip:
1/4 cup yogurt
2 tablespoons mayonnaise
1/2 teaspoon chili powder

DIRECTIONS

Toss the spinach leaves with the olive oil and seasonings.
Bake in the preheated Air Fryer at 350 degrees F for 10 minutes, shaking the cooking basket occasionally.
Bake until the edges brown, working in batches.
In the meantime, make the sauce by whisking all ingredients in a mixing dish. Serve immediately.

494. Romano Zucchini Fries

(Ready in about 20 minutes | Servings 2)

Per serving: 329 Calories; 27.7g Fat; 9.6g Carbs; 12.5g Protein; 3.3g Sugars; 2.9g Fiber

INGREDIENTS

1 zucchini, slice into strips
2 tablespoons mayonnaise
1/4 cup almond meal
1/2 cup Romano cheese, shredded

Sea salt and black pepper, to your liking
1 tablespoon garlic powder
1/2 teaspoon red pepper flakes

DIRECTIONS

Coat the zucchini with mayonnaise.
Mix the almond meal, Romano cheese, and spices in a shallow dish.
Then, coat the zucchini sticks with the cheese mixture.
Cook in the preheated Air Fryer at 400 degrees F for 12 minutes, shaking the basket halfway through the cooking time.
Work in batches until the sticks are crispy and golden brown. Bon appétit!

495. Greek Meatballs with Tzatziki (Keftedes)

(Ready in about 20 minutes | Servings 6)

Per serving: 208 Calories; 15.8g Fat; 8.5g Carbs; 10.3g Protein; 3.3g Sugars; 2.1g Fiber

INGREDIENTS

Greek Keftedes:
1/2 pound mushrooms, chopped
1/2 pound pork sausage, chopped
1 teaspoon shallot powder
1 teaspoon granulated garlic
1 teaspoon dried rosemary
1 teaspoon dried basil
1 teaspoon dried oregano
2 eggs
2 tablespoons golden flaxseed meal

Tzatziki Dip:
1/2 Lebanese cucumbers, grated, juice squeezed out
1 cup full-fat Greek yogurt
1 tablespoon fresh lemon juice
1 garlic clove, minced
1 tablespoon extra-virgin olive oil
1/2 teaspoon salt

DIRECTIONS

In a mixing bowl, thoroughly combine all ingredients for the Greek keftedes.
Shape the meat mixture into bite-sized balls.
Cook in the preheated Air Fryer at 380 degrees for 10 minutes, shaking the cooking basket once or twice to ensure even cooking.
Meanwhile, make the tzatziki dip by mixing all ingredients. Serve the keftedes with cocktail sticks and tzatziki dip on the side. Enjoy!

496. Cheddar Cheese Breadsticks

(Ready in about 30 minutes | Servings 6)

Per serving: 211 Calories; 19.3g Fat; 2.2g Carbs; 8.8g Protein; 0.5g Sugars; 1g Fiber

INGREDIENTS

1/2 cup almond meal
Sea salt and ground black pepper, to taste
1/4 teaspoon smoked paprika
1/2 teaspoon celery seeds

6 ounces mature Cheddar, cold, freshly grated
2 tablespoons cream cheese
2 tablespoons cold butter

DIRECTIONS

Start by preheating your air Fryer to 330 degrees F. Line the Air Fryer basket with parchment paper.
In a mixing bowl, thoroughly combine the almond meal, salt, black pepper, paprika, and celery seeds.
Then, combine the cheese and butter in the bowl of a stand mixer. Slowly stir in the almond meal mixture and mix to combine well.
Then, pack the batter into a cookie press fitted with a star disk. Pipe the long ribbons of dough across the parchment paper. Then cut into six-inch lengths.
Bake in the preheated Air Fryer for 15 minutes.
Repeat with the remaining dough. Let the cheese straws cool on a rack. You can store them between sheets of parchment in an airtight container. Bon appétit

497. Scallops and Bacon Kabobs

(Ready in about 40 minutes | Servings 6)

Per serving: 228 Calories; 15.9g Fat; 5.3g Carbs; 14.6g Protein; 1.9g Sugars; 0.3g Fiber

INGREDIENTS

1 pound sea scallops
1/2 cup coconut milk
1 tablespoon vermouth
Sea salt and ground black pepper, to taste

1/2 pound bacon, diced
1 shallot, diced
1 teaspoon garlic powder
1 teaspoon paprika

DIRECTIONS

In a ceramic bowl, place the sea scallops, coconut milk, vermouth, salt, and black pepper; let it marinate for 30 minutes.
Assemble the skewers alternating the scallops, bacon, and shallots. Sprinkle garlic powder and paprika all over the skewers.
Bake in the preheated air Fryer at 400 degrees F for 6 minutes. Serve warm and enjoy!

498. Bacon, Sausage and Bell Pepper Skewers

(Ready in about 20 minutes | Servings 4)

Per serving: 524 Calories; 48g Fat; 4.6g Carbs; 20.3g Protein; 2.3g Sugars; 0.8g Fiber

INGREDIENTS

16 cocktail sausages, halved
4 ounces bacon, diced
1 red bell pepper, cut into 1 ½-inch pieces

1 green bell pepper, cut into 1 ½-inch pieces
Salt and cracked black pepper, to taste
1/2 cup tomato chili sauce

DIRECTIONS

Thread the cocktail sausages, bacon, and peppers alternately onto skewers. Sprinkle with salt and black pepper.
Cook in the preheated Air Fryer at 380 degrees for 15 minutes, turning the skewers over once or twice to ensure even cooking.
Serve with the tomato chili sauce on the side. Enjoy!

499. Authentic Japanese Yakitori

(Ready in about 15 minutes + marinating time | Servings 4)

Per serving: 206 Calories; 9.9g Fat; 2.7g Carbs; 23.5g Protein; 1g Sugars; 0.5g Fiber

INGREDIENTS

1 pound chicken tenders, cut bite-sized pieces
1 clove garlic, minced
1 teaspoon coriander seeds
Sea salt and ground pepper, to taste

2 tablespoons Shoyu sauce
2 tablespoons sake
1 tablespoon fresh lemon juice
2 tablespoons sesame oil

DIRECTIONS

Place the chicken tenders, garlic, coriander, salt, black pepper, Shoyu sauce, sake, and lemon juice in a ceramic dish; cover and let it marinate for 2 hours.
Then, discard the marinade and tread the chicken tenders onto bamboo skewers.
Place the skewered chicken in the lightly greased Air Fryer basket. Drizzle sesame oil all over the skewered chicken.
Cook at 360 degrees for 6 minutes. Turn the skewered chicken over; brush with the reserved marinade and cook for a further 6 minutes. Enjoy!

500. Saucy Asian Short Ribs

(Ready in about 35 minutes | Servings 4)

Per serving: 222 Calories; 13.6g Fat; 2.1g Carbs; 23.2g Protein; 0.9g Sugars; 0.4g Fiber

INGREDIENTS

1 pound meaty short ribs
1/2 rice vinegar
2 tablespoons soy sauce
1 tablespoons Sriracha sauce
2 garlic cloves, minced

1 tablespoon daenjang (soybean paste)
1 teaspoon kochukaru (chili pepper flakes)
Sea salt and ground black pepper, to taste
1 tablespoon sesame oil
1/4 cup green onions, roughly chopped

DIRECTIONS

Place the short ribs, vinegar, soy sauce, Sriracha, garlic, and spices in Ziploc bag; let it marinate overnight.
Rub the sides and bottom of the Air Fryer basket with sesame oil. Discard the marinade and transfer the ribs to the prepared cooking basket.
Cook the marinated ribs in the preheated Air Fryer at 365 degrees for 17 minutes. Turn the ribs over, brush with the reserved marinade, and cook an additional 15 minutes.
Garnish with green onions. Bon appétit!

DESSERTS

501. Classic Lava Cake

(Ready in about 20 minutes | Servings 4)

Per serving: 408 Calories; 39.5g Fat; 7.2g Carbs; 8.1g Protein; 0.7g Sugars; 4.1g F

INGREDIENTS

4 ounces butter, melted

4 ounces dark chocolate

2 eggs, lightly whisked

2 tablespoons monk fruit sweetener

2 tablespoons almond meal

1 teaspoon baking powder

1/2 teaspoon ground cinnamon

1/4 teaspoon ground star anise

DIRECTIONS

Begin by preheating your Air Fryer to 370 degrees F. Spritz the sides and bottom of a baking pan with nonstick cooking spray.

Melt the butter and dark chocolate in a microwave-safe bowl. Mix the eggs and monk fruit until frothy.

Pour the butter/chocolate mixture into the egg mixture. Stir in the almond meal, baking powder, cinnamon, and star anise. Mix until everything is well incorporated.

Scrape the batter into the prepared pan. Bake in the preheated Air Fryer for 9 to 11 minutes.

Let stand for 2 minutes. Invert on a plate while warm and serve. Bon appétit!

502. Butter Flax Cookies

(Ready in about 25 minutes | Servings 4)

Per serving: 388 Calories; 38.1g Fat; 6.8g Carbs; 7.8g Protein; 1.3g Sugars; 4.4g Fiber

INGREDIENTS

8 ounces almond meal

2 tablespoons flaxseed meal

1 ounce monk fruit

1 teaspoon baking powder

A pinch of grated nutmeg

A pinch of coarse salt

1 large egg, room temperature.

1 stick butter, room temperature

1 teaspoon vanilla extract

DIRECTIONS

Mix the almond meal, flaxseed meal, monk fruit, baking powder, grated nutmeg, and salt in a bowl.

In a separate bowl, whisk the egg, butter, and vanilla extract.

Stir the egg mixture into dry mixture; mix to combine well or until it forms a nice, soft dough.

Roll your dough out and cut out with a cookie cutter of your choice.

Bake in the preheated Air Fryer at 350 degrees F for 10 minutes. Decrease the temperature to 330 degrees F and cook for 10 minutes longer. Bon appétit!

503. Peppermint Mascarpone Cake

(Ready in about 40 minutes | Servings 6)

Per serving: 313 Calories; 31.1g Fat; 7.8g Carbs; 7.9g Protein; 0.7g Sugars; 3.6g Fiber

INGREDIENTS

2 tablespoons stevia

1/2 cup coconut flour

1/2 cup butter

1 cup mascarpone cheese, at room temperature

4 ounces baker's chocolate, unsweetened

1 teaspoon vanilla extract

2 drops peppermint extract

DIRECTIONS

Beat the sugar, coconut flour, and butter in a mixing bowl. Press the mixture into the bottom of a lightly greased baking pan.

Bake at 350 degrees F for 18 minutes. Place it in your freezer for 20 minutes.

Then, make the cheesecake topping by mixing the remaining ingredients. Place this topping over the crust and allow it to cool in your freezer for a further 15 minutes. Serve well chilled.

504. Perfect Mini Cheesecakes

(Ready in about 40 minutes + chilling time | Servings 6)

Per serving: 306 Calories; 27.2g Fat; 9.1g Carbs; 8.2g Protein; 2g Sugars; 2.1g Fiber

INGREDIENTS

1/2 cup almond flour
1 ½ tablespoons unsalted butter, melted
2 tablespoons erythritol

1 (8-ounce) package cream cheese, softened
1/4 cup powdered erythritol
1/2 teaspoon vanilla paste
1 egg, at room temperature

Topping:
1 ½ cups sour cream
3 tablespoons powdered erythritol
1 teaspoon vanilla extract

DIRECTIONS

Thoroughly combine the almond flour, butter, and 2 tablespoons of erythritol in a mixing bowl. Press the mixture into the bottom of lightly greased custard cups.

Then, mix the cream cheese, 1/4 cup of powdered erythritol, vanilla, and egg using an electric mixer on low speed. Pour the batter into the pan, covering the crust.

Bake in the preheated Air Fryer at 330 degrees F for 35 minutes until edges are puffed and the surface is firm.

Mix the sour cream, 3 tablespoons of powdered erythritol, and vanilla for the topping; spread over the crust and allow it to cool to room temperature.

Transfer to your refrigerator for 6 to 8 hours. Serve well chilled.

505. Classic Cookies with Hazelnuts

(Ready in about 20 minutes | Servings 6)

Per serving: 328 Calories; 32.3g Fat; 5g Carbs; 6.7g Protein; 1.9g Sugars; 2.4g Fiber

INGREDIENTS

1 cup almond flour
1/2 cup coconut flour
1 teaspoon baking soda

1 teaspoon fine sea salt
1 stick butter
1 cup swerve

2 teaspoons vanilla
2 eggs, at room temperature
1 cup hazelnuts, coarsely chopped

DIRECTIONS

Begin by preheating your Air Fryer to 350 degrees F.

Mix the flour with the baking soda, and sea salt.

In the bowl of an electric mixer, beat the butter, swerve, and vanilla until creamy. Fold in the eggs, one at a time, and mix until well combined.

Slowly and gradually, stir in the flour mixture. Finally, fold in the coarsely chopped hazelnuts.

Divide the dough into small balls using a large cookie scoop; drop onto the prepared cookie sheets. Bake for 10 minutes or until golden brown, rotating the pan once or twice through the cooking time.

Work in batches and cool for a couple of minutes before removing to wire racks. Enjoy!

506. Chocolate Almond Cookies

(Ready in about 20 minutes | Servings 10)

Per serving: 303 Calories; 29.6g Fat; 8.5g Carbs; 6.5g Protein; 1.6g Sugars; 4.3g Fiber

INGREDIENTS

2 cups almond flour
1/2 cup coconut flour
5 ounces swerve
5 ounces butter, softened

1 egg, beaten
1 teaspoon vanilla essence
4 ounces double cream

3 ounces bakers' chocolate, unsweetened
1 teaspoon cardamom seeds, finely crushed

DIRECTIONS

Start by preheating your Air Fryer to 350 degrees F.

In a mixing bowl, thoroughly combine the flour, swerve, and butter. Mix until your mixture resembles breadcrumbs.

Gradually, add the egg and vanilla essence. Shape your dough into small balls and place in the parchment-lined Air Fryer basket.

Bake in the preheated Air Fryer for 10 minutes. Rotate the pan and bake for another 5 minutes. Transfer the freshly baked cookies to a cooling rack.

As the biscuits are cooling, melt the double cream and bakers' chocolate in the Air Fryer safe bowl at 350 degrees F. Add the cardamom seeds and stir well.

Spread the filling over the cooled biscuits and sandwich together. Bon appétit!

507. Chocolate Fudgy Brownies

(Ready in about 30 minutes | Servings 8)

Per serving: 180 Calories; 17.6g Fat; 5.7g Carbs; 3.5g Protein; 0.8g Sugars; 3.3g Fiber

INGREDIENTS

1 stick butter, melted
1 cup swerve
2 eggs
1 teaspoon vanilla essence
2 tablespoons flaxseed meal

1 cup coconut flour
1 teaspoon baking powder
1/2 cup cocoa powder, unsweetened
A pinch of salt
A pinch of ground cardamom

DIRECTIONS

Start by preheating your Air Fryer to 350 degrees F. Now, spritz the sides and bottom of a baking pan with cooking spray.
In a mixing dish, beat the melted butter with swerve until fluffy. Next, fold in the eggs and beat again.
After that, add the vanilla, flour, baking powder, cocoa, salt, and ground cardamom. Mix until everything is well combined.
Bake in the preheated Air Fryer for 20 to 22 minutes. Enjoy!

508. Fluffy Chocolate and Coconut Cake

(Ready in about 20 minutes | Servings 6)

Per serving: 206 Calories; 20.5g Fat; 6.7g Carbs; 3.7g Protein; 1.3g Sugars; 3.6g Fiber

INGREDIENTS

1/2 stick butter, at room temperature
1/2 cup chocolate, unsweetened and chopped
1 tablespoon liquid stevia
1 ½ cups coconut flour

A pinch of fine sea salt
2 eggs, whisked
1/2 teaspoon vanilla extract

DIRECTIONS

Begin by preheating your Air Fryer to 330 degrees F.
In a microwave-safe bowl, melt the butter, chocolate, and stevia.
Add the other ingredients to the cooled chocolate mixture; stir to combine well. Scrape the batter into a lightly greased baking pan.
Bake in the preheated Air Fryer for 15 minutes or until the center is springy and a toothpick comes out dry. Enjoy!

509. Espresso Brownies with Mascarpone Frosting

(Ready in about 40 minutes | Servings 8)

Per serving: 363 Calories; 33.1g Fat; 9.4g Carbs; 6.6g Protein; 1.1g Sugars; 5g Fiber

INGREDIENTS

5 ounces unsweetened chocolate, chopped into chunks
2 tablespoons instant espresso powder
1 tablespoon cocoa powder, unsweetened
1/2 cup almond butter
1/2 cup almond meal
3/4 cup swerve
1 teaspoon pure coffee extract
1/2 teaspoon lime peel zest
1/4 cup coconut flour
2 eggs plus 1 egg yolk
1/2 teaspoon baking soda

1/2 teaspoon baking powder
1/2 teaspoon ground cinnamon
1/3 teaspoon ancho chile powder
For the Chocolate Mascarpone Frosting:
4 ounces mascarpone cheese, at room temperature
1 ½ ounces unsweetened chocolate chips
1 ½ cups confectioner's swerve
1/4 cup unsalted butter, at room temperature
1 teaspoon vanilla paste
A pinch of fine sea salt

DIRECTIONS

First of all, microwave the chocolate and almond butter until completely melted; allow the mixture to cool at room temperature.
Then, whisk the eggs, swerve, cinnamon, espresso powder, coffee extract, ancho chile powder, and lime zest.
Next step, add the vanilla/egg mixture to the chocolate/butter mixture. Stir in the almond meal and coconut flour along with baking soda, baking powder and cocoa powder.
Finally, press the batter into a lightly buttered cake pan. Air-fry for 35 minutes at 345 degrees F.
In the meantime, make the frosting. Beat the butter and mascarpone cheese until creamy. Add in the melted chocolate chips and vanilla paste.
Gradually, stir in the confectioner's swerve and salt; beat until everything's well combined. Lastly, frost the brownies and serve.

510. Coconut and Orange Cake

(Ready in about 30 minutes | Servings 6)

Per serving: 339 Calories; 33.1g Fat; 7.2g Carbs; 6.8g Protein; 2.4g Sugars; 3.7g Fiber

INGREDIENTS

3/4 cup coconut flour

1/3 cup coconut milk

2 tablespoons orange jam, unsweetened

1 stick butter

3/4 cup granulated swerve

2 eggs

1 ¼ cups almond flour

1/2 teaspoon baking powder

1/3 teaspoon grated nutmeg

1/4 teaspoon salt

DIRECTIONS

Set the Air Fryer to cook at 355 degrees F. Spritz the inside of a cake pan with the cooking spray. Then, beat the butter with granulated swerve until fluffy.

Fold in the eggs; continue mixing until smooth. Throw in the coconut flour, salt, and nutmeg; then, slowly and carefully pour in the coconut milk. Finally, add almond flour, baking powder and orange jam; mix thoroughly to create the cake batter.

Then, press the batter into the cake pan. Bake for 17 minutes and transfer your cake to a cooling rack. Frost the cake and serve chilled. Enjoy!

511. Old-Fashioned Walnut and Rum Cookies

(Ready in about 40 minutes | Servings 8)

Per serving: 228 Calories; 22.3g Fat; 4g Carbs; 3.5g Protein; 0.9g Sugars; 2.3g Fiber

INGREDIENTS

1/2 cup walnuts, ground

1/2 cup coconut flour

1 cup almond flour

3/4 cup swerve

1 stick butter, room temperature

2 tablespoons rum

1/2 teaspoon pure vanilla extract

1/2 teaspoon pure almond extract

DIRECTIONS

In a mixing dish, beat the butter with swerve, vanilla, and almond extract until light and fluffy. Then, throw in the flour and ground walnuts; add in rum.

Continue mixing until it forms a soft dough. Cover and place in the refrigerator for 20 minutes. In the meantime, preheat the Air Fryer to 330 degrees F.

Roll the dough into small cookies and place them on the Air Fryer cake pan; gently press each cookie using a spoon.

Bake butter cookies for 15 minutes in the preheated Air Fryer. Bon appétit!

512. Chocolate and Blueberry Cupcakes

(Ready in about 20 minutes | Servings 6)

Per serving: 303 Calories; 28g Fat; 7.7g Carbs; 8.1g Protein; 3.2g Sugars; 3g Fiber

INGREDIENTS

3 teaspoons cocoa powder, unsweetened

1/2 cup blueberries

1 ¼ cups almond flour

1/2 cup milk

1 stick butter, room temperature

3 eggs

3/4 cup granulated erythritol

1 teaspoon pure rum extract

1/2 teaspoon baking soda

1 teaspoon baking powder

1/4 teaspoon grated nutmeg

1/2 teaspoon ground cinnamon

1/8 teaspoon salt

DIRECTIONS

Grab two mixing bowls. In the first bowl, thoroughly combine the erythritol, almond flour, baking soda, baking powder, salt, nutmeg, cinnamon and cocoa powder.

Take the second bowl and cream the butter, egg, rum extract, and milk; whisk to combine well. Now, add the wet mixture to the dry mixture. Fold in blueberries.

Press the prepared batter mixture into a lightly greased muffin tin. Bake at 345 degrees for 15 minutes. Use a toothpick to check if your cupcakes are baked. Bon appétit!

513. Easy Fruitcake with Cranberries

(Ready in about 30 minutes | Servings 8)

Per serving: 286 Calories; 27g Fat; 9.1g Carbs; 7.8g Protein; 1.1g Sugars; 5g Fiber

INGREDIENTS

1 cup almond flour
1/3 teaspoon baking soda
1/3 teaspoon baking powder
3/4 cup erythritol
1/2 teaspoon ground cloves
1/3 teaspoon ground cinnamon

1/2 teaspoon cardamom
1 stick butter
1/2 teaspoon vanilla paste
2 eggs plus 1 egg yolk, beaten
1/2 cup cranberries, fresh or thawed
1 tablespoon browned butter

For Ricotta Frosting:
1/2 stick butter
1/2 cup firm Ricotta cheese
1 cup powdered erythritol
1/4 teaspoon salt
Zest of 1/2 lemon

DIRECTIONS

Start by preheating your Air Fryer to 355 degrees F.

In a mixing bowl, combine the flour with baking soda, baking powder, erythritol, ground cloves, cinnamon, and cardamom.

In a separate bowl, whisk 1 stick butter with vanilla paste; mix in the eggs until light and fluffy. Add the flour/sugar mixture to the butter/egg mixture. Fold in the cranberries and browned butter.

Scrape the mixture into the greased cake pan. Then, bake in the preheated Air Fryer for about 20 minutes.

Meanwhile, in a food processor, whip 1/2 stick of the butter and Ricotta cheese until there are no lumps.

Slowly add the powdered erythritol and salt until your mixture has reached a thick consistency. Stir in the lemon zest; mix to combine and chill completely before using.

Frost the cake and enjoy!

514. Classic White Chocolate Cookies

(Ready in about 40 minutes | Servings 10)

Per serving: 389 Calories; 36.3g Fat; 9.7g Carbs; 7g Protein; 1.1g Sugars; 5.7g Fiber

INGREDIENTS

3/4 cup butter
1 2/3 cups almond flour
1/2 cup coconut flour
2 tablespoons coconut oil

3/4 cup granulated swerve
1/3 teaspoon ground anise star
1/3 teaspoon ground allspice
1/3 teaspoon grated nutmeg

1/4 teaspoon fine sea salt
8 ounces white chocolate, unsweetened
2 eggs, well beaten

DIRECTIONS

Put all of the above ingredients, minus 1 egg, into a mixing dish. Then, knead with hand until a soft dough is formed. Place in the refrigerator for 20 minutes.

Roll the chilled dough into small balls; flatten your balls and preheat the Air Fryer r to 350 degrees F.

Make an egg wash by using the remaining egg. Then, glaze the cookies with the egg wash; bake about 11 minutes. Bon appétit!

515. Puffy Coconut and Pecan Cookies

(Ready in about 30 minutes | Servings 10)

Per serving: 354 Calories; 36g Fat; 6.3g Carbs; 5.9g Protein; 1.8g Sugars; 3.7g Fiber

INGREDIENTS

3/4 cup coconut oil, room temperature
1 ½ cups coconut flour
1 cup pecan nuts, unsalted and roughly chopped
3 eggs plus an egg yolk, whisked

1 ½ cups extra-fine almond flour
3/4 cup monk fruit
1/4 teaspoon freshly grated nutmeg
1/3 teaspoon ground cloves
1/2 teaspoon baking powder

1/3 teaspoon baking soda
1/2 teaspoon pure vanilla extract
1/2 teaspoon pure coconut extract
1/8 teaspoon fine sea salt

DIRECTIONS

In a bowl, combine both types of flour, baking soda and baking powder. In a separate bowl, beat the eggs with coconut oil. Combine egg mixture with the flour mixture.

Throw in the other ingredients, mixing well. Shape the mixture into cookies.

Bake at 370 degrees F for about 25 minutes. Bon appétit!

516. Flourless Almond and Ginger Cookies

(Ready in about 50 minutes | Servings 8)

Per serving: 199 Calories; 19.2g Fat; 3.8g Carbs; 3.3g Protein; 0.7g Sugars; 2.2g Fiber

INGREDIENTS

1/2 cup slivered almonds
1 stick butter, room temperature
4 ounces monk fruit
2/3 cup blanched almond flour

1/3 cup coconut flour
1/3 teaspoon ground cloves
1 tablespoon ginger powder
3/4 teaspoon pure vanilla extract

DIRECTIONS

In a mixing dish, beat the monk fruit, butter, vanilla extract, ground cloves, and ginger until light and fluffy. Then, throw in the coconut flour, almond flour, and slivered almonds.

Continue mixing until it forms a soft dough. Cover and place in the refrigerator for 35 minutes. Meanwhile, preheat the Air Fryer to 315 degrees F.

Roll dough into small cookies and place them on the Air Fryer cake pan; gently press each cookie using the back of a spoon.

Bake these butter cookies for 13 minutes. Bon appétit!

517. Birthday Chocolate Raspberry Cake

(Ready in about 30 minutes | Servings 4)

Per serving: 217 Calories; 18.8g Fat; 8.6g Carbs; 7.5g Protein; 1.7g Sugars; 4.6g Fiber

INGREDIENTS

1/3 cup monk fruit
1/4 cup unsalted butter, room temperature
1 egg plus 1 egg white, lightly whisked
3 ounces almond flour

2 tablespoons Dutch-process cocoa powder
1/2 teaspoon ground cinnamon
1 tablespoon candied ginger
1/8 teaspoon table salt

For the Filling:
2 ounces fresh raspberries
1/3 cup monk fruit
1 teaspoon fresh lime juice

DIRECTIONS

Firstly, set your Air Fryer to cook at 315 degrees F. Then, spritz the inside of two cake pans with the butter-flavored cooking spray.

In a mixing bowl, beat the monk fruit and butter until creamy and uniform. Then, stir in the whisked eggs. Stir in the almond flour, cocoa powder, cinnamon, ginger and salt.

Press the batter into the cake pans; use a wide spatula to level the surface of the batter. Bake for 20 minutes or until a wooden stick inserted in the center of the cake comes out completely dry.

While your cake is baking, stir together all of the ingredients for the filling in a medium saucepan. Cook over high heat, stirring frequently and mashing with the back of a spoon; bring to a boil and decrease the temperature.

Continue to cook, stirring until the mixture thickens, for another 7 minutes. Let the filling cool to room temperature.

Spread 1/2 of raspberry filling over the first crust. Top with another crust; spread remaining filling over top. Spread frosting over top and sides of your cake. Enjoy!

518. Old-Fashioned Muffins

(Ready in about 20 minutes | Servings 6)

Per serving: 440 Calories; 42g Fat; 9.2g Carbs; 9.4g Protein; 2.9g Sugars; 4.6g Fiber

INGREDIENTS

1/2 cup raspberries
3/4 cup swerve
1/2 cup coconut oil
1 cup sour cream

1 ¼ teaspoons baking powder
2 cups almond flour
2 eggs
1/3 teaspoon ground allspice

1/3 teaspoon ground anise star
1/2 teaspoon grated lemon zest
1/4 teaspoon salt

DIRECTIONS

Grab two mixing bowls. In the first bowl, thoroughly combine the almond flour, baking powder, swerve, salt, anise, allspice and lemon zest. Take the second bowl; whisk coconut oil, sour cream, and eggs; whisk to combine well. Now, add the wet mixture to the dry mixture. Fold in the raspberries.

Press the batter mixture into a lightly greased muffin tin. Bake at 345 degrees for 15 minutes. Use a toothpick to check if your muffins are baked. Bon appétit!

519. Double Chocolate Whiskey Brownies

(Ready in about 55 minutes | Servings 10)

Per serving: 303 Calories; 28g Fat; 9.1g Carbs; 5.5g Protein; 0.7g Sugars; 5.2g Fiber

INGREDIENTS

3 tablespoons whiskey

8 ounces white chocolate

3/4 cup almond flour

1/4 cup coconut flakes

1/2 cup coconut oil

2 eggs plus an egg yolk, whisked

3/4 cup monk fruit

2 tablespoons cocoa powder, unsweetened

1/4 teaspoon ground cardamom

1 teaspoon pure rum extract

DIRECTIONS

Microwave white chocolate and coconut oil until everything's melted; allow the mixture to cool at room temperature.

After that, thoroughly whisk the eggs, monk fruit, rum extract, cocoa powder and cardamom.

Next step, add the rum/egg mixture to the chocolate mixture. Stir in the flour and coconut flakes; mix to combine.

Mix cranberries with whiskey and let them soak for 15 minutes. Fold them into the batter. Press the batter into a lightly buttered cake pan.

Air-fry for 35 minutes at 340 degrees F. Allow them to cool slightly on a wire rack before slicing and serving.

520. Picnic Blackberry Muffins

(Ready in about 20 minutes | Servings 8)

Per serving: 192 Calories; 17.3g Fat; 5.5g Carbs; 5.7g Protein; 2g Sugars; 2.7g Fiber

INGREDIENTS

1 ½ cups almond flour

1/2 teaspoon baking soda

1 teaspoon baking powder

1/4 teaspoon kosher salt

1/2 cup swerve

2 eggs, whisked

1/2 cup milk

1/4 cup coconut oil, melted

1/2 teaspoon vanilla paste

1/2 cup fresh blackberries

DIRECTIONS

In a mixing bowl, combine the almond flour, baking soda, baking powder, swerve, and salt. Whisk to combine well.

In another mixing bowl, mix the eggs, milk, coconut oil, and vanilla.

Now, add the wet egg mixture to dry the flour mixture. Then, carefully fold in the fresh blackberries; gently stir to combine.

Scrape the batter mixture into the muffin cups. Bake your muffins at 350 degrees F for 12 minutes or until the tops are golden brown.

Sprinkle some extra icing sugar over the top of each muffin if desired. Serve and enjoy!

521. Sunday Tart with Walnuts

(Ready in about 20 minutes | Servings 6)

Per serving: 227 Calories; 20.4g Fat; 5g Carbs; 7.1g Protein; 2.9g Sugars; 1.5g Fiber

INGREDIENTS

1 cup coconut milk

2 eggs

1/2 stick butter, at room temperature

1 teaspoon vanilla essence

1/4 teaspoon ground cardamom

1/4 teaspoon ground cloves

1/2 cup walnuts, ground

1/2 cup swerve

1/2 cup almond flour

DIRECTIONS

Begin by preheating your Air Fryer to 360 degrees F. Spritz the sides and bottom of a baking pan with nonstick cooking spray.

Mix all ingredients until well combined. Scrape the batter into the prepared baking pan.

Bake approximately 13 minutes; use a toothpick to test for doneness. Bon appétit!

522. Peanut Butter and Chocolate Chip Cookies

(Ready in about 20 minutes | Servings 8)

Per serving: 303 Calories; 28.5g Fat; 9.8g Carbs; 6.4g Protein; 1.9g Sugars; 4.9g Fiber

INGREDIENTS

1 stick butter, at room temperature
1 ¼ cups swerve
1/4 cup chunky peanut butter
1 teaspoon vanilla paste
1 fine almond flour
2/3 cup coconut flour

1/3 cup cocoa powder, unsweetened
1 ½ teaspoons baking powder
1/4 teaspoon ground cinnamon
1/4 teaspoon crystallized ginger
1/2 cup chocolate chips, unsweetened

DIRECTIONS

In a mixing dish, beat the butter and swerve until creamy and uniform. Stir in the peanut butter and vanilla.
In another mixing dish, thoroughly combine the flour, cocoa powder, baking powder, cinnamon, and crystallized ginger.
Add the flour mixture to the peanut butter mixture; mix to combine well. Afterwards, fold in the chocolate chips.
Drop by large spoonfuls onto a parchment-lined Air Fryer basket. Bake at 365 degrees F for 11 minutes or until golden brown on the top.
Bon appétit!

523. Keto Mixed Berry Crumble Pots

(Ready in about 40 minutes | Servings 6)

Per serving: 155 Calories; 14.3g Fat; 5.1g Carbs; 3.1g Protein; 1.8g Sugars; 2.6g Fiber

INGREDIENTS

2 ounces unsweetened mixed berries
1/2 cup granulated swerve
2 tablespoons golden flaxseed meal
1/4 teaspoon ground star anise
1/2 teaspoon ground cinnamon
1 teaspoon xanthan gum

2/3 cup almond flour
1 cup powdered swerve
1/2 teaspoon baking powder
1/3 cup unsweetened coconut, finely shredded
1/2 stick butter, cut into small pieces

DIRECTIONS

Toss the mixed berries with the granulated swerve, golden flaxseed meal, star anise, cinnamon, and xanthan gum. Divide between six custard cups coated with cooking spray.
In a mixing dish, thoroughly combine the remaining ingredients. Sprinkle over the berry mixture.
Bake in the preheated Air Fryer at 330 degrees F for 35 minutes. Work in batches if needed. Bon appétit!

524. Chocolate Coffee Cake

(Ready in about 40 minutes | Servings 8)

Per serving: 285 Calories; 28.1g Fat; 6.6g Carbs; 4.8g Protein; 1.3g Sugars; 3.1g Fiber

INGREDIENTS

1 ½ cups almond flour
1/2 cup coconut meal
2/3 cup swerve
1 teaspoon baking powder
1/4 teaspoon salt

1 stick butter, melted
1/2 cup hot strongly brewed coffee
1/2 teaspoon vanilla
1 egg

Topping:
1/4 cup coconut flour
1/2 cup confectioner's swerve
1/2 teaspoon ground cardamom
1 teaspoon ground cinnamon
3 tablespoons coconut oil

DIRECTIONS

Mix all dry ingredients for your cake; then, mix in the wet ingredients. Mix until everything is well incorporated.
Spritz a baking pan with cooking spray. Scrape the batter into the baking pan.
Then, make the topping by mixing all ingredients. Place on top of the cake. Smooth the top with a spatula.
Bake at 330 degrees F for 30 minutes or until the top of the cake springs back when gently pressed with your fingers. Serve with your favorite hot beverage. Bon appétit!

525. Peanut Butter Fudge Cake

(Ready in about 30 minutes | Servings 10)

Per serving: 207 Calories; 17.1g Fat; 6.4g Carbs; 8.4g Protein; 1.1g Sugars; 3.4g Fiber

INGREDIENTS

1 cup peanut butter
1 ¼ cups monk fruit
3 eggs
1 cup almond flour

1 teaspoon baking powder
1/4 teaspoon kosher salt
1 cup unsweetened bakers' chocolate, broken into chunks

DIRECTIONS

Start by preheating your Air Fryer to 350 degrees F. Now, spritz the sides and bottom of a baking pan with cooking spray.
In a mixing dish, thoroughly combine the peanut butter with the monk fruit until creamy. Next, fold in the egg and beat until fluffy.
After that, stir in the almond flour, baking powder, salt, and bakers'chocolate. Mix until everything is well combined.
Bake in the preheated Air Fryer for 20 to 22 minutes. Transfer to a wire rack to cool before slicing and serving. Bon appétit!

526. Perfectly Puffy Coconut Cookies

(Ready in about 20 minutes | Servings 12)

Per serving: 304 Calories; 16.7g Fat; 34.2g Carbs; 4.3g Protein; 15.6g Sugars; 2g Fiber

INGREDIENTS

1 cup butter, melted
1 ¾ cups granulated swerve
3 eggs
2 tablespoons coconut milk
1 teaspoon coconut extract
1 teaspoon vanilla extract

1 cup coconut flour
1 ¼ cups almond flour
1/2 teaspoon baking powder
1/2 teaspoon baking soda
1/2 teaspoon fine table salt
1/2 cups coconut chips, unsweetened

DIRECTIONS

Begin by preheating your Air Fryer to 350 degrees F.
In the bowl of an electric mixer, beat the butter and swerve until well combined. Now, add the eggs one at a time, and mix well; add the coconut milk, coconut extract, and vanilla; beat until creamy and uniform.
Mix the flour with baking powder, baking soda, and salt. Then, stir the flour mixture into the butter mixture and stir until everything is well incorporated.
Finally, fold in the coconut chips and mix again. Scoop out 1 tablespoon size balls of the batter on a cookie pan, leaving 2 inches between each cookie.
Bake for 10 minutes or until golden brown, rotating the pan once or twice through the cooking time. Let your cookies cool on wire racks. Bon appétit!

527. Ultimate Chocolate and Coconut Pudding

(Ready in about 20 minutes | Servings 10)

Per serving: 229 Calories; 21.3g Fat; 5.4g Carbs; 4.4g Protein; 0.5g Sugars; 3g Fiber

INGREDIENTS

1 stick butter
1 ¼ cups bakers' chocolate, unsweetened
1 teaspoon liquid stevia

2 tablespoons full fat coconut milk
2 eggs, beaten
1/3 cup coconut, shredded

DIRECTIONS

Begin by preheating your Air Fryer to 330 degrees F.
In a microwave-safe bowl, melt the butter, chocolate, and stevia. Allow it to cool to room temperature.
Add the remaining ingredients to the chocolate mixture; stir to combine well. Scrape the batter into a lightly greased baking pan.
Bake in the preheated Air Fryer for 15 minutes or until a toothpick comes out dry and clean. Enjoy!

528. Chocolate Paradise Cake

(Ready in about 35 minutes + chilling time | Servings 6)

Per serving: 433 Calories; 42.4g Fat; 9.8g Carbs; 8.5g Protein; 0.9g Sugars; 4.9g Fiber

INGREDIENTS

2 eggs, beaten
2/3 cup sour cream
1 cup almond flour
2/3 cup swerve
1/3 cup coconut oil, softened
1/4 cup cocoa powder

2 tablespoons chocolate chips, unsweetened
1 ½ teaspoons baking powder
1 teaspoon vanilla extract
1/2 teaspoon pure rum extract

Chocolate Frosting:
1/2 cup butter, softened
1/4 cup cocoa powder
1 cup powdered swerve
2 tablespoons milk

DIRECTIONS

Mix all ingredients for the chocolate cake with a hand mixer on low speed. Scrape the batter into a cake pan.
Bake at 330 degrees F for 25 to 30 minutes. Transfer the cake to a wire rack
Meanwhile, whip the butter and cocoa until smooth. Stir in the powdered swerve. Slowly and gradually, pour in the milk until your frosting reaches desired consistency.
Whip until smooth and fluffy; then, frost the cooled cake. Place in your refrigerator for a couple of hours. Serve well chilled.

529. Famous New York Cheesecake

(Ready in about 1 hour + chilling time | Servings 8)

Per serving: 245 Calories; 21.2g Fat; 6.5g Carbs; 7.8g Protein; 3.1g Sugars; 1.5g Fiber

INGREDIENTS

1 ½ cups almond flour
3 ounces swerve
1/2 stick butter, melted
20 ounces full-fat cream cheese
1/2 cup heavy cream

1 ¼ cups granulated swerve
3 eggs, at room temperature
1 tablespoon vanilla essence
1 teaspoon grated lemon zest

DIRECTIONS

Coat the sides and bottom of a baking pan with a little flour.
In a mixing bowl, combine the almond flour and swerve. Add the melted butter and mix until your mixture looks like breadcrumbs.
Press the mixture into the bottom of the prepared pan to form an even layer. Bake at 330 degrees F for 7 minutes until golden brown. Allow it to cool completely on a wire rack.
Meanwhile, in a mixer fitted with the paddle attachment, prepare the filling by mixing the soft cheese, heavy cream, and granulated swerve; beat until creamy and fluffy.
Crack the eggs into the mixing bowl, one at a time; add the vanilla and lemon zest and continue to mix until fully combined.
Pour the prepared topping over the cooled crust and spread evenly.
Bake in the preheated Air Fryer at 330 degrees F for 25 to 30 minutes; leave it in the Air Fryer to keep warm for another 30 minutes.
Cover your cheesecake with plastic wrap. Place in your refrigerator and allow it to cool at least 6 hours or overnight. Serve well chilled.

530. Mixed Berries with Pecan Streusel

(Ready in about 20 minutes | Servings 3)

Per serving: 255 Calories; 22.8g Fat; 9.1g Carbs; 7.3g Protein; 3.6g Sugars; 4g Fiber

INGREDIENTS

3 tablespoons pecans, chopped
3 tablespoons almonds, slivered
2 tablespoons walnuts, chopped
3 tablespoons granulated swerve

1/2 teaspoon ground cinnamon
1 egg
2 tablespoons cold salted butter, cut into pieces
1/2 cup mixed berries

DIRECTIONS

Mix your nuts, swerve, cinnamon, egg, and butter until well combined.
Place mixed berries on the bottom of a lightly greased Air Fryer-safe dish. Top with the prepared topping.
Bake at 340 degrees F for 17 minutes. Serve at room temperature. Bon appétit!

531. Easy Fluffy Pancakes

(Ready in about 35 minutes | Servings 3)

Per serving: 315 Calories; 31.3g Fat; 5.3g Carbs; 5.5g Protein; 3g Sugars; 2.1g Fiber

INGREDIENTS

1/2 cup coconut flour
1 teaspoon baking powder
1/4 teaspoon salt
2 tablespoons erythritol
1/2 teaspoon cinnamon
1 teaspoon red paste food color
1 egg

1/2 cup milk
1 teaspoon vanilla
Topping:
2 ounces cream cheese, softened
2 tablespoons butter, softened
3/4 cup powdered swerve

DIRECTIONS

Mix the coconut flour, baking powder, salt, erythritol, cinnamon, red paste food color in a large bowl.
Gradually add the egg and milk, whisking continuously, until well combined. Let it stand for 20 minutes.
Spritz the Air Fryer baking pan with cooking spray. Pour the batter into the pan using a measuring cup.
Cook at 230 degrees F for 4 to 5 minutes or until golden brown. Repeat with the remaining batter.
Meanwhile, make your topping by mixing the ingredients until creamy and fluffy. Decorate your pancakes with topping. Bon appétit!

532. Easy Spanish Churros

(Ready in about 20 minutes | Servings 4)

Per serving: 321 Calories; 31.1g Fat; 4.4g Carbs; 8.4g Protein; 1.1g Sugars; 2.3g Fiber

INGREDIENTS

3/4 cup water
1 tablespoon swerve
1/4 teaspoon sea salt
1/4 teaspoon grated nutmeg

1/4 teaspoon ground cloves
6 tablespoons butter
3/4 cup almond flour
2 eggs

DIRECTIONS

To make the dough, boil the water in a pan over medium-high heat; now, add the swerve, salt, nutmeg, and cloves; cook until dissolved.
Add the butter and turn the heat to low. Gradually stir in the almond flour, whisking continuously, until the mixture forms a ball.
Remove from the heat; fold in the eggs one at a time, stirring to combine well.
Pour the mixture into a piping bag with a large star tip. Squeeze 4-inch strips of dough into the greased Air Fryer pan.
Cook at 410 degrees F for 6 minutes, working in batches. Bon appétit!

533. Mixed Berry Compote with Coconut Chips

(Ready in about 25 minutes | Servings 6)

Per serving: 76 Calories; 4.3g Fat; 9.5g Carbs; 0.6g Protein; 6.1g Sugars; 2.1g Fiber

INGREDIENTS

1 tablespoon butter
12 ounces mixed berries
1/3 cup granulated swerve
1/4 teaspoon grated nutmeg

1/4 teaspoon ground cloves
1/2 teaspoon ground cinnamon
1 teaspoon pure vanilla extract
1/2 cup coconut chips

DIRECTIONS

Start by preheating your Air Fryer to 330 degrees F. Grease a baking pan with butter.
Place all ingredients, except for the coconut chips, in a baking pan. Bake in the preheated Air Fryer for 20 minutes.
Serve in individual bowls, garnished with coconut chips. Bon appétit!

534. Vanilla Coconut Cupcakes

(Ready in about 30 minutes | Servings 4)

Per serving: 177 Calories; 16.9g Fat; 4.6g Carbs; 3.7g Protein; 1.9g Sugars; 2.2g Fiber

INGREDIENTS

1/2 cup coconut flour
1/3 cup coconut milk
2 eggs
1 tablespoon coconut oil, melted

1 teaspoon vanilla
A pinch of ground cardamom
1/2 cup coconut chips

DIRECTIONS

Mix the flour, coconut milk, eggs, coconut oil, vanilla, and cardamom in a large bowl.
Let it stand for 20 minutes. Spoon the batter into a greased muffin tin.
Cook at 230 degrees F for 4 to 5 minutes or until golden brown. Repeat with the remaining batter.
Decorate your cupcakes with coconut chips. Bon appétit!

535. Autumn Walnut Crisp

(Ready in about 40 minutes | Servings 8)

Per serving: 288 Calories; 28.5g Fat; 6.2g Carbs; 5.6g Protein; 1.3g Sugars; 3.4g Fiber

INGREDIENTS

1 cup walnuts
1/2 cup swerve
Topping:
1 ½ cups almond flour
1/2 cup coconut flour

1/2 cup swerve
1 teaspoon crystallized ginger
1/2 teaspoon ground cardamom
A pinch of salt
1 stick butter, cut into pieces

DIRECTIONS

Place walnuts and 1/2 cup of swerve in a baking pan lightly greased with nonstick cooking spray.
In a mixing dish, thoroughly combine all the topping ingredients. Sprinkle the topping ingredients over the walnut layer.
Bake in the preheated Air Fryer at 330 degrees F for 35 minutes. Bon appétit!

536. Vanilla Rum Cookies with Walnuts

(Ready in about 35 minutes | Servings 6)

Per serving: 314 Calories; 32g Fat; 4.7g Carbs; 5.2g Protein; 1.2g Sugars; 2.5g Fiber

INGREDIENTS

1/2 cup almond flour
1/2 cup coconut flour
1/2 teaspoon baking powder
1/4 teaspoon fine sea salt
1 stick butter, unsalted and softened

1/2 cup swerve
1 egg
1/2 teaspoon vanilla
1 teaspoon butter rum flavoring
3 ounces walnuts, finely chopped

DIRECTIONS

Begin by preheating the Air Fryer to 360 degrees F.
In a mixing dish, thoroughly combine the flour with baking powder and salt.
Beat the butter and swerve with a hand mixer until pale and fluffy; add the whisked egg, vanilla, and butter rum flavoring; mix again to combine well. Now, stir in the dry ingredients.
Fold in the chopped walnuts and mix to combine. Divide the mixture into small balls; flatten each ball with a fork and transfer them to a foil-lined baking pan.
Bake in the preheated Air Fryer for 14 minutes. Work in a few batches and transfer to wire racks to cool completely. Bon appétit!

537. Fudge Cake with Pecans

(Ready in about 30 minutes | Servings 6)

Per serving: 253 Calories; 25.5g Fat; 6.4g Carbs; 4.2g Protein; 0.7g Sugars; 3.4g Fiber

INGREDIENTS

1/2 cup butter, melted
1/2 cup swerve
1 teaspoon vanilla essence
1 egg
1/2 cup almond flour
1/2 teaspoon baking powder

1/4 cup cocoa powder
1/2 teaspoon ground cinnamon
1/4 teaspoon fine sea salt
1 ounce bakers' chocolate, unsweetened
1/4 cup pecans, finely chopped

DIRECTIONS

Start by preheating your Air Fryer to 350 degrees F. Now, lightly grease six silicone molds.
In a mixing dish, beat the melted butter with the swerve until fluffy. Next, stir in the vanilla and egg and beat again.
After that, add the almond flour, baking powder, cocoa powder, cinnamon, and salt. Mix until everything is well combined.
Fold in the chocolate and pecans; mix to combine. Bake in the preheated Air Fryer for 20 to 22 minutes. Enjoy!

538. French Blueberry Flan

(Ready in about 30 minutes | Servings 6)

Per serving: 250 Calories; 22.62 Fat; 9.4g Carbs; 6.8g Protein; 4g Sugars; 3.3g Fiber

INGREDIENTS

3/4 cup extra-fine almond flour
1 cup fresh blueberries
1/2 cup coconut cream
3/4 cup coconut milk
3 eggs, whisked
1/2 cup swerve

1/3 cup confectioner's swerve
1/2 teaspoon baking soda
1/2 teaspoon baking powder
1/3 teaspoon ground cinnamon
1/2 teaspoon crystalized ginger
1/4 teaspoon grated nutmeg

DIRECTIONS

Lightly grease 2 mini pie pans using a nonstick cooking spray. Lay the blueberries on the bottom of the pie pans.
In a saucepan that is preheated over a moderate flame, warm the cream along with coconut milk until thoroughly heated.
Remove the pan from the heat; mix in the flour along with baking soda and baking powder.
In a medium-sized mixing bowl, whip the eggs, swerve, and spices; whip until the mixture is creamy.
Add the creamy milk mixture. Carefully spread this mixture over the fruits.
Bake at 320 degrees for about 25 minutes. To serve, dust with confectioner's swerve.

539. Anise and Orange Cake

(Ready in about 30 minutes | Servings 6)

Per serving: 346 Calories; 33.7g Fat; 6.9g Carbs; 7.6g Protein; 1.4g Sugars; 3.8g Fiber

INGREDIENTS

1/3 cup hazelnuts, roughly chopped
3 tablespoons sugar free orange marmalade
1 stick butter
2 eggs plus 1 egg yolk, beaten
5 tablespoons liquid monk fruit
6 ounces unbleached almond flour

1 teaspoon baking soda
1/2 teaspoon baking powder
1/2 ground anise seed
1/2 teaspoon ground cinnamon
1/2 teaspoon ground allspice
Pan oil

DIRECTIONS

Lightly grease a cake pan using a pan oil.
Now, whip the liquid monk fruit and butter in a mixing bowl; whip until pale and smooth. Fold in the eggs, hazelnuts and marmalade; beat again until everything's well mixed.
Throw in the almond flour, baking soda, baking powder, allspice, anise star, and ground cinnamon. Bake in the preheated Air Fryer at 310 degrees F for about 20 minutes.
After that, use a tester to check for doneness. To finish, add the frosting. Bon appétit!

540. Snickerdoodle Cinnamon Cookies

(Ready in about 1 hour | Servings 10)

Per serving: 246 Calories; 23.4g Fat; 6.6g Carbs; 5g Protein; 1.3g Sugars; 3.8g Fiber

INGREDIENTS

4 tablespoons liquid monk fruit
1/2 cup hazelnuts, ground
1 stick butter, room temperature
2 cups almond flour

1 cup coconut flour
2 ounces granulated swerve
2 teaspoons ground cinnamon

DIRECTIONS

Firstly, cream liquid monk fruit with butter until the mixture becomes fluffy. Sift in both types of flour.
Now, stir in the hazelnuts. Now, knead the mixture to form a dough; place in the refrigerator for about 35 minutes.
To finish, shape the prepared dough into the bite-sized balls; arrange them on a baking dish; flatten the balls using the back of a spoon.
Mix granulated swerve with ground cinnamon. Press your cookies in the cinnamon mixture until they are completely covered.
Bake the cookies for 20 minutes at 310 degrees F.
Leave them to cool for about 10 minutes before transferring them to a wire rack. Bon appétit!

541. Boozy Baileys Fudge Brownies

(Ready in about 35 minutes | Servings 8)

Per serving: 277 Calories; 26.6g Fat; 9.7g Carbs; 5.5g Protein; 1.8g Sugars; 3.2g Fiber

INGREDIENTS

1 cup granulated swerve
2 tablespoons unsweetened cocoa powder, sifted
1/2 cup almond flour
1/2 cup coconut flour
1/4 teaspoon salt

1/4 teaspoon baking powder
1/2 cup butter, melted then cooled
2 eggs room temperature
1 teaspoon vanilla
2 tablespoons Baileys
2 ounces unsweetened chocolate chips

1/2 cup sour cream
1/3 cup powdered erythritol
3 ounces Ricotta cheese, room temperature

DIRECTIONS

In a mixing bowl, thoroughly combine granulated swerve, cocoa powder, flour, salt, and baking powder.
Mix in butter, eggs, and vanilla. Add the batter to a lightly-greased baking pan.
Air-fry for 25 minutes at 355 degrees F. Allow them to cool slightly on a wire rack.
Microwave the chocolate chips until everything's melted; allow the mixture to cool at room temperature.
After that, add Ricotta cheese, Baileys, sour cream, and powdered erythritol; mix until everything is blended.
Spread this mixture onto the top of your brownie. Serve well chilled.

542. Orange Swiss Roll

(Ready in about 1 hour 20 minutes | Servings 6)

Per serving: 275 Calories; 25.3g Fat; 7.9g Carbs; 6.3g Protein; 3.1g Sugars; 3.5g Fiber

INGREDIENTS

1/2 cup milk
1/4 cup swerve
1 tablespoon yeast
1/2 stick butter, at room temperature
1 egg, at room temperature
1/4 teaspoon salt

1 cup almond flour
1 cup coconut flour
2 tablespoons fresh orange juice
Filling:
2 tablespoons butter
4 tablespoons swerve

1 teaspoon ground star anise
1/4 teaspoon ground cinnamon
1 teaspoon vanilla paste
1/2 cup confectioners' swerve

DIRECTIONS

Heat the milk in a microwave safe bowl and transfer the warm milk to the bowl of a stand electric mixer. Add the 1/4 cup of swerve and yeast, and mix to combine well. Cover and let it sit until the yeast is foamy.
Then, beat the butter on low speed. Fold in the egg and mix again. Add salt and flour. Add the orange juice and mix on medium speed until a soft dough forms.
Knead the dough on a lightly floured surface. Cover it loosely and let it sit in a warm place about 1 hour or until doubled in size. Then, spritz the bottom and sides of a baking pan with cooking oil (butter flavored).
Roll your dough out into a rectangle.
Spread 2 tablespoons of butter all over the dough. In a mixing dish, combine 4 tablespoons of swerve, ground star anise, cinnamon, and vanilla; sprinkle evenly over the dough.
Then, roll up your dough to form a log. Cut into 6 equal rolls and place them in the parchment-lined Air Fryer basket.
Bake at 350 degrees for 12 minutes, turning them halfway through the cooking time. Dust with confectioners' swerve and enjoy!

543. Ultimate Lemon Coconut Tart

(Ready in about 15 minutes + chilling time | Servings 8)

Per serving: 328 Calories; 29g Fat; 9g Carbs; 11.4g Protein; 2.5g Sugars; 3.8g Fiber

INGREDIENTS

2 eggs plus 6 egg yolks
1/4 cup lemon juice
4 tablespoons unsalted butter
1/2 cup powdered swerve
4 tablespoons heavy cream

Crust:
1 cup blanched almond meal
3/4 cup shredded coconut
1 ¼ cups cream cheese, room temperature

1 teaspoon apple pie spice blend
1 teaspoon pure vanilla extract
1/8 teaspoon salt
1/2 teaspoon ground anise star

DIRECTIONS

In a mixing bowl, whisk the eggs. Add in lemon juice, zest, butter, powdered swerve. Place in a double boiler or place a stainless-steel bowl over simmering water.

Continue to mix until the temperature reaches 170 degrees. Remove from heat and fold in heavy cream.

Place plastic wrap over top and let it cool in your refrigerator.

Next, mix all of the crust ingredients.

Transfer them to the Air Fryer baking dish and bake at 350 degrees F just for 5 minutes. When the edges become golden, they are ready.

Lastly, spread the prepared cream over the crust. Keep them refrigerated until serving time. Bon appétit!

544. Classic Mini Cheesecakes

(Ready in about 30 minutes | Servings 8)

Per serving: 314 Calories; 29.6g Fat; 7g Carbs; 6.8g Protein; 1.4g Sugars; 3.6g Fiber

For the Crust:
1/3 teaspoon grated nutmeg
1 ½ tablespoons erythritol
1 ½ cups almond meal
8 tablespoons melted butter
1 teaspoon ground cinnamon
A pinch of kosher salt

For the Cheesecake:
2 eggs
1/2 cups unsweetened chocolate chips
1 ½ tablespoons sour cream
4 ounces soft cheese
1/2 cup swerve
1/2 teaspoon vanilla essence

DIRECTIONS

Firstly, line eight cups of mini muffin pan with paper liners.

To make the crust, mix the almond meal together with erythritol, cinnamon, nutmeg, and kosher salt.

Now, add melted butter and stir well to moisten the crumb mixture.

Divide the crust mixture among the muffin cups and press gently to make even layers.

In another bowl, whip together the soft cheese, sour cream and swerve until uniform and smooth. Fold in the eggs and the vanilla essence.

Then, divide chocolate chips among the prepared muffin cups. Then, add the cheese mix to each muffin cup.

Bake for about 18 minutes at 345 degrees F. Bake in batches if needed. To finish, transfer the mini cheesecakes to a cooling rack; store in the fridge.

545. 15-Minute Orange Galettes

(Ready in about 15 minutes | Servings 6)

Per serving: 177 Calories; 13.5g Fat; 7.3g Carbs; 7.4g Protein; 3.8g Sugars; 2.6g Fiber

INGREDIENTS

1 cup almond meal
1/2 cup coconut flour
3 eggs
1⁄3 cup milk
2 tablespoons monk fruit

2 teaspoons grated lemon peel
1⁄3 teaspoon ground nutmeg, preferably freshly ground
1 ½ teaspoons baking powder
3 tablespoons orange juice
A pinch of turmeric

DIRECTIONS

Grab two mixing bowls. Combine dry ingredients in the first bowl.

In the second bowl, combine all wet ingredients. Add wet mixture to the dry mixture and mix until smooth and uniform.

Air-fry for 4 to 5 minutes at 345 degrees F. Work in batches. Dust with confectioners' swerve if desired. Bon appétit!

546. Favorite Cupcakes with Peanuts

(Ready in about 15 minutes | Servings 8)

Per serving: 186 Calories; 16.6g Fat; 4.4g Carbs; 6.8g Protein; 1.4g Sugars; 2.1g Fiber

INGREDIENTS

4 egg whites
2 whole egg
1/2 teaspoon pure vanilla extract
1/2 cup swerve
1/2 cup confectioners' swerve
1/3 teaspoon cream of tartar

1/2 stick butter, softened
1/3 teaspoon almond extract
1 cup almond flour
1/2 cup coconut flour
2 tablespoons unsalted peanuts, ground

DIRECTIONS

First of all, beat the softened butter and swerve until it is fluffy.

After that, fold in the egg and mix again; carefully throw in the flour along with ground peanuts; stir in the almond extract and vanilla extract.

Divide the batter among the muffin cups that are lined with muffin papers; air-fry at 325 degrees F for 10 minutes.

Meanwhile, prepare the topping; simply whip the egg and cream of tartar until it has an airy texture.

Now, gradually add the confectioners' swerve; continue mixing until stiff glossy peaks form. To finish, decorate the cupcakes and serve them on a nice serving platter.

547. Vanilla Orange Custard

(Ready in about 35 minutes + chilling time | Servings 6)

Per serving: 247 Calories; 18.8g Fat; 7.8g Carbs; 10.7g Protein; 7.4g Sugars; 0g Fiber

INGREDIENTS

6 eggs
7 ounces cream cheese, at room temperature
2 ½ cans condensed milk, sweetened
1/2 cup swerve

1/2 teaspoon orange rind, grated
1 ½ cardamom pods, bruised
2 teaspoons vanilla paste
1/4 cup fresh orange juice

DIRECTIONS

In a saucepan, melt swerve over a moderate flame; it takes about 10 to 12 minutes. Immediately but carefully pour the melted sugar into six ramekins, tilting to coat their bottoms; allow them to cool slightly.

In a mixing dish, beat the cheese until smooth; now, fold in the eggs, one at a time, and continue to beat until pale and creamy.

Add the orange rind, cardamom, vanilla, orange juice, and the milk; mix again. Pour the mixture over the caramelized sugar. Air-fry, covered, at 325 degrees F for 28 minutes or until it has thickened.

Refrigerate overnight; garnish with berries or other fruits and serve.

548. Blackberry and Cocoa Butter Cake

(Ready in about 30 minutes | Servings 8)

Per serving: 216 Calories; 20.2g Fat; 6.4g Carbs; 6.4g Protein; 0.9g Sugars; 3.4g Fiber

INGREDIENTS

1/3 cup fresh blackberries
1/2 cup butter, room temperature
1/3 teaspoon baking powder
2 ounces swerve
1/2 cup cocoa powder, melted

1 teaspoon baking soda
4 whole eggs
1 cup almond flour
1 teaspoon orange zest

DIRECTIONS

In a bowl, beat the butter, swerve and orange zest with an electric mixer. Carefully fold in the eggs, one at a time; beat well with your electric mixer after each addition.

Next, throw in the almond flour, baking soda, baking powder, cocoa powder, and orange juice.

Pour the prepared batter into a loaf pan. Top with fresh blackberries. Bake in the preheated Air Fryer for 22 minutes at 335 degrees F. Check the cake for doneness; allow it to cool on a wire rack. Bon appétit!

549. Classic Pound Cake

(Ready in about 35 minutes | Servings 8)

Per serving: 193 Calories; 18.7g Fat; 3.2g Carbs; 3.8g Protein; 1.8g Sugars; 1.4g Fiber

INGREDIENTS

1 stick butter, at room temperature
1 cup swerve
4 eggs
1 ½ cups coconut flour
1/2 teaspoon baking powder
1/2 teaspoon baking soda

1/4 teaspoon salt
A pinch of freshly grated nutmeg
A pinch of ground star anise
1/2 cup buttermilk
1 teaspoon vanilla essence

DIRECTIONS

Begin by preheating your Air Fryer to 320 degrees F. Spritz the bottom and sides of a baking pan with cooking spray.
Beat the butter and swerve with a hand mixer until creamy. Then, fold in the eggs, one at a time, and mix well until fluffy.
Stir in the flour along with the remaining ingredients. Mix to combine well. Scrape the batter into the prepared baking pan.
Bake for 15 minutes; rotate the pan and bake an additional 15 minutes, until the top of the cake springs back when gently pressed with your fingers. Bon appétit!

550. Chocolate Rum Lava Cake

(Ready in about 20 minutes | Servings 4)

Per serving: 364 Calories; 33.5g Fat; 8.7g Carbs; 8.4g Protein; 0.8g Sugars; 5g Fiber

INGREDIENTS

2 ½ ounces butter, at room temperature
3 ounces chocolate, unsweetened
2 eggs, beaten
1/2 cup confectioners' swerve

1/2 cup almond flour
1 teaspoon rum extract
1 teaspoon vanilla extract

DIRECTIONS

Begin by preheating your Air Fryer to 370 degrees F. Spritz the sides and bottom of four ramekins with cooking spray.
Melt the butter and chocolate in a microwave-safe bowl. Mix the eggs and confectioners' swerve until frothy.
Pour the butter/chocolate mixture into the egg mixture. Stir in the almond flour, rum extract, and vanilla extract. Mix until everything is well incorporated.
Scrape the batter into the prepared ramekins. Bake in the preheated Air Fryer for 9 to 11 minutes.
Let stand for 2 to 3 minutes. Invert on a plate while warm and serve. Bon appétit!

Printed in Great Britain
by Amazon

18240294R00115